War Matters

War Matters

Material Culture in the Civil War Era

EDITED BY JOAN E. CASHIN

THE
UNIVERSITY OF
NORTH CAROLINA
PRESS

Chapel Hill

© 2018 The University of North Carolina Press
All rights reserved

Designed by Richard Hendel
Set in Miller and Egiziano by Tseng Information Systems, Inc.
Manufactured in the United States of America

The University of North Carolina Press has been a member of
the Green Press Initiative since 2003.

Cover illustration: Civil War–era sword and lace-and-fabric fan from
the Filson Historical Society, Louisville, Ky.

Library of Congress Cataloging-in-Publication Data
Names: Cashin, Joan E., editor.
Title: War matters : material culture in the Civil War era / edited by Joan E. Cashin.
Description: Chapel Hill : The University of North Carolina Press, [2018] |
Includes bibliographical references and index.
Identifiers: LCCN 2018012533 | ISBN 9781469643199 (cloth : alk. paper) |
ISBN 9781469643205 (pbk : alk. paper) | ISBN 9781469643212 (ebook)
Subjects: LCSH: United States—History—Civil War, 1861–1865—
Antiquities. | Material culture—United States.
Classification: LCC E646.5 .W36 2018 | DDC 973.7—dc23
LC record available at https://lccn.loc.gov/2018012533

For all students of the Civil War era

Contents

Acknowledgments / xi

INTRODUCTION. THE IDEA OF THE THING / 1
Joan E. Cashin

1. JOHN BROWN'S PIKES
Assembling the Future in Antebellum America / 13
Jason Phillips

2. RELICS FROM TWO WARS
Revolutionary Artifacts in the Civil War Era / 34
Joan E. Cashin

3. NATURE AS MATERIAL CULTURE
Antietam National Battlefield / 53
Lisa M. Brady and Timothy Silver

4. SAVED BY A TESTAMENT
Books as Shields among Union and Confederate Soldiers / 75
Ronald J. Zboray and Mary Saracino Zboray

5. THE MATERIAL CULTURE OF WEAPONS IN THE CIVIL WAR / 99
Earl J. Hess

6. SCABROUS MATTERS
Spurious Vaccinations in the Confederacy / 123
Robert D. Hicks

7. FITTED UP FOR FREEDOM
The Material Culture of Refugee Relief / 151
Sarah Jones Weicksel

8. THERE'S NO PLACE LIKE HOME
Gender, Family, and the Confederate Alabama Household / 176
Victoria E. Ott

9. THE TROPHIES OF VICTORY AND THE RELICS OF DEFEAT
Returning Home in the Spring of 1865 / 198
Peter S. Carmichael

10. THE STUFF OF DEFEAT
Material Culture and the Downfall of Jefferson Davis / 222
Yael A. Sternhell

Contributors / 245

Index / 249

Figures, Graphs, and Table

FIGURES

1	Cedar Hill, probably late nineteenth century	2
2	John Brown's pike, crafted by bladesmith Charles Blair	12
3	Pohick Church, post-1865	41
4	Map of Antietam battlefield, drawn in 1862 by Robert Knox Sneden	61
5	Charles William Merrill's pocket New Testament	86
6	The gun-inept soldier	105
7	Vaccination kit manufactured by J. H. Gemrig	136
8	Hampton, Virginia, 1864	161
9	*Contraband Quarters, Mason's Island*	167
10	*Alabamians Receiving Rations*, 1866	189
11	Union and Confederate soldiers chopping up apple tree for Appomattox relics	200
12	Jefferson Davis, ca. 1885	224

GRAPHS

1-A, 1-B, and 1-C. The Smallpox Vaccination Process	134

TABLE

1. The Course of Smallpox	129

Acknowledgments

I am delighted to thank the people who kindly helped me assemble this book. For their expertise in arcane matters regarding both manuscripts and photographs, I am grateful to Crystal Castleberry and Randall Jones of the Virginia Department of Historic Resources; Ka'mal McClarin of the Frederick Douglass National Historic Site; James Holmberg of the Filson Historical Society; and Laura Seeger of the Department of History at Ohio State University.

For reading drafts of the introductory essay, I express my warm thanks to Randy Roth and Mark Simpson-Vos. Their shrewd criticisms improved the essay in several important ways.

I am obliged to Cate Hodorowicz, Jay Mazzocchi, Jessica Newman, and the other hard-working staff at the University of North Carolina Press for their friendly assistance during the publication process. They smoothed the way over a number of obstacles with efficiency and good cheer. Many thanks must also go to Mark Simpson-Vos for his acumen, patience, and support throughout the project. He was a generous, thoughtful editor.

Finally, my heartfelt thanks go to the contributors for their erudition and collegiality.

War Matters

Introduction
The Idea of the Thing

JOAN E. CASHIN

In 1838, Frederick Douglass and his wife, Anna Murray Douglass, settled in a two-room house in New Bedford, Massachusetts. They came from Maryland, where he had been a house slave and a field laborer, and she had been a freedwoman and a seamstress. When he fled bondage for the North, Anna Douglass fashioned the sailor's uniform he wore in disguise, and after she joined him in New Bedford, she provided their feather bed, pillows, bed linens, cutlery, and other housewares. They worked hard to make the New Bedford residence what their daughter Rosetta Douglass Sprague called a "well appointed" home. Frederick Douglass, who was highly observant about the material world, remembered that house for a long time. In 1890, when he visited with his daughter, he described "every detail" of the interior, which was "indelibly impressed upon his mind," she said. He remembered the tablecloth, coarse to the touch but white as snow, the neat tableware, and exactly where a towel hung on a nail. When the family moved to Rochester, New York, they took the dishes with them as "souvenirs," according to Sprague. An object can appeal for many reasons, including its design, size, ornamentation, color, texture, or personal association with life experience. Frederick and Anna Douglass cherished their household objects as symbols of their privacy, their liberty, and their ability to create a domestic life together.[1]

The Douglasses also had a keen sense of how material things functioned as signifiers of political issues beyond the household. Some years later, after their house in Rochester burned down, they furnished another house together, Cedar Hill, a two-story structure on a hill in Washington, D.C. They poured their energies into this home, too. They added over half a dozen rooms and filled the domicile with yet more mementos from their lives as free people, including portraits of reformers they admired and precious political artifacts, such as Abraham Lincoln's walking cane, a gift from Mary Todd Lincoln in 1865. Frederick Douglass called it an "object of sacred interest" and said he would keep it as long as he lived, as in fact he did. Anna Douglass, who was very proud of the Cedar Hill house, died there

Figure 1. Cedar Hill, probably late nineteenth century. (Courtesy of the Frederick Douglass National Historic Site, Washington, D.C.)

in 1882. Her widower married Helen Pitts in 1884, and they lived there until Frederick Douglass died in 1895.[2]

Whether they were assembling personal or political artifacts, the Douglasses remind us of the material world's importance in peace and war, for civilians and soldiers, blacks and whites, and women and men in all regions. This book, which is the first collection of essays on material culture of the Civil War era, serves as an introduction to the field. The volume covers the antebellum period, the war, and the postwar years, and all of the essays are grounded in rigorous manuscript research; object research in museums, historical societies, and websites; or research visits to battlefields. The authors employ an impressive variety of methodologies and take an interdisciplinary stance on a range of subjects, with some overlap among the topics. They all address the complex dialectic between ideas, objects, and behavior. As exciting as these essays are, they showcase only a small number of the topics available to historians.

The Civil War generation affords especially rich possibilities for studying the material world. Beginning in the antebellum era, a profusion of objects entered the market via the development of a consumer culture, which had roots in the eighteenth century; the growing consumer culture then stirred the desire to own more things and sparked a sense of pride in ownership. That culture coexisted with an ancient folk culture, in which many people crafted their own objects, such as the clothes they wore, the plates on their tables, and the furniture in their homes, and many others collected artifacts about their family histories. The urge to display material possessions, whether they were new or old, was widespread, evident in such diverse events as the Crystal Palace exhibit in New York City in 1853 and the annual exhibits of the Mechanics' Institute in Richmond in the 1850s. As literacy rates increased, more people could articulate their thoughts on physical objects. Americans used material goods in the antebellum era for many reasons: to ensure their own survival, express their aspirations, prove their social status, preserve their dignity, communicate their political loyalties, and record their experiences. Many people felt strong emotional connections to at least some of their possessions, and they carefully preserved their belongings as the Douglasses did.[3]

Let us begin by defining the phrase "material culture." The term dates from the early 1900s, when anthropologists coined it to describe the study of physical objects as evidence of cultural values. Since then, scholars in a variety of disciplines have disputed exactly how the term should be defined, and there is still no universally agreed-upon definition. The anthropologist James Deetz calls it the "physical environment that we modify through culturally determined behavior," while folklorist Henry Glassie defines material culture as the "tangible yield of human conduct." Christopher Tilley, an archaeologist, remarks that the term "materiality" is typically used to mean the "fleshy, corporeal, and physical" aspects of human existence.[4]

The learned professions have shown an occasional bias against object studies, but there have always been people who understood its importance. The psychologist William James commented in 1890 that each person has multiple identities, including a "material self," and in the last thirty years, specialists in archaeology, anthropology, sociology, psychology, semiotics, geography, the history of science, art history, the history of technology, and the history of architecture have done splendid work on the topic. No one discipline dominates the material studies field, which has porous boundaries and embraces a large scholarship.[5] Vigorous theoretical debates have always characterized the field, and among the most stimulating concepts is actor-network theory, articulated by the philosopher Bruno Latour. He argues that objects themselves have agency—that is, objects by their existence can provoke human action. The archaeologist Ian Hodder disagrees, as have other writers, responding that human beings and objects are dependent on each other. Lorraine Daston, a historian of science, implicitly disputes actor-network theory by contrasting what she calls the "brute intransigence" of the material world with the "plasticity of meaning" assigned to it by human beings, which changes according to time and place.[6]

Inspired by this literature, historians outside the Civil War field have explored the material dimensions of conflicts in the United States and beyond its borders. They focus on brief conflicts, such as the War of 1812, and long wars, such as Vietnam, drawing on multiple disciplines and utilizing many kinds of historical evidence. They study how wars have changed landscapes and altered the built environment in city and country; how wars have caused unexpected shortages in commodities and given rise to black markets; how certain objects have been elevated into potent wartime symbols; and how frenzies of postwar commemoration have broken out, as human beings have tried to forge a sense of collective memory.[7] But most Civil War scholars have yet to make the material turn. Specialists have so many manuscripts to read that they have assumed that no other sources are necessary, while others evidently believe that material culture studies has the stigma of antiquarianism or, strangely enough, the transience of an intellectual fad.[8]

A few Civil War scholars have nevertheless ventured into this field. Michael DeGruccio and I examine relic hunting by soldiers, uncovering a strong desire for artifacts among men in the two armies; I have also portrayed items of female attire as material objects freighted with symbolism for both white and black women. Other historians scrutinize the war's overall impact on the built environment and the natural world. Megan Kate Nelson reports on the damage the war wreaked on Southern cities, houses, and forests, although she notes that the ruins were literally reconstructed after the conflict ended. Lisa M. Brady takes a different tack, arguing that the physical environment, including rivers, bayous, and swamps, was an active force in the Union army's campaigns in the Western and Eastern Theaters, while Brian Allen Drake's book of essays treats wartime landscapes, deforestation, agriculture, and the climate with an emphasis on the wide spectrum of experience. Mark M. Smith has studied sensory perception of the physical world, and he offers fascinating evidence of how the war simultaneously heightened and deadened the senses for soldiers and civilians. These historians use manuscripts, objects, and landscapes as evidence, and they take different positions on agency. Most of them concentrate on human attitudes toward material culture, resulting in a small but compelling body of work, brimming with ideas.[9]

Historians who are interested in material culture in the Civil War era have many sources to pursue. References to three-dimensional objects appear frequently in manuscripts, such as personal correspondence, diaries, memoirs, scrapbooks, newspapers, probate records, court-martial records, the *Official Records of the Union and Confederate Armies*, and the files of the Southern Claims Commission. Objects can turn up inside manuscript collections, sometimes to emphasize a point the writer wanted to make. Margaret Beckwith, a white Virginian, attached a piece of cloth to her memoir to illustrate the wartime increase in prices of women's clothing. The photographic record is also promising, since nineteenth-century Americans often had their daguerreotypes taken while holding a favorite object, such as a guitar, a letter, or a set of surveyor's tools. Historians also have access to a huge, ever-growing array of objects in public institutions. In 2011, the Tennessee State Library and Archives began photographing hundreds of artifacts owned by private residents, and the images are presented in the online project "Looking Back: The Civil War in Tennessee." Additionally, the National Museum of African American History and Culture, which opened in 2016, received many donations of relics never before seen by scholars.[10]

The study of material culture can give us new perspectives on a number of ongoing historical debates, such as the nature of the common soldier's experience, already the subject of an abundant scholarship. The soldier's body was a material entity, as well as a metaphor for prowess, dominance over the enemy, and triumph over death; thinking of the body in this way highlights its fragility, as it could suffer catastrophic damage from disease and amputation. In this volume, Ron J. Zboray and Mary Saracino Zboray attest that pocket-size books could literally save lives in battle, which happened over a hundred times during the conflict; afterward, many soldiers in the two armies preserved the bullet-ridden books as symbols of divine protection. Earl J. Hess discusses the way soldiers used their guns, how they perceived them, and how they sometimes became emotionally attached to them. For many troops in both armies, guns could serve as an extension of the physical self. By adopting the material perspective, all three scholars skillfully represent in different ways the soldier's vulnerability.[11]

Material culture precepts can shed light on long-running debates about the strength of popular allegiance to the Confederacy and the related question of persisting support for the Union within the South. There is no consensus yet on either debate, but my essay finds that white Southern Unionists in the seaboard relished their own artifacts during the war, such as the forbidden United States flag, and that white Unionists, pro-Confederate whites, and former slaves had diverging memories of the war, visible in the souvenirs they preserved. Allegiances could shift during the war, of course. Victoria E. Ott demonstrates how the conflict changed the attitudes of nonelite whites toward their homes and possessions in Alabama. They deployed household objects and tasks to build a Confederate identity until the war's deprivations forced many of them to lose hope in the rebel cause. Ott and I show clearly how tangible objects reflected the cacophony of political loyalties inside the South.[12]

The methods of material culture can supply new approaches to race, bondage, and emancipation, since black Americans often expressed their beliefs with objects, not just documents. Sarah Jones Weicksel argues that fugitive slaves made creative use of material goods in refugee camps in Kentucky, South Carolina, and Virginia as they built shelters and furnished new homes. They salvaged, appropriated, and protected certain artifacts from the past and acquired new objects as they prepared for the future. As newly freed people, they could make choices, enacting their transition out of slavery. In the vast scholarship on bondage, other writers have detailed food, clothing, and housing among slaves in the North and South, but Weicksel's original essay should encourage more work on the emancipation era, when ex-slaves had new access to all kinds of goods.[13]

In a similar vein, the material culture perspective can give us fresh ideas on understanding political behavior. Citizens used physical objects such as kerchiefs and household prints to display their views, although most historians have ignored this feature of political life. Jason Phillips investigates how material objects from the antebellum years could symbolize political intent and military triumph, in particular John Brown's pikes from his famous raid at Harpers Ferry in 1859. Phillips further maintains that the possession of certain objects, such as weapons, could embolden people to take action, and he identifies these pikes as harbingers of the war against slavery. Peter S. Carmichael takes up events in Virginia in 1865, when veterans from both armies gathered military relics to validate their service to their respective causes. He points out that Confederate keepsakes could underscore racial solidarity among whites during Reconstruction, with dangerous implications for white behavior toward African Americans. Phillips and Carmichael suggest entirely new ways to comprehend political motivation before, during, and after the war.[14]

Material culture practices can deepen our understanding of environmental history, broadly defined as people grappling with the physical universe. Lisa M. Brady and Timothy Silver highlight the earthshaking transformations that combat inflicted on Antietam battlefield near Sharpsburg, Maryland. They also prove that the environment played an active role in the war, requiring human beings to adapt to geographic constraints as the forces of war and the forces of nature shaped each other. In his discussion of the war's medical context, Robert D. Hicks shows how vaccine matter figured in the attempt to protect the Southern public from the dreaded smallpox. In the process, Confederate physicians engaged in a fierce struggle with patients, white and black, over the control of their bodies. Brady, Silver, and Hicks expertly convey how human beings confronted the unavoidable parameters of the physical world.[15]

If we turn to the burgeoning scholarship on memory, an awareness of material culture can reveal the workings of private and collective memory all over the country. Because war is an extreme experience, few objects are as powerful as war relics when it comes to preserving or releasing memory. Indeed, most of the essays in this collection touch on memory in some way, shape, or form. Yael A. Sternhell depicts Jefferson Davis's campaign to recoup some of his personal belongings after 1865 as he wrestled with government authorities, friends, and foes to little avail. This strong-willed white man lost most of those possessions, the ultimate symbol of his defeat. Sternhell limns the intensity of his effort, a subtle account of the importance of memory formation in an individual life.[16]

Yet other subjects can benefit from the material culture perspective, beginning with women's history. The field has been thriving for a full generation, but most scholars have neglected the material realities of female existence during the Civil War, in both the North and the South. Once upon a time, museums collected only those relics belonging to elite white men, but institutions have broadened their policies, and many artifacts relating to women's lives—their embroidery, books, and household tools—await the historian. The war's international context, the focus of a growing scholarship, also had a material facet. Americans and western Europeans shared some assumptions about material culture, and they exchanged many goods, including such luxury objects as a Stradivarius, found on the battlefield at Monocacy, Maryland, in 1864. Today the instrument resides in a local historical society, where it fairly cries out for analysis. Moreover, the nation's architecture changed dramatically during the conflict, as the military built forts, camps, prisons, and headquarters in both regions. The housing boom in the North introduced new buildings on a large scale, such as the elegant polygon forts constructed outside of Washington, D.C. Historians can discover how people made these structures, how they perceived them, and how they decided whether to preserve them when peace came.[17]

It should be obvious, then, that material studies can open new vistas on the past, to borrow an environmental image. The war transformed the physical world and ideas about that world in ways that were national in scope yet very personal in effect. Material objects lie at the crux of understanding individual and social relationships in every culture, and nineteenth-century

Americans created, used, preserved, revered, exploited, discarded, mocked, and destroyed objects for a host of reasons. By so doing, they made manifest some of their most significant beliefs about themselves, their communities, and their country, in peacetime and war. The evidence is at our fingertips. If we think more deeply about the physical reality of the past, we can reach a more profound understanding of both people and things in the Civil War generation.[18]

Notes

1. William S. McFeely, *Frederick Douglass* (New York: W. W. Norton, 1991), 69–74; *Life and Times of Frederick Douglass, Written by Himself: His Early Life as a Slave, His Escape from Bondage, and His Complete History*, with a new introduction by Rayford W. Logan, reprinted from the rev. ed. of 1892 (New York: Collier Books, 1971), 271–73, 447–49; John Stauffer, Zoe Trodd, and Celeste-Marie Bernier, *Picturing Frederick Douglass: An Illustrated Biography of the Nineteenth Century's Most Photographed American*, with an epilogue by Henry Louis Gates Jr. and an afterword by Kenneth B. Morris Jr. (New York: Liveright, 2015), 1–5; Rosetta Douglass Sprague, *Anna Murray Douglass: My Mother as I Recall Her* (n.p.: privately printed by Fredericka Douglass Sprague Perry, 1923), 9–10, 17, Frederick Douglass Papers, Library of Congress; Rosemary Troy Krill, *Early American Decorative Arts, 1620–1860: A Handbook for Interpreters*, rev. and enhanced ed. (Lanham, N.Y.: Altamira Press, 2010), 7.

2. Frederick Douglass National Historic Site, Cedar Hill, Washington, D.C., Virtual Museum Exhibit, home page, https://www.nps.gov/frdo/index/htm, accessed 15 August 2016; Frederick Douglass to Mary Todd Lincoln, 17 August 1865, Gilder Lehrman Collection, on deposit at the Pierpont Morgan Library, GLC 2472, www.digitalhistory.uh.edu/exhibits/douglass, accessed 15 August 2016; Sprague, *Anna Murray Douglass*, 20–21.

3. David Jaffee, *A New Nation of Goods: The Material Culture of Early America* (Philadelphia: University of Pennsylvania Press, 2010); Richard L. Bushman, *The Refinement of America: Persons, Houses, Cities* (New York: Vintage Books, 1992); Kenneth L. Ames, *Death in the Dining Room and Other Tales of Victorian Culture* (Philadelphia: Temple University Press, 1992); Bill Cecil-Fronsman, *Common Whites: Class and Culture in Antebellum North Carolina* (Lexington: University Press of Kentucky, 1992), 97, 103, 120; Simon J. Bronner, *Grasping Things: Folk Material Culture and Mass Society* (Lexington: University Press of Kentucky, 1986), 93–95; William Le Duc, *This Business of War: Recollections of a Civil War Quartermaster*, foreword by Adam E. Scher (St. Paul: Minnesota Historical Society Press, 2004), 41–43; "Mechanics' Institute," *Richmond Whig*, 12 August 1859, 3; Harvey Graff, *The Legacies of Literacy: Continuities and Contradictions in Western Culture and Society* (Bloomington: Indiana University Press, 1991), 344; Christopher Bollas, *The Evocative Object World* (London: Routledge, 2009), 80, 89; Judith Flanders, *The Making of Home: The 500-Year Story of How Our Houses Became Our Homes* (New York: Thomas Dunne, 2014), 165–66.

4. *Oxford Dictionary Online*, s.v. "material culture," http://www.oxforddictionaries.com/definition/english, accessed 12 May 2016; James Deetz, *In Small Things Forgotten: An Archaeology of Early American Life*, exp. and rev. ed. (New York: Anchor Books,

1996), 35; Henry Glassie, *Material Culture* (Bloomington: Indiana University Press, 1999), 41; Christopher Tilley, Webb Keane, Susanne Küchler, Mike Rowlands, and Patricia Spyer, eds., *Handbook of Material Culture* (London: Sage, 2006), 3.

5. Daniel Miller, "Why Some Things Matter," in *Material Cultures: Why Some Things Matter*, ed. Daniel Miller (London: University College London Press, 2001), 3, 12; Nigel Rapport, *Social and Cultural Anthropology: The Key Concepts*, 3rd ed. (London: Routledge, 2014), 284; Helga Dittmar, *Consumer Culture, Identity, and Well-Being* (New York: Psychology Press, 2008), 8; Ian Woodward, *Understanding Material Culture* (Los Angeles: Sage Publications, 2007); Steven Lubar and W. David Kingery, eds., *History from Things: Essays on Material Culture* (Washington, D.C.: Smithsonian Institution Press, 1993); Peter N. Miller, "Introduction: The Culture of the Hand," in *Cultural Histories of the Material World*, ed. Peter N. Miller (Ann Arbor: University of Michigan Press, 2013), 6; Tilley et al., *Handbook of Material Culture*, 1; Judy Attfield, *Wild Things: The Material Culture of Everyday Life* (Oxford: Berg, 2000), 1–2; Clifford Geertz, *The Interpretation of Cultures: Selected Essays* (New York: Basic Books, 1973). Starting with the *annales* school, Europeanists have done more work on material culture than Americanists. Among many examples, see Eva Giloi, *Monarchy, Myth, and Material Culture in Germany, 1750–1950* (Cambridge: Cambridge University Press, 2011); and Asa Briggs, *Victorian Things* (Chicago: University of Chicago Press, 1988), 28.

6. Bruno Latour, *Reassembling the Social: An Introduction to Actor-Network Theory* (New York: Oxford University Press, 2005), 63–85; Ian Hodder, *Entangled: An Archaeology of the Relationships between Human and Things* (Malden, Mass.: Wiley-Blackwell, 2012), 3, 10, 16, 33, 215–16; Lorraine Daston, "Speechless," in *Things That Talk: Object Lessons from Art and Science*, ed. Lorraine Daston (New York: Zone Books, 2004), 16. The perceptive work of the anthropologist Clifford Geertz, which had a lasting influence on many social historians, prompted them to examine behavior, rather than material culture; see his *Interpretation of Cultures*.

7. Michael T. Lucas and Julie M. Schlablitsky, eds., *Archaeology of the War of 1812* (New York: Routledge, 2016); Malte Zierenberg, *Berlin's Black Market: 1939–1950* (New York: Palgrave Macmillan, 2015); Steve Maddox, *Saving Stalin's Imperial City: Historic Preservation in Leningrad, 1930–1950* (Bloomington: Indiana University Press, 2015); Meredith Mason Brown, *Touching America's History: From the Pequot War through World War II* (Bloomington: Indiana University Press, 2013); Jane E. Dusselier, *Artifacts of Loss: Crafting Survival in Japanese American Concentration Camps* (New Brunswick, N.J.: Rutgers University Press, 2008); Gerald C. Hickey, *Window on a War: An Anthropologist in the Vietnam Conflict* (Lubbock: Texas Tech University Press, 2002).

8. Michael DeGruccio, "Letting the War Slip through Our Hands: Material Culture and the Weakness of Words in the Civil War Era," in *Weirding the War: Stories from the Civil War's Ragged Edges*, ed. Stephen Berry (Athens: University of Georgia Press, 2011), 27; Robert Blair St. George, "Introduction," in *Material Life in America, 1600–1860*, ed. Robert Blair St. George (Boston: Northeastern University Press, 1988), 8. The David B. Warren Symposium, *American Material Culture and the Texas Experience* (Bayou Bend Collection and Gardens: The Museum of Fine Arts, Houston, 2014), is intriguing but does not cover the war.

9. DeGruccio, "Letting the War Slip," 15–35; Joan E. Cashin, "Trophies of War: Ma-

terial Culture in the Civil War Era," *Journal of the Civil War Era* 1, no. 3 (September 2011): 339–67; Joan E. Cashin, "Torn Bonnets and Stolen Silks: Fashion, Gender, Race, and Danger in the Wartime South," *Civil War History* 61 (December 2015): 338–61; Megan Kate Nelson, *Ruin Nation: Destruction and the American Civil War* (Athens: University of Georgia Press, 2012); Lisa M. Brady, *War upon the Land: Military Strategy and the Transformation of Southern Landscapes during the American Civil War* (Athens: University of Georgia Press, 2012); Brian Allen Drake, ed., *The Blue, the Gray, and the Green: Toward an Environmental History of the Civil War* (Athens: University of Georgia Press, 2015); Mark M. Smith, *The Smell of Battle, the Taste of Siege: A Sensory History of the Civil War* (New York: Oxford University Press, 2015). The Summer 2017 issue of *Civil War History* on material culture came to hand as this book went into production, so it could not be incorporated into this book.

10. Reminiscences of Margaret Stanly Beckwith, 2:28a, Virginia Historical Society, Richmond; *Daguerreian Society Newsletter* 12 (March/April 2000): 1, 5; *Daguerreian Society Newsletter* 11 (January/February 1999): 22; "Looking Back: The Civil War in Tennessee," Tennessee State Library and Archives, sos.tn.gov/tsla/looking-back-civil-war-tennessee, accessed 1 May 2016; Vinson Cunningham, "A Darker Presence: A Museum of African American History Finally Comes to the Mall," *New Yorker*, 29 August 2016, 35–36.

11. Susannah Callow, "The Bare Bones: Body Parts, Bones, and Conflict Behavior," in *"Beyond the Dead Horizon": Studies in Modern Conflict Archaeology*, ed. Nicholas J. Saunders (Oakville, Conn.: Oxbow Books, 2012), 39, 29; Brian Craig Miller, *Empty Sleeves: Amputation in the Civil War South* (Athens: University of Georgia Press, 2015). Among the many books on common soldiers, see Brian Mathew Jordan, *Marching Home: Union Veterans and Their Unending Civil War* (New York: Liveright, 2014); Kenneth Noe, *Reluctant Rebels: The Confederates Who Joined the Army after 1861* (Chapel Hill: University of North Carolina Press, 2010); Joseph T. Glatthaar, *Forged in Battle: The Civil War Alliance of Black Soldiers and White Officers* (Baton Rouge: Louisiana State University Press, 2000); and Reid Mitchell, *Civil War Soldiers* (New York: Viking, 1988).

12. In the most recent work on these debates, Anne Sarah Rubin, *A Shattered Nation: The Rise and Fall of the Confederacy, 1861–1868* (Chapel Hill: University of North Carolina Press, 2005); Mark V. Wetherington, *Plain Folk's Fight: The Civil War and Reconstruction in Piney Woods Georgia* (Chapel Hill: University of North Carolina Press, 2005); and Gary W. Gallagher, *The Confederate War* (Cambridge, Mass.: Harvard University Press, 1997), argue that Confederate nationalism was strong, while Barton A. Myers, *Rebels against the Confederacy: North Carolina's Unionists* (New York: Cambridge University Press, 2014); Margaret M. Storey, *Loyalty and Loss: Alabama's Unionists in the Civil War and Reconstruction* (Baton Rouge: Louisiana State University Press, 2004); David Williams, Teresa Crisp Williams, and David Carlson, *Plain Folk in a Rich Man's War: Class and Dissent in Civil War Georgia* (Gainesville: University Press of Florida, 2002); and Victoria E. Bynum, *The Free State of Jones: Mississippi's Longest Civil War* (Chapel Hill: University of North Carolina Press, 2001), counter that it was weak or that Unionist support persisted.

13. Anne Elizabeth Yentsch, *A Chesapeake Family and Their Slaves: A Study in Historical Archaeology*, illustrations by Julie Hunter (Cambridge: Cambridge University Press, 1994), 4; Katherine Howlett Hayes, *Slavery before Race: Europeans, Africans, and*

Indians at Long Island's Sylvester Manor Plantation, 1651–1884 (New York: New York University Press, 2013); Stephanie M. H. Camp, *Closer to Freedom: Enslaved Women and Everyday Resistance in the Plantation South* (Chapel Hill: University of North Carolina Press, 2004); James Deetz, *Flowerdew Hundred: The Archaeology of a Virginia Plantation, 1619–1864* (Charlottesville: University Press of Virginia, 1995).

14. Robert Fanuzzi, *Abolition's Public Sphere* (Minneapolis: University of Minnesota Press, 2003), 13; Mark E. Neely Jr., *The Boundaries of American Political Culture in the Civil War Era* (Chapel Hill: University of North Carolina Press, 2005), 9–29. Abraham Lincoln's belongings excite great public interest, but historians have yet to treat them as part of material culture; see Philip B. Kunhardt III, Peter W. Kunhardt, and Peter W. Kunhardt Jr., *Looking for Lincoln: The Making of an American Icon*, introduction by Doris Kearns Goodwin, foreword by David Herbert Donald (New York: Alfred A. Knopf, 2008).

15. For related work, see Mark Fiege, *The Republic of Nature: An Environmental History of the United States* (Seattle: University of Washington Press, 2012); Richard P. Tucker and Edmund Russell, eds., *Natural Enemy, Natural Ally: Toward an Environmental History of Warfare* (Corvallis: Oregon State University Press, 2004); Shauna Devine, *Learning from the Wounded: The Civil War and the Rise of American Medical Science* (Chapel Hill: University of North Carolina Press, 2014); and Margaret Humphreys, *Intensely Human: The Health of the Black Soldier in the American Civil War* (Baltimore: Johns Hopkins University Press, 2008).

16. Nicholas J. Saunders, *Killing Time: Archaeology and the First World War* (n.p.: Sutton, 2007), 35, 33; Caroline E. Janney, *Remembering the Civil War: Reunion and the Limits of Reconciliation* (Chapel Hill: University of North Carolina Press, 2013); David W. Blight, *Race and Reunion: The Civil War in American Memory* (Cambridge, Mass.: Harvard University Press, 2001). On memories preserved by individual black Northerners, see Ellen Gruber Garvey, *Writing with Scissors: American Scrapbooks from the Civil War to the Harlem Renaissance* (New York: Oxford University Press, 2012), 100.

17. Sophie White, *Wild Frenchmen and Frenchified Indians: Material Culture and Race in Colonial Louisiana* (Philadelphia: University of Pennsylvania Press, 2012); Moira Donald and Linda Hurcombe, eds., *Gender and Material Culture in Historical Perspective* (New York: St. Martin's, 2000); Patricia West, "Uncovering and Interpreting Women's History at Historic House Museums," in *Restoring Women's History through Historic Preservation*, ed. Gail Lee Dubrow and Jennifer B. Goodman (Baltimore: Johns Hopkins University Press, 2003), 83–85; Catalog numbers A-0067-003, A-1361-359, A-1434-002, Savannah Historical Society; Don H. Doyle, *The Cause of All Nations: An International History of the American Civil War* (New York: Basic Books, 2015); Louise L. Stephenson, *Lincoln in the Atlantic World* (New York: Cambridge University Press, 2015); Catherine Armstrong, *Non-textual Sources: A Historian's Guide* (London: Bloomsbury Academic, 2016), 1–4; Toby Faber, *Stradivari's Genius: Five Violins, One Cello, and Three Centuries of Enduring Perfection* (New York: Random House, 2004); Accession number 89.10, accession file, Historical Society of Frederick County, Maryland; Nelson, *Ruin Nation*, 61–97; Benjamin Franklin Cooling III and Walter H. Owen II, *Mr. Lincoln's Forts: A Guide to the Civil War Defenses of Washington*, foreword by Edwin C. Bearss, new ed. (Lanham, Md.: Scarecrow Press, 2010), 137–250.

18. Woodward, *Understanding Material Culture*, 175.

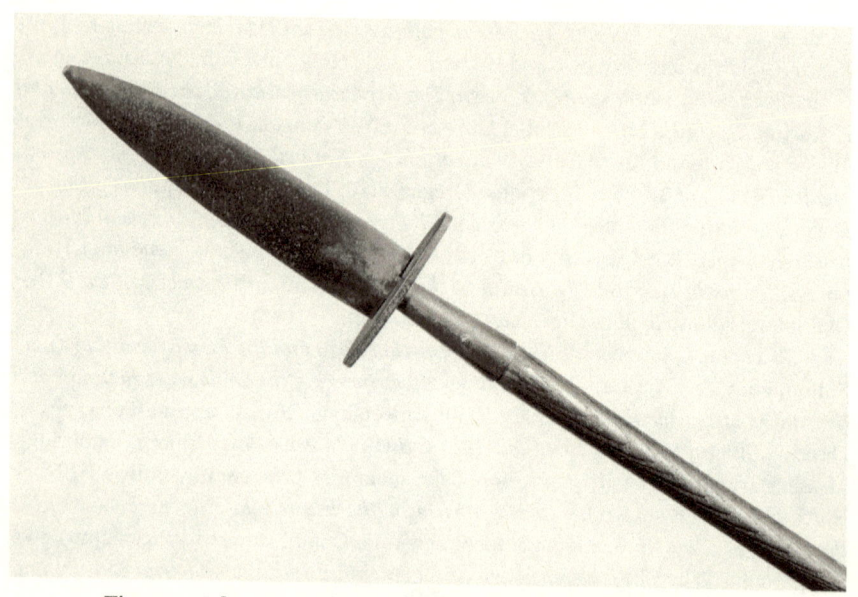

Figure 2. John Brown's pike, crafted by bladesmith Charles Blair.
(Courtesy of the Virginia Historical Society)

John Brown's Pikes
Assembling the Future in Antebellum America

JASON PHILLIPS

When he told friends about Bleeding Kansas, Henry Clay Pate recalled, "I went to take Old Brown, and Old Brown took me." On 2 June 1856, Pate surrendered his Missouri posse to John Brown's company at the battle of Black Jack. Both men recognized the event as the first battle of a looming civil war. Previous violence in the territory had been acts of terror. Black Jack was a pitched firefight between more than 100 men for three hours. To prove that Black Jack meant war, Brown and Pate drafted an article of surrender and prisoner exchange that afternoon. The agreement specified that Pate and his lieutenant, W. B. Brockett, would be exchanged for two of Brown's sons being held by proslavery militia. The document stressed, "The arms particularly the side arms of each one exchanged are to be returned with the prisoners." When U.S. dragoons led by Colonel Edwin Sumner arrived three days later, Brown produced the signed agreement and insisted that Pate and Brockett were his prisoners until proslavery forces released his sons. Sumner told Brown that he would not parley "with lawless and armed men" and demanded that Brown release his prisoners and return their things.[1]

Staring at a column of U.S. cavalry, Brown had no choice but to free Pate and Brockett, but he protested in a striking way. He could not hold the men, so Brown kept Pate's bowie knife and Brockett's sword. "Now, Colonel Sumner," John Brown complained, "I can't undertake to return every man his jack-knife." "Never mind, Captain," said Sumner, "in good faith—in good faith, sir—find all you can, and return these men their property." In "good faith," Brown substantiated the surrender by keeping the sidearms of his captives.[2]

When the Kansas-Nebraska Act gave settlers the power to make a state, it opened the territory to rival assemblies of people and things. French theorist Bruno Latour asks, "*How many participants* are gathered in a *thing* to make it exist and to maintain its existence?" His abstract question was a real concern for Americans who rushed to gather enough people and arms to ensure their future republic in Kansas. These gatherings created more arsenals than representative assemblies. Across the territory and nation, weapons gathered people while people gathered weapons. Latour calls this process *dingpolitik*, or "thing politics." The dominant paradigm in political and military science still relies on *realpolitik*, which insists that material self-interest motivates political movements and military actions. When opponents expect material gains from a conflict, they engage. Latour and other new materialists refuse to reduce conflicts to rational power plays in which humans objectify the material world without being affected in turn by things around them. Latour stresses this point by noting that the root of "republic," *res-publica*, means "public thing." Western thought privileges subjects over objects, but in its Greek origins, things attract and maintain public spheres. As a concept, thing politics suits Civil War America, a time when popular sovereignty meant gathering arms, when a cane spoke louder than a senator, and when war erupted over owning humans.[3]

In Kansas, bowie knives encouraged Southern conquest of the territory through violent intimidation. The famous blades first appeared during the Early Republic after wearing swords went out of fashion. A sign of aristocracy, swords, like wigs, became taboo after the American and French Revolutions. Even British gentlemen stopped wearing them. Social pressures encouraged men to replace swords with concealed weapons, and changes in clothing accommodated this shift by introducing more pockets in men's coats and pants. Concealing arms reflected a more restrained manhood that stressed morality, self-control, domesticity, and temperance. Sword canes and percussion pistols offered discrete forms of self-defense, but both were weak and unreliable. None of the period's weapons replaced the sword's usefulness in a melee until Rezin Bowie sharpened an iron file and gave it to his brother to kill a man. When Bowie died at the Alamo, his knife embodied Southern politics and martial manhood. Jutting from belts in defiance of social propriety, bowies celebrated wildness, adventure, honor, and physical violence. Bowie-knife politics crossed lines and broke laws to assert the supremacy of Southern white men. Even Southern statesmen started wielding bowie knives in legislatures.[4]

In Kansas, proslavery men voted with bowie knives. One Southern adventurer who called himself "General" John Stringfellow told a British reporter in Kansas City that Southern men would "mark every scoundrel that was the least tainted with free-soilism or abolitionism, and exterminate him." According to the reporter, Stringfellow had no qualms about violating state and federal laws to spread slavery to Kansas. It was time, the border ruffian announced, to "enter every election district in Kansas, in defiance of the Governor and his vile myrmidons, and vote at the point of the bowie-knife." When Senator David Atchison led Missouri men to vote in Kansas, he warned the crowd at the precinct, "We came to vote, and we are going to vote, or kill every God-damned abolitionist in the district." While Yankees hid their efforts to arm Kansas behind emigrant groups, Southerners flaunted violence for effect. Filibusters like Alabamian Jefferson Buford advertised plans to conquer Kansas and called for volunteers. Buford sold forty slaves to arm 400 men. He forecast that a "great day of darkness" loomed before Kansas if Southern white men were not "crazy enough to peril even life in the deadly breach." His army marched to Kansas under a flag that read "The Supremacy of the White Race."[5]

The same year that Congress opened Kansas to slavery, Southern evangelist Samuel Baldwin published *Armageddon*. Baldwin prophesied that war in the Midwest would end time and usher the second coming of Jesus Christ. He based his prophecy on the books of Daniel and Revelation and recent filibustering. Baldwin predicted that frontier warfare would ignite America's dominion over the world, burn up the earth's sins, and cauterize the land into God's paradise. American filibustering would usher in the millennium because it manifested "a national itching to extend the area of freedom on the ruins of thrones." White Southerners like Bowie, Buford, and Baldwin looked west and saw the fate of civilization hanging in the balance. For them, frontiers were borderlands where good and evil fought for the future. They expected victory and, as Baldwin predicted, "the total extinction of some inferior races, as for instance, the Mexicans." Weeks before the battle of Black Jack, George Frederick Holmes echoed this sentiment in *De Bow's Review*. "Conquest, extension, appropriation, assimilation, and even extermination of inferior races has been and must be the course pursued in the development of civilization," he explained. Holmes shared Baldwin's belief that exterminating people improved the world. Both men were leading academics. Holmes served as chancellor of the University of Mississippi and later worked at the University of Virginia. Baldwin was president of Soule College in Tennessee. Such leading lights taught a generation of Southern men that violent conquest and destruction would elevate humanity. For them, the point of the bowie knife was the vanguard of progress.[6]

Conquest appealed to Henry Clay Pate. He grew up in Virginia listening to his grandfather's Revolutionary War stories and envied the old man for accomplishing "that greatest of military achievements," spilling blood to secure sovereignty. One of the reasons he left Old Virginia was a sense of frustration that the state focused on the past instead of the future: "My native State seems to be doomed to the rule of enemies of progress, who say daily—let us rest at our ease, and live upon the glory of departed ancestors." The Kansas-Nebraska Act gave Pate a chance to repeat his grandfather's glory. He moved to Missouri, named his newspaper the *Star of Empire*, and crossed the border in search of John Brown. But things did not go as planned for Clay Pate.[7]

When Brown took Pate's knife and Brockett's sword, he acquired trophies. Soldiers often collect souvenirs on battlefields. Nineteenth-century Americans gathered literal pieces of history—locks of Washington's hair, chips from Plymouth Rock. By assembling mementos at Black Jack, Brown anticipated that posterity would value the event as much as he did. His theft of Pate's knife and Brockett's sword also declared dominance by stripping defeated men of their personal possessions. Unlike horses, food, ammunition, or other valuable resources for campaigning, individual sidearms were not spoils of war. Anthropologist Simon Harrison, an expert on battle trophies, notes that a person constitutes more than a body and mind; a "surrounding penumbra" of things evokes a person's life and presence. The most private things, such as diaries, family pictures, and personal objects, have no practical use for an enemy who takes them. Brown suffered from no shortage of swords and knives. Harrison explains that battle trophies seldom remain with their collectors. Soldiers give them to family and friends, gamble them away, or exchange them for luxuries. In the process, trophies circulate from war front to home front, where civilians prize a piece of the war.[8]

Months after Black Jack, Brown paraded his trophies during a fundraising tour across New England. He knew how to impress eastern voyeurs of western violence. Wearing an old-fashioned military cape and fur cap, Brown told bankers, merchants, and doctors how his small army had endured squalor, sickness, hunger, wounds, imprisonment, torture, and death to defend American liberty. All he asked from them was "the money that is *smoked away* during a single day in Boston." Things needed for his war against slavery included "horses, baggage-wagons, tents, harness, saddles, bridles, holsters, spurs, and belts; camp equipage, such as cooking and eating utensils, blankets, knapsacks, intrenching-tools, axes, shovels, spades, mattocks, crowbars," plus ammunition, money to pay for freight expenses, and support for his family. With those things, Brown promised to kill slavery. Without them, God would hold the nation accountable for its unwillingness to provide things to freedom fighters. Mary Stearns, the wife of prominent manufacturer George Stearns, was so impressed by Brown's speech that she asked for "a copy to preserve among my relics." In return, she convinced her husband to write Brown a check for $7,000. As proof of Southern brutality, Brown displayed the shackles that Pate's posse had clamped on his son. But his prized relic was Pate's knife. After listening to Brown's graphic, earnest lectures about Bleeding Kansas, audiences thrilled to see him pull the bowie out of his boot. People came to expect this dramatic flourish. When Ralph Waldo Emerson and Henry David Thoreau met Brown, they asked to see the knife.[9]

After Brown spoke in Collinsville, Connecticut, Horatio Rust, a friend and local reformer, arranged a meeting in his pharmacy between Brown and blacksmith Charles Blair. Brown gave Brockett's sword to Rust as a token of friendship and gratitude. Then he shared Pate's knife with Blair, who admired the blade. "It was a two-edged dirk, with a blade about eight inches long," he remembered. Blair could tell "it was an expensive weapon." An expert in knives, Blair manufactured the finest machetes for Southern sugar plantations. Now slavery's most determined enemy asked him what it would cost to copy Pate's blade and attach it to a thousand six-foot poles. According to Brown, Kansans needed such weapons to defend their homes from "border ruffians or wild beasts." Blair paused. Unsure that he wanted this work, he quoted Brown a stiff price, a dollar each. Brown said he wanted them made.[10]

Why pikes? Brown had already used blades in Kansas when his men hacked to death five Southerners with broadswords. The murders terrified proslavery settlers. Spreading a thousand blades across Kansas would intensify the scare Brown started. His choice of weapon mattered. An avid reader of military history, Brown knew that pikes represented the overthrow of aristocracy. Medieval knights had gained social and military power because few men had had the mettle to stand and receive a cavalry charge. That changed when Swiss peasants skewered charging knights with pikes. A simple edged weapon in the hands of a determined underclass had ended the reign of knights in Europe. Perhaps circulating a thousand pikes to yeomen in Kansas would produce similar results against the "knights" of the South. The pike signified Northerners' determination to stand up to Southern threats. William Lloyd Garrison condemned Southerners' bowie-knife politics and criticized Northerners for being intimidated by men like Pate. "It is only for some few seditious hot-spurs at the South to brandish their cowskins and bowie knives, and shout 'We'll dissolve the Union!' and straightaway we turn pale." If Pate's knife threatened a border war on the frontier, Brown's pike prophesied a class war against the Slave Power.[11]

Turning a bowie into a pike also showed the protean conduct of Yankee radicals. Rifles arrived in Kansas labeled as Bibles. Northern militia called their fort the Free State Hotel. Proslavery settlers had reasons to worry that things were not what they seemed in Kansas. The covertness of Northerners' restrained manhood unnerved them. When Missouri ruffians had "sacked" Lawrence, they had not attacked people, as the Northern press lied. Instead they destroyed Yankee things. After they stole all the weapons they could find, Missourians plundered homes and wore Yankee vests and dresses over their clothing to mock Northerners' pretentions of restrained manhood. They also burned the Free State Hotel and smashed the printing press of the *Herald of Freedom*. After the raid, Northern women gathered the press's scattered type and gave it to free-state militia, who melted it into cannonballs. When Northerners retaliated, they fired the reconstituted type through the enemy's fort. "This is the second edition of the 'Herald of Freedom,'" the militia jeered. "How do you like it?" In more ways than one, things changed in Kansas. Brown continued this tradition by transforming a ruffian's knife into free-state pikes. After receiving prototypes from Blair, Brown modified the design so that the blades and shafts, which were common hoe handles, could be shipped separately to avoid suspicion.[12]

Weeks later the Panic of 1857 doomed Brown's fund-raising tour. Unpaid, Blair left the arms unfinished. The previous panic in 1837 had also ruined Brown's prospects. For twenty years he tried various schemes to overcome bankruptcy. Farming, land speculating, tanning hides, selling wool—each new plan was more ambitious than the last. They all failed. By 1857, Brown was determined to double down on his setbacks by finishing his pike project, but the financial and social support for such schemes had vanished along with so many people's fortunes. He gave up public fundraising and turned to secret donors. But things did not go as planned for John Brown.[13]

In October 1859, pairs of men followed the pikes across the Maryland-Virginia line toward Harpers Ferry. Osborne Anderson, a free black man from Canada, recalled that they marched like "a funeral procession." Brown finally paid for the weapons three years after Black Jack when he returned to Blair's shop unannounced. Blair wondered why Brown wanted them now that Kansas was settled. Brown said, "They might be useful if finished." While Blair found someone to finish Brown's arms, Horatio Rust sent some of Brown's rifles to Samuel Colt for repairs and shipped supplies from his pharmacy to Brown's lieutenant, John Kagi in Chambersburg, Pennsylvania. Working at the center of things, Kagi encouraged his sister not to succumb to a feeling that haunted him, a premonition that "you were singled out by Fate from living chessmen in his game of horror and of death."[14]

Instead of prophesying a border war or class conflict out west, the pikes now threatened a race war down south. This vision featured ironies of befitting justice. The sidearm of a white Virginian from the master class would become a thousand weapons for black Virginians. Hoe handles, a common instrument in slaves' hands, would now work for freedom instead of oppression. Pikes, which displayed the heads of captured insurrectionists across the slaveholding Americas, would now seize masters. For Osborne Anderson, Brown's pikes signified something else. Though an ancient weapon, they were financed by leading capitalists, forged by one of the nation's leading bladesmiths, transported by rail to the band's headquarters, and assembled for swift distribution on-site. This insurrection would not rely on farm implements and random weapons at hand. John Brown's outbreak designed, manufactured, and distributed its own arms. The pike was a harbinger of the modern insurrection. After its metamorphosis, Pate's blade made a different point about conquest and progress.[15]

Anderson was responsible for giving pikes to slaves during the raid on Harpers Ferry. Because he was in charge of *things*, slaves assumed that Anderson was captain of the band. This rumor was reinforced by the fact that Lewis Washington, a great-grandnephew of George Washington, surrendered his ancestor's sword to Anderson, not to Brown. Order 11 of the plan of attack explained why: "Anderson being a colored man, and colored men being only *things* in the South, it is proper that the South be taught a lesson upon this point." Brown exposed the legal fiction that blacks were property by having Washington surrender his prized possession to Anderson. Exchanging arms was Brown's way of proving black humanity. "Give a slave a pike," he said, "and you make him a man." Weapons offered more than freedom; they conveyed virtues that Americans respected. "Nothing so charms the American people as personal bravery," Brown told blacks. While other abolitionists wanted to give slaves freedom, Brown wanted to give them weapons. "Hold on to your weapons, and never be persuaded to leave them," he said.[16]

African Americans at Harpers Ferry understood this advice. Throughout the raid, they handled and exchanged weapons to express allegiance and power. Several enslaved blacks heard about the raid through rumors, traveled to Harpers Ferry, and asked Anderson for pikes. Black men materialized through the night as if they sensed the magnetic possibilities of Anderson's weapons. Armed free blacks stopped a mail express train in Maryland from reaching the Harpers Ferry bridge. Between twenty-five and fifty slaves joined Anderson at the start of the raid. An elderly slave used Lewis Washington's shotgun to kill a white citizen as retaliation for the death of one of the raiders. Some slaves shuttled weapons from Brown's stockpiles in Maryland to the raiders at Harpers Ferry. Others used pikes to guard hostages, including their masters.[17]

The sight of African Americans wielding arms terrified Southerners, who feared a race war. "I saw what, indeed, looked like war," said John Dangerfield, the U.S. paymaster at Harpers Ferry, "negroes armed with pikes, and sentinels with muskets all around." While Anderson gave pikes to assembled slaves, he noticed that white spectators reacted with fear and rage. Blacks understood the scene through biblical allusions to Year of Jubilee, but whites framed the scene as the Apocalypse. As Anderson put it, "Judgment-day could not have presented more terrors, in its awful and certain prospective punishment to the justly condemned." White Southerners spread rumors that multiplied the number of armed blacks by hundreds. Hostages cried and begged for a chance to see their families one last time.[18]

Things got out of hand. Historians have offered many explanations for the raid's failure. Raiders stopped a train and then, inexplicably, let it continue to Baltimore to raise the alarm. Because Brown launched the assault unexpectedly, his support network throughout the region was not prepared to attack. Taking hostages consumed the raiders' time and immobilized them in town when they could have struck the arsenal, gathered arms, and headed for the mountains. Things—and the raiders' obsession over them— also derailed the invasion. Though he carried a thousand pikes and hundreds of firearms to Harpers Ferry, Brown targeted a town stockpiled with weapons. What he needed was a concentration of slaves, not arms. Thousands of slaves lived in the surrounding countryside, but when Brown's men fanned out that night, they gathered more weapons than recruits. Arms seemed to attract the raiders more than the people they needed to succeed.[19]

Most African Americans changed their relationship to weapons the instant the raid failed. When marines charged the engine house, Shields Green, one of five black lieutenants in Brown's party, dropped his rifle and stood beside six slaves, hoping to pass as one of them. When citizens gunned down John Kagi, a nearby slave named Ben threw down his pike and begged for mercy. A clever expression of loyalty was practiced by one of Lewis Washington's slaves. Days after the revolt failed, he showed Washington where he claimed he hid his master's shotgun. He said Brown's men had given him the weapon to aid his escape. But Anderson had given Washington's shotgun to the old slave who had fought throughout the attack. After the raid, Washington's slave recognized the gun and a chance to surrender. By concealing his master's things from Northern thieves, he practiced a ploy that countless blacks would replicate to deflect white suspicions about black loyalties during the Civil War. [20]

While some African Americans returned weapons to save their lives, others hid them as battle trophies. Washington recovered his dress sword and shotgun, but his Belgian bird gun disappeared. Terence Byrne, a Maryland slaveholder who was a hostage during the raid, testified that he saw a black man carrying the fowling piece. In the 1990s, Charles Cephas found a gun that matches its description in his great-grandfather's attic. The Belgian gun has a brass plate with the engraved initial *W*. It was found beside two 1858-model Harpers Ferry rifles. By tracing the story of these weapons, historians Hannah Geffert and Jean Libby have uncovered a complex web of black involvement in the raid. Osborne Anderson hoped that this network would spread a race war. Instead, it helped him escape to Canada along the Underground Railroad. Things did not go as planned for Osborne Anderson.[21]

When marines dragged Brown unconscious from the engine house, Lieutenant J. E. B. Stuart stole his bowie knife, an English blade with a beautiful tortoiseshell handle. Stuart was the only one present who could confirm Brown's identity. Three years earlier he had ridden beside Colonel Sumner into Brown's camp and released Pate's posse after the battle of Black Jack. Stuart detested Brown and encouraged Harpers Ferry citizens to kill him. He singled out David Hunter Strother, an acquaintance and prominent local man, and suggested that Brown was "a man so infamous for his robberies and murders that if the people here knew his antecedents he would not be permitted to live five minutes." An artist and writer, Strother was more interested in sketching than lynching Brown and complained that his subject was too bloody for an accurate portrait. When Stuart ordered someone to clean Brown's wounds, another wounded raider, Aaron Stephens, spoke with more life than Strother thought he had left in him. "If there is any manhood in you and you are not a set of old women you should immediately have him cared for," Stephens remarked. The raider was challenging the martial manhood of the South and Stuart knew it. "You son of a bitch," Stuart snapped. "Your treatment is to that of midnight thieves and murderers not of men taken in honourable warfare," the cavalier retorted.[22]

When things Brown brought with him surfaced across the border hours later, Southerners like Stuart stopped belittling the raiders' intentions. What marines and militiamen found ended all talk about banditry. Brown's

Assembling the Future in Antebellum America

things more than his statements convinced Southerners of his plans to wage war. At noon on the day Brown was captured, the Baltimore Greys investigated a rumor that stores of arms were hidden in the surrounding mountains. Six hours later the militiamen returned to town with two wagons filled with hundreds of revolvers, rifles, torches, percussion caps, gunpowder kegs, and cartridges, proving that Brown had planned to raise an army of race warriors.[23]

Stuart led marines to Brown's headquarters at the Kennedy farm. By the time he arrived, neighbors had already ransacked the place for souvenirs. Maps and military drill manuals littered the farmhouse floor. When Stuart checked an outlying cabin, he found crates filled with tent canvas, axes, hominy mills, men's clothing, and boots throughout the first floor. Climbing to the second story, he discovered counterpanes neatly piled three feet high. Above, in the loft, hundreds of spears lay across the floor and rested against the walls. Stunned, Stuart turned to a local man, John Unseld, who had guided him to the location, and told Unseld to break the attic window and throw the spears down into the yard. Unseld did as he was told, but the work proved too much for him. While he was tossing pikes out the window, citizens reappeared and collected them before Stuart could cart them to town. Overwhelmed by the task at hand, Stuart allowed each person to take five spears, and when that amount did not satisfy civilians or make a dent in the task at hand, he raised each person's quota to fifty. During the spree, white Southerners shattered 175 spear shafts to collect pocket-size relics. People also carried off all the clothing and boots.[24]

White Southerners even vied for pieces of the insurgents themselves. After Dangerfield Newby died in the street, people cut off his ears as trophies, picked his pockets, and stole letters from his wife. Authorities concealed Brown's casket and used decoy hearses to throw off relic hunters. The body of his son Watson did not make it north until the 1880s. When it arrived, fingers and toes were missing. Medical students from Winchester dug up the bodies of two raiders minutes after they were interred and carried them to anatomy class. When one of the raider's parents asked the faculty for their son's remains, the students refused to surrender the body. White Southerners collected things to make sense of the raid, uncover its supporters, and predict its consequences. They also savored trophies that flaunted its failure. A Virginia slaveholder mailed a lock of John Brown's hair to Wendell Phillips and inadvertently gave the abolitionist a cherished relic.[25]

Agricultural reformer and ardent secessionist Edmund Ruffin believed from the start that Brown invaded Virginia to wage civil war. In his opinion, Brown's invasion deserved a Southern declaration of war, but the slave states lacked unity of vision and purpose. During the hysteria surrounding Brown's raid, Ruffin acquired "one of the spears which Brown had brought to arm the slaves." Instead of recognizing European pikes as Brown intended, Ruffin and other white Southerners saw African spears. The federal bookkeeper who listed things captured after the raid counted "a large quantity of spears, sharp iron bowie knives fixed upon poles, a terrible looking weapon, intended for the use of the negroes." He gave one to his wife as a souvenir.[26]

Edged weapons were at the heart of slave revolts. Toussaint L'Ouverture fashioned iron spears for his 1791 overthrow of French slavers in Santo Domingo. In 1800, Gabriel Prosser's plot for a revolt in Virginia included a plan to arm slaves with swords made by Gabriel and his brother Solomon, both trained blacksmiths. In 1822, Denmark Vesey plotted to raid the Charleston, South Carolina, arsenal to gather and circulate hundreds of pikes and bayonets. In 1831, Nat Turner's insurrection resulted in the murder of Virginians with knives and sharp farm implements. When authorities captured Turner, he was carrying a sword. In history and physical attributes, pikes were civilized, defensive arms, whereas spears were barbaric, offensive weapons. Ruffin appreciated the difference and exploited every chance to display his trophy. The sight of Ruffin, a little old man clutching a seven-foot spear through the streets of Charlestown, attracted crowds, and he used "every suitable occasion to express disunion sentiments." The secessionist appropriated Brown's weapon to start his own war, one that would defend, not end, slavery.[27]

Ruffin hatched a plan to circulate Brown's spears across the South to start a revolution for Southern independence. He gave one spear to each governor of a slaveholding state to display in the legislature. Ruffin was a famous agronomist and relentless secessionist, but he alone could accomplish little. His spears would "serve as a most eloquent and impressive preacher" in his absence. Ruffin's words could convey only so much. He understood how these things expressed a visceral power that surpassed his best writing. His plan echoed something Ruffin did during Andrew Jackson's Bank War, when he cleverly attached calls for financial reform to the backs of bank notes before returning them to circulation. With Ruffin's artful additions, each note would "instruct by its back as many persons as it cheats by its face," Ruffin quipped. He enjoyed appropriating the enemy's objects for his own ends. The label Ruffin attached to each spear ensured that they conveyed his message:

Assembling the Future in Antebellum America

To the State of _____.
SAMPLE OF THE FAVORS DESIGNED FOR US BY OUR NORTHERN BRETHREN.
The most precious benefit derived from the Northern States, by the Southern, if rightly using it, "out of this nettle *danger*, we pluck the flower *safety*."²⁸

Ruffin was addressing slave owners who received many samples from Northern manufacturers. Samples of cloth, tools, and other items moved south for masters to inspect before placing orders. Samples were promises about the future that Northerners made to Southerners. Ruffin wanted the master class to know that Brown's spear was the genuine article, the very thing that Yankees would send south in bulk. Brown's spears belonged to a long tradition of insurrectionary violence, but one critical fact distinguished his weapons: white Northerners financed and forged Brown's weapons. Ruffin's samples damned the Yankee origins of the raid and prophesied a looming civil war. While war trophies verified the enemy's defeat, they also exposed his intentions.²⁹

The things that captivated Americans when they anticipated civil war mattered. People, white and black, did not focus on modern weapons like rifles, pistols, and cannons when they collected relics of the future. Brown could have kept Pate's revolver but preferred his knife. Stuart and Ruffin could have collected Brown's handguns but preferred his knife and spear. The grim sharpness of edged weapons appealed to these men and spoke volumes about the kind of war they projected. These visceral totems foretold a brutal war of close combat and personal killings. Things were more than symbols of imagined outcomes—these weapons materialized the future. As Lorraine Daston explains, without things people would literally have nothing "to describe, or to explain, remark on, interpret, or complain about.... Without things, we would stop talking. We would become as mute as things are alleged to be."³⁰

The quotation Ruffin attached to the pike, "out of this nettle danger, we pluck the flower safety," is from Shakespeare's *Henry IV*, and it illustrates how Ruffin imagined himself as a fomenter of rebellion. Nineteenth-century Americans would have recognized the line spoken by Henry "Hotspur" Percy, the chief rebel against the king. As his nickname suggests, Hotspur was also Shakespeare's most famous fire-eater. Portrayals of Hotspur have changed over time, but literary scholar Roberta Barker notes that "the readings of Hotspur's role that dominate page and stage at a given time will most likely be those that reproduce their own culture's normative concepts of masculine heroism." In nineteenth-century America, Hotspur was considered a tragic hero, a swashbuckling nobleman who dies avenging his insulted honor on the field of battle. The character resonated among Southern slave owners dedicated to martial manhood and honor. A military hero from the countryside, Hotspur represented the older feudal order and rebelled against the king's more modern style of rule that courted the masses. Hotspur is a nonpolitical man who was born too late and suffered in an age fascinated by image and prone to deception. The current government had used guile and deceit to usurp the throne. Hotspur sought to restore justice and reconstruct the legitimate older order by purging the nation of corruption in a bloody civil war. Imagining enemy hordes arrayed against him, Hotspur exclaims,

> They come like sacrifices in their trim,
> And to the fire-eyed maid of smoky war
> All hot and bleeding shall we offer them.
> The mailed Mars shall on his altar sit
> Up to the ears in blood.[31]

In the scene Ruffin quoted, Hotspur performs the same task that consumed Ruffin, corresponding with sympathizers in an attempt to galvanize a rebel alliance. His efforts failed in his home state of Virginia. When Ruffin asked Albert Rust to deliver a pike, he took one look at the weapon, read Ruffin's message, and declined the honor. Rust objected to "having any thing to do with the pike," because he feared its presence would inspire slave revolts. In Rust's view, the pike was too real, and Ruffin's label could not erase its original meaning and intentions. When Ruffin sent a pike to the incoming governor of Virginia, John Letcher, he stressed how it was "sent from the North to arm slaves, and to be imbrued in the blood of the whites of the South." Ruffin asked Letcher to display it in the capital, "as impressive and abiding evidence of the fanatical hatred borne by the dominant party of the North to the institutions and people of the Southern States." For Ruffin, this object proved the objects of his enemy's designs. Letcher ignored the request.[32]

The fire-eater's gift received a warmer reception in South Carolina. When South Carolinians seceded, Ruffin and his spear were honored guests at the secession convention. Ruffin, like Hotspur, started a quest to restore a static past. The president of the convention, David Flavel Jamison, was a planter and amateur scholar of French history. A month before John Brown's raid, Jamison publically berated his fellow South Carolinians for not uniting against the abolitionists' threat. Instead of anticipating danger and checking it like men, Carolinians waited with expectation, submissively like women: "We are looking to some sudden turn of fortune we know not what to rescue us from the doom we have not the courage to avert." The following year, Jamison urged manly anticipation at the secession convention. He told delegates "to dare! And again to dare! And without end to dare," a line first spoken by Georges Jacques Danton during the French Revolution. In the same speech, Danton outlined a war strategy that John Brown would have approved: "One portion of our people will proceed to the frontiers, another will throw up intrenchments, and the third with pikes will defend the hearts of our cities." Jamison did not catch the irony of his remark, nor did he consider it strange that conservative South Carolina should evoke the French Revolution when leaving the Union.[33]

Americans across the nation sought Brown's pikes as relics of the future, harbingers of a revolution to end or defend slavery. Within months of the raid, almost half of all the pikes circulated the nation as personal souvenirs. Horatio Rust cherished his pike and the role he played in creating it. After escorting John Brown's widow, Mary Brown, to and from Charlestown, James Miller McKim received the pike that Brown's son Oliver carried and gave it to Wendell Phillips. A Harpers Ferry clerk mailed one to Samuel Colt as a gift. The B&O Railroad sold pikes to passengers at the Harpers Ferry station until a company official ended "this pike trade" because it "only adds to the excitement." Even William Lloyd Garrison, a paragon of pacifism and restrained manhood, prized the pike he received from John Hopper in May 1860. Brown had given the sample to Hopper as a token of friendship. Sawn short to facilitate shipping, Garrison's pike lacked a rivet or screw to attach the ferrule, indicating that it was among the first pikes that Blair crafted before Brown modified the design. For Garrison, the pike embodied "Virginia Herself, who, by her coat of arms, with its terrible motto, 'Sic semper tyrannis,' asserts the right of the oppressed to trample their oppressors beneath their feet, and, if necessary, consign them to a bloody grave!" The man who would make Virginia's motto famous a few years later, John Wilkes Booth, attended Brown's execution and took home a Harpers Ferry pike as a memento. Virginia's state seal displayed a man conquering his oppressor by wielding a pike.[34]

During the aftermath of the raid, Virginian John Floyd served Southern interests by exploiting his position as secretary of war to distribute the remaining pikes. His father had been governor of Virginia during Nat Turner's insurrection. Weeks after Brown's execution, the younger Floyd used his cabinet position to transfer thousands of weapons from Northern to Southern arsenals. More than 100,000 muskets moved from Massachusetts to North Carolina, South Carolina, Georgia, Alabama, and Louisiana. Floyd collected crates of Harpers Ferry pikes and shipped them to a Texas armory, where they eventually armed a Confederate regiment. Virginia secessionists looted Harpers Ferry in April 1861 after Federal troops evacuated and burned the arsenal. David Hunter Strother, a Unionist, watched the spectacle and criticized his friend Turner Ashby for participating in it. Young men like Ashby sensed the looming war and wanted a piece of it. These developments confirmed Ruffin's suspicion that circulating weapons increased passion for war. Despite his best efforts, Ruffin's rebellion, like Hotspur's revolt, ended with his death. Things did not go as planned for Edmund Ruffin.[35]

Henry Clay Pate spent years trying to recover his knife. As Kariann Yokota writes, "Once they are put into circulation, objects consort with people on both sides of any political divide; their makers cannot control how they will be used or by whom." Pate would have appreciated that insight. Things also asserted the manliness of their possessors and unmanned people who lost them. Pate understood this too. In November 1859, he visited John Brown in jail and demanded the return of his knife. Brown confessed that he had given it to friend, a gentleman from Massachusetts. When Pate pressed him for a name, Brown refused. So Pate published a pamphlet calling for the return of his knife. "If Brown's friend will send my weapon to me, I shall be obliged to him," he said. Pate even offered to purchase it. Recovering his knife was the only way Pate could escape Brown's shadow.[36]

He never did. To restore his honor, Pate reversed Brown's course. If Brown could leave his home in New York and attack Southern honor in Virginia, Pate could leave his home in Virginia and attack Brown's character in New York. Five days after Brown's execution, a time when church bells tolled and millions mourned the martyr, Pate denounced Brown in a speech at the Cooper Institute in New York City. Standing before hundreds of New Yorkers, Pate predicted a terrible civil war if the North continued its campaign against slavery. You "might as well try to abolish death as to abolish slavery," he said. Both "existed from the beginning of the world." He defended his honor at Black Jack by drawing a large map of the fight and exaggerating his heroism against five-to-one odds. When he welcomed questions from the audience, a young man in a military overcoat shot from his seat and asked, "Do you think that if I were to go to Virginia I would be allowed to speak as you speak here tonight?" "Certainly, sir, you would," Pate replied, but everything about his lecture supported the accusation within the stranger's question. Pate and his fellow Virginians would not allow Northern prophecies of border war, class war, or race war in the Old Dominion. The pointer Pate carried said as much. He stood before his heckler armed with a pike he had snatched at Harpers Ferry. The fact that his missing blade formed the point of the pike escaped him.[37]

Before Brown left for Virginia, he asked his family to give Pate's knife to one of his stalwart supporters in Massachusetts. Unlike most friends who betrayed Brown in the initial aftershock of the attack, this man praised him. He argued that Brown's raid shocked Americans, because they were too accustomed to wielding weapons in ignoble affairs, like dueling, waging foreign wars, killing Indians, and hunting fugitive slaves. "For once the Sharps' rifles and the revolvers were employed in a righteous cause," and Americans considered it an outrage. Eager to fashion Northern reaction to the news, he repeated the speech in Worcester and Boston. "I think we should express ourselves at once, while Brown is alive," he told a friend. When Frederick Douglass declined to appear at a Boston rally for Brown, this man took his place on the program. Newspaper summaries of his speech edited out its boldest points. James Redpath asked him to provide a definitive account of Black Jack for his book about Brown and dedicated the volume to him. His name was Henry David Thoreau.[38]

As they circulated the country, iterations of Pate's knife assembled different people and futures. How these things were made and what they meant were not separate concerns but the same matter. In Kansas, Southern filibusters who wielded bowie knives threatened a border war over sovereignty and white supremacy. In Connecticut, reformers who turned a bowie knife into pikes sought a class war to level Southern aristocracy. In Virginia, African Americans carried pikes to assert manhood and threaten a race war. In South Carolina, secessionists displayed spears to forecast civil war and foment disunion. Twice these things crossed borders and sparked conflicts for freedom. Both invasions failed, and the enemy captured things as trophies and circulated them to promote radical politics—first abolition and then secession. This national circulation of things accomplished more than a series of thefts and gifts. The men who invaded Kansas and Virginia found courage, resolve, and identity in the things they carried. They could not have pressed forward without such things. The men who took those things to Connecticut and South Carolina gained a false sense of security by disarming their enemies. They too could not have pressed forward without such things. More than ideas distinguished the politics of border ruffians, abolitionists, slaves, and secessionists. They understood things differently and associated with things in diverse ways.

Researching the material cultures of Civil War Americans will uncover more than artifacts preserved beside manuscripts in archives. Focusing on things shows how the power of possessions, particularly weapons, can goad people into action and make history. Perhaps even immaterial acts—like remembering and expecting—rely on things to form and spread. From mementos to monuments, things materialize the past by recalling personal and historical memories. While much scholarship has explained how relics and statues reinforced Civil War memories, this chapter has shown how things realized antebellum expectations of the war too. Competing visions of settlement in Kansas relied on bowie-knife politics and crates of concealed weapons. Captured arms circulated in New England and the South substantiated the enemy's intentions by making their schemes tangible. By assembling things, antebellum Americans crafted competing futures. Among these harbingers of war, John Brown's pikes, in all their forms, spread the most powerful prophecies. These weapons proved to be more than mute props. Their mere presence caused alarms, triggered controversies, and divided Americans without shedding blood. Pate's knife and Brown's pikes harmed the body politic without piercing a single soul. Their story compels us to take *things* seriously.

Notes

1. Henry Clay Pate, *John Brown, as Viewed by H. Clay Pate* (New York: the author, 1859), 34. Pate called Black Jack "the first time American citizens, of different States, professing different politics, had met in battle array" (36). Brown described Black Jack as "the first regular battle fought between Free State & pro Slavery men." See John Brown to wife and children, June (no date) 1856, in John Stauffer and Zoe Trodd, eds., *The Meteor of War: The John Brown Story* (Maplecrest, N.Y.: Brandywine, 2004), 87–88. Terms of surrender: John Brown, Articles of Agreement for the Exchange of Prisoners following Battle of Black Jack, John Brown Collection #299, box 1, folder 16, item number 4272, Kansas Historical Society, accessed online at kansasmemory.org, 18 May 2015. Sumner quoted in Stephen B. Oates, *To Purge This Land with Blood*, 2nd ed. (Amherst: University of Massachusetts Press, 1984), 155.

2. Alex Hawes, "In Kansas, with John Brown," 1881–1882, bound in Boyd B. Stutler, John Brown Pamphlets, vol. 4, pp. 70, Boyd Stutler Collection, West Virginia State Archives. For more Civil War scholarship that takes things seriously, see Simon Harrison, "Bones in the Rebel Lady's Boudoir: Ethnology, Race and Trophy-Hunting in the American Civil War," *Journal of Material Culture* 15 (December 2010): 385–401; Joan E. Cashin, "Trophies of War: Material Culture in the Civil War Era," *Journal of the Civil War Era* 1, no. 3 (September 2011): 339–67; Michael DeGruccio, "Letting the War Slip through Our Hands: Material Culture and the Weakness of Words in the Civil War Era," in *Weirding the War: Stories from the Civil War's Ragged Edges*, ed. Stephen Berry (Athens: University of Georgia Press, 2011), 15–35; Megan Kate Nelson, *Ruin Nation: Destruction and the American Civil War* (Athens: University of Georgia Press, 2012); and Virginia Scharff, ed., *Empire and Liberty: The Civil War and the West* (Berkeley: University of California Press, 2015).

3. Bruno Latour, "Why Has Critique Run Out of Steam? From Matters of Fact to Matters of Concern," *Critical Inquiry* 30 (Winter 2004): 246 (italics in original). Bruno Latour and Peter Weibel, *Making Things Public: Atmospheres of Democracy* (Cambridge, Mass.: MIT Press, 2005); Bruno Latour, *Politics of Nature: How to Bring the Sciences into Democracy*, trans. Catherine Porter (Cambridge, Mass.: Harvard University Press, 2004); Jane Bennett, *Vibrant Matter: A Political Ecology of Things* (Durham: Duke University Press, 2010).

4. Michael Zakim, *Ready-Made Democracy: A History of Men's Dress in the American Republic, 1760–1860* (Chicago: University of Chicago Press, 2003), 203; Amy S. Greenberg, *Manifest Manhood and the Antebellum American Empire* (Cambridge: Cambridge University Press, 2005), 11–15; Norm Flayderman, *The Bowie Knife: Unsheathing an American Legend* (Lincoln, R.I.: Andrew Mowbray, 2004); Steve Shackleford, ed., *Blade's Guide to Knives and their Values*, 7th ed. (Iola, Wisc: Krause, 2009), 307; William C. Davis, *Three Roads to the Alamo* (New York: HarperCollins, 1998).

5. T. H. Gladstone, *The Englishman in Kansas: Squatter Life and Border Warfare* (New York: Miller and Company, 1857), 251–52; Dr. G. A. Cutler testimony, "Report of the Special Committee Appointed to Investigate the Troubles in Kansas," *House Documents*, volume 89 (Washington: Cornelius Wendell, 1856), 357; Buford quoted in Walter L. Fleming, "The Buford Expedition to Kansas," *American Historical Review* 6 (October 1900): 40, 43.

6. Samuel D. Baldwin, *Armageddon* (Cincinnati: Applegate, 1854), 162, 161; George Frederick Holmes, "Relations of the Old and the New Worlds," *De Bow's Review*, May 1856, 529.

7. H. Clay Pate, *American Vade Mecum* (Cincinnati: Morgan, 1852), 78, 75. Pate joined an exodus of a million Virginians who left for western horizons during the antebellum years, a total that dwarfed the population lost by any other state during this time. See Daniel Walker Howe, *What Hath God Wrought: The Transformation of America, 1815–1848* (New York: Oxford University Press, 2007), 158. Surviving descriptions of Pate's knife make it likely that the weapon was an expensive one made in England. Franklin Sanborn claimed that Pate's Virginia friends gave him the knife as a gift before he left for Kansas: "a magnificently mounted Bowie-knife, presented to Pate by his friends in Virginia, when he started out to subjugate the wicked abolitionists who had presumed to migrate to Kansas, and there oppose negro slavery." See Sanborn, *Recollections of Seventy Years*, vol. 1 (Boston: Richard G. Badger, 1909), 103–4.

8. Simon J. Harrison, "War Mementos and the Souls of Missing Soldiers: Returning Effects of the Battlefield Dead," *Journal of the Royal Anthropological Institute* 14 (December 2008): 774–90 (quotation on 785).

9. Brown and Stearns quoted in Franklin B. Sanborn, ed., *The Life and Letters of John Brown: Liberator of Kansas, and Martyr of Virginia* (Boston: Roberts Brothers, 1891), 508–10; David S. Reynolds, *John Brown, Abolitionist: The Man Who Killed Slavery, Sparked the Civil War, and Seeded Civil Rights* (New York: Alfred A. Knopf, 2005), 222.

10. Boyd Stutler to Donald B. Webster Jr., 3 May 1958, Boyd Stutler Collection, West Virginia State Archives; James Redpath, *The Public Life of Captain John Brown* (Boston: Thayer and Eldridge, 1860), 193. Blair quotes from his testimony in the "Mason Report," *U.S. Senate Committee Reports*, 1859–1860, II (Washington, D.C.: no publisher, 1860), 121–29.

11. Garrison quoted in Reynolds, *John Brown*, 162. Theodore Dwight Weld, *American Slavery as It Is* (New York: American Anti-slavery Society, 1839), 189–90. According to John Keegan, "The pike, or thrusting spear, was a simpler tool of war, and in the hands of hardy and fractious peasant communities from areas where the knightly class was small, such as Switzerland, could be wielded to oppose a dense barrier to cavalry attack, as long as the pikemen kept their nerve in the face of a charge." During the fifteenth century, Swiss pikemen asserted their superiority against mounted knights in a series of battles that fostered Switzerland's reputation as the motherland of mercenaries. The Swiss pike thwarted Hapsburg overlords and "destroyed Burgundian power for good." See John Keegan, *A History of Warfare* (New York: Knopf, 1993), 329.

12. Edward Payson Bridgman and Luke Fisher Parsons, *With John Brown in Kansas* (Madison: J. N. Davidson, 1915), 16.

13. John Stauffer, *The Black Hearts of Men: Radical Abolitionists and the Transformation of Race* (Cambridge, Mass.: Harvard University Press, 2001), 95–133; Oates, *To Purge This Land with Blood*, 49.

14. Osborne Anderson, *A Voice from Harper's Ferry* (Boston: the author, 1861), 32; "Mason Report," 128; Oates, *To Purge This Land with Blood*, 286. Kagi quoted in Stauffer and Trodd, *Meteor of War*, 100–101.

15. Anderson, *Voice from Harper's Ferry*, 8; Weld, *American Slavery as It Is*, 23; Adam Rothman, *Slave Country: American Expansion and the Origins of the Deep South* (Cambridge, Mass.: Harvard University Press, 2005), 115.

16. Anderson, *Voice from Harper's Ferry*, 31 (italics in original). Brown quoted in Reynolds, *John Brown*, 306; John Brown, "League of Gileadites," 15 January 1851, in *The Tribunal: Reponses to John Brown and the Harpers Ferry Raid*, ed. John Stauffer and Zoe Trodd (Cambridge, Mass.: Harvard University Press, 2012), 8–9.

17. Anderson, *Voice from Harper's Ferry*, 38, 52; Jean Libby, ed., *John Brown Mysteries* (Missoula: Pictorial Histories, 1999), 36; Hannah Geffert with Jean Libby, "Regional Black Involvement in John Brown's Raid on Harpers Ferry," in *Prophets of Protest: Reconsidering the History of American Abolitionism*, ed. Timothy Patrick McCarthy and John Stauffer (New York: New Press, 2006), 165–82.

18. Dangerfield quoted in Richard J. Hinton, *John Brown and His Men* (New York: Funk and Wagnalls, 1894), 300; Anderson, *Voice from Harper's Ferry*, 37.

19. Tony Horwitz, *Midnight Rising: John Brown and the Raid That Sparked the Civil War* (New York: Henry Holt, 2011); Reynolds, *John Brown*; Oates, *To Purge This Land with Blood*.

20. Horwitz, *Midnight Rising*, 179, 163; "Mason Report," 39.

21. "Mason Report," 16; Geffert with Libby, "Regional Black Involvement."

22. Bowie knife and sheath, object number 1983.31, Virginia Historical Society, Richmond; undated entry, Journal 3, 1857–1859, David Hunter Strother Papers, West Virginia and Regional History Collection, Wise Library, West Virginia University.

23. Robert W. Baylor to Governor Henry Wise, 18 October 1859, in Robert M. De Witt, *The Life, Trial and Execution of Captain John Brown* (New York: Robert M. De Witt, 1859), 43, 38.

24. Ellis Turner, "Terrible Swift Sword: The Edged Weapons of John Brown's War on Slavery," *Man at Arms*, December 2012, 34. There is conflicting evidence about whether

Assembling the Future in Antebellum America   { 31

Stuart or Lieutenant Israel Green found the spears and distributed them. John C. Unseld testified that Lieutenant Green found and distributed the weapons, but Robert E. Lee reported that he ordered Green to escort the prisoners to Charlestown and sent Stuart to Brown's headquarters. In his postwar recollection of the raid, Green did not mention finding the spears. See "Mason Report," 42, 11, 12; and Israel Green, "The Capture of John Brown," *North American Review*, December 1885, 564–65.

25. James Monroe, *Thursday Lectures, Addresses and Essays* (Oberlin, Ohio: Edward J. Goodrich, 1897), 170; Horwitz, *Midnight Rising*, 282; James Brewer Stewart, *Abolitionist Politics and the Coming of the Civil War* (Amherst: University of Massachusetts Press, 2008), 165. Grave robbing for anatomy classes was common in the nineteenth century; however, the students' attachment to the raiders' corpses was political. Though this essay concentrates on inanimate things, it is worth pointing out that corporeal trophies from Bleeding Kansas and Harpers Ferry linked old practices and customs rooted in slavery and Indian wars. See Michael Fellman, *Inside War: The Guerrilla Conflict in Missouri during the American Civil War* (New York: Oxford University Press, 1990); Peter Silver, *Our Savage Neighbors: How Indian War Transformed Early America* (New York: W. W. Norton, 2008); and Daina Ramey Berry, *The Price for Their Pound of Flesh: The Value of the Enslaved, from Womb to Grave, in the Building of a Nation* (Boston: Beacon Press, 2017).

26. Entries of 8 December 1859 and 7 December 1859, *The Diary of Edmund Ruffin*, ed. William Kauffman Scarborough, vol. 1 (Baton Rouge: Louisiana State University Press, 1972), 377, 375–76; De Witt, *Life, Trial and Execution of Captain John Brown*, 38; Stan Cohen, *John Brown: "Thundering Voice of Jehovah"* (Missoula: Pictorial Histories, 1999), 151.

27. Turner, "Terrible Swift Sword," 25; entry of 1 December 1859, *Diary of Edmund Ruffin*, 368.

28. Ruffin quoted in Avery Craven, *Edmund Ruffin, Southerner: A Study in Secession* (Baton Rouge: Louisiana State University Press, 1932), 178, 69. Entry of 10 December 1859, 17 July 1860 (last quotation), *Diary of Edmund Ruffin*, 378, 443.

29. For economic ties between Northern manufacturers and Southern slaveholders, see Sven Beckert and Seth Rockman, eds., *Slavery's Capitalism: A New History of American Economic Development* (Philadelphia: University of Pennsylvania Press, 2016).

30. Lorraine Daston, ed., *Things That Talk: Object Lessons from Art and Science* (New York: Zone Books, 2008), 9.

31. Roberta Barker, "Tragical-Comical-Historical Hotspur," *Shakespeare Quarterly* 54 (Autumn 2003): 299; William Shakespeare, *Henry IV, Part 1*, ed. David Scott Kastan (London: Arden Shakespeare, 2002), 287.

32. Albert Rust to Edmund Ruffin, 21 June 1860, and Ruffin to John Letcher, 1 January 1860, Edmund Ruffin Papers, Virginia Historical Society.

33. Jamison quoted in Stephen A. Channing, *Crisis of Fear: Secession in South Carolina* (New York: W. W. Norton, 1974), 82, 83; Jamison quoted in William W. Freehling, *The Road to Disunion, Volume II: Secessionists Triumphant, 1854–1861* (New York: Oxford University Press, 2007), 421; Danton quoted in William Jennings Bryan, ed., *The World's Famous Orations, Volume VII: Continental Europe, 380–1906* (New York: Funk and Wagnalls, 1906), 130–31.

34. Turner, "Terrible Swift Sword," 35 (first quotation), 47; William E. Cain, ed., *William Lloyd Garrison and the Fight against Slavery* (New York: Bedford, 1994), 158–59; Terry Alford, *Fortune's Fool: The Life of John Wilkes Booth* (New York: Oxford University Press, 2015), 81.

35. John T. Thompson, *A Descriptive Catalogue of the Ordnance Museum* (West Point: U.S. Military Academy Press, 1898), 158; David Hunter Strother, "Personal Recollections of the War, by a Virginian, First Paper," *Harper's New Monthly Magazine*, June 1867, 14.

36. Kariann Yokota, *Unbecoming British: How Revolutionary America Became a Postcolonial Nation* (New York: Oxford University Press, 2014), 29; Pate, *John Brown*, 38. As anthropologist Simon Harrison explains, "Gifts . . . are concerned with the creation and maintenance of social relations and connections, while restitutions are concerned with the reinstatement or reinforcement of boundaries." See Harrison, "War Mementos and the Souls of Missing Soldiers," 775.

37. *New York Herald*, 9 December 1859, 2.

38. Henry David Thoreau, "A Plea for Captain John Brown," 30 October 1859, in Stauffer and Trodd, *Tribunal*, 108; Henry David Thoreau to H. G. O. Blake, 31 October 1859, in *The Correspondence of Henry David Thoreau*, ed. Walter Harding and Carl Bode (New York: New York University Press), 563; James Redpath to Henry David Thoreau, 6 February 1860, in *Correspondence of Henry David Thoreau*, 574. Pate suspected that Brown gave the knife to Samuel Gridley Howe, but there is no evidence of Howe receiving a knife from Brown or his family. According to multiple sources, Brown's family gave Thoreau "a huge knife that had belonged to Brown" in 1859. See Walter Harding, *The Days of Henry Thoreau* (New York: Knopf, 1970), 423; Larry J. Reynolds, "The Cimeter's 'Sweet' Edge: Thoreau, Contemplation, and Violence," in *More Day to Dawn: Thoreau's Walden for the Twenty-First Century*, ed. Sandra Harbert Petrulionis and Laura Dassow Walls (Amherst: University of Massachusetts Press, 2007), 65; and Janet Kemper Beck, *Creating the John Brown Legend: Emerson, Thoreau, Douglass, Child and Higginson in Defense of the Raid on Harpers Ferry* (Jefferson, N.C.: McFarland, 2009), 163.

Relics from Two Wars
Revolutionary Artifacts in the Civil War Era

JOAN E. CASHIN

In the spring of 1861, newspapers in the North and South reported that George Washington's body had disappeared from the graveyard at Mount Vernon. Allegedly the body had been reburied in Lexington, Virginia, over a hundred miles away, to protect it from desecration by Yankees. The story spread like wildfire, amplified by Washington's fame and the public's reverence for his home, one of the country's most beloved houses. The prime suspect was John Augustine Washington II, a grandnephew who had sold the edifice to the Mount Vernon Ladies Association in the late 1850s but maintained control of the tomb and the family graveyard; much to the chagrin of Unionists, he joined the Southern army. Further newspaper reports contradicted the original allegation about the president's corpse, however, and statements from U.S. general Winfield Scott and Confederate general Robert E. Lee confirmed that the body was still in the Mount Vernon vault. That finally convinced the public, in both regions.[1]

Washington's body was both artifact and symbol, and as such it was highly significant in a conflict in which both sides claimed to uphold the Revolution's legacy. The contest over Revolutionary artifacts was part of the all-out political and cultural struggle during the Civil War between the North and the South. Almost any object associated with the Revolution could be involved, although disputes about human remains were rare; more often, the struggles concerned such things as a church pew, a statue, or a house. Both armies tried to take possession of these objects if they could and shield them from the enemy. All of them were proxies for the central question of which side truly upheld the legacy of the Revolution. This essay explores a topic that scholars have neglected: how ordinary citizens in the post-Revolutionary generations perceived artifacts and what happened to those things during the Civil War. It focuses on the Confederate states of Virginia, North Carolina, South Carolina, and Georgia, which numbered among the thirteen original colonies. Loyalists, who had their own memories of the conflict and their own relics, are omitted. The terms "artifact" and "relic" are defined as objects made by human beings in the past, and "material culture" is defined as the "tangible yield of human conduct," to borrow a phrase from the folklorist Henry Glassie.[2]

Well before 1861, white Southerners had developed a distinctive set of ideas about the Revolutionary War and its material culture. Many of the Revolution's leaders hailed from the South, and much of the fighting happened there; most Americans believed that the war ended when Lord Cornwallis surrendered at Yorktown, Virginia, in 1781. Historical knowledge was communicated afterward by print culture, oral tradition, and material culture, the latter being a particularly memorable way to convey information. The region was filled with historic places, both renowned battlefields and the sites of skirmishes known only to local people. The homes of Revolutionary figures survived long past the war, as did Patrick Henry's estate, Red Hill, still standing in the 1840s. Less notable dwellings from the Revolutionary period also lasted a long time. The Cayce family of South Carolina moved into an abandoned British fort and transformed it into a private home, where they lived for nearly a hundred years.[3]

The Southern landscape was filled with artifacts, embedded in the terrain itself. Revolutionary objects, as well as Native American relics and colonial mementos, turned up in the same sandbank, as a South Carolinian discovered one day in 1859. Other farmers routinely plowed up Revolutionary artifacts in their work, finding gun parts near such places as Guilford Courthouse, North Carolina. Private residences also contained objects belonging to prominent revolutionaries, including the bookcase owned by Richard Henry Lee, a signer from Virginia, kept by his descendants until the 1840s. Many other citizens, not related to the famous names, preserved their own artifacts. For three generations, the descendants of one Colonel William Roane of Virginia saved a pair of his crutches from the war.[4]

Many white people from different backgrounds—yeoman farmers, shoemakers, planters—owned these artifacts. They brought out their relics on the Fourth of July, and they donated objects to historical societies, particularly military objects, which often surface at archaeological sites because the metals are so durable. In fact, white Southerners had so many artifacts that it sometimes militated against an attitude of reverence. They could decide to repurpose these objects for use in their own lives, as did a farmer who unearthed parts of a British weapon near Cedar Springs, South Carolina, in 1858. He asked a gunsmith to reassemble the parts so he could use the weapon himself.[5]

The concept of historic preservation as we understand it—that things associated with significant events or prominent figures should be set apart, preserved, and curated—did not become widespread until the twentieth century. This held true for local, state, and national governments. The U.S. government was reluctant to pay for memorials to the founding generation, with the exception of George Washington, and his monument was finished more than thirty years after construction began in the nation's capital in 1848. The first national preservation society was founded only in 1853, by private citizens, and the purpose was to save Mount Vernon. In the vacuum, a dynamic folk culture developed. Whites in the Old South perceived historic relics as objects to be cherished, of course, but they also thought that artifacts should be shared, exhibited, and employed in daily life.[6]

Eyewitnesses to the Revolution also mattered a great deal, and into the 1850s, hundreds of veterans and their widows resided in the South. These people literally embodied the uprising, their contemporaries believed, as walking manifestations of the past. Veterans appeared at public gatherings, toasting the Founders, and some of them wore their Continental uniforms. Many of them enjoyed talking about the war, as did John Haimes, who regaled his neighbors with stories about Francis Marion, the so-called Swamp Fox of South Carolina. The press described these white men as "relics"—not "relict," the ancient term for widow, but "relic," as in Theodoric Lee, brother of Richard Henry Lee, who died in 1849. The state governments felt some obligation to assist the aging survivors. Between 1840 and 1860, the state of Georgia paid pensions to over 300 Revolutionary widows.[7]

Some objects had more power than others, and the most cherished Revolutionary objects belonged to George Washington, a rich man who owned many material possessions. As numerous scholars have noted, he is the Revolution's ultimate symbol. He had an acute self-awareness as a historic figure, and he understood the importance of display in public life. He carefully preserved his belongings, ranging from his surveying instruments to his military regalia, and he gave away many of his possessions, handing out mementos to combat veterans who visited him at Mount Vernon. After Charles Willson Peale painted his portrait, Washington gave the ceremonial sash he wore to the artist. In his will of 1799, Washington distributed many objects to relatives, as did his widow, Martha, before she died in 1802. Then the executors had a public sale of yet more of their belongings. This helps explain the number of Washington-related artifacts in the hands of so many people.[8]

Washington's relatives played an important role in the cultural transmission, whether they were his nieces, nephews, grandnieces, grandnephews, great-grandnieces, great-grandnephews, step-grandchildren, or cousins. They also had a keen sense of history, as well as family identity, and they owned a variety of the president's objects. No one owned more than Parke Custis, Martha Custis Washington's grandson from her first marriage who grew up at Mount Vernon. He had many of the president's military effects (such as his battle flags) and his household goods (a china set, vases, and a tea table, among other things), which Custis kept at his plantation, Arlington, in northern Virginia. He was a one-man publicity machine, talkative and gregarious, appearing frequently in the press into the 1850s. He donated some objects to museums, but he was not much of a curator for his own collection, unperturbed as visitors cut souvenir pieces of silk from the battle flags. George Washington's other relatives, many of whom lived in Virginia, readily showed their artifacts to strangers who asked to see them. They made sure to bequeath their relics to the next generation, but they too felt free to make use of them. A great-nephew attended a Fourth of July ceremony in 1859 wearing one of Washington's rings with the initials "G. W." set in pearls, which he showed to fellow celebrants.[9]

Many people mentioned the tactile pleasure they derived from holding artifacts. Most human beings want to have contact with evocative objects—therefore the silk samples cut from Arlington's flags—and because the fingers of the hand have so many nerve endings, holding an object can light up the pleasure centers of the brain. Touching something seems to be a confirmation of reality itself, and many nineteenth-century Americans assumed that the tactile experience was superior to looking at an object. A reporter exulted that grasping one of Washington's dress swords, a gift from Frederick the Great and owned in 1855 by great-grandnephew Lewis Washington, gave him intense "pleasure." Holding a drum from the battles of Saratoga, Cowpens, and Eutaw Springs excited very "pleasing emotions" in another journalist after members of the Savannah militia permitted him to hold it one day in 1857. Moments of physical contact with these things could fire the historical imagination. A yeoman farmer, name unknown, enjoyed holding a musket lock that turned up in his field because, he said, it brought the Revolution "somehow ... nearer to us."[10]

So far we have concentrated on relics created by white men, collected by white men, and handled by white men. They dominated the cultural discourse, yet white women could play a part in relic collecting and the creation of public memory. Gender matters in material culture, and many women owned traditional female objects: a linen tablecloth captured from a British officer, given as a wedding present to Mrs. Chinoe Smith in 1799 and still used by her family in the 1850s; a quilt made with the help of Mrs. George Washington, handed down in the female line in Constance Cary's family through the 1850s; a calico dress, made by Mrs. John Austin during the Revolution, preserved by her family into the 1850s. Southerners asked white women who lived through the event, such as Mary Kershaw, to tell their stories. Lord Cornwallis seized her childhood home in Camden, South Carolina, in 1780 to use as his headquarters, and eleven years later she met George Washington when he toured the state. Until her death in 1848, relatives, neighbors, and strangers asked for her memories of the two men, which local historians recorded. These white women were praised so long as they celebrated the Revolution and did not raise any uncomfortable questions about gender inequities during or after the uprising.[11]

The same was true to some degree for African Americans. Race matters in material culture, and slaves could play a role, albeit a secondary role, in the creation of public memory. Bondmen and bondwomen laboring in the fields sometimes discovered Revolutionary artifacts, although they were not allowed to keep what they found, since those things became the master's property. We cannot know what they thought as they handed over the artifacts or what they said to the master, but other slaves could be taken seriously as custodians of oral tradition if they stuck to a conventional military narrative. An elderly slave known only as Abel, the son of a slave who had died in combat with his master in 1777, often talked about the uprising with a white boy, Alfred Waddell, who listened closely. Another slave, Jerry, once owned by George Washington, held his white listeners rapt with accounts of battles he had observed during the war. These black men were accepted as witnesses so long as they did not raise difficult questions about the British offer of freedom for slaves who joined their ranks or the hundreds of masters, including Washington, who later freed their slaves because bondage seemed to contradict the Revolution's best ideals.[12]

Objects can serve either progressive or conservative purposes, as anthropologist Grant McCracken has observed, and white Americans defined the war with Great Britain in profoundly different ways. Some of them perceived it as a singular, one-time event, no matter how glorious, while others saw it as the beginning of a new, more equitable social order. Parke Custis took a rather narrow view of the Revolution, focused tightly on the military victory over England and on one person, his ancestor George Washington.

Custis was not the only one, of course, and historian Seth Bruggeman has compared the Washington phenomenon to a cult. That has happened in other societies (Garibaldi and Lenin come to mind), but the obsessive focus on him was probably not what Washington intended, since he told his male kinfolk to make their own mark in the world rather than live off their relationship with him. Yet the Revolution clearly meant a great deal to a great many people, no matter how they interpreted the event, and they wanted things associated with it.[13]

As for the antebellum North, there is little scholarship on how ordinary people discovered, collected, or perceived Revolutionary artifacts. Yet the primary sources suggest that the same kind of dynamic folk culture developed in the region, with the same vernacular impact. The landscape had many relics buried in its soil, which farmers plowed up on a regular basis, just as they did in Dixie. These white families preserved their mementos and passed them on to the next generation, and sometimes they donated their objects to museums. They too had personal acquaintance with combat veterans well into the antebellum era, as did the young Oliver Wendell Holmes of Massachusetts. Their local historians recorded the memories of white women who lived through the Revolution. Most white Northerners of both sexes revered George Washington as the preeminent Founder, just as white Southerners did, and they too celebrated the Revolution's glory.[14]

Free black Northerners served in the Revolution, of course, which formed part of the region's historical memory, and their service helped inspire the beginning of Yankee abolition. (The fact that some black Southerners served was largely forgotten in the post-Revolutionary South.) Northern emancipation occurred on a halting, state-by-state basis, through legislation and court decisions, starting in 1780 and continuing into the 1860s. Some slaves were listed in every New England census up to 1840; New Jersey's census of 1860 listed at least eighteen slaves; and in Delaware slavery lasted until 1865. Some whites tried to thwart emancipation, refusing to register their slaves as the law required or kidnapping free blacks to work for them, while others tried to forget that Northern bondage ever existed. The region's museums hold a tiny number of artifacts that celebrate regional emancipation—for example, a necklace belonging to Elizabeth Freeman, who sued for her freedom in Massachusetts in the 1780s. This small number of museum artifacts could be the result of choices made by museum staff who did not remember slavery or did not wish to acquire its relics, or it could be that these objects remained in private hands.[15]

During the secession crisis of 1860–61 and the ensuing war, many parties claimed the Revolution as their inspiration, whether they were Confederates and Unionists in the South or the war's supporters and opponents in the North. In the military realm, cultural symbols mattered to both armies, and both sides frequently invoked George Washington; his image was on the official Confederate seal, and passages from his Farewell Address were read aloud at every Yankee military post in 1862. The troops wanted to see the places associated with the landmark battles and the leading military figures, particularly Washington. Throughout the war, soldiers left camp to visit places in the countryside associated with his personal history and military service. Soon a protracted struggle broke out over the South's object-laden landscape, which everyone saw as imbued with meaning.[16]

Yet neither army had a policy on securing artifacts or historic buildings, regardless of who once owned them or lived in them. In 1861, both armies adopted the Articles of War, composed in 1806, which banned plunder and pillage of citizen property, with no specifics on relics or historic properties. The *Revised United States Army Regulations of 1861* added that safeguards could be provided to property owners "whom it may be in the interest of the army to respect," which gave soldiers a lot of leeway in the field. The Lieber Code, drawn up by Francis Lieber and issued by the Northern army in the spring of 1863, protected "museums of the fine arts" and "libraries" but did not define either term. Did Arlington plantation, the residence of Parke Custis, qualify as a museum? Apparently not, as we shall see.[17]

Nor did the Confederate government try to protect the South's historic properties, which is bewildering. Jefferson Davis quickly abandoned his states' rights philosophy when he became chief executive and exercised his powers to the full. He imprisoned several thousand white Southerners for criticizing the Confederacy or supporting the Union. He rarely consulted his Congress on policy questions of any kind, and he ignored Vice President Alexander Stephens of Georgia, a former Unionist whom he distrusted. He saw the Founders as his models, yet he issued no executive orders to preserve their homes, many of them located a few miles from his Richmond residence, and he did not ask the Congress to initiate legislation on the issue. Perhaps he expected the South to win the war easily, thus rendering the issue moot. In any case, he did nothing, and he said nothing about the damage that men in gray inflicted on historic sites. None of the Confederate states moved to defend their landmarks, either. The civilian population, even if they descended from the Founders, had to look after things themselves.[18]

George Washington was still in a category by himself, although the Founders as a group had strong appeal. In the fall of 1861, Union forces took over Mount Vernon to much rejoicing in the North and dejection in the South, and they maintained custody of it until the war concluded. The sym-

*Figure 3. Pohick Church, post-1865.
(Courtesy of the Virginia Department of Historic Resources)*

bolism was unavoidable, giving hope to the Union for an ultimate victory. The property attracted a lot of wartime visitors, its historic interest seemingly enhanced by the regional strife. President Lincoln's cabinet members and U.S. senators toured the grounds and admired the house, as did some Federal soldiers. Officers encouraged such outings by the troops. U.S. major general Jacob Cox thought that close contact with any kind of Washington artifact "strengthened" the zeal of Union soldiers for fighting the war.[19]

Washington-related places other than Mount Vernon did not fare so well during the war because of the paradoxical desire to have and hold relics. His pew in Pohick Church, the Episcopal church he attended near his home, was cut to pieces by Yankee troops by the spring of 1862. Other "relic-hunters" from both armies chipped marble pieces off the tombstone of Mary Ball Washington, George's mother, near Fredericksburg, Virginia. Individual soldiers condemned these actions, as did several journalists, but the search went on, involving some objects that required a great deal of labor. In 1864, Federal troops captured a life-size statue of George Washington at the Virginia Military Institute in Lexington. They planned to ship it to West Point Military Academy, but Colonel David Strother, a Southern Unionist in the Federal army, advised that the statue be diverted to Wheeling, West Virginia, to celebrate that state's departure from the Confederacy to rejoin the United States, so it was moved there instead.[20]

The desire to touch a historic artifact ran wide and deep among men in the armies, just as it had in peacetime. Individual soldiers wanted physical contact with relics—firsthand evidence, so to speak—and they wanted to possess those things. They grabbed articles of furniture from buildings associated with the famous, including the courthouse in Hanover County, Virginia, where Patrick Henry supposedly made his first political speech. We have no idea how they managed to transport the furniture, but their behavior attests to the overpowering desire for a relic. Horatio Taft, a clerk in the U.S. Patent Office, longed for his own artifact but opted for something smaller. Musing on what he called the "usual Yankee desire for Relics," he pocketed a stone fragment from the foundation of Braddock House, a hotel built in northern Virginia before the Revolution and used as a military hospital.[21]

Many Federal soldiers sent their relics home, despite orders to the contrary, while other troops sold their Revolutionary souvenirs to any interested party. In 1863, a U.S. Navy clerk visiting Yorktown purchased from an unidentified Northern soldier a group of artifacts, including a signet ring owned by the French major general the Comte de Rochambeau, who served there in 1781. The price was five dollars, but if the ring was genuine, it alone was worth a lot more than five dollars. Yankee civilians who set up informal partnerships with U.S. officers occasionally sent some of these relics directly to Washington, D.C. When the Federal army occupied Arlington plantation in 1861, civilian Caleb Lyon, a former congressman from New York, persuaded the officers to let him rummage through the house for Washington's belongings. With no authority beyond his own avid interest, he collected dozens of objects and sent them to the Smithsonian and the U.S. Patent Office.[22]

Union soldiers on their own initiative sometimes protected the homes of public figures. If a Founder's descendants still lived in the residence, that could tip the balance in favor of preserving the building. In the spring of 1862, Yankee officers issued a special order safeguarding the mansion of Revolutionary War hero Nathanael Greene, whose grandson lived in the house on Cumberland Island, Georgia. But other historic dwellings met very different fates. In Virginia, Federal troops seized the 200-year-old residence of former president William Henry Harrison, whose father signed the Declaration of Independence, and turned it into an army hospital. Both armies spared Monticello, even though the owner (not a Jefferson descendant) joined the Union army and the Southern government confiscated the house. There was no obvious logic to the fates of these different houses, the result of officers improvising in the field.[23]

In the war's chaos, with no effective regulations in place, many other historic structures were destroyed. Federal officers put up guards around White House, Martha Custis Washington's first home on the York River in Virginia, but the house burned soon afterward in 1862. Union chaplain William Corby blamed the fire on Mars, the god of war, while rebel troops blamed it squarely on human beings, namely the Yankees. Southern lieutenant colonel William T. Martin insisted that the devastation of White House and the surrounding estate proved that the enemy would spare nothing. The truth is, some troops in both armies felt uneasy at the damage done to so many buildings by their comrades. Pohick Church, where George Washington worshipped, was eventually ruined, all of the interior objects (not just his pew) carried away by what Union soldier Charles Wills called "relic maniacs" in both armies. The artifact hunting by both sides continued nonetheless.[24]

The living relatives of the Founders were still perceived as the embodiments of the Revolution, although the bloodlines diverged in some unexpected ways. The newspapers closely tracked the military records of the best-known descendants, such as George Washington's kinsmen. Most of his kinfolk who were of age joined the rebel military, to the glee of Confederates, as did Edgar Macon, James Madison's nephew. The Northern press retorted that U.S. colonel Benjamin Harrison (the future president) was a direct descendant of the Harrisons of Virginia, who included a signer of the Declaration of 1776, and that General William T. Sherman was a collateral descendant of a signer, Connecticut's Roger Sherman. Various civilians in the North and South explained their loyalties by claiming Revolutionary ancestors, and sometimes they appealed to fellow citizens in the region on those grounds. When South Carolina governor Francis W. Pickens asked for Robert E. Lee's help in strengthening defenses around Charleston, he reminded the general that his grandfather Andrew Pickens fought alongside Lee's father during the Revolution.[25]

White Southern Unionists naturally held a distinctive view of history, and the war, and they had their own experience with material culture after 1861. Several Confederate states banned the ownership of the United States flag, turning it into an instant relic, yet some Unionists managed to wave it whenever Federal soldiers appeared, as those troops observed with pleasure. Unionists were happy to give information to Yankee soldiers about the location of such historic landmarks as General Nathanael Greene's field headquarters in South Carolina, and they deeply enjoyed sharing their personal histories with Federal troops. Members of the Putnam family came out to talk to soldiers marching through the Virginia countryside in 1864. The family moved down from Connecticut before the war, bringing with them artifacts belonging to General Israel Putnam, a Revolutionary hero from New England. In 1864, one elderly Mr. Putnam of Virginia, probably the general's grandson, brought out a powder horn belonging to his illustrious ancestor and showed it to the delighted troops. The incident fuses elements of antebellum culture in a wartime context: the living representatives of a historic figure, the sharing of the object itself, and the bonding over its display.[26]

Most pro-Confederate whites had the opposite perspective, of course, and attempted to hide their artifacts from the armies. When it came to looting, they feared the Northern host much more than the rebel army. Grace Beard concealed a Masonic emblem from the Revolution under some logs in the South Carolina lowcountry, and in Richmond, John Lange buried in his yard a sword used by French troops at Yorktown. The image of the thieving Yankee was soon fixed in the popular imagination, but the historical record is more complicated than stereotype would indicate, for the troops did not always destroy relics. The Chesnut family owned a portrait of Charles Cotesworth Pinckney, a Founder, at Mulberry plantation in South Carolina, and at the war's beginning, Pinckney's ancient daughter Harriott asked the Chesnuts to take good care of it. The painting survived the war, even though Northern soldiers looted the property when the Chesnuts were absent from the house.[27]

Many white Confederate women, with their menfolk in uniform, became custodians of the family relics. Mary Custis Lee, the daughter of Parke Custis and wife of Robert E. Lee, is a high-profile case. She saw herself as the guardian of the Arlington mansion, the mother lode as it were, and after she married Lee in 1831, she stayed there much of the time rather than joining him at his frontier postings. When the war started, she gave some of the Washington relics, such as the Charles Willson Peale portrait, to an aunt who lived nearby, and she concealed others in the cellar. She departed Arlington in May 1861 just before Yankee troops arrived, so a female cousin persuaded the Northern officers to let her take yet more household objects to her home elsewhere in Virginia. But Robert E. Lee's rejection of the offer to run the U.S. war effort, tendered in Washington, D.C., in April 1861, and his decision to join the Confederacy infuriated many Northerners, so Arlington became a target for pillaging troops. Although Union general Winfield Scott issued a special order that Arlington's "unique" Washington-related artifacts should be protected, Federal troops took every single object from the house by the war's conclusion. The fury at Lee was so great that his Unionist cousin U.S. major Lawrence A. Williams could not convince Federal authorities to give the objects to his own relatives in Washington, D.C.[28]

Confederate soldiers took war relics, too, motivated by the same drive to touch, hold, and keep artifacts from the Revolution. As we know, they seized nuggets of rock from Mary Ball Washington's tombstone. When Yankee shelling destroyed some of George Washington's furniture, including a bureau in a great-niece's house in the Shenandoah Valley, troops from both armies snatched up the pieces as mementos. Rebel soldier George Neese lamented that villainous Northerners inflicted so much damage on Virginia, Washington's native state, but it was not just Northerners, of course. And if Robert E. Lee's Pennsylvania campaign had succeeded in 1863 with the capture of Harrisburg, the state capital, followed by the seizure of Philadelphia—which was the original plan, not the battle at Gettysburg—then his soldiers would have collected objects from Independence Hall and other historic buildings in the Quaker City. They probably would have cleaned out Independence Hall as thoroughly as Northerners cleaned out Arlington.[29]

Some white Southern civilians had the same utilitarian attitudes toward making use of artifacts as they had before the war. They reckoned that the demands of the current conflict sometimes had to take precedence over the splendid past. In 1862, the *Richmond Examiner* called on the public to melt down the Revolutionary cannons lying half-buried in their yards and use the metals in the ongoing war. The paper added that citizens should take down the cannons used as pillars in private homes, with no advice on how to prop up the buildings afterward. We do not know how many residents followed this advice, but the journalist called for the public to make this sacrifice for what he called "the war of our second independence." Individual whites could be ruthless when it came to leaving things behind as they left home. The Ford family of South Carolina owned a sofa that dated from the Revolution; George Washington sat on it when he visited their house in 1791. When the sofa broke in 1864 as they tried to move it, Marion Ford almost cried, but her mother told her not to be sentimental because they were living through their own revolution.[30]

The Civil War did have revolutionary outcomes regarding emancipation, beyond anything that most Confederates expected in 1861. The extension of freedom to African Americans converted certain material objects into meaningful relics. Slaves sometimes initiated these transformations, pulling off their collars and handing them to Yankee troops, as did a slave known only as Old Steve, who gave his to Wisconsin soldier John Perry before joining the Northern army. In other encounters, abolitionist soldiers took an active role. Some of them personally removed shackles from individual slaves they met, as New Yorker William Badger did for Mary Horn of Georgia. Both artifacts now reside in museums in Wisconsin and New York. These exchanges happened before and after the preliminary Emancipation

Proclamation in September 1862, and they seem to have occurred spontaneously when black Southerners and white soldiers met in the field. Other Federal troops deliberately sought out objects associated with slavery. The future president Rutherford B. Hayes, a diligent collector, found shackles in a slave trader's office in Virginia.[31]

Yet other Federal soldiers felt curious about slavery as an institution and valued artifacts for that reason, with little regard for African Americans as human beings. R. L. Maynard and several comrades entered a slave cabin near Hilton Head, South Carolina, to see "how they lived" and stood staring at the kitchenware and the clothes before a slave woman chased them out, giving them what Maynard admitted was a "good cursing." More disturbing encounters took place, one of them at Arlington. John Fowle, a Yankee veteran, owned a dress "taken" from an anonymous female slave who fled to the plantation after the U.S. army occupied it; later he donated it to a historical society in Dorchester, Massachusetts. The language is troubling, suggesting that he or someone else seized it against her will. These incidents remind us that some white troops did not support racial equality, much less gender equality, which differed from emancipation. None of these soldiers, regardless of their political views, mentioned emancipation in the prewar or wartime North.[32]

By the time the guns fell silent in 1865, the country was filled with eyewitnesses who wanted to share what they saw, just as the Revolutionary generation did, and they told their stories with gusto in conversation and in print. The war also created a huge body of new artifacts, reflecting the scale of the upheaval, just as the Revolution did. Millions of Civil War–related things were distributed within the entire population, as the antebellum folk culture expanded to cover more collectors and more relics. In a rich irony, Robert E. Lee became an icon for white Southern conservatives, his mementos collected by Lost Cause devotees with the same eagerness that people showed for his wife's great-grandfather. Any relic pertaining to Lee had value, even something as banal as a square of cloth taken from his rug. If an object harked back to his wife's famous ancestor, all the better. The belt from his dressing gown, made by Mary Custis Lee from cloth belonging to George Washington, is currently archived in the Virginia Historical Society.[33]

Americans saved all kinds of mundane objects pertaining to the common soldier and the average civilian: sabers, revolvers, rings, blankets, and tintypes in Tennessee, and drums, fifes, canteens, bullets, spurs, and hospital linens in Maine. White people in both regions acquired these objects much as they had obtained Revolutionary artifacts: from their own wartime service, by purchasing them, or by digging them out of the ground at battlefields or campsites. They preserved their relics, just as citizens preserved their Revolutionary objects, and they gave them to their relatives. Yet other people donated their Civil War objects to historical societies, in all parts of the country. Well after the conflict ended, many people believed in their evocative power, and they enjoyed the tactile contact with relics. In the 1880s, Cora Berry, a white woman in Georgia, thought that donning a Confederate badge brought the wearer symbolically closer to rebel soldiers.[34]

The material record reflects the complexity of political loyalties in the South's population, and it often contradicts the simplifying tendencies of collective memory. White Southern Unionists like Jesse Gambill had their own military artifacts (such as his cap box), their own memories, and their own interpretation of the war, even though their part in the fight was largely forgotten until the twentieth century. And race still mattered in material culture. The contributions of black Southerners who served in the Union ranks were forgotten for almost as long, but their families remembered. Arthur Boone, who had roots in North Carolina, ran away from his master and joined the Yankee army, and after the war his oldest son preserved Boone's rifle and his uniform for decades. He took "particular" care of them, his relatives said. Now African Americans could generate and keep their own relics, which was deeply satisfying after bondage ended.[35]

Gender mattered in material culture, too, and white women of all political persuasions had their own artifacts. They continued to preserve traditional feminine objects, just as they did after the Revolution. Confederate Fanny Waddell saved a pincushion made out of tiny rebel flags, which is now located in the North Carolina Museum of History. In New Hampshire, Harriet Dame's collection of war-related souvenirs features a needle case made by some white women for a departing soldier. African American women also made use of objects that signified the end of slavery. Willie Doyld's grandmother of Mississippi, her name unknown, removed the mistress's bed from the house and slept on it the rest of her life. That, too, must have been deeply satisfying.[36]

Americans from diverse backgrounds savor relics from the two wars, many of them now carefully preserved, which was not always the case before 1861. The public debate on the Civil War and the meaning of its artifacts remains as fervent as ever, with no agreement on the war's purpose. More than 150 years later, the object lessons go on. The collection of all these things demonstrates yet again how much human beings have coveted relics, how much they have enjoyed them, and how insistently they have used them to express their political beliefs, as they perceive them anew in new contexts.

The study of material culture can illuminate yet other undiscovered aspects of politics and memory in the long sweep of American history.[37]

Notes

1. "Remains of Washington," *Atlantic Democrat* [N.J.], 25 May 1861, 2; no title, *Staunton (Va.) Spectator*, 14 May 1861, 2; "Miscellaneous News of Importance," *Philadelphia Inquirer*, 25 May 1861, 1; "The Sacred Remains," *Philadelphia Inquirer*, 25 May 1861, 7; "Washington Items," *Baltimore Sun*, 17 May 1861, 1; Lydia Mattice Brandt, *First in the Homes of His Countrymen: George Washington's Mount Vernon in the American Imagination* (Charlottesville: University of Virginia Press, 2016), 20-30, 49-54; "Miscellaneous Dispatches," *Augusta (Ga.) Chronicle*, 6 June 1861, 1.

2. Loyalist's coat, "Connecticut: 50 Objects/50 Stories," Connecticut Historical Society, http://chs.org/50objects, accessed 10 January 2016; *Oxford Living Dictionaries*, s.v. "artifact" and "relic," http://www.oxforddictionaries.com/us/, accessed 13 February 2016; Henry Glassie, *Material Culture* (Bloomington: Indiana University Press, 1999), 41.

3. Robert Middlekauff, *Washington's Revolution: The Making of America's First Leader* (New York: Alfred A. Knopf, 2015), 278; Jules David Prown, "The Truth of Material Culture: History or Fiction?," in *History from Things: Essays on Material Culture*, ed. Steven Lubar and W. David Kingery (Washington, D.C.: Smithsonian Institution Press, 1993), 2-3; Alfred Moore Waddell, *Some Memories of My Life* (Raleigh: Edwards and Broughton, 1908), 8-9; "Historical Collections of Virginia," *Southern Patriot* [Charleston, S.C.], 29 September 1845, 2; "About the Museum," Cayce Historical Museum, www.cityofcayce-sc.gov/museum.asp, accessed 1 November 2015.

4. James Axtell, *The Indians' New South: Cultural Change in the Colonial Southeast* (Baton Rouge: Louisiana State University Press, 1997), 1-3, 5-24; "Indian Relics in South Carolina," *Charleston Mercury*, 30 March 1859, 1; Porte Crayon, "North Carolina Illustrated," *Harper's Monthly*, July 1857, 164; "Household Furniture, Trunks, &c., by William S. Hull," *Charleston Courier*, 23 May 1843, 3; Museum of the Confederacy, *Catalogue of the Confederate Museum of the Confederate Memorial Literary Society* (Richmond, Va.: Ware and Duke, 1905), 43, located in the Virginia Historical Society, Richmond (hereafter VHS).

5. "Revolutionary Relic," *Charleston Mercury*, 7 August 1858, 2; Memoirs of John Gottfried Lange, 1:218, VHS; Mrs. Burton Harrison, *Recollections Grave and Gay* (New York: Charles Scribner's Sons, 1911), 32; "For the Mercury," *Charleston Mercury*, 30 March 1859, 1; Ivor Noel Hume, *A Guide to Artifacts of Colonial America* (New York: Alfred A. Knopf, 1970), 211, 219.

6. G. Kurt Piehler, *Remembering War the American Way* (Washington, D.C.: Smithsonian Institution Press, 1995), 27-29, 183; Michael Kammen, *Digging Up the Dead: A History of Notable American Reburials* (Chicago: University of Chicago Press, 2010), 55-56; Norman Tyler, Ted J. Ligibel, and Ilene R. Tyler, *Historic Preservation: An Introduction to Its History, Principles, and Practice*, 2nd ed. (New York: W. W. Norton, 2009), 29; Charlene Mires, *Independence Hall in American Memory* (Philadelphia: University of Pennsylvania Press, 2002), 31-32.

7. Karal Ann Marling, *George Washington Slept Here: Colonial Revivals and Ameri-*

can Culture, 1876-1986 (Cambridge, Mass.: Harvard University Press, 1988), 9-10; "Celebration at Campbell Court House," *Richmond Whig*, 18 July 1843, 4; Rebecca Harding Davis, *Bits of Gossip* (Boston: Houghton, Mifflin, 1904), 15; "A Revolutionary Soldier," *Savannah Republican*, 10 November 1851, 2; "A Revolutionary Relic," *Richmond Whig*, 17 April 1849, 2; National Archives and Records Administration, *Final Revolutionary War Pension Payment Vouchers* (Washington D.C.: Georgia Genealogical Society and National Archives and Records Administration, 1994).

    8. Michael F. Conlin, *One Nation Divided by Slavery: Remembering the American Revolution while Marching toward the Civil War* (Kent: Kent State University Press, 2015), 72-73, 84; Piehler, *Remembering War*, 12; Sandra Moats, *Celebrating the Republic: Presidential Ceremony and Popular Sovereignty, from Washington to Monroe* (DeKalb: Northern Illinois University Press, 2010), 35-62; "Interesting Relics," *Alexandria (Va.) Gazette*, 5 May 1855, 2; James Thomas Flexner, *Washington: The Indispensable Man* (New York: Back Bay Books, 1974), 379; George Washington Parke Custis, *Recollections and Private Memoirs of Washington* (New York: Derby and Jackson, 1860), 415-16; Laurel Thatcher Ulrich et al., *Tangible Things: Making History through Objects* (New York: Oxford University Press, 2015), 76, 160; Flora Fraser, *The Washingtons: George and Martha, "Join'd by Friendship, Crowned by Love"* (New York: Alfred A. Knopf, 2015), xi-xii.

    9. Fraser, *Washingtons*, xiv-xv; "Revolutionary Trophies," *Augusta Chronicle*, 27 May 1854, 2; U.S. House of Representatives, *Mount Vernon Relics* (Washington, D.C.: n.p., 1870), 2; "Interesting Relics," *Alexandria Gazette*, 5 May 1855, 2; John W. Wayland, *The Washingtons and Their Homes* (Stanton, Va.: McClure, 1944), 291; Mary Pastor to John Cochran, 6 July 1859, Valley of the Shadow Project, Valley Personal Papers, http://valley.lib.virginia.edu, accessed 1 November 2015.

    10. Christopher Bollas, *The Evocative Object World* (London: Routledge, 2009), 84; Tiffany Field, *Touch*, 2nd ed. (Cambridge, Mass.: MIT Press, 2014), 5, 14, 88-89, 96, 115; Ashley Montagu, *Touching: The Human Significance of the Skin*, 3rd ed. (New York: Harper and Row, 1986), 124; "Interesting Relics," *Alexandria Gazette*, 5 May 1855, 2; "An Old Drum," *Charleston Courier*, 18 July 1857, 2; Crayon, "North Carolina Illustrated," 164.

    11. "An Interesting Revolutionary Relic," *Charleston Mercury*, 12 January 1859, 1; Harrison, *Recollections*, 31; "Times Have Changed," *Alexandria Gazette*, 22 December 1856, 2; Thomas J. Kirkland and Robert M. Kennedy, *Historic Camden, Part One: Colonial and Revolutionary* (Columbia, S.C.: State Company, 1905), 274-78, 310. For noncelebratory narratives, see Kathleen DuVal, *Independence Lost: Lives on the Edge of the American Revolution* (New York: Random House, 2015).

    12. "A Revolutionary Relic," *Charleston Courier*, 10 January 1857, 1; Waddell, *Some Memories*, 10-11; "An Old Negro—a Servant of Washington," *Charleston Courier*, 16 June 1858, 1.

    13. Grant McCracken, *Culture and Consumption: New Approaches to the Symbolic Character of Consumer Goods and Activities* (Bloomington: Indiana University Press, 1988), 133-34; Piehler, *Remembering War*, 13; Seth Bruggeman, *Here, George Washington Was Born: Memory, Material Culture, and the Public History of a National Monument* (Athens: University of Georgia Press, 2008), 55; Lorri Glover, *Founders as Fathers: The Private Lives and Politics of American Revolutionaries* (New Haven: Yale University

Press, 2014), 103–5, 122–25; Andrew M. Schochet, *Fighting over the Founders: How We Remember the American Revolution* (New York: New York University Press, 2015), 11–12.

14. "Revolutionary Relic," *New London (Conn.) Democrat*, 30 September 1848, 2; Thomas A. Chambers, *Memories of War: Visiting Battlegrounds and Bonefields in the Early American Republic* (Ithaca: Cornell University Press, 2012), 73–74; Prescott and Linzee Swords, description, MHS Gallery, Massachusetts Historical Society, http://www.mass.hist.org/gallery/artifacts, accessed 16 February 2016; *The Occasional Speeches of Justice Oliver Wendell Holmes*, comp. Mark DeWolfe Howe (Cambridge, Mass.: Belknap Press of Harvard University Press, 1962), 78–79; Elizabeth F. Ellet, *The Women of the American Revolution*, 2 vols., 5th ed. (New York: Baker and Scribner, 1819), 1 (frontispiece), 57–61, 74–106; Bruggeman, *Here, George Washington Was Born*, 55; Alfred F. Young, *The Shoemaker and the Tea Party: Memory and the American Revolution* (Boston: Beacon Press, 1999), 117.

15. William Cooper Nell, *The Colored Patriots of the American Revolution* (Boston: Robert F. Wallcutt, 1855), 21–25, 28–37, 50–52, 119–40, 160–81, 198–200, on black Northerners, and 216–18, 223, 232–35, 237–43, on black Southerners; Joanne Pope Melish, *Disowning Slavery: Gradual Emancipation and "Race" in New England, 1780–1860* (Ithaca: Cornell University Press, 1998), 76, xiii; James J. Gigantino II, *The Ragged Road to Abolition: Slavery and Freedom in New Jersey, 1775–1865* (Philadelphia: University of Pennsylvania Press, 2014), 240; Edgar J. McManus, *Black Bondage in the North* (Syracuse: Syracuse University Press, 1973), 163, 181–82; Conlin, *One Nation Divided by Slavery*, 147, 152–53; Bracelet made of gold beads from necklace of Elizabeth Freeman ("Mumbet"), Massachusetts Historical Society, http://www.masshisto.org/2012/collections/online, accessed 10 February 2016.

16. Walter Lenoir to Rufus Lenoir, 20 February 1862, Lenoir Family Papers, University of North Carolina–Chapel Hill (hereafter UNC); "Testimony against War," *Hillsborough (N.C.) Recorder*, 29 August 1860, 1; U.S. War Department, *The War of the Rebellion: A Compilation of the Official Records of the Union and Confederate Armies*, 128 vols. (Washington, D.C.: GPO, 1880–1901), ser. 1, vol. 2, 782 (hereafter *OR*); *OR*, ser. 2, vol. 6, 65; Shearer Davis Bowman, *At the Precipice: Americans North and South during the Secession Crisis* (Chapel Hill: University of North Carolina Press, 2010), 13; *OR*, ser. 3, vol. 1, 893; Isaac Bevier to Dear Parents, 8 May 1862, Correspondence of Isaac Bevier, Lincoln Museum Research Library, Fort Wayne, Indiana.

17. *Revised United States Army Regulations of 1861, with an Appendix Containing the Changes and Laws Affecting Army Regulations and Articles of War to June 25, 1863* (Washington, D.C.: GPO, 1863), 113; Articles 34, 35, Lieber Code, The Avalon Project: Documents in Law, History, and Diplomacy, Yale University Law School, http://avalon.law.yale.edu/19th-century/lieber, accessed 9 March 2016.

18. Paul D. Escott, *After Secession: Jefferson Davis and the Failure of Confederate Nationalism* (Baton Rouge: Louisiana State University Press, 1978), 54–93, 203–5; Mark E. Neely Jr., *Southern Rights: Political Prisoners and the Myth of Confederate Constitutionalism* (Charlottesville: University Press of Virginia, 1999), 1–2; William C. Davis, *Jefferson Davis: The Man and His Hour* (New York: HarperCollins, 1991), 308.

19. "Our Dispatches from Washington," *New York Times*, 12 November 1861, n.p.; "News from Washington," *New York Times*, 14 December 1861, n.p.; Abner R. Small, *The*

Road to Richmond: The Civil War Memoirs of Major Abner R. Small of the 16th Maine Volunteers with His Diary as a Prisoner of War, ed. Harold Adams Small (Berkeley: University of California Press, 1957), 28–29; Jacob Dolson Cox, *Military Reminiscences of the Civil War, Volume One, April 1861–November 1863* (New York: Charles Scribner's Sons, 1900), 1:274–75.

20. "Our Lower Potomac Correspondence," *New York Times*, 16 March 1862, n.p.; J. T. Trowbridge, *The South: A Tour of Its Battle-Fields and Ruined Cities* (Hartford, Conn.: L. Stebbins, 1866), 112–13; Keith E. Gibson, "The Capture of George Washington, June 12, 1864," 3–4, unpublished manuscript, Virginia Military Institute Archives, Lexington, cited with the author's permission.

21. George Alfred Townsend, *Rustics in Rebellion: A Yankee Reporter on the Road to Richmond, 1861–65*, with an introduction by Lida Mayo (Chapel Hill: University of North Carolina Press, 1950), 67; Diary of Horatio Taft, 5 October 1863, Library of Congress.

22. *OR*, ser. 1, vol. 45, pt. 1, 410; "An Interesting Relic Brought to Light," *Hartford Daily Courant*, 4 January 1864, 2; "Relics of the Washington Family," *New York Evening Post*, 8 January 1862, 1.

23. *OR Navy*, ser. 1, vol. 12, 598; Townsend, *Rustics in Rebellion*, 180; *Visitors to Monticello*, ed. Merrill D. Peterson (Charlottesville: University Press of Virginia, 1993), 4–6, 144–45.

24. William Corby, *Memoirs of Chaplain Life: Three Years Chaplain in the Famous Irish Brigade, Army of the Potomac* (Chicago: La Monte, O'Donnell and Co., 1893), 53; *OR*, ser. 1, vol. 11, pt. 2, 529; Charles W. Wills, *Army Life of an Illinois Soldier, Including a Day by Day Record of Sherman's March to the Sea, Compiled and Published by His Sister* (Washington, D.C.: Globe Printing Company, 1966), 382.

25. Wayland, *Washingtons*, 277; Conlin, *One Nation Divided by Slavery*, 162; "The 'Fatal Valley'—Its Battle Mark," *Macon Telegraph*, 7 October 1864, 1; "Alexandria," *Fayetteville (N.C.) Observer*, 6 August 1861, n.p.; "Epitome of the Week," *Frank Leslie's Illustrated Newspaper*, 18 March 1865, 403; "The Shermans," *Lowell (Mass.) Daily Citizen and News*, 8 February 1865, n.p.; *OR*, ser. 2, vol. 1, 732; *OR*, ser. 1, vol. 14, 515–16; John B. Edmunds Jr., *Francis W. Pickens and the Politics of Destruction* (Chapel Hill: University of North Carolina Press, 1986), 5.

26. Thomas G. Dyer, *Secret Yankees: The Union Circle in Confederate Atlanta* (Baltimore: Johns Hopkins University Press, 1999), 96; Enoch Colby Jr. to Enoch Colby, 19 June 1862, Francelia Colby Collection, Chicago History Museum; Mary A. Livermore, *My Story of the War: A Woman's Narrative of Four Years of Personal Experience* (Hartford: A. D. Worthington, 1892), 698; "A Revolutionary Relic," *Alexandria Gazette*, 9 June 1858, 2; Robert Ernest Hubbard, *Major-General Israel Putnam: Hero of the American Revolution* (Jefferson, N.C.: McFarland, 2017), 2–7, 191–202; Charles H. Lynch, *The Civil War Diary 1862–1865 of Charles H. Lynch, 18th Conn. Vols.* (n.p.: privately printed, 1915), 94.

27. Grace Pierson James Beard, "A Series of True Incidents Connected with Sherman's March to the Sea," 6, UNC; Memoirs of Lange, 1:218, VHS; *Mary Chesnut's Civil War*, ed. C. Vann Woodward (New Haven: Yale University Press, 1981), 43, 80.

28. Elizabeth Brown Pryor, *Reading the Man: A Portrait of Robert E. Lee through His Private Letters* (New York: Viking, 2007), 73–74, 85–88, 302–6, 289–91; Robert E. Lee,

Recollections and Letters of Robert E. Lee (New York: Doubleday, Page, 1904), 354, 32, 34, 190n; U.S. House of Representatives, *Mount Vernon Relics*, 2.

29. "'Fatal' Valley," 1; George M. Neese, *Three Years in the Confederate Horse Artillery* (New York: Neale, 1911), 299–300; Edwin B. Coddington, *The Gettysburg Campaign: A Study in Command* (New York: Touchstone, 1968), 8–9; Mires, *Independence Hall*.

30. "Revolutionary Relics," *Richmond Examiner*, 4 August 1862, 2; Arthur Peronneau Ford and Marion Johnstone Ford, *Life in the Confederate Army: Being Personal Experiences of a Private Soldier in the Confederate Army; and Some Experiences and Sketches of Southern Life* (New York: Neale, 1905), 116.

31. Slave shackles, object 1921.20, unidentified newspaper clippings, Museum Collections Dept., New-York Historical Society, New York City; Fugitive slave collar, museum object 1961.73, Wisconsin Historical Society, http://www.wisconsinhistory.org, accessed 11 March 2016; "Diary and Letters of Rutherford B. Hayes," vol. 5, app. C, p. 450, Rutherford B. Hayes Presidential Center, http://apps.ohiohistory.org/hayes, accessed 11 March 2016.

32. R. L. Maynard to E. C. Maynard, 9 June 1864, Maynard Family Civil War Letters and Diaries, Erie County [N.Y.] History Center; Dorchester Historical Society, *Catalogue of Civil War Relics, 1862–1863–1864* (Dorchester, Mass.: Old Blake House, 1906), 9–10.

33. Joan E. Cashin, "Trophies of War: Material Culture in the Civil War Era," *Journal of the Civil War Era* 1, no. 3 (September 2011): 355; Rug, object 1969.26, and dressing gown belt, object 1951.7, museum catalog, VHS.

34. Objects, Wilson Co., Williamson Co., Tenn., "Looking Back: The Civil War in Tennessee," Tennessee State Library and Archives, http://sos.tn.gov/tsla/looking-back-civil-war-tennessee, accessed 20 February 2016; Objects, Maine Memory Network, Maine Historical Society, https://www.mainememory.net/sitebuilder/site/2428/slideshow/1474/display, accessed 3 August 2016; Artillery shell, object 2014.010.11, medal, object 2013.019.03, pipe, object 1937.013, needle case, object 1963.062.02, "Harriet Dame: New Hampshire's Angel of Mercy" exhibit, New Hampshire Historical Society, https://www.nhhistory.org, accessed 3 August 2016; "A Regular Revival," *Columbus (Ga.) Enquirer-Sun*, 26 July 1888, 1.

35. Cap box of Jesse Gambill, U.S.A., objects, Washington Co., Tenn., "Looking Back," accessed 28 February 2016; *The American Slave: A Composite Autobiography*, ed. George P. Rawick (Westport, Conn.: Greenwood Press, 1977), Arkansas, vol. 2, pt. 1, 210–11.

36. "North Carolina and the Civil War," online exhibit, North Carolina Museum of History, http://moh.ncdcr.gov/exhibits/civilwar/artifacts.html, accessed 20 February 2016; Needle case, object 1963.062.02, "Harriet Dame" exhibit; *Lay My Burden Down: A Folk History of Slavery*, ed. B. A. Botkin, foreword by Jerrold Hirsch (New York: Delta Book, 1994), 245, 302.

37. Civil War Family—Artifacts—Heirlooms, http://www.civilwarfamily.us/artifacts-heirlooms, accessed 3 August 2016.

Nature as Material Culture
Antietam National Battlefield

LISA M. BRADY & TIMOTHY SILVER

It was a cold, windy morning as we trudged along the edge of the cornfield. The grain had not yet been planted, so the field looked bleak and brown, uninviting. We huddled close together so we could hear each other over the gusting wind and share a little body heat. It was a morning much like many others in the rural agricultural district around Sharpsburg, Maryland. From our position just off the Hagerstown Pike, about half a mile north of the Dunker Church, we could see the Mumma farm. Just beyond lay the Sunken Road. A few miles farther south was our ultimate destination, the Lower Bridge over Antietam Creek. There were about twenty of us hardy souls moving over the rolling ground that morning, driven by a firm purpose. Our intent was to cross the stubbly field, reconnoiter at the old market road, and march on to the banks of the creek. It would have been a difficult trek under the best of circumstances, but the raw weather of early spring promised an especially bitter few hours. No doubt each of us, even though we didn't admit it out loud, was thankful for the tour bus that could take us where we needed to go.

Unlike our Civil War soldier counterparts, who over a century and a half ago fought the elements and each other on the bucolic landscape that is now Antietam National Battlefield (ANB), we—a group of environmental historians—were there to explore the ways that war and nature shaped each other during the conflict. We had notable advantages over those men who preceded us: we had reliable transportation; most of us had fleece jackets or windbreakers; all of us had box lunches packed by the hotel catering staff; and, perhaps most important, we had the consoling knowledge that we weren't expected to shoot at the other people roving across the park. We also had National Park Service (NPS) maps and interpretive materials that enabled us to find our way easily from spot to spot and that put such landmarks as Antietam Creek into the larger context of Civil War history and strategy.

Although the technologies available to us were dramatically different from those of the mid-nineteenth century, the landscape across which we moved was not. Excepting the improved roads and the memorials erected since the battle, the built and natural geographies of Antietam were remarkably similar in April 2015 to what they were in September 1862. The NPS actively manages Antietam's landscape, seasonally planting and harvesting crops, tending orchards, and thinning wooded areas, replicating 1862 conditions as best it can so that visitors may gain a better sense of what Union and Confederate troops encountered and experienced. Moreover, the NPS tries to eradicate invasive species, control animal populations, and save witness trees (those that were alive at the time of battle) at Antietam and other Civil War battle sites because the agency is committed to preserving the nation's symbolic landscapes as close to their historical states as possible. In attempting to stop time, the NPS works toward transforming the living, material world into static, cultural sites.[1]

At first blush, such efforts might appear to be a boon to scholars who wish to study the material culture of the Civil War. Here are entire landscapes preserved almost exactly as they were during the conflict, allowing us to see what our subjects saw, walk along their paths, and feel what they touched, thereby increasing our ability to imagine and interpret what Civil War soldiers experienced on that day, in that place. Visually and tactilely, ANB merges the material with the cultural—that is, the physical, living world with the various meanings we've ascribed to it—in important ways, not only recreating the 1862 sight lines but also capturing a moment in time that has many layers of significance for the nation's history.

As an artifact—and landscapes are unquestionably artifacts—ANB does what Michael DeGruccio suggests material culture can do: it helps us "reckon with the symbolic and spiritual power of things." Many who visit the site feel some sense of awe, perhaps when they look up at the heights over Burnside's Bridge and imagine how difficult it must have been for Union soldiers to push forward under the concerted fire of Toombs's Confederate troops, or perhaps it's when they visit Antietam National Cemetery and attempt to visualize 6,000 corpses. As an artifact, ANB presents a view to the past, preserving a landscape imbued with meaning drawn out of military sacrifice and political rhetoric. Its existence exemplifies Joan Cashin's astute argument that people want artifacts "to make permanent the fleeting nature of experience" and to "establish dominion over time itself."[2]

Even so, ANB differs from most historical artifacts. It is not kept in an archive or museum, protected from drastic changes in temperature or humidity, or displayed only under ideal conditions. It is not an inanimate object but is instead part of the natural world, a living, evolving landscape subject to countless external and internal pressures that affect its appearance and stability. The NPS is well aware of this yet is bound by its mission to present the site as a static representation of the past. Treating the preserved landscape as material culture can lay bare the physical realities that affected the battle and turned an ordinary patch of ground into a commemorative site. That is only one part of a more complicated story, though. The landscape's physical features—including those that proved so crucial to the military encounter—resulted from a long history of interaction between people and a changing environment. Nature also loomed large in the experiences of individual soldiers on that September day, and when the fighting stopped, civilians returned to find that a once-familiar natural world had been torn asunder by battle and strained to its ecological limits by the demands of an occupying army.

To get at that story, to understand Antietam as more than a passive geographical or physical entity, it helps to combine an analysis of material culture with the methodology of environmental history. In addition to viewing the preserved landscape as an artifact, we also need to know how nature *functioned* in the past, both on its own and as influenced and manipulated by people. Equally important are the ways in which people of the past imagined and defined their place in nature, how they gave meaning to the natural world. When we add those perspectives, ANB emerges as more than a war artifact or commemorative site. As we contemplate both nature and human nature, we become keenly aware of what can and cannot be recovered from that bloody September day in 1862. Moreover, our efforts to preserve the natural world in which the battle occurred reveal as much about the values of the present as they do those of the past.

The Place

Long before it became an artifact of war, Antietam existed as an artifact of nature. The land on which so much human blood would be spilled had been shaped by geologic events that occurred so slowly and so long ago that people have trouble imagining the process. Reduced to a simplistic time-lapse narrative more suited to the capabilities of human brains, the story began maybe 500 million years ago as sand and silt collected on the floor of an ancient sea. That giant basin, known to geologists as the Iapetus Ocean, eventually closed and disappeared as continents drifted together and then apart. The sediments, however, endured to be thrust up and over younger formations to create the underlying layers of the Appalachian Mountains. Some 200 or so million years ago, during the age of dinosaurs, volcanic activity added igneous rocks to the geologic structure and the highlands began to erode, a process that continues to the present.[3]

As the mountains yielded to the unrelenting pressures of wind and precipitation, various layers of rock broke down at different rates. Sandstone formations lasted longer, creating the highest ridges and mountains. Other deposits, including shale- and carbonate-based rocks known as dolomite, wore down quicker, leaving wide swaths of lower-lying ground between the peaks. One such region, known as the Great Appalachian Valley, extended north from western Maryland into Pennsylvania (where it becomes the Cumberland Valley) and south into Virginia (where it takes the name Shenandoah Valley). Situated in the wet climes of eastern North America, the Great Valley gave rise to numerous springs and creeks, each of which cut its own small watershed within the larger landform. One of these lesser streams, now called Antietam Creek, flowed over such ground as it made its way to the Potomac River. That eroded landscape, now called Hagerstown Valley, makes up the Antietam battlefield.[4]

In this peculiar geographic setting, the term "valley" can be misleading. The land along Antietam Creek is not flat. The uneven pattern of erosion makes for higher ridges, rolling hills, and sunken hollows. Rocky outcrops are common, sometimes jutting out above low-lying terrain. The land's undulating character owes much to the prevalence of limestone, one of the softest materials in the ancient geologic deposits. Limestone is far less resistant to the elements than sandstone or dolomite. Over time, precipitation worked its way through the softer limestone, leaving behind a honeycomb of caves, sinkholes, and long, shallow ditch-like depressions.[5]

Antietam Creek sliced through those same deposits. Flowing fast and deep in all but the driest seasons, the stream could be crossed only at a few natural fords. During flooding rains, the creek collected dirt and gravel eroded from nearby hillsides. On less porous terrain, the alluvial soil left behind by the floodwaters might have been highly acidic. Because Antietam Creek carried limestone from the underlying formations, however, the soil along its banks routinely got a dose of natural buffer that made for fertile ground and lush natural vegetation. Northern red oak, American beech, and bitternut hickory flourished on drier high ground. Along the stream and in other low-lying areas, riparian forests of sycamore, black walnut, and red maple often grew right to the water's edge. It would be wrong, though, to imagine the woods as a giant, dense stand of trees. Ecologists and environmental historians have long known that weather, insect depredations, natural deaths of trees, and a host of other factors bring myriad alterations in forest patterns, including those of Antietam.[6]

Because archaeologists have been most concerned with the Civil War battle and its aftermath, we know comparatively little about the first people on the now-famous landscape. For Native Americans, it seems to have served as a kind of middle ground or buffer zone between various groups migrating north and south. Assuming Indian subsistence practices mirrored those in nearby regions, we can guess that native hunters used fire to open the woods for travel and hunting. Perhaps abandoned agricultural fields left small plots of relatively open land scattered across the forested terrain. Natives also fought each other over the region's abundant wildlife, especially as trade with Europeans transformed deerskins into valuable commodities for the world market. In the early eighteenth century, disputes over hunting rights apparently led to a prolonged conflict between the Delawares and the Catawbas, including one especially gruesome battle along Antietam Creek in the 1730s. In all likelihood, scores of Native people died along the waterway 130 years before it became synonymous with the wholesale slaughter of Civil War soldiers.[7]

European settlers arrived in the 1740s. Mostly farmers of English, German, Scotch-Irish, and Swiss descent, they ascribed new values to the natural world. Low-lying tracts where natural vegetation sprouted from limestone-enriched soils promised level cropland. The usually swift waters of Antietam Creek might provide power for gristmills and sawmills. Clearing the forests from hillier ground could turn woodland into suitable pasture for livestock. Native peoples resisted the intrusion, but by the time of the American Revolution, white settlers secured their place on the landscape and gave it new meaning based on agrarian ideals and the commodification of nature.[8]

To make the natural world comprehensible, the new human occupants drew lines on maps and assigned familiar names to prominent physical features. Surveyors set the boundaries for Washington County and selected sites for various towns, including one called "Sharps Burgh" about three miles from a prominent ford on the Potomac River. Laid out in 1763, Sharpsburg drew its water from a large limestone spring located nearby. Such efforts slowly turned the countryside into an irregular grid of plots and acreage, transforming the land itself into a commodity that could be sold at a profit.[9]

Religion, too, helped the newcomers give meaning to daily life on the land. From its founding as a British colony that welcomed Catholics, Maryland had a reputation for religious tolerance. The various churches in and around Sharpsburg bore witness to that ideal. German settlers, mostly members of the Lutheran or Reformed Lutheran denominations, first built simple log structures alongside the more ornate churches of Anglicans and Roman Catholics. In addition, Sharpsburg attracted "Sect People," including Dunkers, Amish, and Mennonites, all of whom built simple churches of stone or clapboard. The architectural distinctions between the denominations were as recognizable as their doctrinal variances, but whatever their differences over baptism, communion, and the proper places for worship, most of the residents shared the basic Christian idea that the natural world should be subdued, civilized, and made to benefit the children of God.[10]

Reimagined as a place of agrarian order, productivity, and profit, Antietam underwent a stunning transformation as residents replaced large swaths of natural vegetation with crops and pastures. Like the natural world out of which it evolved, the new agricultural landscape was not static. Between 1820 and 1850, American agriculture experienced its own revolution. Inspired by writers who advocated improvement and reform, many American farmers, including those around Sharpsburg, began to strive for better efficiency and higher profits. Increasingly, they sought the finest breeds of livestock for beef and dairy products. They planted the best seed, saved manure for fertilizer, rotated crops, and made use of the latest tools and technology. Neatness mattered, too. Stout fences, clean barns, well-kept outbuildings, and spacious dwellings became as important as bumper crops and fat cattle.[11]

As archaeologists working around Antietam have discovered, the reform movement even altered local methods of garbage disposal. The earliest settlers in the region simply threw household trash and refuse into the yard. Chickens or hogs might consume some of the waste, but items such as broken glass, old wood, and pottery could be found scattered around most farmhouses. By the early 1860s, however, many residents buried their garbage in pits located well away from their dwellings, keeping yards and fields clear of debris. Appearances mattered, reformers believed, because "the agrarian landscape had to reflect the nation's prosperity and importance."[12]

By all accounts, the farmers of Antietam did their part to clean up the countryside. Near the north end of what would become the battlefield, David Miller worked a large plot carved out of two forests known as the North and East Woods. Visitors to his farm could not help but be impressed with his neat house and huge cornfield. A bit farther south, within sight of a Dunker church, Samuel and Elizabeth Mumma operated another prominent farm of 324 acres, replete with lush fields, large barns, and an impressive two-and-half-story house. The Mummas and their thirteen children worked that land for twenty-five years. East of there, William and Margaret Roulette supported their family of seven in similar fashion. But farming was not the area's only thriving enterprise. An ironworks sprang up along Antietam Creek. Weavers and dye-makers established operations in Sharpsburg. Several major wagon roads on the outskirts of town provided farmers and merchants with direct routes to the markets of Hagerstown and other communities.[13]

However powerful and transformative they might be, human ideas about order, productivity, and profit still had to make accommodations for nature. Antietam Creek provided waterpower, but with few natural fords, its deep currents stood in the way of farmers' access to various markets. In 1836, a group of Dunker farmers built a 125-foot stone bridge to facilitate transport of goods and livestock across the stream. Constructed of limestone from nearby sources and named for a local farmer, Rohrbach's Bridge (also called Lower Bridge to distinguish it from two similar structures farther upstream) provided much easier and more direct access to Sharpsburg and the wagon thoroughfares beyond. Seeking ever more efficient avenues for commerce, residents also laid out a network of smaller side roads that zigzagged between fields and farms. Some of those routes, including one known as the "Hog Trough" or "Sunken" Road, followed natural depressions in limestone and other soft deposits laid down millions of years before. According to nearly every contemporary description, by 1862 the human presence had turned Sharpsburg into a model agricultural and mercantile community, one that local residents had come to cherish and visitors admire. It was a typical landscape both in its history, as a place wrought by nature and remade by human ingenuity, and in its residents' affinity for it. Its transition had taken only a hundred years, a mere eye blink compared to the vast expanse of geologic time. In the fall of 1862, people would again give new meaning to the landscape. This time the transformation required only a single day.[14]

The Battle

Arriving some time after noon on 15 September 1862, General Jacob Cox described the view from the Union line:

> Immediately in front the Antietam wound through the hollow, the hills rising gently on both sides. In the background on our left was the village

of Sharpsburg, with fields inclosed by stone fences in front of it. At the right was a bit of wood (since known as the West Wood), with the little Dunker Church standing out white and sharp against it. Farther to the right and left the scene was closed in by wooded ridges with open farm lands between, the whole making as pleasing and prosperous a landscape as can easily be imagined.

The bucolic scene held hidden dangers, however; a brief exchange of cannon fire revealed the general location of Confederate positions along the Hagerstown Pike, but, Cox noted, "the undulations of the rolling ground" hid the enemy's infantry from sight. Union lines stretched along the eastern bank of Antietam Creek from Rohrbach's Bridge to Samuel Price's mill near Keedysville, about three miles to the northeast. Cox expected the battle to commence the following day, and when two Union corps, under Major General Joseph Hooker and Major General J. F. K. Mansfield, took up positions on Joseph Poffenberger's farm across the creek early on the sixteenth, it could have, but commanding general George B. McClellan, ever cautious, waited to attack until dawn on 17 September.[15]

The delay enabled General Robert E. Lee time to choose his ground and for reinforcements to arrive. Lee, commanding 38,000 Confederate troops, anchored his left flank on Nicodemus Hill, north of the town between a bend in the Potomac River and the Hagerstown Pike, and placed his center along the Sunken Road south of Samuel Mumma's farm, using woodlands, stone walls, and the naturally rolling topography as cover along the entirety of his line. He set his right flank on the heights overlooking the southernmost bridge over Antietam Creek. Strangely, Lee did not claim all the high ground available to him; running parallel to his lines and between him and the Potomac was a small ridge, from which Union forces, if they managed to get to his rear, could envelop and destroy his entire army. Despite claiming some natural advantages, Lee was in a tenuous position: he was cut off from Virginia and easy retreat by the Potomac, which lay at his back, with only one accessible ford available to him; he had high ground between him and that single possible escape route; and he had an army twice the size of his own to his front.

The morning of the battle, 17 September 1862, was chilly and damp, thick with fog. As the sun rose, the fog lifted, and the battle began with Union forces under Hooker's command leading the first of three disjointed attacks. The first set of engagements took place against Lee's left flank, in the woodlands south and east of Poffenberger's farm, where after two hours Union

Figure 4. This 1862 map, drawn by Union soldier Robert Knox Sneden, depicts the topography of the Antietam battlefield as well as the positions of the Union and Confederate forces. The Potomac runs along the bottom of the map and Sharpsburg sits just left of center. The East Woods, the Dunker Church, and the Sunken Road lie slightly up and left from the town site. The J. Poffenberger farm is in the upper left corner, with the Corn Field immediately to its right. Burnside's Bridge crosses Antietam Creek just above and to the right of Sharpsburg, labeled on this map as "Bridge No. 3." (Courtesy of the Virginia Historical Society)

troops claimed the ground. The fight quickly moved into David Miller's cornfield, immortalized now as *the* Corn Field, where the worst of the day's fighting took place, claiming 8,000 casualties in less than three hours. The final assault of phase one came at about 9:15 A.M., led by General Edwin Sumner. The plan was for the entire Second Corps to attack, but the effort of fording the swift waters of Antietam Creek slowed its advance, and only one of the three divisions moved toward the Confederate forces positioned near the Dunker Church, in a forested area known today as the West Woods. The delay gave Lee time to shore up his positions there, and in under twenty minutes over 2,200 of Sumner's 5,300 men were lost to injury or death.

The second phase of the battle, beginning around 9:30 A.M., focused on Lee's center, hunkered down in the Sunken Road south of the Mumma and Roulette farms. The two remaining divisions of Sumner's Second Corps, approximately 9,000 men led by Generals William French and Israel Richardson, attacked Colonel John Brown Gordon's 2,200 Confederate troops; after more than three hours of desperate fighting and 5,000 dead or wounded, Richardson's men broke through the Confederate line and took the Sunken Road, which, in the aftermath of the battle, became known as Bloody Lane. Simultaneously, but without real coordination, the third phase of the battle commenced on Lee's right flank. This was McClellan's opportunity to get behind Confederate lines, take the ridge and cut Lee off from Virginia, and, perhaps, end the war. General Ambrose Burnside commanded this part of the battle, throwing brigade after brigade of his Ninth Corps against General Robert Toombs's small Confederate force of fewer than 500 men, who held the heights above Rohrbach's Bridge and stymied the Union advance for over three hours. Burnside's troops ultimately succeeded—today the bridge is named for the commander—and engaged Confederate positions near Sharpsburg, only to find them reinforced by General A. P. Hill's division, which had arrived from Harpers Ferry around 2 P.M. Burnside's corps fell back across Antietam Creek. The battle ended at sunset, twelve hours later. It was the war's single bloodiest day, with 23,000 casualties—6,000 dead, 17,000 wounded—littering a landscape that had begun the day as the epitome of American agrarian progress. The following evening Lee pulled back across the Potomac; McClellan declined to follow.[16]

Modern visitors to Antietam can clearly see how the landscape shaped the battle. The creeks, the woods, and even the slight dips and swells of the ground affected both sides' abilities to maneuver and presented either lifesaving protection or deadly obstructions. David Thompson of Company G, Ninth New York Volunteers, placed "natural obstacles and the inequalities of the ground" (random anomalies resulting from the region's long and varied geologic history) second only to the human enemy in terms of consequence. He wrote, "A slight rise of ground in an open field, not noticeable a thousand yards away, becomes, in the keep of a stubborn regiment, a powerful headland against which the waves of battle roll and break," pointing to the sunken roads over ancient limestone deposits—like Bloody Lane—as evidence. If the terrain shaped the battle, the battle also changed Sharpsburg's landscape. The Confederates burned the Mumma farmhouse to the ground, and the Dunker Church and many other buildings suffered extensive damage from rifle and cannon fire. The tens of thousands of men and animals that encamped, fought, and died on the pastoral landscape left forests and crops in shambles. According to an archeological study of the site, "while the rural landscape was significantly changed by the battle of Antietam, this altered world was not acceptable or tenable to the people of Sharpsburg, who strived to return it to its previous condition." Their devotion to the agricultural landscape would, years later, make Antietam an ideal candidate for battlefield preservation.[17]

The Park

Even before Lee's surrender at Appomattox, various groups sought to memorialize the sacrifice and bravery demonstrated by those who fought the war. The first efforts were spearheaded by individuals or military units and included small memorial markers placed just after the battle identifying where a beloved commander or comrades-in-arms fell. Most of these were temporary, but others, such as the 1863 marble monument honoring Union colonel William B. Hazen and the men of his brigade who died at the battle of Stones River, near Murfreesboro, Tennessee, still exist. Large-scale memorialization also occurred during the war in the form of the creation of national cemeteries. As a matter of expediency—both sides simply buried their dead where they lay—these makeshift burial grounds gained legitimacy, at least for the Union dead, when the Thirty-Seventh Congress passed a law in 1862 authorizing the president to purchase those lands from their private owners and declare them national cemeteries. This marked, according to historian Timothy B. Smith, "the first time actual sites of conflict were preserved to honor the fallen."[18]

Because of its notoriety as the bloodiest day of the war and, for Union sympathizers, its association with Lincoln's Emancipation Proclamation, memorialization at Antietam began early. On 10 March 1864, the Maryland legislature attempted to purchase land east of Sharpsburg to set it aside as a state and national cemetery for Union soldiers killed in the battle. Legal issues prevented the completion of the transfer of land until 23 March

1865, when the state officially established the Antietam National Cemetery and a board of trustees to administer it. Twelve years later, with costs mounting and funds dwindling, the trustees turned to Congress, which on 2 March 1877 assumed fiscal responsibility for and administration over the site, placing its management under the War Department. This structural transition coincided with the official end of Reconstruction and a shift in American politics that encouraged efforts to remember and commemorate those who fought on both sides. Civil War veteran organizations and their affiliate groups, such as the United Daughters of the Confederacy and the Sons of Union Veterans of the Civil War, raised funds to erect memorials and hold reunions and also lobbied Congress to purchase land where major battles took place. Those efforts resulted in the expansion of memorialization beyond cemeteries toward the preservation of entire fields of battle, not only transforming the physical territory that was thereby protected but also creating entirely new landscapes with new meanings. The first battle site to gain national protection was the 6,000-acre Chickamauga and Chattanooga National Military Park, created by Congress on 19 August 1890. Antietam was the second, becoming a National Battlefield Site on 30 August 1890, when President Benjamin Harrison signed into law H.R. 10844.[19]

The Congressional Committee on Military Affairs gave a succinct reason for its support for Antietam's protection: "A nation should preserve the landmarks of its history." Furthermore, the committee explained in its report to the U.S. House of Representatives in 1891, it was "absolutely necessary that the lines of both sides to the persistent struggle should be marked." The Antietam site was an ideal setting for such commemoration because, as the report suggested, "the field on which the battle took place is practically unchanged from what it was on the day of the action, save the cutting down of some trees, and presents to-day, as it did in 1862, the most open field on which was fought any of the great battles of the rebellion." Antietam presented a unique opportunity to commemorate the struggle with little effort because the war-era landscape remained largely intact. It was not just the battle that was important at Antietam, however; while the committee warned against making battlefield preservation too political (and reigniting the sectional strife the nation was attempting to put behind it), they claimed, "Antietam forms an exception, for upon the result on that field depended the greatest political stroke of modern times, the promulgation of the policy of emancipation by the President of the United States." It was not just sacrifice, therefore, that would be commemorated, but also the moral high ground the Union claimed through Lincoln's proclamation.[20]

For the most part, those charged with preserving Antietam's symbolic importance believed that the physical landscape should be maintained to appear as it did on the day of the battle. Administrators of the National Battlefield Site took up that cause in 1877, and that basic philosophy endured when responsibility for Antietam passed from the War Department to the Interior Department and the National Park Service in 1933. That goal, however, has been difficult to attain, not least because of the need to acquire the large tract of land on which the battle took place. The original purchase in 1877 secured only 10 acres that made up the military cemetery. Another acquisition in 1896 added 22 acres, but the tract still included only .004 percent of the 8,000 acres affected by the battle. As late as 1960, the site included just over 193 acres. Congress authorized significant increases in NPS holdings at Antietam throughout the next two decades, but by 1983, the NPS still held only 814 acres of the battlefield in fee, with scenic easements on just under 900 additional acres. Today, the NPS has title to only 1,937 of Antietam's 3,263 acres; the remaining land is privately owned, with easements restricting the types and scale of development that can take place on 820 of those 1,326 acres (the 500 acres without easements are protected through general goodwill of the landowners). Compare that with Gettysburg National Battlefield, where the majority of the site's 5,733 acres is owned outright by the federal government, which exerts full control over their management and disposition. The fragmentary and haphazard acquisition of land at Antietam has meant that, since the day after the battle ended, private owners and the local government have been free to develop much of the area for residential and commercial purposes, leaving important aspects of the site lost to history.[21]

Physical territory is not the only aspect of the battle that remains elusive at ANB. Although visitors to the park can observe reconstructed buildings, stand beneath witness trees, walk the Bloody Lane, and cross Burnside's Bridge, we can never recover the experience of that day. Certain sensory elements have not been replicated. The NPS cannot reproduce the weather patterns of 1862, and the park has no sound system to broadcast the boom of cannon and the sharp reports of rifle fire. No hidden aerosol containers add the acrid smell of black powder weapons. We also cannot know the anticipation and anxiety soldiers felt as they waited for battle. Consider the men who served under Confederate general John Bell Hood. They awoke early that morning, well before daylight, not in expectation of a fight but because at long last they had a chance to cook a proper breakfast. When cannon boomed at dawn, Hood ordered the troops to the front, and they made their way toward David Miller's cornfield. The fighting there proved so fierce that gunfire soon turned the six-foot cornstalks into stubble. Many of Hood's men died with their stomachs still empty. The suddenness of that turn of events, from lighthearted campfire banter and the camaraderie of meal preparation to the horror and death of the cornfield, is something that we can never hope to duplicate.[22]

The plight of Hood's men also suggests that, unlike bridges, roads, and farmhouses, one of the most basic elements of nature's material culture — the availability of food — cannot be recreated. By the summer of 1862, the Confederate commissary system had already demonstrated that it could not provide adequate rations for troops on the move. In the weeks before they ventured into Maryland, Lee's men had survived on provisions taken from several counties in northern Virginia. Farms there had been nearly picked clean. If the Confederate army lingered in the Old Dominion, Lee feared that civilians might also starve. As yet untouched by war, Maryland had barns "as big as Noah's ark" and might provide the army with sustenance to reach Pennsylvania.[23]

Even the most dedicated Civil War reenactors, including those who fast for several days before an event, cannot begin to experience the near-starvation and poor health of Lee's soldiers as they left Virginia. Civilians who saw the troops cross the Potomac that September often struggled for words to describe the emaciated crew. "When I say they were hungry," one woman explained, "I convey no impression of the gaunt starvation that looked from their cavernous eyes." Gazing upon the men from afar, some civilians wondered if scarecrows from all the fields of Maryland had somehow assembled in one place. "A most ragged, lean and hungry set of wolves," another observer called them.[24]

On their way to Frederick, the Confederates subsisted mainly on immature corn and green apples, poor substitutes for the meat and bread their bodies so desperately needed. With their high-fiber and high-sugar content, the unripe fruits and vegetables caused excessive water to accumulate in the large intestines of human digestive systems, fluid that had to be evacuated via the bowels. As Private Alexander Hunter described it, after six days, "there was not a man whose form had not caved in, and who had not had a bad attack of diarrhea." Lacking spare garments, many soldiers soon discovered that their "underclothes were foul and hanging in strips." Civilians along Lee's route could smell the approaching troops before they saw them. "I have never seen a mass of such filthy strong-smelling men," one witness noted. "Three in a room would make it unbearable." Thanks to sickness and malnutrition, some 10,000 of Lee's 55,000 troops fell out of the ranks before they reached the battlefield. Those who made it in time to fight battled gastric distress throughout the engagement. A few days after the battle, one visitor to Antietam noted that he could trace the movements of Confederate soldiers "by the thickly strewn belt of green corn husks and cobs" and the "ribbon of dysenteric stools just behind."[25]

The victors fared better but still faced living conditions and health problems that modern reenactors and visitors seldom contemplate. For six weeks after the battle, some 50,000 Union troops remained close to the battlefield. Their presence instantly transformed rural Sharpsburg into a metropolis, with a human population comparable to cities like Pittsburgh, Detroit, Milwaukee, Rochester, and Cleveland. Those municipalities relied on food produced elsewhere, primarily in the hinterlands of the American West and the Ohio Valley. Sharpsburg, with only about 1,300 permanent residents, had its own well-established commercial and transportation networks, but those connections now proved woefully inadequate to sustain the burgeoning population. Thousands of stragglers from both armies who drifted into the region in the days after the battle only compounded the problem. Civilians returning home quickly discovered that anything edible—crops, livestock, smoked meats, canned vegetables, jellies and jams—had vanished. Amid the scarcity, food prices soared. Rations helped sustain the Union army, but others sometimes had to buy from feckless speculators who brought in victuals from other regions. By late September, a newspaper noted, Sharpsburg had "been eaten out of food of every description."[26]

The region was also ill equipped to deal with another common municipal problem: waste disposal. Though the Union's Sanitary Commission made it clear that soldiers "should never be allowed to void their excrement elsewhere than in the regularly established sinks," enforcing the regulation in camp proved impossible. For the most part, soldiers relieved themselves wherever and whenever they pleased. People were not the only source of ordure. The North lost scores of horses and mules in the battle, but as of 1 October, the occupying army still had upwards of 33,000 animals. Modern estimates suggest that a healthy 1,000-pound horse or mule produces an average of 50 pounds of manure and six gallons of urine in a typical day. Those numbers can vary about 30 percent up or down, depending on an individual animal's food and water intake. Allowing for inadequate nourishment among warhorses and taking the lowest possible estimate (35 pounds of manure and two gallons of urine per animal per day), Union horses and mules left at least 575 *tons* of solid waste and more than 65,000 *gallons* of liquid effluent on the landscape around Sharpsburg *every day* during the six-week occupation.[27]

By the 1860s, the sixteen largest American cities, including some with populations smaller than post-battle Sharpsburg, employed water-carriage systems of sewage disposal. Simply stated, those systems used water pumped from distant locales to carry waste out of the cities, usually into rivers and streams. These sewer systems created their own set of environmental hazards, and urban pollution from horse manure remained a serious problem throughout the century, but in the short run, city health improved. Sharpsburg had no such infrastructure. Prior to the battle, residents had relied on outhouses and used surplus manure to fertilize their fields. Now tons of waste simply accumulated on the landscape.[28]

Sharpsburg also had to deal with another public health issue, one that most Northern cities had never contemplated. When the shooting stopped, some 23,000 soldiers lay dead or wounded on the landscape. As environmental historian Ellen Stroud reminds us, death is the point at which "human bodies most clearly become components of their environments," both "as organic material ... and as health hazards." Civilians and the surviving soldiers worked day and night to bury human corpses and amputated limbs in shallow graves, hoping (correctly as it turns out) that the remains might later be interred in a proper cemetery. Yet even those heroic efforts could not keep up with nature's own processes for disposing of the dead. Roughly a week after the battle, one Union surgeon saw "at least a thousand corpses with blood and gas protruding from every orifice, and maggots holding high carnival over their heads." Oddly enough, an individual rotting corpse probably posed little threat to the health of the living. Those who moved the bodies had a slight risk of contracting tuberculosis, hepatitis, and blood-borne diseases, but only if the dead man suffered from those contagions and only if the corpse was fresh; organisms that cause such diseases cannot survive for more than a day or two after death. As the International Committee of the Red Cross explains it, when lots of people die from trauma (in this case war wounds), "it is those who have survived who are more likely to be spreading disease."[29]

Nineteenth-century Americans, however, did not know that. Ideas about the causes of sickness varied widely the 1860s, but many American physicians and army surgeons still put stock in the miasmatic theory of disease. Simply stated, the theory held that sickness resulted from breathing in toxic matter suspended in the air. Such noxious fumes might come from swampy ground (as in the case of malaria) or from general filth and poor sanitary practices. Experts believed that whatever its source, a potentially lethal miasma could be identified by its putrid odor. It was natural to assume that a decomposing body, with its unmistakable stink, released rotten matter into the atmosphere. As a result, whenever people died en masse, removing the reeking bodies from contact with air became a priority.[30]

Equally problematic were the animal carcasses that lay rotting in the September sun. Soldiers and townsfolk covered dead horses with lamp oil and set fire to the remains. Everywhere the burning horseflesh and decomposing corpses combined to produce a stench that seemed fit to "breed a pestilence." The real threat, however, probably came not from the miasma but from contamination of the water supply. Dry summer conditions left Antietam Creek and its tributaries running low. Without prolonged rains to flush them out, local water sources became susceptible to contamination from bacteria that flourished amid the heat, accumulated excrement from the occupying troops and animals, and decomposing flesh.[31]

Though exact diseases are difficult to identify, local people and visitors alike described Antietam as a sickly place throughout the winter of 1862–63. Residents noted outbreaks of typhoid, chronic diarrhea, and even cholera, a disease that rarely surfaced elsewhere during the war. All of these, Sharpsburg's citizens believed, resulted directly from the battle. Only after spring rains flushed and replenished local groundwater did conditions improve. Indeed, the town retained its reputation for sickness until well after the war ended.[32]

For the moment, a once-thriving agricultural community had been transformed into a near ecological wasteland. We may never know the full extent of that devastation. In all likelihood, excessive demand for firewood depleted forests; army horses and mules overgrazed local pasturelands. Birds and other wildlife disappeared, chased off by the boom of artillery or killed for food by half-starved soldiers and civilians. As one resident noted, "You couldn't hear a dog bark nowhere. You couldn't hear a bird whistle or a crow caw.... We didn't even a see a buzzard with all the stench.... When night come I was so lonesome that I see I didn't know what lonesome was before. It was a curious silent world."[33]

Conclusion

Antietam is no longer silent. Today, an average of over 350,000 people visit the park each year, seeking information, insight, and perhaps inspiration. In April 2015, our small group of scholars was among those thousands, with many of the same expectations. We went to learn about the battle and the soldiers' experiences and to understand the Civil War in all its complexities. Its landscape offered the best way for us, as environmental historians, to see and sense the place of nature, especially physical geography, in the larger conflict. We went to Antietam because, although participants' and witnesses' diaries, letters, and reports can be enlightening, they cannot substitute for *place* in revealing how the material and the cultural come together.[34]

Antietam National Battlefield, the place, exemplifies the interplay between natural and social forces and epitomizes Civil War material culture. ANB is an artifact writ large, interpreted across multiple generations and imbued with both physical and intellectual significance. Its terrain, made by nature, reveals the power of the material world to shape human experience. Its historical landscapes, created by human labor and made meaningful through human ideas, illuminate the myriad ways culture shapes nature. Both together created the conditions in 1862 that Civil War soldiers encountered and, in their turn, transformed.

We went to Antietam to sort through the layers that nature and culture contributed to the events on 17 September 1862. Like those who traveled to Antietam in the 1870s, visitors today expect to see what the soldiers did in 1862. To an extent, they do. The goal of the NPS is to recreate the landscape on the "eve of battle." As such, Antietam shows visitors a romanticized version of the region's nineteenth-century agriculture: cornfields, quaint farm buildings, and stately forests. That is not all bad. Indeed, that agrarian way of life—so important that civilians immediately sought to restore it on the battle-scarred landscape—reflects an idyllic agricultural world that Union soldiers fought to protect. The site also allows visitors to understand something about the role of the material world in war, especially visible in the worn limestone deposits that gave the land its undulating character and created conditions for the carnage in the Bloody Lane. Various memorials, signage, and its designation as a National Battlefield add details about strategy, troop movements, and casualties, leaving visitors (except on reenactment days) to imagine the fighting. As a tactile artifact, Antietam best represents what the war was about as much as, and perhaps even more than, it represents how it was fought.[35]

Digging into the site's environmental history can help complete that picture by pointing us toward some of the less savory aspects of the complex relationship between people, nature, and war. Acknowledging the environment as an active force in history also shows that the natural world moves to its own peculiar rhythms and frequently shapes historical events in ways that humans cannot anticipate. Perhaps most important, taking the long view of the site's history reveals that, as it exists today, Antietam is as much a memorial to the present as it is to the past. At the moment, a major problem confronting the NPS is an exploding white-tailed deer population, created by restrictions on hunting, the decline of natural predators, and the availability of food and habitat in the neatly maintained fields and forests. The prevalence of so many deer, which in 1862 might have provided venison for starving Civil War soldiers, is an ironic reminder that people of the past interacted with nature in ways that no restored landscape can ever recapture—and in ways that most of us, even if we could, would not care to duplicate.[36]

Notes

1. J. E. Thomas, J. Calzarette, J. P. Campbell, T. J. B. Carruthers, D. Cohen, W. C. Dennison, L. Donaldson, A. Landsman, M. Lehman, M. Nortrup, and E. Wenschhof, *Antietam National Battlefield Natural Resource Condition Assessment: National Capital Region*, Natural Resource Report NPS/NCRN/NRR—2011/413 (Fort Collins, Colo.: National Park Service, 2011).

2. Michael DeGruccio, "Letting the War Slip through Our Hands: Material Culture and the Weakness of Words in the Civil War Era," in *Weirding the War: Stories from the Civil War's Ragged Edges*, ed. Stephen Berry (Athens: University of Georgia Press, 2011), 29; Joan E. Cashin, "Trophies of War: Material Culture in the Civil War Era," *Journal of the Civil War Era* 1, no. 3 (September 2011): 349. In 2006 the *Journal of Material Culture* did a special double issue on landscape as material culture. Particularly useful is Christopher Tilley's "Introduction: Identity, Landscape, Place and Heritage," *Journal of Material Culture* 11, no. 1/2 (September 2006): 7–32. Other scholars interested in landscape or other aspects of the physical or natural world as part of material culture have also contributed to that journal. Although their arguments are not directly pertinent to analysis of Antietam, they are nevertheless important indices that this is a growing subject that deserves greater attention. See, for example, Esteban Ruiz-Ballesteros, José Maria Valcuende, Victoria Quintero, José Antonio Cortes, and Elena Rubio, "Naturalizing the Environment: Perceptual Frames, Senses and Resistance," *Journal of Material Culture* 14 (June 2009): 147–67; and Roderick B. Salisbury, "Engaging with Soil, Past and Present," *Journal of Material Culture* 17 (March 2012): 23–41. Barbara Bender's work is also useful for understanding the political and social aspects of how landscapes are created and understood. See especially Barbara Bender, "Place and Landscape," in Christopher Tilley, Webb Keane, Susanne Küchler, Mike Rowlands, and Patricia Spyer, eds., *Handbook of Material Culture* (London: Sage, 2006), 303–14.

3. National Park Service, U.S. Department of the Interior, Geologic Resources Division, *Antietam National Battlefield, Chesapeake and Ohio Canal National Historic Park, & Harpers Ferry National Historic Park, Geologic Resource Evaluation Report* (Denver: NPS Geologic Resources Division, January 2005), 27–28, http://www.nature.nps.gov/Geology/parks/anti/anti_choh_hafe_gre_rpt_view.pdf, accessed 5 June 2016.

4. National Park Service, Geology Field Notes Antietam National Battlefield, http://www.nature.nps.gov/Geology/parks/anti/index.cfm, accessed 8 June 2016.

5. National Park Service, U.S. Department of the Interior, Geologic Resources Division, *Geologic Resource Evaluation Report*, 15.

6. National Park Service, "Geology Field Notes Antietam"; National Park Service, "Antietam National Battlefield, Maryland/Nature/Natural Features and Ecosystems/Forests," https://www.nps.gov/anti/learn/nature/forests.htm, accessed 7 June 2015.

7. National Park Service, "Archaeology at Antietam, Archaeological Survey of New Lands, 2011–2013," https://www.nps.gov/rap/archeology/PDFs/ANTI%20Archeology AtAntietamPoster.pdf, accessed 8 June 2015; Ted Alexander, *The Battle of Antietam: The Bloodiest Day* (Charleston: History Press, 2011), Kindle ed., location 658.

8. Alexander, *Battle of Antietam*, location 666–73.

9. Kathleen Ernst, *Too Afraid to Cry: Maryland Civilians in the Antietam Campaign* (Mechanicsburg, Penn.: Stackpole Books, 2007), 3–5.

10. Alexander, *Battle of Antietam*, location 677; National Park Service, "Who Were the Dunkers?," https://www.nps.gov/anti/learn/historyculture/who-were-the-dunkers .htm, accessed 7 June 2015; Harvey H. Kaiser, *The National Park Architecture Sourcebook* (New York: Princeton Architectural Press, 2008), 457; Carl Lounsbury, "God Is in the Details: The Transformation of Ecclesiastical Architecture in Early Nineteenth-Century America," *Perspectives in Vernacular Architecture* 13, no. 1 (2006): 1–21.

11. Elise Manning-Sterling, "Antietam: The Cultural Impact of Battle on an Agrarian Landscape," in *Archeological Perspectives on the American Civil War*, ed. Clarence R. Geier and Stephen R. Potter (Gainesville: University Press of Florida, 2000), 188–216. More general treatments of agricultural developments during the early to mid-nineteenth century confirm this. See, for example, Jack Temple Kirby, *Poquosin: A Study of Rural Landscape and Society* (Chapel Hill: University of North Carolina Press, 1995); and Steven Stoll, *Larding the Lean Earth: Soil and Society in Nineteenth-Century America* (New York: Hill and Wang, 2002).

12. Manning-Sterling, "Antietam," 189.

13. Alexander, *Battle of Antietam*, location 798–845; Ernst, *Too Afraid to Cry*, 4.

14. Alexander, *Battle of Antietam*, location 725, 839; Ernst, *Too Afraid to Cry*, 4; Manning-Sterling, "Antietam," 213. There is an extensive literature on the cultural history of landscapes, with Simon Schama's *Landscape and Memory* (New York: Knopf, 1995) among the most sweeping. For more specific works on the subject as it relates to the United States during the nineteenth century and beyond, see, for example, Joan E. Cashin, "Landscape and Memory in Antebellum Virginia," *Virginia Magazine of History and Biography*, October 1994, 477–500; Megan Kate Nelson, *Ruin Nation: Destruction and the American Civil War* (Athens: University of Georgia Press, 2012); Megan Kate Nelson, *Trembling Earth: A Cultural History of the Okefenokee Swamp* (Athens: University of Georgia Press, 2005); and John R. Stilgoe, *Landscape and Images* (Charlottesville: University of Virginia Press, 2005).

15. Jacob D. Cox, "The Battle at Antietam," in *North to Antietam: Battles and Leaders of the Civil War*, ed. Robert Underwood Johnson and Clarence Clough Buel, vol. 2 (New York: Castle Books, 1956), 630–31.

16. There are a number of excellent studies of Antietam, both from military and political history perspectives. A few of these are Gary Gallagher, ed., *The Antietam Campaign* (Chapel Hill: University of North Carolina Press, 1999); James M. McPherson, *Battle Cry of Freedom: The Civil War Era* (New York: Oxford University Press, 1988), 537–45; James M. McPherson, *Crossroads of Freedom: Antietam* (New York: Oxford University Press, 2002); Stephen W. Sears, *Landscape Turned Red: The Battle of Antietam* (New Haven: Ticknor and Fields, 1983); and Russell F. Weigley, *A Great Civil War: A Military and Political History, 1861-1865* (Bloomington: Indiana University Press, 2000), 144–54.

17. David L. Thornton, "With Burnside at Antietam," in *North to Antietam*, 660; Manning-Sterling, "Antietam," 216; Judy Ehlen and R. C. Whisonant, "Military Geology of Antietam Battlefield, Maryland, USA—Geology, Terrain, and Tactics," *Geology Today* 24, no. 1 (January–February 2008): 20–27.

18. Timothy B. Smith, *The Golden Age of Battlefield Preservation: The Decade of the 1890s and the Establishment of America's First Five Military Parks* (Knoxville: University of Tennessee Press, 2008), 16. The monument to Hazen is the oldest surviving Civil War memorial; see p. 14.

19. On the general history of Civil War battlefield park creation, see Smith, *Golden Age of Battlefield Preservation*. For Antietam's evolution as a memorial site, see the chapter "'The Experiment at Antietam': Antietam National Battlefield, 1890–1933," in Smith, *Golden Age of Battlefield Preservation*, 87–114; and Charles W. Snell and Sharon A. Brown, *Antietam National Battlefield and Cemetery, Sharpsburg, Maryland: An Administrative History* (Washington, D.C.: U.S. Department of the Interior, National Park Service, 1986).

20. H. R. Rep. No. 51-4019, at 1-3 (1891).

21. Franklin Delano Roosevelt issued two Executive Orders, 6166 on 10 June 1933 and 6228 on 28 July 1933, transferring administration over Antietam and forty-seven other sites from the War Department to the Interior. See National Archives, "Executive Orders: Executive Order 6166—Organization of executive agencies," http://www.archives.gov/federal-register/codification/executive-order/06166.html, accessed 8 June 2015; "The New Deal Years, 1933–1941," in *America's National Park System: The Critical Documents*, ed. Lary M. Dilsaver (New York: Rowman and Littlefield, 1994), available online at https://www.nps.gov/parkhistory/online_books/anps/anps_3b.htm, accessed 8 June 2015. For details on land acquisitions to expand the Antietam National Battlefield, see Snell and Brown, *Antietam National Battlefield*.

22. Keith Bohannon, "'Dirty, Ragged, and Ill-Provided For': Confederate Logistical Problems in the 1862 Maryland Campaign and Their Solutions," in *The Antietam Campaign*, ed. Gary W. Gallagher (Chapel Hill: University of North Carolina Press, 1999), 117.

23. Robert E. Lee to Jefferson Davis, 3 September 1862, in *The Wartime Papers of Robert E. Lee*, ed. Clifford Dowdey and Louis H. Manarin (Boston: Little Brown, 1961), 293; Ernst, *Too Afraid to Cry*, 40.

24. McPherson, *Crossroads of Freedom*, 88–94, 98; Sears, *Landscape Turned Red*, 65–67; Ernst, *Too Afraid to Cry*, 39.

25. W. H. Van Buren, *Rules for Preserving the Health of the Soldier* (Washington, D.C.: Sanitary Commission, 1861), 5; Margaret Humphreys, *Marrow of Tragedy: The Health Crisis of the American Civil War* (Baltimore: Johns Hopkins University Press, 2013), 98; Michael C. C. Adams, *Living Hell: The Dark Side of the Civil War* (Baltimore: Johns Hopkins University Press, 2014), 43.

26. Ted Alexander, "Destruction, Disease, and Death: The Battle of Antietam and the Sharpsburg Civilians," *Civil War Regiments* 6, no. 2 (1998): 151, 152, 155; "Population of the 100 Largest Urban Places: 1860," https://www.census.gov/population/www/documentation/twps0027/tab09.txt, accessed 7 June 2015; Ernst, *Too Afraid to Cry*, 160, 185.

27. Jing Tao and Karen Manci, "Estimating Manure Production, Storage Size, and Land Application Area," Fact Sheet, Agricultural and Natural Resources, Ohio State University Extension (2008), http://ohioline.osu.edu/aex-fact/pdf/0715.pdf, accessed 15 June 2015).

28. Joel Tarr, *The Search for the Ultimate Sink: Urban Pollution in Historical Perspective* (Akron: University of Akron Press, 1996), 113–14. Even in cities, residents relied

on privies, outhouses, and cesspools before the advent of running water systems. Buffalo, with a population of 80,000 (just slightly larger than the Union encampment at Sharpsburg), experienced its last serious cholera epidemic in 1854. Installation of a sewer system in Chicago required that all of the buildings be raised (sometimes as much as fourteen feet) above the level of Lake Michigan, and by the 1880s, that remarkable engineering effort had all but eliminated cholera from that city.

29. Ellen Stroud, "Reflections from Six Feet under the Field: Dead Bodies in the Classroom," *Environmental History* 8, no. 4 (2003): 618; Oliver Morgan, "Infectious Disease Risks from Dead Bodies Following Natural Disasters," *Rev Panam Salud Publica/ Pan Am Journal of Public Health* 15 (2004): 5, 307–12, http://publications.paho.org/pdf/dead_bodies.pdf.

30. Humphreys, *Marrow of Tragedy*, 78–79.

31. Daniel M. Holt, *A Surgeon's Civil War: The Letters and Diary of Daniel M. Holt, M.D.*, ed. James M. Greiner, Janet L. Coryell, and James R. Smither (Kent: Kent State University Press, 1994), 28.

32. Alexander, "Destruction, Disease, and Death," 156–58.

33. Quoted in Ernst, *Too Afraid to Cry*, 194.

34. National Park Service, "Visitor Use Statistics, Annual Visitation By Park (1979–Last Calendar Year)," https://irma.nps.gov/Stats/SSRSReports/National%20Reports/Annual%20Visitation%20By%20Park%20(1979%20-%20Last%20Calendar%20Year), accessed 4 October 2016.

35. Thomas et al., *Antietam National Battlefield Natural Resource Condition Assessment*, ix. Adam Wesley Dean makes the case for "agrarian republicanism"—small farming—as motivations for both the Republican Party and Union soldiers in his book *An Agrarian Republic: Farming, Anti-slavery Politics, and Nature Parks in the Civil War Era* (Chapel Hill: University of North Carolina Press), 2015.

36. Brian Black has made several of the same arguments about Gettysburg National Battlefield; see Brian Black, "The Nature of Preservation: The Rise of Authenticity at Gettysburg," *Civil War History* 58 (September 2012): 348–73; and Black and Richard B. Megraw, *Gettysburg Contested: 150 Years of Preserving America's Cherished Landscapes* (Staunton, Va.: George F. Thompson, 2016).

4

Saved by a Testament

Books as Shields among Union and Confederate Soldiers

RONALD J. ZBORAY & MARY SARACINO ZBORAY

On 4 September 1861, the *Boston Investigator* in its "Things in General" column published an item titled "Saved by a Testament." It recounted the story of Private George K. Ingalls of Company B, Second Maine Volunteer Infantry Regiment, who "was saved from death" when a bullet accidentally fired from an adjacent tent lodged in his breast-pocket Testament instead of his heart. "The bullet struck the Testament with great force, but fortunately did not go through it," the report explained. Shortly after the seemingly miraculous incident in camp at Willett's Point, Long Island, Company B's Captain Seth K. Devereaux sent the punctured book with a thank-you letter to the Bangor Young Men's Bible Society, the organization that donated the volume to Ingalls, who happened to be his nephew. Captain Devereaux wrote that the near-death experience "made an impression on the members of my company which will not soon wear off." His greenhorn troops apparently had become less reckless with their weapons and more devout in their faith. Perhaps they began placing Bibles in their pockets.[1]

It had been less than a month after the war began on 12 April 1861 when this American Bible Society publication took a bullet for Private Ingalls. Throughout the Civil War's next four years, many other pocket-size books carried by soldiers in camp, on picket guard, or to the battlefield would be pierced by minié balls, grapeshot, and shrapnel. Accounts of soldiers whose lives were purportedly saved by an assortment of Bibles, New Testaments, diaries, and songbooks appeared in such diverse printed sources as newspapers, magazines, and religious tracts. But stories spread by word of mouth, too. Americans on both sides of the conflict gossiped in letters about life-saving printed materials or related their wondrous deeds in diaries. Soldiers often sent the curious relics home so that civilians could contemplate the vicissitudes of war through these damaged books. Although books that saved lives in wartime had been commemorated in English-language print since at least 1691, bullet-in-the-book stories entered the consciousness of Americans on both sides of the conflict to an unprecedented degree during the Civil War because the sheer magnitude of firepower meant that a far greater number of books would be struck than ever before. Still, among the vast array of American Civil War relics changing hands, books struck by bullets were relatively rare. But that was what made them so fascinating to contemporaries. They were, perhaps, the most mysterious, intriguing, and awe-inspiring of all the material manifestations of war soldiers and civilians encountered.[2]

Yet the book-as-shield phenomenon has received no systematic scholarly study. Civil War historians and print culture specialists have noted it, but only incidentally. Sustained attention to the war's bullet-laden books is more likely to be located, today, on museum placards, in internet blogs and on comment boards, and at auctions in which such volumes command bids of $15,000, and perhaps more. This popular interest suggests a reason for the topic's lack of academic investigation. As Michael DeGruccio surmises, Civil War historians have made "a self-conscious attempt to distance 'serious' scholarship from the quaint (if mildly embarrassing) zeal of modern-day bullet collectors and hobbyists." When that distancing is combined with a reluctance among Civil War historians to engage material culture studies in general, book-shields are easily overlooked. There are other reasons for the lack of study. Being only one type of relic involved in what Joan E. Cashin calls the "massive traffic in objects" engendered by a war that "transformed the material culture of the entire country," these books have, unsurprisingly, resisted special treatment.[3]

In this essay we will focus upon these neglected remnants of Civil War material culture and examine bullet-in-the book episodes for the light they shed upon how and why books were refashioned into talismans against harm by soldiers, upon the loved ones who gave them books, and upon those who wrote about these incidents. We also explore the contemporary meaning-making system in which books played a fated role in protecting lives and, in the case of religious material, fulfilled a spiritual mission to enact divine providence. Turning volumes into pieces of armor was only one way that printed materials' usages were transformed during the Civil

War. But it was an important way—one that was imbricated in maintaining larger religious belief systems, addressing the war's massive dislocation of people, and coping with its incomprehensible destruction.[4]

We have been collecting research material on book-shields for about fifteen years. So far we have been able to document 108 cases involving both Union (70) and Confederate (38) soldiers and chaplains, but new examples will, no doubt, come to our attention in the future. That only 1 in 6 Confederate soldiers owned a Bible may account for the greater number of Unionist cases, but certainly the South's tenuous publishing industry and interrupted wartime reportage explains the imbalance in contemporary records upon which to draw. Privates or noncommissioned officers made up 69 percent of the soldiers in this group—we located no naval personnel—and 26 percent were commissioned officers. For 6 soldiers we have not been able to identify rank. We have located no certain instances of black soldiers' books being struck by bullets, although African Americans, too, carried print with them onto the battlefield. For example, some soldiers of South Carolina's First Regiment evidently had the 1863 Emancipation Proclamation with them when they met fire for the first time.[5]

Evidence for our cases derives from many sources, including the books themselves, some of which we examined in libraries, archives, and museums, and others of which we viewed in digital online galleries and illustrated printed sources, which sometimes represent the only remaining visual traces of discarded or lost volumes. We tapped into printed accounts of book-shields appearing in primary sources such as Civil War–era periodicals and published memoirs but also in secondary sources, including regimental and local histories, museum newsletters, and digital archives. Military records, including those compiled as the *Official Records of the Union and Confederate Armies*, as well as manuscript pension files at the National Archives and Records Administration, provided other sources of documentation. We also searched our extensive database of transcriptions taken from over 5,500 manuscript diaries and letters authored during the Civil War by 1,100 ordinary men, women, and children on both sides of the conflict who commented on their own and other readers' engagement with printed matter. Because of this database, which has been constructed for our larger project on reading during the war, we were able to both augment our file of case studies and situate shielding among the many other wartime usages of reading material.[6]

These diverse resources have allowed us not only to discover examples of book-shields but to learn more about their owners and histories. Without supporting documentation, the material objects themselves present only prima facie evidence of shielding. While substantiating claims to these books' life-saving powers is far from the purpose of this essay—indeed, many soldiers died when projectiles penetrated through books or glanced off of them to inflict wounds—it remains true that the era's relatively low-powered, black-powder igniting rifles would not have consistently fired bullets with enough force to enter and exit objects such as thick volumes; likewise, spent bullets would not have ripped entirely through a book. As such, we maintain that these books' authenticity should not be easily dismissed.[7]

Regardless of their effectiveness as armor, such books serve as grim reminders of a war in which 750,000 or more soldiers died. If, at times, the only thing that stood between life and instantaneous death was a leather cover and a stack of printed pages, then these sad little books embody, still today, the precariousness of fate so painfully experienced by Civil War soldiers and those who saw them off to war.[8]

We organize our essay in light of that fated, lived experience and its trajectory—from Americans conceiving of print matter as shield, to their fashioning of a volume into armor, to their transforming of scarred books into material mnemonics of the war. We begin with a consideration of the cultural-intellectual history of shielding and how Civil War–era Americans may have heard about it. Then we investigate the ways soldiers acquired a book-shield, how they positioned it on the body, and their experiences going into battle with the printed armor. After that we assay reactions to printed armor by those who published news pieces about book-shields during the war. Finally, we examine the ways these books were enshrined as either testaments to fated destinies and divine interventions or relics of wartime's horrors and human follies.

Conceiving of Shielding

Refashioning books into armor was not peculiar to the Civil War, nor was the idea then new. By the time the war began, the association of pocket-size books with shielding had already been established through the circulation of printed accounts about life-saving Bibles and the folklore these stories engendered. An early—perhaps the first—English-language record was published in 1691 by English Puritan theologian Richard Baxter in his *Certainty of the World of Spirits*. He simply stated that during "our late War"—the English Civil War—someone, but implicitly a Parliamentarian soldier, "had a small Bible in his Pocket, and a Musket-Bullet shot into his Bible, which saved his Life." Baxter seemed as enthralled with "one credible Person [who] had a Bullet shot through the felt of his Hat, and stopp'd at the Lining," as he was with the miraculous Bible, yet it became the inspiration for subsequent stories. American ministers and laity may have known Baxter through the prominent Boston Puritan Cotton Mather, whose *Wonders of the Invisible World* (1693) was appended to several early nineteenth-century editions of *Certainty*.[9]

Baxter's minimalist statement was embellished by Welsh divine John Evans in his 1721 sermon "The Serious Consideration of a Future Judgement Recommended to Youth." In it, Evans recalled a conversation he had when young with an old veteran of the English Civil War, a captain who carried a Bible only because it was "fashionable" to do so in the army. After storming a royal fort, the captain "found a musket-ball lodged in his Bible, which lay in his pocket on such a part of his thigh, that it must necessarily have proved mortal to him, had it not been for this ... well placed piece of armour." The bullet burrowed its way through to Ecclesiastes 11:9 — "a passage ... which providence in so remarkable a way pointed to his observation [and] made the deepest and the best impression on his mind," according to Evans. "From that time he minded religion in earnest" and often said how "his Bible had been the salvation of his Soul and his body too." It had been an instrument of divine providence.[10]

Evans's sermon became the foundation for variants printed in the United States. One of the earliest, "The Bullet and Bible: An Anecdote," written "for the *Albany Chronicle*, &c.," appeared in that paper on 16 October 1797. In the hands of author "G," Evans's soldier becomes "a profligate youth, who for the sake of plunder and dissipation, had abandoned his parents who lived very respectably in London." Oliver Cromwell is introduced as the commander of the Parliamentarian army who "ordered each of his soldiers to carry a Bible." The rest of the story remains true to Evans except in its being appended by a six-line poem celebrating the "Sacred Volume."[11]

The Cromwell Bible story with new variants resurfaced in 1811. In "Buck's" version the poem is missing, the Bible's edition ("Field's") is provided, and the soldier becomes a "wild, wicked young fellow, who ran away from his apprenticeship in London." Buck also introduced the lines from Ecclesiastes 11:9 upon which the bullet landed: "Rejoice, O young man, in thy youth and let thy heart cheer thee in the days of thy youth, and walk in the ways of thy heart, and in the sight of thine eyes; but know thou that for all these things God will bring thee into judgment." This story was reprinted several times just prior to and during the War of 1812 and throughout its aftermath in 1815. But Evans's narrative reappeared then as well. In May 1812, one writer for the *Evangelical Magazine* excerpted the part of it concerning the Bible and prefaced it with this: "The present exertions of the Naval and Military Society, occasioned my recollections of what I had read several years ago." Clearly, America's war with Britain had summoned up the earliest Bible-shield stories.[12]

English Civil War Bible tales popped up occasionally in print until the American Civil War's outbreak. Circulating, too, were excerpts from the 29 May 1854 speech of Massachusetts governor Emory Washburn about Oliver Cromwell's soldiers keeping Bibles in their knapsacks. Newspapers juxtaposed Washburn's words with Cambridge rare book collector George Livermore's refutation that the *Souldier's Pocket Bible* (1643) "was generally buttoned between the coat and vest, next to the heart, proving perhaps, sometimes, a defense from the weapons of the enemies of their bodies." Throughout the first half of the nineteenth century, periodicals published accounts of biblical shielding during the Seven Years' War, the French and Indian War, the battle at Waterloo, the American Revolution, and the U.S.-Mexican War, in addition to generalized tributes to the Bible's protective powers. Some histories were entirely fictionalized, such as the prize-winning short story about ill-fated love during the American Revolution, "Caroline Gray." In addition to miraculous Bible stories, reports of interventionist newsprint appeared. "Saved by a Newspaper," for example, tells how a superintendent, upon having his coattail caught in the cogs of a steam pump, was saved from injury by the "tightly folded" sheet in his pocket, which jammed the cogs, "throwing the band off the pullies."[13]

Collectively, these diverse narratives fashioned over time a consciousness among white Americans that the Bible, and to a lesser degree other reading material, had been rescuing people from harm ever since the earliest hand presses began mass-producing print. In this cultural formulation's deepest resonances, print has interceded most earnestly in wartime. With the Civil War's approach, ordinary Americans began drawing upon their association of embattlement with printed armor to prepare for the coming conflict. When it arrived, their faith in the protective power of books was put to the test.

Turning Books into Shields

As soon as the war began, religious publishers began tapping into popular beliefs about Bibles and shielding. Sometimes they alluded directly to the English Civil War by issuing the 1643 *Souldier's Pocket Bible*. The American Tract Society (ATS) first reprinted the rare item courtesy of George Livermore, who owned one of two extant copies and who, as we have seen, perpetuated assumptions that this was the edition Cromwell's men—and by extension Evans's and Baxter's iconic soldier—wore for protection. "This is just the Book every Soldier needs in his pocket," one ATS advertisement read. By September 1861 the ATS had published 20,000 copies, and by December the Young Men's Christian Association had distributed "a large number" to Pennsylvania regiments. Others reprinted it, including the Tract Society of Charleston, South Carolina, and Livermore himself, who made a facsimile edition from his personal copy. None of the Bibles in our research sample that we were able to identify by edition was the *Soldier's Pocket Bible*—which was not actually a Bible but rather a sixteen-page collection of scriptural excerpts relevant to the soldier. Both the facsimile and the twenty-five-or-so-page reprint were simply too thin for armor and may have shredded to pieces when struck. Most pocket books, however, were thicker.[14]

If the cases we have examined are representative, thicker religious books were the most common kinds of volumes to be penetrated by a bullet during the Civil War and therefore the most likely to have been used as shields. Of the 113 printed artifacts in our set (some soldiers stacked them with other items), 79 are sacred volumes. The majority (73) are King James Bibles and New Testaments, and of these, most are pocket editions. Soldiers carried other denominational books, too. At least two Union troops in our study set owned the Anglican *Book of Common Prayer*. An Irish-American corporal in the Sixty-Ninth Pennsylvania, John Cassidy, kept close his Catholic *Manual of the Christian Soldier*, an omnibus of prayers, devotionals, and lessons, published by the Society of St. Vincent De Paul. A Seventeenth Connecticut private, John Collins, had an illustrated Roman Catholic prayer book with him at Gettysburg. We also came upon two hymnals. To save their bodies and souls, soldiers embraced sacred words in a variety of formats.[15]

Although soldiers carried denominational volumes, the relationship between faith and type of book remains indeterminate. Of four known Catholics, two pocketed denominational texts (mentioned just above). One of the remaining carried an account book and a presumably Protestant New Testament; the other, a notebook. Given the paucity of Catholic chaplains and limited degree of organized Catholic book production and distribution for soldiers, it is not surprising that they should resort to secular or Protestant books. Harassment by officers and other forms of prejudice, however, may have discouraged Catholic soldiers from practicing faith through reading.[16]

Among the numbers of holy texts, we found thirty-four secular books. Union soldiers were more likely to own these. Only five of the Confederate-owned book-shields in our sample—a notebook, a blank book, a diary, Walter Scott's narrative poem *Lady of the Lake*, and a dictionary—were nonreligious. Other secular items included songbooks, a pamphlet Emancipation Proclamation, a dime novel, a folded-up *Harper's Weekly*, a law book, and an unidentified pocket-size volume. So, while it is clear that spiritual books predominated, it is important to keep in mind that because other types of reading materials were in soldiers' pockets, religiosity was not the only factor in play. Memoranda books, for example, were pocketed for convenience's sake rather than for spiritual protection. Still, they became pieces of armor in battle.

The book-shields soldiers carried varied in size, but most were under five inches in height. The average height for pocket Bibles and Testaments for which we could establish an edition was just over four and a half inches; individually, they fell within the range of thirty-twomo to sixty-fourmo—the numbers of leaves created when a large printed sheet was folded to create page gatherings for binding. Numbers of pages and, therefore, thickness varied, too. Some small-size books in our group were 300 pages or more. At Fair Oaks, Virginia, a bullet penetrated 600 pages of the Bible that Ninety-Third Pennsylvania captain Eli Dougherty carried, after first shattering the gold watch next to it in his vest pocket. Evidently in response to demand for thick volumes, the American Bible Society increased its production of "larger books" and decreased its issuance of parts of the Bible, such as the book of Psalms or the Gospels, between May 1862 and May 1863. Larger books made better shields.[17]

Pocket volumes were inexpensive. Private George P. Howard of the Ninth Iowa paid only sixty cents for his leather-bound pocket diary, which was blasted through at Pea Ridge on 7 March 1862. At the American Bible Society's bottom end, a sixty-fourmo roan (sheepskin) New Testament cost only fourteen cents, while at the top end, a thirty-twomo morocco gilt Bible cost one dollar in 1863. The elegant Eyre and Spottiswoode English Bible that one Confederate soldier in our set owned probably cost more.[18]

But money was usually no object since soldiers often received religious volumes gratis or carried their own well-worn books into battle. Some new book-shields were donated by religious and benevolent organizations. Private Ingalls's Testament, for example, came compliments of the Bangor Young Men's Bible Society. The auxiliary paid for it but instructed the New York home institution, the American Bible Society, to distribute it to Ingalls's company when it marched through the city. Chaplains, too, handed out religious books. Private Cassidy received his *Manual of the Christian Soldier* from Reverend Michael F. Martin, chaplain of the Sixty-Ninth Pennsylvania. That publishing houses sometimes gave lower rates for bulk buying or shipped for free only aided gratis dissemination. Soldiers found even more ways to procure a free book. Tenth West Virginia private Harrison Mollohan stole his prayer book from a soldier's corpse at Harpers

Ferry two months before the volume would take a bullet for its new owner at Winchester on 19 September 1864.[19]

Almost one-quarter of the book-shields in our set were given as gifts from mothers, sisters, sweethearts, friends, or pastors before a soldier's departure from home or by chaplains and orderlies in camp. Loved ones' gifting may account for the likelihood of spiritual volumes remaining always in place, close to soldiers' hearts, and therefore, by chance, caught in fire. Inscriptions only enhanced these books' sentimental value. Before giving Second Lieutenant William Preston Mangum, Sixth North Carolina State Troops, a Bible, Martha Mangum inscribed it with "To my brother. He will read a portion of this blessed word every day, and remember his sister." Rosa Shuler inscribed her name, date, and the place presented on the Bible she gave her brother, Sergeant Walter Henry Counts, Thirteenth South Carolina. One New England minister personalized his Bible gift by writing on its recto flyleaf, "Charles W. Merrill [F]rom your aff. Pastor Davis Foster West Newbury *Mass* Aug. 12 1862." Even sparse lines, like this, meant the world to soldiers; after all, they were imprints from the hand of loved ones. "When you see Mr Foster remember me to him[.] [H]ardly a day passes without my thinking of him," Private Merrill, Nineteenth Massachusetts, wrote his mother from Falmouth, Virginia. Civilians generally eschewed giving embattled loved ones secular tokens of affection. There were no evident secular wartime gifts in our set.[20]

That soldiers had ample resources for acquiring books to pocket is clear. But did they intentionally wear their books as shields? Weaponizing secular books posed no moral qualms. One Forty-Seventh Alabama sergeant readily admitted he tucked his diary into his pocket after premonitions of being struck. Soldiers, however, were generally reluctant to confess that shielding was the primary reason for carrying a religious book, but evidence suggests they sometimes had it uppermost in mind. One private deliberately used a Bible for protection, according to Private Levi Fritz of the Fifty-Third Pennsylvania. "The life of a member of Co. F. was saved at the Battle of Chancellorsville in a remarkable manner while on picket," Fritz began his diary entry. "He was shot fair in the region of the heart," but the "shell struck the booke and bored its way through to the inner br'd [board]." Fritz noted that "the young man ... said that the book would save his life in just the manner it did and several weeks before the fight, he had the Bible sewed into the side pocket of his coat, covering his heart."[21]

More commonly, shielding was accepted as a side benefit but not the principal advantage of carrying a Bible. With that in mind, the men of the 100th Pennsylvania, famous for pocketing Bibles, called themselves the "Roundheads" in reference to English Civil War Parliamentarians. Colonel Daniel Leasure reportedly claimed his men, "when laying off their knapsacks to go into battle, were accustomed to open them and take out their Bibles and put them into the breast pocket of the blouse, right over the heart." He noted "several instances ... in which the balls of the enemy had either glanced from or lodged in the Bibles of his men, which else had pierced their hearts." One editor concluded, "It thus proved to some a shield to stay the fatal bullets of the enemy." The resonances with age-old folklore were too pointed to be ignored.[22]

Civilians sometimes had shielding in mind when they gave soldiers Bibles. Martha Mangum, for example, "had read about the Bible turning away balls," and in handing a Bible to her brother purportedly said, "This might do so some day." Some women gave instructions for strategic placement. Lucy Jones sewed a pocket in her stepson's blouse expressly for the Bible that she gave the private upon his departure with the Eighth New York Cavalry Regiment. Private Jones recalled her words "*It will do you no harm, and sometime it may do you some good*" after the Bible absorbed not one but two bullets. Like Jones, a group of Cheneyville, Louisiana, seamstresses, who furnished each member of an Eighth Louisiana company with a pocket Bible, also sewed each a new coat equipped with an inside breast pocket "so that each one can carry [the Bible] very near his heart, and thus it will act the double purpose of protecting the vital parts of his person ... and guiding or solacing him." If Bibles could provide both armor for the body and fortification for the soul, so much the better.[23]

Armed with books often before they even left home, soldiers prepared themselves spiritually and physically for battle with the aid of print. Most soldiers positioned their books in the breast or side pocket of a coat, jacket, vest, or shirt. As we have seen, some had special pockets made for them. But soldiers who feared their volumes would fall out stitched pockets shut. One Fireman Zouave (Eleventh New York) evidently fastened his Testament with needle and thread to his shirt so that the book would lie next to his heart. Sewn-in volumes were not handy for reading, but they remained securely in place.[24]

Some books resisted pocketing if they were large or chunky. Flimsy print items presented their own problems, especially unwieldy newspapers. George Fletcher, a Fifteenth Massachusetts private, folded his *Harper's Weekly* sheets sixteen times to make a thirty-twomo stack that would fit in his blouse pocket. But some paper-covered books, too, required manipulation to make them useful as shields. A private in the Fifth North Carolina State Troops sandwiched his rolled-up, paper-covered Sabbath school hymnbook between his vest and shirt. Some soldiers with odd-sized items abandoned pocketing altogether. One Illinois private had his songbook stashed in his cap when it was hit. When all else failed, soldiers tossed their books into a knapsack or haversack with other items.[25]

Soldiers frequently stacked books with other items to form a thick, layered barrier. In knapsacks, heaping was inevitable. But stacking in pockets required thought and strategy. Auxiliary pocketed items were diverse. Our set included a belt and cap box, wallet, tintype, cartridge box, rag for wiping rifles, handkerchief, documents, map, pay voucher, watch, and photo. In four cases, secular books combined forces with religious ones to create a barrier.

What happened when a projectile encountered printed barricades? In many of the cases we found, bullets entered books, burrowed through them, and implanted themselves somewhere in the cover or pages without exiting. A piece of grapeshot remains nestled inside Private Merrill's Testament, just as it did 150 years ago. Civil War–era books' leather bindings, sturdy boards, and strong, high-rag-content paper provided ample resistance to long-range fire and bullets nearing the end of their trajectories. When drenched, a book's good-quality pages melded together into an impassable block of concrete-like mush. The Testament of Sixtieth Ohio sergeant Wilton B. Logan was so "thoroughly saturated with water by exposure to a rain of several day's continuance" that a bullet "did not penetrate so as to do him any serious injury," one periodical divulged. Soldiers spared from injury sometimes felt a projectile's impact, nonetheless; General James Hewett Ledlie of the First Division, Ninth Corps, Army of the Potomac, felt "stunned" though unhurt when his stack of memoranda book, papers, and other items was hit during the siege of Petersburg in 1864. Others, like the mythical Parliamentarian, scarcely knew their books were hit until they took them out and discovered bullets lodged inside.[26]

Although many soldiers were spared from death by pocketed print matter, about 15 percent of those in our sample set died from wounds received the day that projectiles struck their book-shields. Sometimes bullets pierced entirely through books to enter the body, causing instant death or death within days. Confederate captain James Keith Boswell, for example, died on the spot when his pocketed notebook gave way to fire at Chancellorsville. At other times bullets were slowed down or redirected by books to inflict serious wounds responsible for eventual death from infection. Struck by a minié ball that glanced off his Bible at First Manassas, Lieutenant Mangum lingered on a week with a chest wound the size of his hand before passing away. Some soldiers expressed gratitude for the extra time on earth book-

Figure 5. Charles William Merrill's pocket New Testament, which was struck by grapeshot on 3 May 1863 at Fredericksburg, Virginia. (Courtesy of the Charles William Merrill Papers, Fam. MSS 611, Phillips Library, Peabody Essex Museum, Salem, Massachusetts; photography by Walter Silver)

shields afforded them to prepare for death or to see family members for one last time. Before expiring, Twenty-First Virginia private Thomas Cox had a fellow prisoner inscribe in his Testament, "It saved instant death & will be the means of saving my soul. Blessed are the dead that die in the Lord." Books in these cases granted spiritual, eternal life.[27]

In fusing together physical shielding with divine protection, soldiers and civilians attributed power to the religious book's physical materiality as well as to its intangible sacredness. But even with secular books, soldiers necessarily replayed folkloric and historical dramas in which the Bible as material artifact had saved lives in wartime. As the American Civil War persisted on, soldiers bore witness to an ever-increasing number of contemporary re-enactments of the Parliamentarian's fated encounter with a bullet. In drawing lessons from these incidents, they kept the practice alive throughout the war, so much so that by its end, the Cromwellian origin stories, superseded by scores of contemporary testimonies, had faded from memory.

Testifying to Shielding

As more and more soldiers' books came under fire during the war, stories about them for the national population, which by then was highly literate, became regular features in the press. The new crop nudged the Cromwell tale out of circulation. In contemporary accounts, mutilated books of any sort, not just Bibles, were considered noteworthy. These stories played down print matter's physical features in terms of size, bindings, and ornamentation but emphasized page numbers for the part they played in shielding and, most important, in biblical divination. Books' materiality was often paired with soldiers' corporeality. Both were physically victimized by invasive bullets, and together they were bonded through strange twists of fate.[28]

Bibles were the most commonly featured book in newspaper articles. In reporting upon them, editors and news correspondents usually deployed a rhetoric of wonder that can be traced back to the seventeenth century, when it was enmeshed in beliefs in divine providence, as revealed through the exceptional occurrence; consequently, American news coverage, David Paul Nord argues, has been fixated upon the strange and unusual ever since the colonial era. In drawing upon this rhetoric, Civil War–era newsmen inadvertently reinforced popular beliefs about divine intervention through scripture.[29]

Some column headers or news item titles were obvious in their allusions to the extraordinary: "Providential," "Remarkable Preservation," "Mysterious Virtues of the Common Prayer Book," "Life Saved by a Bible," "Saved by a Testament," and "Narrow Escape." These stories situated the dreadful everydayness of war casualties within a higher plane of the preternatural, the improbable, and the astonishing. To enact this transformation, some papers referred candidly to the mystical. "We have another of those remarkable occurrences showing a special Providence," a Savannah, Georgia, paper wrote of the previously mentioned private who rolled up his hymnbook between his vest and his shirt. "A ball entered this book, and penetrated through the outer folds, lodging in the center, thus unquestionably saving his life." In some stories, a book's placement was directed from on high. Of a New Hampshire officer, one paper announced, "The many friends of Lieut. Colonel Hapgood will be rejoiced to learn of his wonderful escape from danger ... receiving a bullet in his Bible, which providentially was directly over his heart." Editorial copy often retraced the unnatural, convoluted paths bullets took when confronted by a holy text. Such was the case for Twenty-Seventh Pennsylvania major Peter A. McAloon: "A minie ball struck his right side, going through an account book to a Testament which was in his pocket, and glancing off on this shield, went through his vest and the other side of his coat without doing him the slightest injury." Of the items in this printed stack, the account book was rendered useless—the bullet penetrated it easily. But the Bible, which was described as a "shield," flicked off the minié ball as if it were an annoying mosquito.[30]

The same hierarchy of effectiveness can be seen in Captain Dougherty's layered shield. The bullet "went through his coat, vest and shirt. It smashed a gold watch (which he had bought for his sister) all to pieces. The ball went into a Bible and dug its way through the lid and through about six hundred pages. At the beginning of the 4th C[h]apter of 2d Timothy, it went out of the Bible and inflicted a slight wound in his breast." The bullet created a material dyad of afflicted soldier-Bible, uniting in readers' minds the war cause with religious mission.[31]

As can be seen in the Dougherty case, periodicals indirectly alluded to English Civil War stories by pinpointing a chapter and verse that stopped a careening projectile. Although contemporaries must have been hard put to target exact landing points—bullets often nested in clusters of cracked or mangled pages—the variety of biblical verses cited suggests that those practicing this kind of biblical divination were in earnest and not simply parroting Evans's sermon. Stoppage points from our set of cases came from Revelation, Matthew, Malachi, 2 Timothy, Luke, and Psalms. Editors delighted in reprinting the biblical passages that seemed to have been divinely selected for their special messages. Of 125th Massachusetts private Edward R. Graton's book, a magazine editor wrote, "Curious enough, the bullet passed between the two following stanzas of the third Psalm, as if selecting them to be sung:—'Thou, gracious God, art my defense, / On thee my hopes rely ...'" In citing chapter and verse, newspapers sometimes set in motion constitutive acts of patriotic reading founded in popular religious practice. In one exposition of Lieutenant Mangum's mutilated Bible, "a rifle ball ... penetrat[ed] to the 98th Psalm." The editor asked that the "reader ... turn to the Psalm above alluded to" and locate "these words: 'O sing unto the Lord a new song: for He hath done marvelous things: His right hand, and his holy arm hath gotten Him the victory.'" Rather than a holy passage, an engraving bore the earthly trace of divine providence in Private Collins's Catholic prayer book. "A minnie ball penetrated Collins' clothing, and passed through the prayer book to the 199th page," one newspaper recounted. "Between this page and the next, is a picture of our Saviour teaching a child. On this picture not the slightest impression of the ball is visible." The pristine state of the image apparently sent its own message about the impenetrable power of the divine. Beyond suggestive wording, editors seldom, if ever, attempted interpretation of words or images that stopped bullets dead in their tracks and instead left exegesis to readers.[32]

Secular book-shields were treated somewhat less reverently by newsmen, who spiced their stories with a dash of wit, sarcasm, or parody. One editor prefaced a column about a stacked shield that included an account book with the snide quip, "Here is an item for the tract societies." Sensationalist printed items gave editors license to act even more derisively. In such cases, they omitted unseemly titles or genres and left it up to the reader to fill in the blanks. One editor parodied biblical divination while commenting on the trashy books soldiers sometimes read. Of a bullet that penetrated a popular music book, perhaps a minstrel songster, he wrote, "The verses of the songs were so execrable that the ball, like any reader of good taste, could not, by any possibility, get more than half way through the extremely stupid contents." Titles with puns, such as "Firing into the Laws," about a punctured *Laws of the State of Missouri*, signaled less-than-weighty reportage about "curiosities."[33]

Bullet-in-the-Bible stories tended to receive more serious, even reverent treatment. When they were about prominent soldiers, they held mass appeal and could spread like wildfire. Accounts of Lieutenant Mangum, son of North Carolina ex-senator Willie P. Mangum, spread from Raleigh to Memphis, Fayetteville, Charlotte, New Orleans, Nashville, and Augusta within only eleven days of his 21 July 1861 wounding. These alluded to his sister Martha and her inscription, still visible through the bloodstains, and how the life-saving Bible providentially redirected the bullet to inflict "a severe but not dangerous wound." By the end of August, Richmond, Philadelphia, Baltimore, and San Francisco had picked up the thread. Patriotic rhetoric crept in to eventually strip Mangum's story of wonderment, to downplay his Bible, and to extol the soldier as symbol of the Confederate cause. "When the rallying cry for the defense of our insulted South fell upon his ears," one memorial declared, "he told the loved ones at home that *that* call was to him the voice of duty."[34]

In writing about bullet-in-the-book incidents, editors were challenged to represent through words the intercession of material objects—bullets, books, and soldiers—in the enactment of fate or providence. Books mediated while bullets antagonized, yet together they worked didactically, alerting observers to the extraordinary workings of providence, directing attention to pointed biblical passages, or creating heroes for the war cause. Although newsmen were often shown the damaged books they wrote about, they tended to downplay the artifact itself while amplifying the event surrounding it, its role in the divine scheme of things, or its novelty. Yet, ultimately, it was the book-shield itself, and not its story, that became enshrined. During and after the war, soldiers and civilians worked to preserve the artifact as a material reminder of life rescued from death, but they failed to look ahead to a time when the object could be decontextualized as mere curiosity. The consequence has been that while many of these life-saving books remain with us today—in archives, on display at museums, in digitized form, or in private collections—the stories behind them, and those who once cherished them, have been long forgotten.

Enshrining Book-Shields

Many soldiers could not part with their punctured books or even the bullets that struck them. In the process of being assaulted, the volumes were transformed in the eyes of soldiers from reading material into reliable bodyguards, trusted friends, and sacred messengers. They opted to still hold them near throughout enlistment and to inscribe upon them the events of their everyday life. Private Frederick Watkins, Fourth New York Light Artillery Battery, continued to write around the hole in his diary after it was shot through the spine at Gettysburg. So, too, did Tenth Wisconsin sergeant Frank Ingersoll. "Got a ball through my coat tail and damaged this book as you see," he wrote in his pocket journal, although its bottom half had been eaten away by a minié ball at Stones River on 31 December 1862. Sergeant Mollohan became so attached to his looted prayer book after his brush with death that he feared someone else lifting it, as he once did. To send a clear warning to plunderers, he jotted inside, *"Steal not this Book for fear of shame may come upon you for it saved my life in the Bloody battle at Winchester."* As soldiers added their marginalia to the printed page, book-shields became laden with layers of meaning.[35]

While the war still raged, soldiers exhibited their printed armor to others so that they could pay homage to, memorialize, or spread the word about the chivalrous books. These showings sometimes became the source of copy for periodicals that, as we have seen, fed inspirational stories of wonder to the public. Private Collins, for example, allowed a writer for the Connecticut *Stamford Advocate* to see his revered prayer book in August 1863, about a month after it was blasted at Gettysburg. Roving religious emissaries were always willing to examine Bible-shields, for they made excellent tools for proselytizing. One Union soldier waiting to cross a stream took the opportunity to show his bullet-studded Bible to Christian Commission agents traveling from Belle Plain to Fredericksburg. "'See what His word did for me,'" he reportedly said as he drew out his precious book from his bloodstained shirt. In similarly spontaneous fashion, life-saving books were displayed by soldiers in trains, on steamships, in camp, and on the battlefield, only to enter official records. In writing up his casualty report for the First Virginia Battery after the battle of Kernstown, Virginia, Captain David Benjamin Bridgford referenced Captain Joseph Pembroke Thom's protective book. "He received a ball against his left breast, which was prevented from penetrating his body by a small copy of the New Testament in a pocket of his shirt, and one through the fleshy part of the palm," Captain Bridgford disclosed. Why he included this inessential detail remains puzzling, but it stands as a rare example of shielding's sanctioned imprint upon the military record.[36]

Rather than retain badly mangled book-shields, some soldiers retired them to family and friends who could safeguard them or exhibit them to the inquisitive. At the war's beginnings, when tested book-shields were still a novelty, even generals were interested in them. After one Union picket guard's book was struck, it was delivered to General Nathaniel P. Banks at Fort Henry. Chaplains sometimes directed injured books home. "His Bible, which I send with this [letter]—saved his life," Reverend Junius Moore wrote to Willie Mangum of his son's volume. Soldiers obliged beloved companions who coveted the tiny but potent shields. Captain Dougherty told one news correspondent that he had given his mangled pocket Bible "to a friend who begged it of him." Well-wishers might try to replace a damaged book with a new one, but substitutes were sometimes shunned.[37]

Those who lived to muster out brought their treasured shields home with them. Some veterans kept them for years. Corporal Samuel R. Gettig, 148th Pennsylvania, still had his Bible "with the missile embedded therein" with him when the regiment's history came out in 1904. Sometimes trusting veterans would let ministers borrow their precious lifesavers for evangelical purposes. "He has only loaned it to me that I may use it in my appeals in behalf of the claims of the American Bible Society," Reverend William Herr wrote of Sergeant Logan's edition, the Bible that was so drenched with rain it proved a formidable shield. Some soldiers tried to house their books in museums before passing away. But several veterans clung to their books until death. So priceless were these books that no amount of money could wrest them from old soldiers' hands. Book-shields, after all, were one-of-a-kind relics. They were repositories of memories upon which life stories were indelibly imprinted.[38]

Conclusion

Over the years, those life stories have been mostly forgotten, along with the books that embodied them. While some of these "wounded" volumes are in libraries, with private collectors, or with the families of long-gone soldiers, many others have been evidently lost or destroyed—and with them, remnants of history. But even those that have been preserved are often lacking a past. In museums or archives, book-shields have been detached of their personal narratives and are often cataloged or displayed without much information about their Civil War–era owners, the events in which they were caught up, or their biographies after the war. Book-shields that have become commodified and put on auction, too, are often given only minimal genealogies. Still, they sell at steep prices. It is not so difficult to understand why. With their bullets still peeking out from torn pages, these tiny books have the power to astonish and amaze as material artifacts—in and of themselves—without the encumbrance of historical context. Yet, they were forged in the blood of history.

The pathway back in time with these precious objects, however, is not a simple one. It leads through now-lost webs of cultural and personal meaning that are linked inextricably to popular religious practices, customs of social exchange, the traffic in war relics, varieties of book usage, and journalistic practice. Reconstructing these complex networks, the "cultural biographies of things," as we have attempted to do here, involves resisting the lure of these books' intriguing facades and following the often-somber and broken paper trails they left behind in published and manuscript memoirs, periodical stories, diaries, correspondence, military records, and photographs. Some of these trails are only dimly articulated and fraught with obstacles, wrong turns, and detours. But they lead inevitably to a greater understanding of book-shields—one that lifts them out of the domain of quaintness into a sphere of meaning that was once formulated by soldiers and civilians struggling to endure a long war with the aid of material objects at hand.[39]

Notes

1. *Boston Investigator*, 4 September 1861, 158; *Cincinnati Enquirer*, 10 June 1861, 1; William E. S. Whitman and Charles H. True, *Maine in the War for the Union: A History of the Part Borne by Maine Troops in the Suppression of the American Rebellion* (Lewiston, Maine: Nelson Dingley Jr., 1865), 39; "Life Saved by a Testament," with excerpts

from S. K. Devereaux to [Bangor Young Men's Bible Society, n.d.], *Bible Society Record*, July 1861, 103.

2. Whitman and True, *Maine in the War*, 38–39; "Life Saved by a Testament," 103. On the diversity of trophies, relics, and practices related to them, see Joan E. Cashin, "Trophies of War: Material Culture in the Civil War Era," *Journal of the Civil War Era* 1, no. 3 (2011): 339–67.

3. See, for example, David Kaser, *Books and Libraries in Camp and Battle: The Civil War Experience* (Westport, Conn.: Greenwood Press, 1984), 51; Steven E. Woodworth, *While God is Marching On: The Religious World of Civil War Soldiers* (Lawrence: University Press of Kansas, 2001), 71–72; John Fea, *The Bible Cause: A History of the American Bible Society* (New York: Oxford University Press, 2016), 82–83; Michael DeGruccio, "Letting the War Slip through Our Hands: Material Culture and the Weakness of Words in the Civil War Era," in *Weirding the War: Stories from the Civil War's Ragged Edges*, ed. Stephen Berry (Athens: University of Georgia Press, 2011), 26; James M. McPherson, *For Cause and Comrades: Why Men Fought in the Civil War* (New York: Oxford University Press, 1997), 63; Civil War and Militaria Auction #6083, 8 December 2012, Heritage Auctions, http://historical.ha.com/itm/military-and-patriotic/civil-war/incredible-bullet-struck-bible-from-sailors-creek/a/6083-52157.s, accessed 26 October 2017; and DeGruccio, "Letting the War Slip," 27–29. On Civil War material culture studies, see Jennifer Roth Bucci, ed., *The Civil War and the Material Culture of Texas, the Lower South, and the Southwest* (Houston: Bayou Bend Collection and Gardens, the Museum of Fine Arts, Houston, 2012); Joan E. Cashin, "Hungry People in the Wartime South: Civilians, Armies, and the Food Supply," in *Weirding the War*, 160–75; Cashin, "Trophies of War," 339–67; Drew Gilpin Faust, "Equine Relics of the Civil War," *Southern Cultures* 6, no. 1 (March 2000): 23–49; Simon Harrison, "Bones in the Rebel Lady's Boudoir: Ethnology, Race and Trophy-Hunting in the American Civil War," *Journal of Material Culture* 15, no. 4 (December 2010): 385–401; Anna Denov Rusk, "Collecting the Confederacy: The Civil War Scrapbook of Henry M. Whitney," *Winterthur Portfolio* 47, no. 4 (Winter 2013): 267–95; Amanda Jane Townes, "Material Culture as a Primary Source for Understanding Bedford County, Tennessee in the Civil War Era" (Ph.D. diss., Middle Tennessee State University, 2011); and Cashin, "Trophies of War," 339. On scavenged and looted books, see Ronald J. Zboray and Mary Saracino Zboray, "The Bonds of Print: Reading on Home Front and Battlefield," in *Massachusetts and the Civil War: The Commonwealth and National Disunion*, ed. Matthew Mason, Katheryn P. Viens, and Conrad Edick Wright (Amherst: University of Massachusetts Press, 2015), 203; and Ronald J. Zboray and Mary Saracino Zboray, "Beyond the Market and the City: The Informal Dissemination of Reading Material during the American Civil War," in *Print Culture Histories beyond the Metropolis*, ed. James J. Connolly, Patrick Collier, Frank Felsenstein, Kenneth R. Hall, and Robert G. Hall (Toronto: University of Toronto Press, 2016), 137–39.

4. Ronald J. Zboray and Mary Saracino Zboray, "Cannonballs and Books: Reading and the Disruption of Social Ties on the New England Homefront," in *The War Was You and Me: Civilians in the American Civil War*, ed. Joan E. Cashin (Princeton: Princeton University Press, 2002), 237–61.

5. Fea, *Bible Cause*, 79; J. Cutler Andrews, *The South Reports the Civil War* (Prince-

ton: Princeton University Press, 1970), 41–45; Thomas Wentworth Higginson, *Army Life in a Black Regiment* (Boston: Fields Osgood, 1870), 71.

6. U.S. War Department, *The War of the Rebellion: A Compilation of the Official Records of the Union and Confederate Armies*, 128 vols. (Washington, D.C.: GPO, 1880–1901) (hereafter *OR*). We consulted the Ohio State University Department of History's online-searchable digitized *OR*, "The War of the Rebellion: Original Records of the Civil War," on the ehistory website, http://ehistory.osu.edu/books/official-records. Ronald J. Zboray and Mary Saracino Zboray, "Research Essay: A Database of Civil War Readers," *AJHA Intelligencer* 31, no. 3 (2015): 2–3.

7. Jack Coggins, *Arms and Equipment of the Civil War* (Garden City, N.Y.: Doubleday, 1962), 28; Reviel Netz, *Barbed Wire: An Ecology of Modernity* (Middletown, Conn.: Wesleyan University Press, 2004), 8; Vincent J. Cirillo, *Bullets and Bacilli: The Spanish-American War and Military Medicine* (New Brunswick, N.J.: Rutgers University Press, 2004), 49–50. On spent bullets striking Bibles, see Fea, *Bible Cause*, 82–83. On popular skepticism, see "Bibles Stopping Bullets," 1 January 2014, Civil War Talk, http://civilwartalk.com/threads/bibles-stopping-bullets.93779/, accessed 26 October 2017.

8. J. David Hacker, "A Census-Based Count of the Civil War Dead," *Civil War History* 57, no. 4 (December 2011): 307–48.

9. Richard Baxter, *The Certainty of the World of Spirits and Consequently, of the Immortality of Souls* ... (London: T. Parkhurst, 1691), 162–63; Richard Baxter and Cotton Mather, *The Certainty of the World of Spirits Fully Evinced* (London: Joseph Smith, 1834); Richard Baxter and Cotton Mather, *Certainty* (London: Howell, 1840); Richard Baxter and Cotton Mather, *Certainty* (London: S. Cornish and Co., 1841).

10. John Evans, *Sermons upon Various Subjects, Preach'd to Young People*... (London: J. Clark and R. Hett, 1725), 62–78, quotes on 62–63.

11. *Albany Chronicle*, 16 October 1797; *Albany Chronicle* quoted in *Newport Mercury*, 7 November 1797, 2.

12. Buck, "When Oliver Cromwell ...," *Middlesex Gazette*, 14 March 1811, reprinted as "Anecdote" without attribution in *Rural Visitor* [Burlington, N.J.], 29 April 1811. See also *Herald of Gospel Liberty* [Philadelphia], 19 March 1813; *New York Weekly Museum*, 12 June 1813; *The Yankee* [Boston], 18 June 1813; "Remarkable Providential Visitations, Selected," *Christian Visitant* [Albany, N.Y.] 29 July 1815; *Orange County Patriot* [Goshen, N.Y.], 15 August 1815; *New Jersey Journal* [Elizabethtown], 22 August 1815, 10; *Centinel of Freedom* [Newark, N.J.], 22 August 1815; *Western Monitor* [Lexington, Ky.], 15 September 1815; *Northern Post* [Salem, N.Y.], 21 September 1815; *Washington Reporter*, 9 October 1815; *National Aegis* [Worcester, Mass.], 11 October 1815; *Evangelical Magazine*, May 1812, 177.

13. "The Bible a Shield," *Hudson (Ohio) Observer and Telegraph*, 15 July 1830; "Remarkable Conversion," *The Friend* [Honolulu, Hawaii], 1 December 1859, 92; "Singular Conversion," *Pittsburgh Gazette*, 28 July 1835, 2; "Singular Conversion," *Charlotte Journal*, 8 April 1836, 4; *Hillsborough (N.C.) Recorder*, 29 February 1860; William C. Conant, "The Bullet's Text," *Narratives of Remarkable Conversions and Revival Incidents* ... (New York: Derby and Jackson, 1858), 182–83; "Cromwell's Soldiers' Bible," *Deseret News* [Utah], 16 November 1854; "Cromwell's Soldier's Bible," *Washington (D.C.) Evening Star*, 16 September 1854, 1; "Cromwell's Soldier's Bible," *Albany Evening Journal*, 9 Septem-

ber 1854, 4. It remains improbable that Cromwell issued this sixteen-page pamphlet of scriptural excerpts, for he was relatively unknown at the time of its publication. Robert Thomas Fallon, *The Christian Soldier: Religious Tracts Published for Soldiers on Both Sides during and after the English Civil Wars, 1642–1648* (Tempe: Arizona Center for Medieval and Renaissance Studies, 2003), 2. On the Seven Years' War, see the *Evangelical Magazine* 16 (1808): 343. On the French and Indian War, see Theophilus, "Story of the Pilgrims," in *Berkshire Star* [Stockbridge, Mass.], 7 November 1822, 1. On the Revolution, see "Keep That Testament in Your Vest Pocket over Your Heart," *Weekly Nashville Union*, 10 June 1846. On the War of 1812, see "The Soldier's Life," *Daily National Intelligencer*, 14 April 1813. On Waterloo, see "The Soldier and His Bible," *Religious Messenger* [Norwich, Conn.], 14 April 1832, 3; and "An Incident of the Battle of Waterloo," *Boston Traveler*, 22 November 1839, 1. On Mexico, see *Brooklyn Daily Eagle*, 24 November 1847, 2; *Trenton State Gazette*, 1 January 1848, 2; *Charleston (S.C.) Southern Patriot*, 8 February 1848, 2; and *Raleigh Register, and North-Carolina Gazette*, 1 December 1847. "The Bible," *Daily National Intelligencer*, 25 October 1860; *Hillsborough Recorder*, 14 November 1860, 1; "The Bible," *Spirit of the Age* [Raleigh, N.C.], 12 December 1860, 1; [Louisa Park Hall], "Caroline Gray," *Boston Pearl and Galaxy*, "Prize Papers," supplement (after April 1837), 15; *Lowell Daily Citizen and News*, 11 February 1859. See also "A Man's Life Saved by a Newspaper," *Newport Mercury*, 31 January 1846, 1.

14. "Preface to This Edition," *The Soldier's Pocket Diary* (New York: American Tract Society, 1861), printed in *New York Herald*, 1 September 1861, 2. See also *Philadelphia Press*, 14 September 1861; *Philadelphia Inquirer*, 16 September 1861; *Daily State Gazette and Republican* [Trenton, N.J.], 2 July 1861; *Philadelphia Inquirer*, 12 November 1861; *Philadelphia Press*, 9 December 1861; Fallon, *Christian Soldier*, 2; *Vermont Chronicle*, 27 August 1861, 138; *Boston Daily Advertiser*, 16 August 1861.

15. Jack McCormack, "John Cassidy: 69th Pennsylvania Infantry Philadelphia Brigade," *Military Images Magazine*, March/April 1985, 6–7; Randall M. Miller, "Catholic Religion, Irish Identity, and the Civil War," in *Religion and the American Civil War*, ed. Randall M. Miller, Harry S. Stout, and Charles Reagan Wilson (New York: Oxford University Press, 1998), 271; *Hartford Daily Courant*, 29 August 1863.

16. Miller, "Catholic Religion," 271–74; William B. Kurtz, *Excommunicated from the Union: How the Civil War Created a Separate Catholic America* (New York: Oxford University Press, 2015), 53–55, 68–69, 78.

17. *Reading (Pa.) Times*, 11 June 1862; *Lebanon (Pa.) Daily News*, 30 March 1917, 7; Historical Society of Pennsylvania, "Coincidences or Acts of Divine Intervention? Accounts of the Bible Saving Soldiers on the Battlefield," *Hidden Histories* (blog), 11 May 2011, https://hsp.org/blogs/hidden-histories/coincidence-or-acts-of-divine-intervention-accounts-of-the-bible-saving-soldiers-on-the-battlefield, accessed 16 February 2018; *Forty-Seventh Annual Report of the American Bible Society Presented May 14 1863* (New York: American Bible Society, 1863), 26.

18. George T. [*sic*, P.] Howard, Civil War diary, [3], Manuscripts and Archives Division, New York Public Library; *Forty-Seventh Annual Report*, 14–15; George H. Stuart, *The Life of George H. Stuart Written by Himself* (Philadelphia: J. M. Stoddart, 1890), 355.

19. "Life Saved by a Testament," 103; McCormack, "John Cassidy," 6; *Farmer's Cabinet* [Amherst, N.H.], 27 September 1861, and advertisement in *Boston Traveler*, 18 Decem-

ber 1861; B. M. Mollohan and Bernard Mollohan, *By the Banks of the Holly: Notes and Letters from the Desk of Bernard Mollohan* (New York: iUniverse, 2005), 328, 371. On Dallas M. Rigler, Thirty-Seventh North Carolina, taking a Unionist's book, only to be saved by it, see Clement Anselm Evans, *Confederate Military History: A Library of Confederate States History* (Atlanta: Confederate Publishing Company, 1899), 4:713-14.

20. *Raleigh Weekly Standard*, 31 July 1861, 2; Robert E. Taylor, ed., "Lucky Escapes," *The Bugle 38: Australian International Newsletter*, July/August 2012, 10; inscription, *New Testament of Our Lord and Savior Jesus Christ* (American [Tract?] Society, 1862), Charles William Merrill Papers, Fam. MSS 611, Phillips Library, Peabody Essex Museum, Salem, Massachusetts (hereafter PEM). On "social imprints" and books, see Ronald J. Zboray and Mary Saracino Zboray, *Everyday Ideas: Socioliterary Experience among Antebellum New Englanders* (Knoxville: University of Tennessee Press, 2006), ch. 11. Charles William Merrill to Catharine Pearson Merrill, 22 February 1863, PEM. Giftgivers sometimes converted nonbelievers prior to deployment; see Edward Parmelee Smith, *Incidents among Shot and Shell: The Only Authentic Work Extant Giving the Many Tragic and Touching Incidents . . .* (Philadelphia: Edgewood, 1868), 263.

21. "Presentiments in Battle Realized," *Confederate Veteran* 6, no. 2 (February 1898): 52; Levi J. Fritz Diary, [c. May 1863], Levi Fritz Papers #05442-z, Southern Historical Collection, Wilson Library, University of North Carolina at Chapel Hill (hereafter UNC). The soldier is probably Roscoe Selwin Loomis, Company F, 141st Pennsylvania, also at Chancellorsville; see David Craft, *History of the One-hundred Forty-First Regiment Pennsylvania Volunteers, 1862-1865* (Towanda, Penn.: published by the author, Reporter-Journal Printing Company, 1885), 88.

22. "Religious Items," *Boston Recorder*, 11 December 1862, 198; Living History Club, Company E "Slippery Rock Volunteers," History (website), http://www.100thpenn.com/default.html, accessed 26 October 2017.

23. *Fayetteville Observer*, 5 and 6 August 1861; Walter G. Jones, *History of a Testament My Stepmother Gave Me before Going to the War* (McDonough, N.Y.: privately printed, 1899); *Times Picayune* [New Orleans],22 May 1861.

24. Fritz Diary, [c. May 1863], UNC; *Centinel of Freedom*, 30 July 1861, 3.

25. Ted Alexander, *The Battle of Antietam: The Bloodiest Day* (Charleston: History Press, 2011), 78; Jim Buchanan, "Only 9 Were Left Standing: Company H, 15th Massachusetts in the West Woods," Walking the West Woods: Ramblings on the West Woods at Antietam National Battlefield Park (blog), 23 February 2011, http://walkingthewestwoods.blogspot.com/2011/02/only-9-were-left-standing-company-h.html, accessed 20 February 2018; *Savannah Daily Morning News*, 27 June 1862; *Detroit Free Press*, 21 March 1862.

26. *Bible Society Record*, December 1863, 189; *Philadelphia Inquirer*, 3 August 1864. See, for example, Charles W. Merrill to Charles Merrill and Catherine Pearson Merrill, 7 May 1862, PEM.

27. A. Wilson Greene, "Where a Hundred Thousand Fell," in *Fredericksburg Battlefields: Fredericksburg and Spotsylvania County Battlefields Memorial National Military Park, Virginia* (Washington, D.C.: U.S. Department of the Interior, 1998), 44; William Preston Mangum to Martha P. Mangum, 25 July 1861, Willie Person Mangum Papers, Library of Congress, Washington, D.C.; Phil Gast, "'Saving My Soul,'" Civil War Picket

(blog), 1 April 2016, http://civil-war-picket.blogspot.com/2016/04/saving-my-soul-bullet-struck-bibles.html, accessed 26 October 2017.

28. The 1860 national adult (over twenty, white and free black) literacy rate was nearly 92 percent; Harvey Graff, *The Legacies of Literacy: Continuities and Contradictions in Western Culture and Society* (Bloomington: Indiana University Press, 1991), 344.

29. David Paul Nord, "Teleology and News: The Religious Roots of American Journalism, 1630–1730," *Journal of American History* 77, no. 1 (1990): 9–38.

30. *Lansing (Mich.) State Republican*, 8 Oct. 1862; *Lowell Daily Citizen and News*, 15 May 1863; *Philadelphia Inquirer*, 2 and 3 August 1864; *Monthly Religious Magazine*, April 1862, 265; *New Orleans Daily True Delta*, 30 July 1861; *Boston Investigator*, 4 September 1861; *Savannah Daily Morning News*, 27 June 1862; *Farmer's Cabinet*, 14 May 1863; "Escape of Major M'Aloon," *New York Herald*, 12 May 1863.

31. *Reading Times*, 11 June 1862.

32. *Monthly Religious Magazine*, April 1862, 265. It is a poetical version of the psalm. *Weekly Mississippian* [Jackson], 7 August 1861; *Hartford Daily Courant*, 29 August 1863.

33. *New York Herald*, 12 May 1863; *Weekly Wisconsin Patriot* [Madison], 29 March 1862; *Wisconsin Daily Patriot* [Madison], 25 January 1862.

34. *Raleigh Daily Register*, 27 July 1861; *Fayetteville Observer*, 29 July 1861; *Daily True Delta* [New Orleans], 30 July 1861; *Memphis Daily Appeal*, 28 July 1861; *Daily Nashville Patriot*, 1 August 1861; *Nashville Union and American*, 30 July 1861; *Augusta Chronicle*, 31 July 1861; *Charlotte (N.C.) Western Democrat*, 30 July 1861; *Richmond Examiner*, 2 August 1861; *Philadelphia Inquirer*, 2 and 13 August 1861; *Baltimore Sun*, 8 August 1861; *San Francisco Daily Evening Bulletin*, 26 August 1861; A. W. Mangum, "William Preston Mangum," *Weekly Raleigh Register*, 28 August 1861.

35. Simon Tomlinson and Meghan Keneally, "Archivists Have Collected …," 27 December 2011, DailyMail.com, http://www.dailymail.co.uk/news/article-2078938/A-treasure-trove-American-history-Massive-collection-Civil-War-artifacts-unearthed-basements-attics-mark-150th-anniversary-conflict.html, accessed 26 October 2017; Frank Ingersoll Diary (TS), 31 December 1862, transcribed by Jeff Javid, Wisconsin Veterans Museum, Madison; Mollohan and Mollohan, *By the Banks*, 371.

36. "Narrow Escape," reprinted in *Hartford Daily Courant*, 29 August 1863; Smith, *Incidents among Shot and Shell*, 263; William Archibald Waugh, *Reminiscences of the Rebellion*, 5th Massachusetts Battery E, http://fifthmass.org/research/RebellionWaugh.htm, accessed 26 October 2017; "Saved by a Bible," *Reading Times*, 11 June 1862; D. B. Bridgford, Captain, Commanding First Va. Batt., Report, 26 March 1862, *OR*, ser. 15, ch. 24, 407.

37. *Philadelphia Inquirer*, 1 July 1861; Junius Moore to Willie P. Mangum, 26 July 1861, Willie Person Mangum Papers, Library of Congress; *North American*, 5 June 1862. On replacements, see, for example, Austin Dickinson, "The Prayer-Meeting," *National Preacher and Village Pulpit*, 3d ser., 1, no. 11 (November 1862): 352.

38. James F. Weaver, "The Lieutenant Colonel's Story and Incidentally the Story of Company B," in *The Story of Our Regiment: A History of the 148th Pennsylvania Vols.*, ed. J. W. Muffly (Des Moines: Kenyon, 1904), 157; W. Herr, [letter to ABS], excerpted in "An Excellent Shield," *Bible Society Record*, December 1863, 189; Edwin C. Hall to William Johnson, 1 April 1898, "Community Collection," Ohio History, http://www.ohio

memory.org/ cdm/ref/collection/ p15005coll41/id/212, accessed 26 October 2017; *Chenango American* [Greene, N.Y.], 28 May 1896.

39. Igor Kopytoff, "The Cultural Biography of Things: Commoditization as Process," in *The Social Life of Things: Commodities in Cultural Perspective*, ed. Arjun Appadurai (Cambridge: Cambridge University Press, 1986), 64–90.

5

The Material Culture of Weapons in the Civil War

EARL J. HESS

Material culture methodology is especially suited to the study of warfare, an activity heavily dependent on weapons and material resources in general and infused with important strains of social and cultural implications. Scholars who study the connection between artifacts and how and why people use them are poised to understand how soldiers use weapons, what they think about those weapons, and the impact those tools of war have had on society. In fact, material culture is an interesting bridge between the sometimes disparate genres of traditional military history (the study of strategy, tactics, weapons, and generalship) on the one hand and social and cultural analysis of societies at war. The study of weapons has been so neglected even by academic Civil War scholars that it has become the exclusive preserve of amateur historians who focus narrowly on the hardware without paying attention to how the weapons were used or to the cultural implications associated with those weapons.[1]

The theory behind material culture applies equally well to warfare as to any other activity. According to Jules David Prown, it is "the study through artifacts of the beliefs—values, ideas, attitudes, and assumptions—of a particular community or society at a given time." All artifacts "reveal intention." Devices, as opposed to art objects, have as their aim an external intent, and weapons certainly fall into this category. Writing in 1988, Prown asserted that devices have "cultural significance" in that, although largely utilitarian, they also "incorporate some decorative or aesthetic elements." In listing examples of devices, Prown did not mention weapons. Moreover, he too narrowly defined cultural significance, believing that "purely utilitarian objects provide only limited cultural insights." Prown thought that art and decorative items were at the heart of material cultural studies, overemphasizing the aesthetic aspects of artifacts as worthy of study.[2]

Prown represented a typical attitude among the early practitioners of material culture; they ignored armed conflict. One can search the pages of the *Journal of Material Culture*, the primary scholarly publication in the field, from its inception in 1996 until recent years and find nothing on warfare.

Only in the past couple of decades have scholars awakened to the potential in applying material culture methods to the many and varied aspects of warfare. Most of this awakening has taken place in World War I studies, but some of it has branched out to embrace a variety of twentieth-century conflicts as well. Nicholas J. Saunders has pioneered this approach to the Western Front of 1914–18. His core work lies in the study of trench art—war material (especially used artillery shells) transformed into works of art by soldiers during their idle hours. Saunders, however, has rightly identified the destruction of built and natural environments by armies; the construction of earthworks, wayside calvaries, and crucifixes; and commemorative activity long after 1918 as fit subjects for the material culture approach.[3]

Other scholars have studied the artifacts that civilian internees of World War I made while held in camps; the manufacture of prostheses and how society viewed amputees after the war; the interesting German tradition of encouraging citizens to drive a nail into a wooden block displayed at a prominent place in order to form a patriotic symbol with the nail pattern (as a way to draw society toward a common purpose); and the impact on landscapes of massive army bases, training grounds, and home defenses. Even a brief survey of trajectories in the developing scholarship on materiality and World War I is both encouraging and exciting; the approaches are not only varied but imaginative, fresh, and compelling.[4]

World War II has not yet come under the steady gaze of material culture scholars, although the potential is even greater than for World War I. Gabriel Moshenska's study of how children collected fragments of British antiaircraft artillery (often soon after they fell into their own neighborhoods) is an interesting exploration of one small aspect of a huge conflict, opening a new front in the study of war relics.[5]

Initial explorations of the material culture of twentieth-century conflicts occurring after 1945 displays still more variety in the approach. Much of it tends to focus on archaeological investigations of fortifications, nuclear testing sites, battlefields, monuments, medals, concentration camps, the Berlin Wall, and forensic investigations of the remains of service members listed as missing in action or civilian victims of human rights abuses. In fact, the material culture approach is already being broadened so much that it has in many cases lost its tight focus on the study of artifacts. The interaction between armed conflict and landscapes is a popular approach, as is the idea of broadening our definition of war to include violence of all kinds, such as that associated with the troubles in Northern Ireland and the enforcement of apartheid in South Africa.[6]

Civil War scholars are a long distance behind the curve in these developments. Prior to this anthology, the material culture focus in Civil War studies tended to be on relics and ruins.[7] Very little has been done concerning trench art in the Civil War. Soldiers certainly did while away their time making objects. A Texas soldier who served in the siege of Vicksburg carved a miniature armchair from a minié ball and presented it to a woman who lived in the town. When Federal soldiers dug the mine gallery at Petersburg that was used to blow up a section of Confederate earthworks (producing the famous battle of the Crater on 30 July 1864), they used the clay coming out of the gallery to fashion a variety of objects. Pipes, crosses, marbles, and a representation of the Ninth Corps badge resulted from this activity. Children caught in the siege of Vicksburg excitedly collected fired minié balls and shell fragments even as those projectiles had narrowly missed killing or injuring them.[8]

Still, despite the promising developments in applying material culture theory to warfare, weapons have been given little attention. Stéphane Audoin-Rouzeau and Annette Becker have complained that World War I historians know little about weapons and argue that familiarity with instruments of destruction is as important as knowing what the trench system was like and how the environment influenced the experience of soldiering.[9] There certainly are a handful of studies that focus on some particular type of weapon, even individual pieces of ordnance, to produce, for example, a "cultural history" of a gun. The bayonet has been given more attention in this regard than guns; its symbolism to the soldier has been thoroughly explored. But material culture studies of weapons in general are yet in their infancy, despite the handful of good works on a few aspects of this large and complex topic.[10]

The purpose of this essay is to chart new approaches to the material culture of weapons by exploring some ways in which Civil War soldiers perceived and were emotionally affected by the small arms and artillery they employed. It is important to recognize that a significant gun culture existed in pre-Civil War America, with a substantial proportion of the population owning, using, and valuing weapons for many reasons. This gun culture played into the experience of soldiering as men accustomed to and naturally adapted to their use became superb shooters on the battlefield and those who had no prewar affinity became only indifferent gunmen. Civil War soldiers can be divided into men who were intimately familiar with firearms and used them well and those who were very inexperienced in their use. Applying an awareness of sensorimotor skills to this topic can help us understand why some men fell into one or the other category. This essay also examines the degree to which Civil War soldiers were aware of themselves as shooters and as targets of other shooters. They not only developed an awareness of the lethal potential of their weapons for the enemy they fought on the battlefield but also recognized how they themselves could be affected by shooters on the other side of the war. Many soldiers also became aware of how their weapons could be used in unintended ways, to kill fellow comrades out of anger or through accidental discharges. Growing out of these intertwined themes is an understanding of why some soldiers relied on talismans to protect them in battle or adopted manufactured protection, such as bulletproof vests. Those who felt good about their weapons often developed emotional attachments to them, naming their rifles or artillery pieces, while others hated their weapons and were glad to get rid of them at the war's end. Finally, an awareness of international comparisons reminds us that the Civil War was far from unique in these themes.

We start with the emerging gun culture of pre–Civil War America. That conflict predated the mass production of cheap firearms that created the modern gun culture by the turn of the twentieth century, but many of the emotional and cultural strains in it were becoming evident before 1861.[11]

While growing up in Georgia, future artillery officer Edward Porter Alexander was "perfectly devoted to shooting & fishing" and counted his gun as his "dearest possession on earth." In Ohio, future Union infantryman John Calvin Hartzell reveled in his family's devotion to hunting and shooting matches. "They always spoke of them in the feminine gender," Hartzell recalled of the family's weapons. His father and brother did not participate in this family tradition; "books ruined them both that way," Hartzell concluded.[12]

When the war broke out, many volunteer companies adopted names to indicate their supposed prowess with weapons. Moreover, some soldiers saw pistols as important for the safety of those they left behind. Captain James Innes Davidson of the Seventy-Third Illinois worried about his wife back home in Griggsville, Illinois, and purchased a revolver specially designed and marketed for the use of ladies. He included 100 rounds of ammunition and presented it to her as a Christmas gift, arranging for a friend to teach her how to use it. "It will prove your safe friend at any time but be sure to keep it out of Minnie's way and do not handle it carelessly," Davidson noted. "If it should [drop] and hit on the hammer it will go off."[13]

Davidson fully understood that every weapon was potentially dangerous to user and friends as well as to enemies. Careless handling was uppermost in his mind as he coached his wife about the problems of keeping a loaded revolver in the house. This advice was highly relevant for soldiers as well. Training in the Civil War mostly focused on learning the intricate set of formations and maneuvers designed to allow officers to control masses of men on the battlefield. There were no lessons in how to handle a gun other than for show when in formation and on parade. Even when Civil War units engaged in target practice, which was comparatively rarely, the officers failed to give their men lessons in how to estimate distance and adjust the rather crude sighting mechanism on the rifle musket then in use.[14]

But learning how to handle a weapon was vital to the art of soldiering. Like any tool or implement, guns have to be adapted to human capabilities, and men have to adapt to them as well. Jean-Pierre Warnier has pointed out that to be effective, a tool has to be linked to the body's senses and its musculature. He writes of "a dynamic synthesis of sensori-motricity in a given materiality." Warnier offers a telling example by writing of a blind person using a cane as an extension of his senses, integrating the cane into his "sensori-motor apparatus to such an extent that the blind person's perception is not projected from his/her hand, but from the tip of the cane; where it comes into contact with the sidewalk, the walls or the stairs." He notes that the boundaries of the body are therefore quite expansive and can include many objects within a person's perception. Warnier concludes that "it is not possible to divorce material culture studies from the study of the body, and vice versa."[15]

Warnier's praxeological approach to objects is highly relevant for the study of weapons. Some Civil War soldiers were peculiarly adept at using their small arms, enjoyed firing them, and were admired by their less-adept comrades. Soldiers developed a habit of relying on these gun-adept men in the heat of battle. Less capable comrades reloaded the single-shot muzzle-loading rifles for the good shooters in their company to maximize the volume of well-directed fire on the enemy. Most likely these gun-adept men had also enjoyed the use of firearms before the war and were happy participants in the emerging gun culture of America. According to Warnier's view, these skilled men also were those who adapted their "sensori-motor apparatus" to the use of firearms more readily and naturally than their comrades. Like the blind man and his cane, the end of the muzzle-loader's barrel became an extension of the soldier's nerves, senses, and muscles.[16]

But these gun-adept men certainly were in a minority. There is evidence that an equally small proportion of the troops occupied the opposite end of the spectrum, never developing an aptitude for the use of small arms. J. B. Polley of the Fourth Texas wrote about this phenomenon after the war. His regiment was lodged in the extensive earthworks protecting Petersburg during the last few months of the conflict, and boredom sometimes was oppressive. The men often called on two comrades to provide entertainment. J. C. Jordan was a particularly good shot and proud of his ability to elicit admiration from the men; he happily fired when they called on him to shoot at the enemy across no-man's-land. But Levi S. Pogue, a nervous man who never adapted to his gun, provided entertainment of a different sort. When called on for a shot, Pogue tried to please but could not bring himself to aim properly. "'Lower the muzzle of your gun,'" his comrades would yell, "'for you will hit nothing but a quartermaster or commissary that way.'" Pogue ineffectually fired into the air and then sank back to safety, covered with sweat and pale in the face, and tried to enjoy the good-natured laughs of his comrades.[17]

Undoubtedly every regiment in the Union and Confederate armies had a few men like Pogue. David Holt described a comrade in the Sixteenth Mississippi named Theobold Foltz as "an everlastingly good soldier and a sporting old numbskull that knew more about a yardstick than he did about a gun." In the Seventy-Seventh Illinois, John G. Phillips was the prominent gun-inept man. He tripped so much during an advance by the regiment at the battle of Chickasaw Bayou that his comrades were afraid his gun would go off and hurt someone. They told their captain to send him away, "for if they had to be shot they wanted it to be by the enemy and not by that d——d fool." The captain obliged them.[18]

J. W. Gaskill of the 104th Ohio was quite honest in his memoirs about the fact that he had trouble adapting to firearms. He subtitled his book *Everyday Life of the Man under a Musket on the Firing Line and in the Trenches*. Emphasizing the negative import of the phrase "under a musket," Gaskill included an illustration titled "Austrian Musket in Action," which showed how it kicked and hurt every time he fired it. The picture presented him as dazed by the action of this old, outdated weapon that was issued to many regiments early in the conflict.[19]

To a degree, Gaskill's troubles stemmed from having to use a poor example of a musket, but his reaction to it was emblematic of how all gun-inept soldiers felt about having to use an implement of war that they never grew to like. Most soldiers, upon enlisting, very much wanted the latest in weapons technology, which in 1861 was the rifle musket. Introduced only a

Figure 6. The ultimate image to represent the gun-inept soldier, a man who could not adapt to his weapon, appeared as the frontispiece of J. W. Gaskill's Footprints through Dixie: Everyday Life of the Man under a Musket on the Firing Line and in the Trenches, 1862–1865.

few years before for general issue, its only improvement over the previous smoothbore musket was the introduction of rifling inside the barrel, which imparted a spin on the lead bullet. That spin increased the carrying power of the projectile to about 500 yards, as opposed to the effective range of the smoothbore at about 100 yards.[20]

Northern and Southern solders exulted when they received brand-new rifle muskets. Robert Lewis Bliss bragged that he carried "the best gun in the service" after the Thirty-Third Mississippi obtained British-made Enfield rifles. Finley P. Curtis thought his comrades in the First North Carolina "could 'lick' the entire Federal army" with modern rifle muskets. Members of the Third Louisiana no longer had to endure the taunts of Union skirmishers for their bad shots after new Enfield rifles replaced their old Mississippi rifles partway through the siege of Vicksburg.[21]

Faced with death on the battlefield, soldiers naturally felt a desire to use the best weapon they could find. But a deeper source of this desire for the latest small arm was a peculiarly American faith in new technology. Merritt Roe Smith has described this faith as "a trickle of enthusiasm for technology in the late eighteenth century," which "became a rivulet by the Civil War and continued to surge thereafter." Technological devices were viewed "both as instruments of power and as triumphant symbols of human progress." Smith also identified evidence of technological determinism, a belief "that changes in technology exert a greater influence on societies and their processes than any other factor."[22]

Most Northern and Southern recruits saw the new rifle as an important development in war making and very much wanted it. They generally disdained old guns as worthless. Federal artilleryman William T. Shepherd made fun of abandoned Confederate small arms as "old flintlock rifles that have hung in the kitchens of the western pioneers" and that were fit only as relics and souvenirs. "Language fails when attempting to describe the grotesque worthlessness of these so-called arms," wrote the historian of the Fifty-Fifth Illinois about the German weapons the regiment was forced to use. "They were of foreign make having scarcely the similitude of guns."[23]

Ironically, while most soldiers wanted modern long-range rifles, they did not want to use them to deliver long-range fire on the enemy. Most soldiers and officers alike had an abiding faith in close-range fire as more effective than long-range aiming. The evidence coming from countless battles in the Civil War proves that they were right. Many factors complicated long-range firing, and it took a particularly gun-adept soldier to master them; the average soldier who fell somewhere between the two extremes of gun-able and gun-incompetent had a far better chance of firing effectively at ranges of 100 yards or less. Battle reports as well as personal accounts testify to the fact that most combat took place at ranges roughly consistent with that of the old smoothbore musket that soldiers disdained rather than at ranges consistent with the long-range capabilities of the new weapon they admired. Even at battles such as Franklin, where the terrain offered defending Federals a view of the approaching Confederates stretching for hundreds of yards into the distance, the overwhelming majority of bodies that littered the ground lay within a space only fifty yards from the Union line of defense.[24]

This anomaly represents an interesting example of cognitive dissonance in the experience of Civil War soldiering. The only advantage of the rifle musket over the smoothbore was its longer range; soldiers very much wanted the weapon, but they did not evaluate that desire based on its longer range. They judged a weapon on whether it was "new," whether it was light enough so as not to become a burden to handle, and whether it was effective when fired at the distance they preferred. In fact, Civil War soldiers typically never acknowledged that they failed to achieve the long-range fire that the rifle musket was technically capable of delivering. Short-range firing challenged their sensorimotor capabilities far less than aiming at long distances, and they overwhelmingly used the weapon for close combat. The only soldiers who achieved some degree of success at long-range fire were those gun-adept men who served as snipers. According to the evidence, many of them were able to hit targets at incredibly long range, but it has to be reiterated that they numbered only a few thousand troops out of millions who served in the Civil War.[25]

Thus far we have looked at the subject of small arms from the standpoint of the user, but Civil War soldiers also became aware of themselves as targets of small arms and artillery while engaged in battle. Of course they knew in a generic way that once in combat they were liable to be hit, but the emotional realization of it in their first action often took them by surprise. The result could be a sudden surge of fear that led them to run away or a sudden resolve to stay the course and endure their initiation into the ultimate experience of soldiering. Adjusting to being a target, most soldiers could accept the fact that they had a general chance of getting hit, but the idea that a man on the other side of the field deliberately targeted them often seemed little less than murder. In short, there were stages in the soldier's expanding self-awareness of his role as a military target of enemy fire, and each stage had its unique characteristics that influenced the man's conception of himself as an element on the complicated field of battle.[26]

Most soldiers did not think about another aspect of combat, which was being accidentally shot by their own comrades. Unfortunately, friendly fire in some form or another was a common occurrence during the Civil War. It also was common in all other wars in which contending armies employed projectile weapons. Amicide probably also occurred in classical warfare, given the tightly packed nature of combat by armies using hand-held weapons.[27]

The army did not tabulate deaths due to friendly causes in the Civil War, but personal accounts and rosters indicate that literally every unit suffered at least a few cases of this pernicious problem. It often occurred through careless handling of weapons in camp. When an infantry regiment conducted target practice near the camp of the Fifth Massachusetts Battery, someone carelessly pointed his weapon in the direction of the artillerymen's cook house. The bullet came very close to striking the head of a man in the shack. "They are bad things to trifle with," the battery's historian later wrote of rifle muskets.[28]

Captain Francis T. Moore recalled a poignant accidental death in the Second Illinois Cavalry. Lieutenant James K. Catlin examined a Smith and Wesson revolver belonging to Captain Sterling P. Delano one day. "'It is easier on the trigger than mine, I do not like it so well on that account,'" he said. Just then Catlin's thumb slipped off the trigger and the gun fired a bullet into Delano's back, who was sitting only ten feet away. Delano never blamed Catlin, even though the shot took his life two weeks later. "Catlin was almost beside himself with grief," Moore reported.[29]

Weapons could also become deadly for companions in ways that were not accidental. Their presence often turned a personal confrontation into a deadly affair. Guns influence behavior, according to an interesting study conducted by psychologists concerning the "aggressive cue value" of weapons in 1967. They paired 100 male students at the University of Wisconsin into teams, asked them to exchange ideas about a trumped-up project, and then tasked one member of the team to administer electric shocks to his partner as punishment for failing to think of good ideas. The psychologists placed unloaded weapons within sight of some of the victims; when all of the victims had a chance to return the shocks, those who saw guns tended to administer significantly more shocks to their tormentors than the others. The study concluded that guns served as "aggression-eliciting stimuli, causing an angered individual to display stronger violence than he would have shown in the absence of such weapons."[30]

We can see links between the Wisconsin experiment in 1967 and the experience of soldiering more than 100 years before by looking at the phenomenon of interpersonal violence within Civil War armies. With so many young men living together in uncomfortable conditions, it was inevitable that personal disputes could escalate into violence, accentuated by the fact that these young men were armed with modern weapons. Jacob T. Foster recalled that during a particularly difficult march through the mountains of eastern Kentucky, an exhausted infantryman was imposed on by a comrade who accidentally stepped on his foot. The aggrieved soldier lost his temper and used his rifle musket to shoot the other fellow, killing him instantly. He was court-martialed that same day, found guilty, and shot for his crime. After a quick burial, the troops moved on.[31]

The point is that the presence of a weapon in this incident certainly made the situation far worse than if the angry soldier had had no access to a gun at the moment he became enraged. Guns are more than just devices; they are agents that shape human action. Elders in the Mankon Kingdom of the Cameroon Grassfields clearly understood this aspect of weapons. Their culture evolved a practice of segmenting warfare into three levels of conflict. Within the household or the descent group, confrontation rarely resulted in physical violence, perhaps because no weapons were involved. Conflict among members of the larger kingdom was allowed but only with wooden weapons, sticks, or clubs to minimize physical harm. Conflict between the kingdom and neighboring kingdoms involved deadly iron weapons, machetes, spears, and even guns. Mankon elders were cognizant of the aims of violence and evaluated the potential harm to the victim by carefully selecting weapons to achieve a proper resolution of conflict according to who the participants happened to be.[32]

Faced with serving as a visible target for men armed with modern weapons, some Civil War soldiers relied on talismans as an emotional support. In this way they connected with many warriors in conflicts ranging across the globe and spanning time. A wide variety of items became important in their minds as a way to ward off danger or ensure survival. No matter the culture, nationality, time period, or religious beliefs, soldier talismans are a universal feature of warfare.

While conducting research in the Grassfields of Cameroon in the 1970s, Jean-Pierre Warnier discovered numerous cases of African warriors who invested pebbles, mummified hawks, and other objects with special magic to protect them in battle. Warnier was quick to point out that these men were in fact good soldiers; they learned the techniques of combat and attuned their bodies to the needs of their weapons quite well. But they blended elements of magic and practicality in their soldiering in equal measure. Warnier argued strenuously that the material culture scholar must look beyond the material and appreciate the warrior's subjectivity, his inner self, to truly understand the link between spirit and object that goes deep into the way men use weapons, as well as how they try to protect themselves from those weapons.[33]

Paul Richards discovered that dress played a large role in talismanic approaches to combat. During the civil war in Sierra Leone from 1991 to 2002, he saw a rebel soldier wearing under his shirt a *ronko*, or warrior's jacket, made of traditional country cloth and with medicine applied to make the wearer "invisible" to the enemy. The insurgent forces that Richards was observing were not well organized into a standing army, and therefore they had more leeway in choosing battle dress. Culture as well as their subjective approach to dealing with the dangers of combat produced the *ronko*.³⁴

But becoming a member of a regularly organized military force did not prevent Civil War soldiers from choosing unusual battle dress in an attempt to protect themselves from enemy weapons. Quite a few enterprising businessmen tried to sell bulletproof vests to Northern soldiers through advertisements in newspapers as well as by hawking them in army camps. At least some of the soldiers bought them. Captain William Vermilion of the Thirty-Sixth Iowa purchased a vest but explained to his wife that he intended to wear it "not through cowardice but because I consider it my duty to protect myself in every manner possible." But Vermilion told her not to tell anyone. "The boys here don't know it," he admitted. While a handful of soldiers apparently trusted the utility of these vests, most others ridiculed them. A peddler who solicited the First Wisconsin Battery ran away when a member of the company agreed to buy a vest if the hawker would wear it and allow him to test its usefulness by firing a pistol at him.³⁵

It is tempting to conclude that Civil War Americans lived in a culture too sophisticated to put trust in either the practical benefits of wearing a thin plate of metal or in any kind of magical formula to protect them from bullets. But there is ample proof that quite a few of them quietly used talismans of one kind or another. Frank L. Richardson of the Thirteenth Louisiana kept a small Bible he had used since childhood; it "was intended to serve as a kind of talisman from the enemy's bullets." Captain Elliot N. Bush of the Ninety-Fifth Illinois had a motto inscribed on the sheath of his sword that he often repeated to himself while steeling his nerves for battle: "The Lord is on my side. I will not fear; what can man do with me?"³⁶

In the Trans-Mississippi Theater of operations, Captain George Washington Grayson commanded a company of Creeks in the Confederate army. He was surprised to see his men prepare for action at the battle of Cabin Creek by passing around some medicine that they rubbed "on and about the clothing of the body and limbs as thoroughly as they could." Grayson's lieutenant offered some to him, but he refused. Although a Creek himself, Grayson preferred to rely on "the impulses of my innate courage" rather than on the "supposed protection afforded by medicines or talismans."³⁷

The most important point about talismans is not whether they work but the fact that they are a persistent feature of soldiering that cuts across time periods. But even among cultures less "modern," such as the Creeks or the rebels of Sierra Leone, not everyone believed in them. Those who did believe in them had a tendency to invoke the power of talismans in a quiet way. The rebel warrior whom Richards saw in 1992 wore his *ronko* tightly around his torso under his shirt, not outside it.[38] Vermilion and every other Civil War soldier who admitted later to using a bulletproof vest kept it a secret at the time. They did not want their comrades to think they lacked bravery.

For the warrior in Sierra Leone, that protection was afforded by a coarse cotton cloth typically made by older women in his family to serve as gifts or funeral shrouds. It came from the rural culture of village life and, with a little magic spread over its rough texture, served the purpose of protecting the family son. For the Creeks, it was some kind of powder applied to the clothing and skin. For Vermilion from Iowa, it was a manufactured product of thin steel emblematic of the modern culture of America. There was no overt magic to the bulletproof vest except perhaps in the hope-against-hope of the wearer that it could be effective. There actually is no evidence of any kind that such a vest ever saved the wearer's life and substantial proof that it did not. One need only ponder a bulletproof vest taken from the body of Colonel William P. Rogers of the Second Texas, killed at the battle of Corinth and currently displayed at the Wisconsin Veterans Museum in Madison. It has a very large hole through the center.[39]

European warriors have used talismans as a way to ease the fears of combat. British soldiers facing the challenges offered by the Western Front of World War I latched onto the Catholic crucifix as a talismanic symbol. This phenomenon seems to have been widespread, even among Protestants, and one sees crosses made out of discarded war materials as trench art, which flourished within the extensive system of field fortifications that sliced across western Belgium and northeast France. Roadside calvaries also proliferated during the war, offering large examples of the cross to soldiers who understood that it somehow provided sacred ground where one could at least hope to survive the storm of steel that characterized combat on the Western Front.[40]

Today, with the extended military commitments in Afghanistan and Iraq, we see the further commercialization of soldier talismans. Amazon markets a "Wiccan Dragon Shield Knot Pendant Talisman for Soldiers," a necklace made of zinc alloy that sells for $15.99.[41]

"Fighting is all about the body and its material setting," Jean-Pierre Warnier has argued. "I contend that one way to explore the practice of warfare is by having access to the fighter's subjectivity, and that the best way to access this is by investigating the bodily/material culture of the fighter." To understand not just the body motions needed to use a particular weapon but the emotions that are associated with its use and with the obverse—having a similar weapon used by the other side against you—is vital in apprehending the link between object and man. "In other words, not the material culture," Warnier writes, "but the bodily/material culture" of fighting in any war, or "the daily practice of armed violence, on the battlefield and also in the daily routines behind the battle lines," is an important new avenue of investigation.[42]

Another aspect of this "embodied material culture of fighting" lies in the need for soldiers to domesticate their weapons by giving them names or engraving mottos on them. This practice could be viewed as a way to further link the object with the user, making the cold metal familiar and comfortable in an emotional way that contributes to the employment of sensorimotor skills when the weapon is used. The Civil War soldiers who named their guns most likely were the more gun-adept men whose acclimation to shooting encouraged such a familiar practice. Most often the names they chose were feminine—Hannah, Mary Jane, and Silver Sue—rather than the aggressive names that entire companies adopted as their monikers, such as Sharpshooters, Marksmen, or Targeteers.[43]

We reach a new stage of discussion when beginning to ponder why soldiers named their weapons. As Martin Heidegger pointed out in 1971, there is a distinction between an object and a thing. The object remains impersonal with only a superficial, utilitarian connection to the person using it. For most soldiers, we assume, their weapons probably remained an object. But a thing is an object with which someone has developed personal connections.[44]

In an interesting discussion of a Distinguished Flying Cross awarded her grandfather in World War II, Jody Joy has described how a mass-produced object was treated by the soldier and his family during the passage of generations after 1945. The way in which the veteran and various relatives thought about and took care of the medal changed over time and differed with each person, but the end result was that nearly everyone developed some sort of personal attachment to it for different reasons. Joy's point was that performative action by each individual led to this mass-produced object becoming a thing for that person. "Even objects associated with war ... are not pre-programmed," Joy concludes; "they still need to be constituted performatively by social action." Personal engagement is at the heart of performative social action, and gun-adept soldiers certainly engaged their weapons in a personal way that gun-inept men and the average soldier failed to do.[45]

Giving a name to a Springfield rifle musket certainly can be seen within the light of these conclusions, but why give it a feminine name? One can interpret this in more than one way. Gender scholars may be tempted to see it as an example of inequality: dominant male mastering a firearm and giving it the name of a woman as a symbol of his gender-based domination of the home and of the public sphere. One cannot dispute the validity of this interpretation for at least some men who gave names to their guns, but it has to be admitted that for others, assigning a feminine name to their weapon carried more positive connotations of honoring a gender he admired. The practice of naming military things generally was honorific, not repressive—for example, when forts were named for officers who were killed in battle.

We can suggest another view of naming objects in order to turn them into things, and it ties in with an often unstated recognition that weapons can be as dangerous to friends as to enemies. There is no doubt that many soldiers never really acclimated themselves to weapons and could not learn how to use them effectively. Although soldiers rarely wrote of their fears of getting shot by their own comrades, there is also no doubt that this awareness existed to some degree. The evidence strongly suggests that literally every regiment had at least one or two cases of amicide in its war experience. Was the soldier trying to master his sublimated fear of the gun by choosing a feminine name for it, a name to connote happy, comforting associations of the domestic circle rather than the aggressive names associated with killing that he could have chosen?

The practice of naming weapons seems to have been more widespread among artillerists than infantrymen. Gun crew detachments operated as a team to serve one large weapon; their training and corporate identity were tied to working that large gun efficiently, and thus most of their war experience centered on taking care of it. No wonder they had a tendency to fixate on the weapon—to love it, admire it, and take pride in performing their task well.

Some of these artillery pieces received names associated with their performance in action. The Confederates had a large gun at the siege of Vicksburg that made a peculiar noise when fired and was dubbed Whistling Dick. Long Tom was a common name for large artillery pieces; one Confederate gunner asserted that such a gun was given that name because of its "far reaching and accurate firing" at the battle of First Bull Run.[46]

Guns that performed well or peculiarly in battle received masculine names, but most artillery pieces received feminine names: Crazy Jane, Betsy Bell, Mary Gray, and Do Do Baby. More formal types of feminine names included those to honor the wives of famous men; these included Lady Davis and Lady Bowen.[47]

Lieutenant James P. Douglas certainly viewed the naming process as an important way to strengthen his connection with the home front. Upon joining a Texas battery early in the war, he named one of the two guns in his section after his fiancée, Sallie. Another officer in the battery named a gun after his girlfriend, Texana Walker. Douglas was severely disappointed that neither of these weapons participated in the battle of Wilson's Creek. "They would have been a terror to the enemy," he told Sallie; "be assured that my life will be imperiled before I give up the gun which bears your name." Douglas finally was able to bring "Sallie" to bear on the enemy at the battle of Pea Ridge. "I had the pleasure of pointing and ranging 'Sallie' in the fight, ... and I can assure you that as her loud voice died away sweepingly among the distant hills the enemy felt the effect of her shot."[48]

For Douglas, the cannon became a surrogate for his beloved Sallie. He brought her symbolically with him to the field and allowed her to participate in his war making and to share in his defiance of the enemy. We do not know how much Sallie appreciated this, but it obviously was important to Douglas as a way to compensate for his detachment from her. There can be no sense of gender domination here; what Douglas offered Sallie was something like gender equality, or at least the opportunity to feel she was part of the actual war effort on the battlefield. Merely by giving his cannon a name, Douglas incorporated the home front with the battlefront. He made sure Sallie knew what was going on so she had the opportunity to understand his purpose.

What Douglas did was only one aspect of the multifaceted topic of naming weapons. Another was the practice of naming big guns as a direct result of battle. A three-inch rifle captured by the Confederates at the battle of Glendale was inscribed with the name of Union general George A. McCall because he had been captured in that engagement. In another example, following the battle of Stones River, Confederate general Braxton Bragg authorized Brigadier General George Maney to select four brave men from Tennessee in his brigade who had died in the engagement. He wanted their names engraved on artillery pieces attached to the brigade in an effort to boost morale and honor the fallen.[49]

Warriors have often adorned their weapons with mottos or symbols designed to inspire fighters in combat or remind them of why they fought. In studying the Wola Highlanders of Papua New Guinea, Paul Sillitoe was intrigued by the decorations they applied to war shields. They painted a variety of symbols from the anthropomorphic (to represent men) to the abstract ("distorted human elements"), but one enigmatic figure consisted of "a diagonal cross of two sticks." Even the painters could not tell Sillitoe why they chose this design, even though they were convinced it was necessary to do so. Sillitoe concluded it was an especially abstract symbol of a man because for the Wola, a premodern society, revenge was the key to warfare. With no higher political organization, members of the village had to react to the killing of one of their members to maintain social order. Their designs tended to be simple and graphic and functioned to remind the Wola of why they fought and whom they fought, in comparison to other premodern societies that had more sophisticated designs on their shields, such as North American Plains Indians, whose shield designs were linked to dreams and visions.[50]

If one wonders whether there is relevance to comparing the culture of a tribe in New Guinea with that of Civil War America, ponder this example. When the Federals captured Fort Henry in February 1862, they found an abandoned bowie knife that had been made from an old rasp. Crudely inscribed on it were the words "deth to all ablishners." In his own way, the unknown Confederate who left this weapon behind was reminding himself of why he fought and whom he fought, as well as providing himself with a ready source of inspiration to steel his nerves when the clash came.[51]

The converse of adorning weapons is to produce them with clean lines that serve a utilitarian and aesthetic purpose at the same time. Many artillerymen keenly appreciated the look of their weapons. The Napoleon had been developed in France only a few years before the outbreak of the Civil War with deliberately clean lines, eliminating all ornamental aspects that had adorned artillery tubes for centuries. "They were beautiful," remembered Philip Daingerfield Stephenson of the Fifth Company, Washington Artillery, "perfectly plain, tapering gracefully from muzzle to 'reinforce' or 'butt,' without rings, ridges or ornaments of any kind. We were proud of them and felt towards them almost as if they were human."[52]

Yet, all artillerymen were just as keenly aware that the weapon they admired could kill and maim its own gun crew. If one member made a mistake in the precisely timed movements each performed on the piece, it could result in a fearful accident that tore off the arm of his comrade through premature discharge. Every battery suffered a handful of unintended casualties, and they acted as severe lessons reminding everyone to be careful with their dangerous weapons.[53]

Likewise, many infantry units assigned to positions near a battery learned that friendly fire constituted one of many hazards on the battlefield. Although we have no statistics on this phenomenon, there is little doubt that friendly artillery fire accounted for more cases of amicide than did small-arms fire. That was certainly true of modern conflicts such as World War I, where 75,000 Frenchmen died as result of fire from their own artillery. Charles R. Shrader has estimated that friendly fire amounted to

The Material Culture of Weapons in the Civil War

about 1.5 percent of all French military deaths from 1914 to 1918. He also believes that 1.6 percent of American deaths in the Korean War and 2.85 percent of American deaths in Vietnam could be blamed on accidental killings by American weapons.[54]

It is likely the percentage might be a bit lower for the Civil War, given that twentieth-century operations so heavily involved a variety of long-range weapons compared with warfare during the 1860s, but that assumption hardly diminishes the impact of friendly fire on the troops. Whenever men happened to be positioned in front of friendly batteries, they suffered unintended casualties. Members of the Tenth New York Cavalry "talked hard against us" for a long while after they lost a handful of men because some shells prematurely exploded when fired by the Sixth New York Battery during the Overland campaign.[55]

Federal troops besieging Vicksburg often encountered this problem because the nature of their operations required most of the Union artillery to be located to the rear of the infantry. In general the Yankee artillery dominated the siege lines and inspired Federal troops with confidence every time they witnessed counter-battery fire that resulted in silencing the Confederate guns.[56] But many Union shells exploded prematurely, and the friendly casualties began to mount. Friendly bursts killed or injured one or two men at a time, increasing the survivors' anger and fear with each incident.[57]

"We have more danger from a battery of regulars on the hill behind us than from the enemy's bullets," complained Edward H. Ingraham of the Thirty-Third Illinois to his aunt. "Our boys declare they will go up and spike their guns if they don't throw away that bad ammunition." Other members of the regiment admitted that they shuddered every time the battery opened fire "for fear of the sad results." A man was hit almost every day, and the growing realization of the danger from their comrades "did more to pull the regiment down" than did their contest with the enemy.[58] Bad manufacturing of the shells at arsenals was generally accounted as the cause of this problem.[59]

Infantrymen had little choice but to endure the danger from friendly artillery. While the gunners felt bad about the results, they nevertheless grew to love their guns with a passion hardly attainable by the infantrymen. "None but a soldier can 'sense' the affection with which a cannoneer regarded his gun," wrote two officers of the First Wisconsin Battery. They described the "pungent scent of battle" that a veteran gunner could bring to his senses when examining a gun long after the conflict, a scent that elicited emotions and memories that were both comforting and horrifying.[60]

When a veteran of the First Wisconsin Battery visited Marshalltown,

Iowa, to see Grand Army of the Republic friends, he was stunned to find that one of the four twenty-pounder Parrotts displayed on the courthouse lawn had been served by his battery. He knew that because he was able to match the identification number engraved on the tube with information in a memo book he carried. "I was kneeling, facing the gun and my forehead went down on to the iron face, the tears jumped to my eyes and I thought more in a minute than I can write in an hour."[61]

Several strands of discussion in this essay help to chart a path toward constructing a material culture approach to weapons in the Civil War. An appreciation of this approach should start with the recognition that a considerable gun culture embraced a certain proportion of Americans in the antebellum period, a culture that venerated weapons, added symbolic importance to the objects, and encouraged its adherents to rely on them for a variety of reasons. It is quite possible that the men who embraced this gun culture were those whose sensorimotor skills were particularly attuned to the use of weapons, and these men became superb gunmen after they joined the Union and Confederate armies. We also need to recognize that a certain proportion of the military-age men of both the North and the South had no affinity at all with the gun culture and possessed no innate ability to use weapons. They became gun-inept soldiers in the ranks of both armies. Everyone else fell at some point along the spectrum between those two extremes.

In addition to being aware of themselves as shooters, soldiers also became aware of themselves as targets of other men with guns. They had to deal with the emotional effect of becoming victims of enemy fire and, to a lesser degree, of becoming victims of friendly fire by their own comrades. No wonder that some Union and Confederate soldiers adopted talismans to serve as an emotional crutch in battle or purchased body armor in the hope of using commercialized products to save their skin.

Finally, many soldiers embraced their weapons in an emotional way by giving them names, by acknowledging the aesthetics of individual guns and artillery pieces, and by remembering those weapons with positive feelings of one kind or another long after the war ended.

A cross-cultural perspective helps greatly to achieve a well-rounded view of the material culture of weapons, exposing common trends that link conflicts and the soldiers who served in them. Warriors even in such disparate cultures as the Wola of New Guinea and the American Civil War shared a number of attitudes toward and practices concerning the tools of destruction they used. War devices also share common characteristics with devices used for peacetime purposes. Finally, it is important when studying

The Material Culture of Weapons in the Civil War

weapons to understand that they are material objects laden with a wide variety of meanings and relationships to their users, which is to say that they fill the same role in material culture studies as any other man-made object.

Notes

1. For example, see James C. Hazlett, Edwin Olmstead, and M. Hume Parks, *Field Artillery Weapons of the Civil War*, rev. ed. (Urbana: University of Illinois Press, 2004). For a discussion of the importance of studying how weapons were actually employed, see Earl J. Hess, *The Rifle Musket in Civil War Combat: Reality and Myth* (Lawrence: University Press of Kansas, 2008).

2. Jules David Prown, "Mind in Matter: An Introduction to Material Culture Theory and Method," in *Material Life in America, 1600-1860*, ed. Robert Blair St. George (Boston: Northeastern University Press, 1988), 18-19, 31-32.

3. Nicholas J. Saunders, *Trench Art: Materialities and Memories of War* (Oxford: Berg, 2003); Nicholas J. Saunders, "Matter and Memory in the Landscapes of Conflict: The Western Front, 1914-1999," in *Contested Landscapes: Movement, Exile and Place*, ed. Barbara Bender and Margot Winer (Oxford: Berg, 2001), 37-53; Nicholas J. Saunders, "Crucifix, Calvary, and Cross: Materiality and Spirituality in Great War Landscapes," *World Archaeology* 35, no. 1 (June 2003): 7-21; Nicholas J. Saunders, "Material Culture and Conflict: The Great War, 1914-2003," in *Matters of Conflict: Material Culture, Memory and the First World War*, ed. Nicholas J. Saunders (London: Routledge, 2004), 5-25.

4. See the essays in Saunders, *Matters of Conflict*.

5. Nicholas J. Saunders, "Apprehending Memory: Material Culture and War, 1919-1939," in *The Great World War, 1914-1945, Vol. 2: The People's Experience*, ed. Peter Liddle, John Bourne, and Ian Whitehead (London: HarperCollins, 2001), 483; Gabriel Moshenska, "A Hard Rain: Children's Shrapnel Collections in the Second World War," *Journal of Material Culture* 13, no. 1 (March 2008): 107-25.

6. John Schofield, William Gray Johnson, and Colleen N. Beck, eds., *Matériel Culture: The Archaeology of Twentieth-Century Conflict* (London: Routledge, 2002).

7. Joan E. Cashin, "Trophies of War: Material Culture in the Civil War Era," *Journal of the Civil War Era* 1, no. 3 (September 2011): 339-67. Simon Harrison, "Bones in the Rebel Lady's Boudoir: Ethnology, Race and Trophy-Hunting in the American Civil War," *Journal of Material Culture* 15, no. 4 (December 2010): 385-401, focuses on one particular aspect of Civil War relic collecting and predated Cashin's article by a few months.

8. Saunders, *Trench Art*, 25; [Mary Ann Loughborough], *My Cave Life in Vicksburg, with Letters of Trial and Travel* (New York: D. Appleton, 1864), 107; D. S. Way, "The Battle of the Crater," *National Tribune*, 3 June 1904; Earl J. Hess, *Into the Crater: The Mine Attack at Petersburg* (Columbia: University of South Carolina Press), 2010, 12-13; William W. Lord Jr., "A Child at the Siege of Vicksburg," *Harper's Monthly*, December 1908, 50; Winchester Hall, *The Story of the 26th Louisiana Infantry, in the Service of the Confederate States* (n.p.: n.p., n.d.), 86-87.

9. Stéphane Audoin-Rouzeau and Annette Becker, *14-18: Understanding the Great War*, trans. Catherine Temerson (New York: Hill and Wang, 2002), 19-20.

10. Nicholas J. Saunders, "The Ironic 'Culture of Shells' in the Great War and Beyond," in *Matériel Culture: The Archaeology of Twentieth-Century Conflict*, ed. John Schofield, William Gray Johnson, and Colleen N. Beck (London: Routledge, 2002), 22–40; David Pearson and Graham Connah, "Retrieving the Cultural Biography of a Gun," *Journal of Conflict Archaeology* 8, no. 1 (January 2013): 41–73; Lawrence E. Babits, Christopher F. Amer, Lynn Harris, and Joe Beatty, "The Tale of a Gun—IX-inch Dahlgren #FP573: It's Not Just a Cannon, It's a Story," in *From These Honored Dead: Historical Archaeology of the American Civil War*, ed. Clarence R. Geier, Douglas D. Scott, and Lawrence E. Babits (Gainesville: University Press of Florida, 2014), 238–46; Brandon Olson, "The Dedication of Roman Weapons and Armor in Water as a Religious Ritual, *CJA: Anthrojournal* 1 (October 2011): not paginated, http://anthrojournal.com/issue/october-2011/artilce/the-dedication-of-roman-weapons-and-armor-in-water-as-a-religious-ritual, accessed 21 October 2017; Paul Hodges, "'They Don't Like It Up 'Em!' Bayonet Fetishization in the British Army during the First World War," *Journal of War and Culture Studies* 1, no. 2 (2008): 123–38; John Stone, "The Point of the Bayonet," *Technology and Culture* 53, no. 4 (October 2012): 885–908.

11. Glenn H. Utter and James L. True, "The Evolving Gun Culture in America," *Journal of American and Comparative Cultures* 23, no. 2 (Summer 2000): 67–79; Michael A. Bellesiles, *Arming America: The Origins of a National Gun Culture* (New York: Alfred A. Knopf, 2000), 305–71, 383–87, 430–44.

12. Gary W. Gallagher, ed., *Fighting for the Confederacy: The Personal Recollections of General Edward Porter Alexander* (Chapel Hill: University of North Carolina Press, 1989), 3; Charles I. Switzer, ed., *Ohio Volunteer: The Childhood and Civil War Memoirs of Captain John Calvin Hartzell, OVI* (Athens: Ohio University Press, 2005), 10–12.

13. Hess, *Rifle Musket*, 63; Davidson to Annie C. Davidson, 11 and 21 January 1863, James Innes Davidson Papers, Alabama Department of Archives and History, Montgomery.

14. Hess, *Rifle Musket*, 31–32, 68–71, 91–93, 139.

15. Jean-Pierre Warnier, "A Praxeological Approach to Subjectivation in a Material World," *Journal of Material Culture* 6, no. 1 (March 2001): 6–7, 10.

16. Hess, *Rifle Musket*, 97.

17. J. B. Polley, *A Soldier's Letters to Charming Nellie* (New York: Neale, 1908), 242–44.

18. Thomas D. Cockrell and Michael B. Ballard, eds., *A Mississippi Rebel in the Army of Northern Virginia: The Civil War Memoirs of Private David Holt* (Baton Rouge: Louisiana State University Press, 1995), 282; Terrence J. Winschel, ed., *The Civil War Diary of a Common Soldier: William Wiley of the 77th Illinois Infantry* (Baton Rouge: Louisiana State University Press, 2001), 29.

19. J. W. Gaskill, *Footprints through Dixie: Everyday Life of the Man under a Musket on the Firing Line and in the Trenches, 1862–1865* (Alliance, Ohio: Bradshaw, 1919).

20. Hess, *Rifle Musket*, 35–59, 85–119.

21. Bliss to mother, 21 April 1862, Robert Lewis Bliss Papers, Alabama Department of Archives and History, Montgomery; Finley P. Curtis, "The Black Shadow of the Sixties," *Confederate Veteran* 24 (1916): 353–54; W. H. Tunnard, *A Southern Record: The History of the Third Regiment Louisiana Infantry* (Dayton: Morningside Bookshop, 1970), 242.

22. Merritt Roe Smith, "Technological Determinism in American Culture," in *Does*

Technology Drive History? The Dilemma of Technological Determinism, ed. Merritt Roe Smith and Leo Marx (Cambridge, Mass.: MIT Press, 1994), 2, 5, 6, 8.

23. Kurt H. Hackemer, ed., *To Rescue My Native Land: The Civil War Letters of William T. Shepherd, First Illinois Light Artillery* (Knoxville: University of Tennessee Press, 2005), 93, 97; Hess, *Rifle Musket*, 36–39; *The Story of the Fifty-fifth Regiment Illinois Volunteer Infantry in the Civil War, 1861–1865* (Clinton, Mass.: W. J. Coulter, 1887), 41–42.

24. Hess, *Rifle Musket*, 107–15.

25. Hess, 175–96.

26. Earl J. Hess, *The Union Soldier in Battle: Enduring the Ordeal of Combat* (Lawrence: University Press of Kansas, 1997), 1–21.

27. Geoffrey Regan, *Back Fire: The Tragic Story of Friendly Fire in Warfare from Ancient Times to the Gulf War* (London: Robson, 1995), 29–39. On pages 67–74, Regan discusses the American Civil War, but his evidence comes mostly from secondary sources.

28. Diary, 14 July 1863, Thomas B. Byron Papers, William L. Clements Library, University of Michigan, Ann Arbor; *History of the Fifth Massachusetts Battery* (Boston: Luther E. Cowles, 1902), 143.

29. William H. Runge, ed., *Four Years in the Confederate Artillery: The Diary of Private Henry Robinson Berkeley* (Chapel Hill: University of North Carolina Press, 1961), 21; Thomas Bahde, ed., *The Story of My Campaign: The Civil War Memoir of Captain Francis T. Moore, Second Illinois Cavalry* (DeKalb: Northern Illinois University Press, 2011), 77, 79.

30. Leonard Berkowitz and Anthony Le Page, "Weapons as Aggression-Eliciting Stimuli," *Journal of Personality and Social Psychology* 7, no. 2 (October 1967): 202–7.

31. Jacob T. Foster Memoirs, 32, Wisconsin Historical Society, Madison.

32. Jean-Pierre Warnier, "Bodily/Material Culture and the Fighter's Subjectivity," *Journal of Material Culture* 16, no. 4 (December 2011): 361.

33. Warnier, 359–60, 363.

34. Paul Richards, "Dressed to Kill: Clothing as Technology of the Body in the Civil War in Sierra Leone," *Journal of Material Culture* 14, no. 4 (December 2009): 496.

35. Hess, *Rifle Musket*, 79–82; Dan Webster and Don C. Cameron, *History of the First Wisconsin Battery Light Artillery* (n.p.: n.p., 1907), 35–36.

36. Frank L. Richardson, "War as I Saw It, 1861–1865," *Louisiana Historical Quarterly* 6, no. 1 (January 1923): 96; Elliot N. Bush to Father and Mother and All, 29 May 1863, Elliot N. and Henry M. Bush Papers, William L. Clements Library, University of Michigan, Ann Arbor.

37. W. David Baird, ed., *A Creek Warrior for the Confederacy: The Autobiography of Chief G. W. Grayson* (Norman: University of Oklahoma Press, 1988), 102.

38. Richards, "Dressed to Kill," 504.

39. Hess, *Rifle Musket*, 79–82.

40. Nicholas J. Saunders, *Killing Time: Archaeology and the First World War* (Stroud, Gloucestershire, UK: Sutton, 2007), 36–37, 72.

41. https://www.amazon.com/Pendant-Talisman-Soldiers-Military-Necklaces/dp/B01BAML43S, accessed 21 October 2017.

42. Warnier, "Bodily/Material Culture," 360, 363, 366, 371.

43. Hess, *Rifle Musket*, 63–64.

44. Martin Heidegger, *Poetry, Language, Thought* (New York: Harper and Row, 1971), 167–168; Jody Joy, "Biography of a Medal: People and the Things They Value," in *Matériel Culture: The Archaeology of Twentieth-Century Conflict*, ed. John Schofield, William Gray Johnson, and Colleen N. Beck (London: Routledge, 2002), 132.

45. Joy, "Biography of a Medal," 141. See also Igor Kopytoff, "The Cultural Biography of Things: Commodization as Process," in *The Social Life of Things: Commodities in Cultural Perspective*, ed. Arjun Appadurai (Cambridge: Cambridge University Press, 1986), 66–68, 73–74, 87–88.

46. Samuel H. Lockett to C. C. Memminger, 26 July 1863, in U.S. War Department, *The War of the Rebellion: A Compilation of the Official Records of the Union and Confederate Armies*, 128 vols. (Washington, D.C.: GPO, 1880–1901), ser. 1, vol. 24, pt. 2, 331–32 (hereafter *OR*); [Frederick S. Daniel], *Richmond Howitzers in the War: Four Years Campaigning with the Army of Northern Virginia* (Richmond, 1891), 29.

47. James E. Moss, ed., "A Missouri Confederate in the Civil War: The Journal of Henry Martyn Cheavens, 1862–1863," *Missouri Historical Review* 57, no. 1 (October 1962): 42–43; Robert K. Krick, *Parker's Virginia Battery, C.S.A.*, 2nd ed. (Wilmington, N.C.: Broadfoot Publishing, 1989), 152; "The Civil War Diary of Charles Henry Snedeker," 8 July 1863, Special Collections and Archives, Auburn University, Alabama; Edwin C. Bearss, ed., "Diary of Captain John N. Bell of Co. E, 25th Iowa Infantry, at Vicksburg," *Iowa Journal of History* 59, no. 2 (April 1961): 221.

48. Lucia Rutherford Douglas, ed., *Douglas's Texas Battery, CSA* (Tyler, Tex.: Smith County Historical Society, 1966), 3, 9, 31.

49. R. Prosper Landry, "The Donaldsonville Artillery at the Battle of Fredericksburg," *Southern Historical Society Papers* 23 (1895): 198; Hypolite Oladowski to George Maney, 8 April 1863, *OR*, ser. 1, vol. 16, pt. 2, 1003.

50. Paul Sillitoe, "The Art of War: Wola Shield Designs," *Man* 15, no. 3 (September 1980): 483, 490, 493–97.

51. George H. Woodruff, *Fifteen Years Ago: Or the Patriotism of Will County* (Joliet, Ill.: Joliet Republican, 1876), 399.

52. Nathaniel Cheairs Hughes Jr., ed., *The Civil War Memoir of Philip Daingerfield Stephenson, D.D.* (Conway: University of Central Arkansas Press, 1995), 165.

53. Hackemer, *To Rescue My Native Land*, 71.

54. "The Civil War Diary of Charles Henry Snedeker," 20 June 1863, Special Collections and Archives, Auburn University, Alabama; Sylvester Strong to brother, 23 June 1863, Sylvester and Albert Strong Civil War Letters, Wisconsin Historical Society, Madison; J. H. Jones, "The Rank and File at Vicksburg," *Publications of the Mississippi Historical Society* 7 (1903): 30; Saunders, "Ironic 'Culture of Shells,'" 24; Charles R. Shrader, *Amicide: The Problem of Friendly Fire in Modern War* (Leavenworth, Kans.: Combat Studies Institute, 1982), xii.

55. Richard N. Griffin, ed., *Three Years a Soldier: The Diary and Newspaper Correspondence of Private George Perkins, Sixth New York Independent Battery, 1861–1864* (Knoxville: University of Tennessee Press, 2006), 234.

56. Reese to Tissee, 4 June 1863, John Reese Papers, Special Collections Research Center, Southern Illinois University, Carbondale.

57. Wood to wife, 14 June 1863, Edward Jesup Wood Papers, Indiana Historical Society, Indianapolis; J. J. Kellogg, *War Experiences and the Story of the Vicksburg Campaign from "Milliken's Bend" to July 4, 1863* (Washington, Iowa: Evening Journal, 1913), 43; Seth J. Wells, *The Siege of Vicksburg* (Detroit: William H. Rowe, 1915), 73, 78; Jenkin Lloyd Jones, *An Artilleryman's Diary* (Madison: Democrat Printing, 1914), 66; Joseph A. Saunier, ed., *A History of the Forty-Seventh Regiment Ohio Veteran Volunteer Infantry* (Hillsboro, Ohio: Lyle Printing, [1903]), 156; R. L. Howard, *History of the 124th Regiment Illinois Infantry Volunteers* (Springfield, Ill.: H. W. Rokker, 1880), 111; diary, 2 and 7 June 1863, Hugh Boyd Ewing Papers, Ohio Historical Society, Columbus; William G. Christie to brother, 23 June 1863, Christie Family Letters, Minnesota Historical Society, St. Paul.

58. Edward H. Ingraham to aunt, 29 May 1863, Edward H. Ingraham and Duncan G. Ingraham Letters, Abraham Lincoln Presidential Library, Springfield, Illinois; Edgar L. Erickson, ed., "With Grant at Vicksburg: From the Civil War Diary of Captain Charles E. Wilcox," *Journal of the Illinois State Historical Society* 30, no. 4 (January 1938): 492; Virgil G. Way, *History of the Thirty-Third Regiment Illinois Veteran Volunteer Infantry* (Gibson City, Ill.: Gibson Courier, 1902), 45.

59. Ord to wife, 27 June 1863, Edward Otho Cresap Ord Letters, Special Collections and University Archives, Stanford University, Palo Alto, California; Charles A. Dana to Edward M. Stanton, 16 June 1863, *OR*, ser. 1, vol. 24, pt. 1, 100.

60. John D. Billings, *The History of the Tenth Massachusetts Battery of Light Artillery in the War of the Rebellion, 1862–1865* (Boston: Hall and Whiting, 1909), 431–32; Dan Webster and Don C. Cameron, *History of the First Wisconsin Battery Light Artillery* (n.p.: n.p., 1907), 257–58.

61. Webster and Cameron, *First Wisconsin Battery*, 171.

Scabrous Matters
Spurious Vaccinations in the Confederacy

ROBERT D. HICKS

Introduction

During 1863–64, smallpox had become epidemic throughout the South. "Panic-stricken by the spread of the disease," the Confederate army urgently required the vaccination of both soldiers and civilians. Desperate because of the scant supply of vaccine, surgeon James Bolton, MD, quickly vaccinated employees and soldiers of the Confederate government in Richmond, Virginia. Fearful that vaccine shipped from abroad would not reach the South through the Federal blockade of ports, Bolton cut the arms of healthy children and inserted lymph (liquid that appears in blisters called vesicles) taken from the sores of people who had been infected with the disease through the vaccine. Ideally, the children would experience a milder form of the disease (called vaccinia) and *their* lymph would furnish new vaccinating material. At the time, smallpox was the only disease that could be prevented by this method. Physicians used lymph and scabs—termed vaccine matter—to vaccinate soldiers and government workers who, after they endured vaccinia, would enjoy immunity against infection, at least for a time. Of the 1,300 persons vaccinated, Bolton claimed only one failure of it to "take."[1]

Vaccine matter was not just a pestiferous substance used to immunize people; it is historical evidence that can be examined through the lens of material culture. In this essay, I employ this lens to understand how Confederate doctors created new knowledge about a natural, biological material—vaccine virus—that they circulated through live human and bovine hosts in order to immunize soldiers. Smallpox vaccination involves the manipulation of the human body to achieve a very specific outcome: immunity from a worse disease. This manipulation is a material process wherein we see "reflections of underlying mental constructs," to quote anthropologist Rita P. Wright. These constructs can be glimpsed through extant reports by Confederate doctors, particularly when vaccination did not appear to work. Although most Confederate medical records were destroyed when Richmond burned near the war's end, later, ex-Confederate surgeons resurrected lost reports through correspondence to analyze what they had learned.[2]

Material culture study is an interdisciplinary inquiry based on the presumption that human-made things—artifacts—are historical evidence. Civil War studies have made little use of material culture, and the extant scholarship has favored analyses of battlefield relics, military hardware, patterns of production and consumption of domestic goods, and the evolution of specific technologies such as telegraphy. The material culture of vaccination, however, examines substances removed from and placed within human bodies. Scrutinizing the material process of vaccination within the context of the medical ideology of the Civil War shows how doctors created and modified knowledge about disease transmission, especially when vaccination failed. Its failure heightened physicians' self-scrutiny about vaccination and modified subsequent practice.[3]

Bolton's experience was positive, but when vaccination failed, the results were disastrous. For example, Chimborazo Hospital in Richmond—the largest hospital during the war, in the North or the South—housed smallpox victims but also soldiers whose vaccinations coincided with the appearance of other diseases. Twenty-two-year-old private W. J. Smith, Sixtieth Georgia Infantry, was vaccinated in both arms in Danville, Virginia, in January 1863. He subsequently appeared to undergo the predictable course of vaccinia, but after he returned to duty, pustules formed around the scar on the left arm. He entered Chimborazo in May 1863. Eruptions appeared elsewhere on the arm and near the wrist, "covered with thick elevated scabs." "Ichorous [foul smelling] pus" seeped from the pustules. Had Smith somehow acquired a new disease while laboring through vaccinia? Was some other malady introduced into his body along with the vaccine matter from another person? How did surgeons appraise this problem as it appeared in many regiments under similar circumstances?[4]

In January 1863, Chief Surgeon W. S. Mitchell of Rodes's Division, Army of Northern Virginia, reported 227 instances of "spurious vaccinia" among soldiers of the Forty-Fourth Georgia Infantry. Vaccinations that did not take or appeared to go awry (especially when other disease symptoms appeared) were termed "spurious." In this case, a soldier home on furlough was inoculated with his wife's skin eruptions, and he subsequently got infected and used his own lymph or scabs to inoculate fellow soldiers without the involvement of physicians. Soon, vesicles appeared on the men and turned into ulcerous sores with large scabs. Even when the scabs disappeared following treatment with potassium iodide or mercury, sores erupted again with subsequent scabs. These symptoms transformed soldiers' bodies into quarantined, disabled, isolated, barely recognizable patients. Similar phenomena occurred in other regiments.[5]

Northern and Southern armies confronted smallpox in essentially similar ways, although Confederate physicians apparently experienced worse vaccination misadventures that seemingly had no effect or were "spurious." Confederate doctors noted the coincident appearance of syphilis and erysipelas (bacterial infection producing red, raised sores on skin surfaces) with sufficient prevalence to justify heightened scrutiny of vaccination practices. The prevalence of spurious outcomes led the Confederate surgeon general to issue special orders demanding adherence to a strict vaccination protocol.

Material Culture and Vaccination

Material culture studies span the interdisciplinary spectrum. What these studies have in common is an examination of things and the materials things are made of to discover "the beliefs—the values, ideas, attitudes, and assumptions—of a particular community or society at a given time." The locus of study is the artifact, the human-designed, -built, -modified, or -adapted thing, and the thing's progress through time and space as cultural evidence. Borrowing from anthropology, material culture studies assume that the things we make and use can be interrogated as informants. As such, artifacts can be read as texts. They tell us about the extraction of raw materials to make the thing, its design, its manufacture or assembly by artisans (if not the user), and its user or consumer.[6]

I argue that lymph and crusts are artifacts. Natural or biological materials are artifacts if modified or used by people. Material culture scholars have included natural or biological materials to illuminate historical questions. For example, the DNA of American *Phlox* was sequenced in order to identify species planted by eighteenth-century naturalist John Bartram, and similar analysis determined the contents of "seed boxes" created by Bartram and sent to Europe from America.[7]

I argue, too that the artifact of vaccine matter expresses Wright's "mental constructs" of the culture that made and used it. Most instruments within the nineteenth-century doctor's bag cut, severed, or probed as specialized extensions of human hands. These tools attested to the surgeon's dexterity in removing diseased or damaged body parts to save lives and are thus metaphors for the doctor's learning and skill. Tools functioned as emblems of the doctor's prerogative to invade or destroy parts of the human body without fear of criminal transgression. Medical tools reflected the shared ideology between nineteenth-century doctors and patients about healing, violent manipulation of the body to maintain life, and confronting death. The Civil War doctor's vaccination kit was one such tool that embodies all of these meanings. The kit's key vaccination instrument was the lancet, with which the doctor pierced a diseased body's vesicle to obtain lymph. He then used the same tool to cut the skin of a healthy person to introduce lymph and induce infection. Lancets combined with specialized components, including a tin box for lymph or scabs and two glass plates between which lymph was spread into a film for temporary storage. The kit captured and harbored vaccine matter until the doctor manipulated it before placing it within another body.[8]

Civil War doctors applied therapies that, like artifacts, reflected beliefs and values, thus creating a cognitive framework. Within this framework, vaccination was a cultural ritual of disease prevention that affirmed the authority and experience of the doctor. It assured the patient that a cycle of manageable symptoms had commenced that would lead to immunity from smallpox. The insertion of vaccine matter into a physician-made cut required a shared understanding between doctor and patient that the therapy would work. To both the patient and a knowledgeable and skilled doctor, lymph and scabs were lifesaving materials. Knowing when and how to vaccinate and how to evaluate its result depended on the doctor's observations of the amount, density, opacity, color, and odor of lymph and similar observations about scabs.[9]

Doctors judged the value of vaccine matter according to the visible changes it caused in the body. Civil War doctors obtained lymph or crusts from medical purveyors in the formal army medicine supply system or directly from senior medical authorities or harvested them from afflicted soldiers or nearby civilians. How doctors harvested vaccine matter affected the probability of a successful vaccination. Just as artisans make choices in selecting materials out of which to create artifacts, doctors accepted or rejected vaccine matter based on color, shape, odor, length of time since it was obtained from donor bodies, and how it was stored before use.[10]

Confederate doctors expected vaccine matter to function as *materia medica*, the collective term for remedies derived from plants, animals, or minerals. According to professor of materia medica Joseph Carson, to prescribe drugs, doctors had to know their "*sources* or *localities of production, their natural history*, the *modes of collecting and preparing them*, for the market, and their *sensible properties*." Once a drug was applied, the doctor monitored its physical, chemical, and "vital" effects as the medicine performed its work "by nervous communication." Doctors monitored a drug's effectiveness, which varied according to the patient's life circumstances, attitude or temperament, age, and sex and also to the climate. For soldiers, doctors commonly cited fatigue and diet as militating against successful vaccination.[11]

Vaccination happened within a social and material context. This context considers the relationships between doctors and other medical professionals (such as stewards or assistants), purveyors of medicine, soldiers, government officials, and civilian citizens in the creation and use of vaccine matter. Embedded within this story are questions about knowledge creation: Did military doctors share common perceptions about the nature of smallpox contagion and the effectiveness of vaccination? Did they share criteria for selecting and applying vaccine material? How did they evaluate the success or appraise the failure of vaccination? Did patients independently question the source of vaccine material and negotiate the process with doctors? Under what conditions did patients prefer to self-vaccinate and avoid physicians? What does vaccination tell us about the human body and the material world? Examining the spurious vaccination cases in the Confederacy affords some answers.[12]

Understanding Smallpox

For over two millennia, smallpox, the "exemplar of contagiousness," was the most contagious disease with the highest mortality (up to 40 percent) in history until its official eradication by 1980. Its introduction by Europeans to North America possibly reduced native populations by upwards of 90 percent. Most doctors were aware that variolation—the process of introducing lymph or scabs from smallpox-infected persons directly into healthy persons—conferred immunity following a comparatively mild illness. At the end of the eighteenth century, Edward Jenner (who had been variolated as a child) in England noticed that milkmaids contracted cowpox while milking infected cows. The maids developed and survived mild smallpox-like symptoms and upon recovery seemed to achieve immunity from smallpox infection. Jenner discovered that vaccinating healthy persons with cowpox conferred smallpox immunity. His insights represented state-of-the-art understanding at the outset of the Civil War, although few public vaccination programs existed. Smallpox remained endemic in most urban areas, not only in American cities but in many places worldwide.[13]

If vaccine matter is an artifact, then acute observation of the progress of phenomena (see Table 1) was essential to determining vaccination's efficacy. In order to know how and when to vaccinate, the doctor had to understand how the patient experienced disease, how the sequence of symptoms in smallpox and vaccinia progressed, and how medicines worked. Vaccine matter therefore was an artifact that represented knowledge about the behavior of a virus, the environment, and the patient's physiology. By and large, Civil War physicians identified diseases by symptoms that converge with those identified today. *Infection* denoted the presence of disease, however acquired. *Virus* denoted the presence of a specific disease, however it was contracted. *Vaccination* usually meant the insertion of vaccinia or cowpox (also known as kine-pox) lymph or scabs, whereas *inoculation* involved the insertion of smallpox matter from human or bovine hosts.[14]

Consistent with a complex scheme of environmental and physiological contributors to disease, smallpox could be contracted by inhaling "effluvia" exhaled by diseased persons or by inoculation with smallpox matter. No two people experienced disease in precisely the same way because of environmental, cultural, and physiological variables. Diet, the general atmosphere, fitness, sleep or lack of it, mental state, "moral condition," family (heredity), and vocation determined susceptibility to disease and its progress. When diseases first appeared, they produced common symptoms such as fevers, aches and pains, or general malaise. Precise diagnosis might not have been possible until specific symptoms had well advanced. To those who observed this eruptive skin disease in the 1860s, smallpox resulted in a truly frightful bodily transformation.[15]

The smallpox and vaccinia cycle represented a temporary partnership of the doctor and sick soldier as the former observed and tried to palliate symptoms, later removing vaccine matter for use in a healthy body. Smallpox first manifested itself as fever, followed by eruptions progressing from pimple to vesicle. Vesicles had characteristic sizes and appearances and contained lymph. Vesicles changed into pustules, around which an areola formed, and its color, shape, and size were noted in relation to the timing of the withdrawal of lymph. As pustules appeared, they assumed a distinctive hardness, opacity, and change in size. Lymph became clear, then turned opaque and milky, and later disappeared. Finally, pustules became scabs that eventually fell off and left pits or scars. Smallpox had two varieties, distinct and confluent. Distinct referred to a constellation of isolated pustules, whereas the more severe form, confluent, involved the coalescence of the

TABLE 1. THE COURSE OF SMALLPOX

Stage	Day	Distinct	Confluent
1 (Eruptive)	1–3	Skin hot, accelerated pulse, thirst, nausea, vomiting, headache, joint pain, weakness	Fever more violent Pains more severe
	3	Bright red spots appear on face, chest, neck	Convulsions delirium, stupor frequent
	4–5	Fever abates, pulse normal, pimples become pocks	
2 (Maturation)	3–4	Full eruption of pocks, including arms, extremities Pocks become vesicles; areola appears Vesicles hard to the touch, areola inflamed	Eruptions preceded by "roseolous" excrescence on face, trunk
	5–6	Vesicles become pustules Lymph turns opaque, purulent; pustules are convex, distended	
	8+	Pustules mature, secondary fever	Entire face becomes "a mask" of eruptions; fetor; blindness a risk
	11+	Small, round, white spots appear (no pus or lymph) Sore throat, swelling, salivation, burning, sensation on skin, body odor	Boils and/or sores appear Death possible
3 (Decline)	11+	Pustules become brown/dry, may break, liquid oozes, yellow-brown crust (scab) forms, pustules desiccate and become dry scabs, swelling subsides	"Disorganizing" inflammations appear
	14–21	Crusts fall off, blotches of red/brown remain, pits and scars develop, appetite returns	

Sources: Wood, *Treatise on the Practice of Medicine*, 1:387–418; Beach, *American Practice of Medicine*, 1:455–64.

Note: At the onset of infection, precise identification of the disease is uncertain. Initial symptoms could be smallpox, erysipelas, scarlet fever, or measles. Similarly, varioloid, or modified smallpox, may be difficult to distinguish.

pustules into large patches of sores and higher mortality. Doctors scrutinized the progress from pimples to vesicles to pustules and crusts to verify that the smallpox was genuine. Doctors knew when to intervene with therapies at precise moments. They had to know when to capture lymph or crusts to ensure their viability for vaccination.[16]

Physicians distinguished smallpox from similar diseases by observing the frequency, duration, and intensity of symptoms. Varioloid or modified smallpox, for example, could be discerned in a previously vaccinated person by the relatively brief cycle of skin eruptions and the lack of odor. Vaccinia, synonymous with cowpox, was communicated through atmospheric effluvia but also through vaccination. It presented milder symptoms than smallpox, for which the three stages of the disease shown in Table 1 lasted shorter periods. Symptoms were not always predictable, however, and vaccination did not always prevent smallpox. It might, however, modify the disease by making it survivable in milder form.[17]

Confederate Vaccination Experience

The earliest significant smallpox outbreak among Confederate soldiers occurred after Antietam in 1862. A second epidemic occurred in Richmond, Virginia, and within Robert E. Lee's Army of Northern Virginia during the fall of 1863. During the same year, smallpox began to spread throughout the Mississippi Valley, and by 1864 every Confederate division had cases. Northern and Southern doctors agreed that the Confederacy experienced the more severe smallpox challenge. Statistics on the mortality of Confederate soldiers are rough estimates. Confederate surgeon Joseph Jones noted that mortality among infected soldiers ranged from 1 in 5 or 6 to 1 in 14, depending on how people contracted the disease. By comparison, among Northern troops, smallpox afflicted 5.5 soldiers per 1,000, resulting in about 2 deaths per 1,000. Following the Antietam campaign, smallpox produced a case fatality rate of 28.5 percent.[18]

Among a core group of Confederate doctors who analyzed smallpox cases and vaccination problems, Jones, after the war, when a professor of physiology and pathology at the University of Nashville, compiled a key study of spurious cases to replace one lost during the war. He had received an undergraduate degree from Princeton and later a medical doctor degree from the University of Pennsylvania. Well connected in the medical profession, Jones, unusually, served in a research capacity during the war rather than as a regimental doctor, with a mandate to study diseases, their etiology, and hospital care throughout the South. He occupied an ideal position from which to study the Confederate experience with smallpox. He had an ally and patron in Confederate surgeon general Samuel Preston Moore, who expected surgeons to create knowledge and therefore established a professional society, the Association of Army and Navy Surgeons of the Confederate States. He also founded the *Confederate States Medical and Surgical Journal*, which, during its brief run, encouraged scientific inquiry among Confederate States Army doctors. Moore supported Jones's research and encouraged other doctors to emulate his example. By the end of the war, apart from Moore, Jones probably knew more about the Confederate medical service than any other doctor.[19]

Like the North, the South selected physicians with a common ideology of medical practice. Over time, both sides developed testing and screening criteria for applicants. Implicit to the selection of doctors was a desire to employ allopathic or "regular" physicians (those who prescribed medicines that produced symptoms opposite to those produced by the disease), as opposed to homeopaths, Thomsonians, or eclectics. Since Confederate regulars trained at the same institutions and participated in a common discourse about health, they shared a consensus about why vaccination was necessary and how to accomplish it. Their discourse about vaccination, exercised through practice, created a system of knowledge production.[20]

Although the Confederate army required vaccination of all recruits, it was not always accomplished or reliably performed. Many men coming into the army had not been vaccinated, although by 1860 vaccination was available through most private physicians. Urban recruits were more likely to have been vaccinated than rural ones. Inadequate vaccine supply hampered this policy. Although the supply system did not require doctors to independently evaluate the source of vaccine they obtained, they came to do so when vaccinations went awry. Given the responsibility of physicians to evaluate a drug's effect on bodies of soldiers of disparate backgrounds, habits, and constitutions, it is no surprise that they occasionally rejected vaccine matter provided by medical purveyors and instead found sources that they themselves could monitor and control. Eventually, Surgeon General Moore stepped in to regulate vaccination practices and provide vaccine matter directly from his office.[21]

Vaccine matter did not appear on the standard drug supply list for the Confederacy. In fact, the Confederacy lacked large-scale drug manufacturing facilities, so its ability to supply vaccine was limited. Surgeons requisitioned drugs from the approved supply list from medical purveyors, doctors who were assigned control over regional drug depots. Purveyors obtained medicines by purchasing wholesale supplies on the commercial market, but the Northern blockade made regular and reliable imports impossible. Advertisements for vaccine matter appeared in trade periodicals and highlighted the features important to purveyors: the quality of the vaccine matter, standard doses, and methods of administering them.

For example, the January 1862 issue of the New York *American Druggists' Circular and Chemical Gazette* carried two advertisements for vaccine. One offered "virus of all kinds, perfectly pure, and most reliable, used by the leading physicians of this city; put up in the best form for transmission to any part of the world." The vendor, Eastern Dispensary on Grand Street, New York City, sold vaccine matter as single crusts, lymph in single tubes, a three-tube package, or a "single charge of eighth day lymph on pointed quills." Commercially obtained lymph frequently came in the form of goosequill points or small, conical pieces of carved bone impregnated with it. The surgeon placed the bone or quill point into a small incision to introduce the virus into a body. [22]

Graphs 1-A through 1-C depict the material vaccination sequence as experienced in the Confederate army. The figures outline all key stages of vaccination, whether administered by doctors or by soldiers themselves, and address spurious outcomes. The sequence was simplified if cowpox spontaneously appeared among healthy cows, just as smallpox may have spontaneously appeared among soldiers. Spontaneity did not yield a dependable supply of vaccine, however, so doctors deliberately infected both humans and cows (the latter with humanized vaccine virus) from which to harvest vaccine matter. From the moment of infection, doctors observed, monitored, and recorded bodily changes. In this process, doctors applied Edward Jenner's precepts. In his research, Jenner used minute quantities of vaccine matter as both experiment and therapy to achieve dramatic results.[23]

Once the doctor vaccinated his patient, he began a multiweek sequence of observing and recording phenomena, ameliorating or restricting symptoms through medication, and probing and inspecting lymph and scabs. The doctor effectively shaped vaccine matter as an artifact just as a farmer sows seeds, grows crops, attends to their health, harvests them, and modifies his practice to achieve improved crops in the future.

Following vaccination, the surgeon awaited the crop of reddish pimples on the body. For the first few days of vaccinia, soldiers experienced generalized symptoms common to a variety of illnesses, including general malaise, fever, nausea, and pain (see Table 1). Once the pimples became pocks (a term applied to enlarged pimples) and vesicles, the doctor knew that vaccinia infection had occurred and applied remedies to ameliorate the symptoms. He inspected the soldier's body frequently to note odor, color, shape, and texture of skin eruptions and how these characteristics changed day to day. At the puncture site, the skin showed "an elevated edge and depressed centre" (a pock) by days three or four, changing into a vesicle. By day eight, "its day of greatest perfection, [the vesicle] is circular and pearl-colored: its margin is turgid, firm, shining, and wheel-shaped." Later, an areola formed and surrounded the vesicle, its evolution, color, and shape acutely observed. In a few more days, the vesicle acquired hardness as it turned into a pustule and the areola eventually disappeared. Before these symptoms appeared, lymph ("perfectly pure and limpid") was drawn for vaccination. Surgeons learned never to draw lymph from a vesicle with the areola present. Critically, physicians remained alert to the presence of other cutaneous diseases that could alter the vaccinia sequelae (pathological conditions resulting from infection) and retard immunization.[24]

While the lymph was at its "greatest perfection," the doctor pierced the vesicle with a lancet, taking care not to poke too deeply and cause blood to flow into the lymph. Against the cut, he held a tiny glass tube to capture the lymph. The doctor may have had to pierce multiple vesicles to obtain sufficient lymph to fill one tube, which he then sealed with a candle flame. Other methods included emptying lymph onto a glass plate, whereupon the physician sandwiched lymph under another glass plate and sealed both with wax, the lymph assuming a filmlike consistency. Confederate surgeon Josiah C. Nott cautioned, however, that dipping a lancet into the lymph mixture, then into an arm, and into the mixture again necessarily introduced blood, which might convey other diseases.[25]

Once the physician collected lymph, he and the patient were not done. By days eleven to fifteen, lymph in the body desiccated and the pustule became "a hard round scab of a reddish-brown color." Eventually the scab fell off, leaving a cicatrix (scar). Commonly, physicians stored scabs until needed and believed them to sustain a much longer shelf life than lymph, although they disagreed about appropriate storage protocols and longevity. Some recommended pulverizing scabs and mixing with glycerin before storing the mixture in a small tube. Jones cautioned danger in mixing powdered scabs and water because warm weather might putrefy the vaccine matter into a poison. Mixing the powdered scabs and water also risked inadvertently introducing "pus, blood, lymph and cellular tissue" that communicated new diseases, especially syphilis. Jones cited a method of preserving entire scabs in wax until needed, but fresh lymph was always preferred.[26]

Vaccinia and smallpox may have required a more intimate relationship with the soldier's body than other diseases owing to the long list of contingent symptoms and their evolution. Doctors vaccinated soldiers with lancets or points or quills and monitored the patients' pulse, respiration, uri-

GRAPH 1-A. THE SMALLPOX VACCINATION PROCESS, PART 1

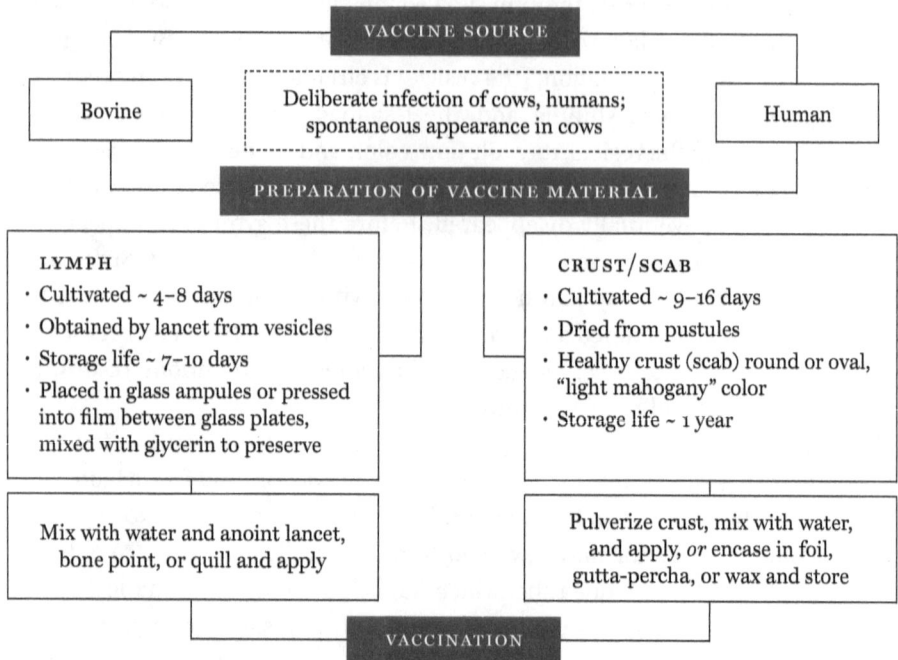

GRAPH 1-B. THE SMALLPOX VACCINATION PROCESS, PART 2

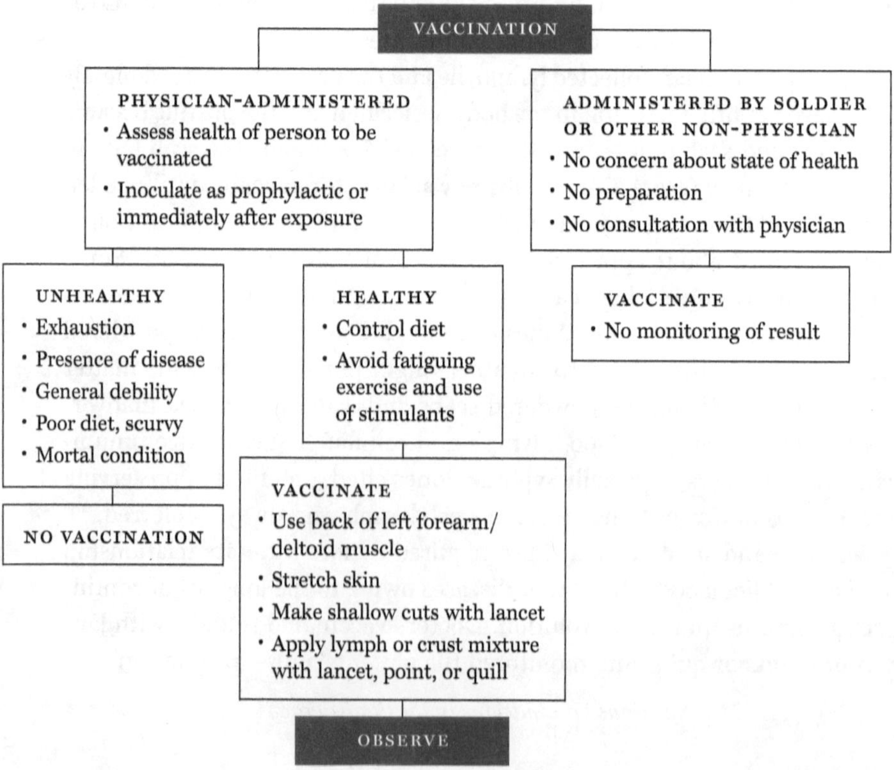

GRAPH 1-C. THE SMALLPOX VACCINATION PROCESS, PART 3

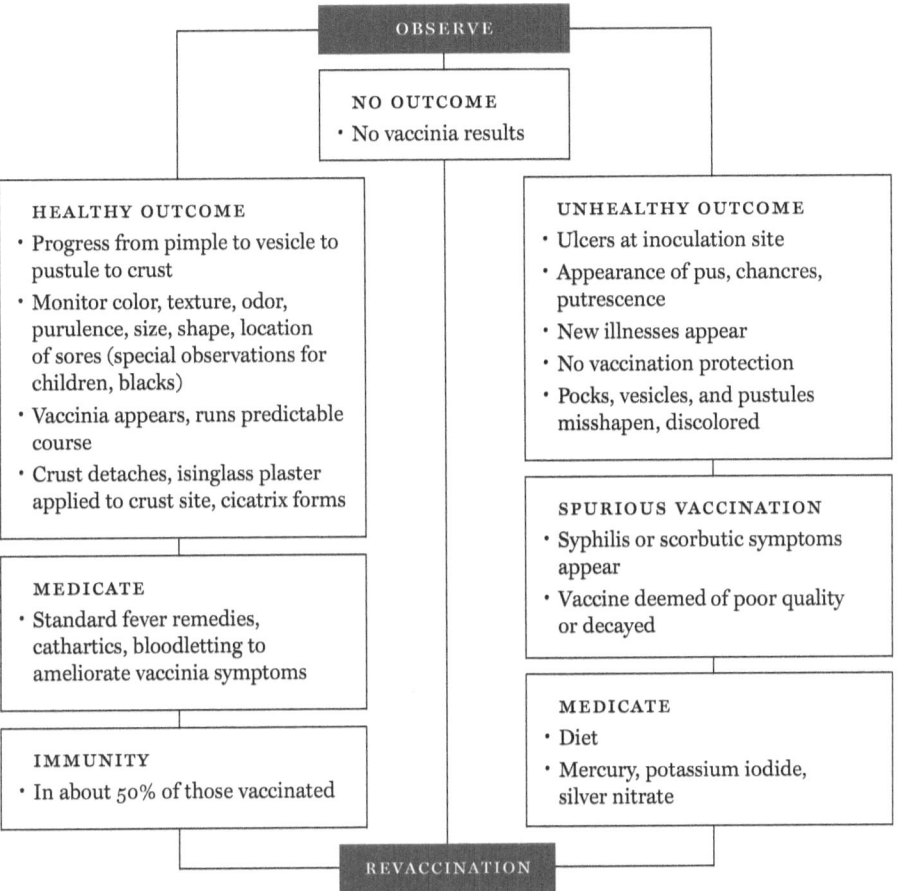

Sources: Jones, *Researches upon "Spurious Vaccination"*; Wood, *Treatise on the Practice of Medicine*, 1:387–418.

Figure 7. Vaccination kit manufactured by J. H. Gemrig, a major supplier of medical instruments to the U.S. Army during the Civil War. The components of this kit provided the tools to collect vaccinia scabs and lymph and to vaccinate using the two lancets that flank the kit. The lancets stored under the loop of the upper and inner flap of the case; the two identical glass plates, used for depositing lymph and mixing a lymph- or scab-water mixture, are shown above the leather case, removed from the rectangular recess that includes the manufacturer's label; and to the right of the recess is a tin box with sliding cover (which pops out of the case with a tug of the ribbon, partially shown) for storing scab material. (Courtesy of the Mütter Museum of the College of Physicians of Philadelphia)

nation, and defecation. Introducing vaccine matter into the body meant managing the whole body for weeks, assessing health according to vital signs and waste, and administering therapies to ease discomfort. Doctors employed many therapies during the course of the disease. They might encourage or limit bleeding, urination, or salivation in order to help the body achieve equilibrium. They ordered soldiers to rest, avoid strenuous exercise, and observe dietary restrictions. In short, doctors absorbed vaccination's unique process within the ideology of materia medica, thus expanding their discourse about disease etiology. Doctors came to realize that they needed to vaccinate *everyone* prophylactically. Further, experience with vaccination affirmed for Confederate doctors what European armies had discovered, that soldiers who thought themselves protected from smallpox may never have been properly vaccinated, if at all. Revaccination had not been advocated until the war showed both armies it was necessary.[27]

Children, Cows, and Race

The preferred Confederate source for vaccine matter was healthy white and black plantation children. Isolated from urban areas, children were presumed to be uninfected by diseases common to adults, particularly syphilis. Jones maintained that other diseases could be avoided "by adhering rigidly to the rule of using lymph from the arms of healthy children and infants." Surgeon S. F. Stout, Army of Tennessee, obtained vaccine matter from healthy children who had not been previously vaccinated and distributed it to regional hospitals with the assistance of Surgeon General Moore. Surgeon S. P. Crawford, who supervised a hospital in Tennessee, maintained access to healthy children and vaccinated one every few months to ensure a constant supply of vaccine matter. In Richmond, Surgeon-in-Charge S. E. Habersham, Chimborazo Hospital, found the supply of vaccine prone to give abnormal results, so he arranged to propagate vaccinia among local healthy infants. What the children's parents thought of this procedure was not recorded. No protocols existed regarding vaccinating or harvesting lymph or scabs from children.[28]

Confederate doctors used cows not only as a source of cowpox matter but also to harvest human virus through bovine vaccination. The use of cows to obtain vaccine matter for human use was not straightforward because some humanized viruses would not cycle through cows. Surgeon Frank A. Ramsey found cowpox more distinguishable from smallpox than Jenner's observations would allow. Surgeon General Moore ordered the procurement of bovine vaccine, but experiments in inoculating cows in and near the teats and nose did not yield crusts, "the much sought treasure." It may have been possible that many doctors, frustrated with unreliable vaccine material procured through military channels, made arrangements with local farmers to vaccinate cows to harvest vaccine matter under their own supervision. The Confederacy, however, pronounced its trials with cows a failure. One reason was that vaccine matter circulated through cows soon degenerated quickly into poison. Jones documented experiments with cows to create cowpox but described them as inconclusive, given the abrupt ending of the war.[29]

The Confederacy's need for pure vaccine superseded racial boundaries. Before the war, for instance, the catalog of medical tools published by Philadelphia firm Bullock and Crenshaw in 1853 promised vaccine matter cultivated from "healthy *white* children." In the absence of wartime exigency, white people doubtless preferred their vaccine matter from white bodies. But the Confederacy could not afford to discriminate, and many Confederate soldiers might have been surprised to discover that their bodies had been infected with vaccine matter from African Americans. Some military doctors attended to pox-infected white and black people equally, while others ascribed outbreaks of smallpox among black people as "a natural outcome" of the North's proclaimed emancipation. Further, newly freed people, like soldiers, vaccinated themselves or resorted to unusual therapies, such as coating their bodies with tar to ward off the illness. Disease in black populations presented a potential to destabilize military strategy because they posed an infection risk to the Confederate armies on the move.[30]

Spurious Vaccination

Mass immunization throughout the South as a war measure afforded protection to many Confederate soldiers but also challenged military doctors with mobile armies, black people migrating, and urban white populations deprived of food and medicines. In 1862, Surgeon General Moore ordered the vaccination of all soldiers, and Chimborazo Hospital was designated the receiving hospital for soldiers suffering from "a peculiar eruptive disease, supposed to be the consequence of vaccination." The ward population grew rapidly. Surgeon Ramsey, while medical director in Knoxville, reported on vaccination sequelae consequent to the use of impure vaccine matter, symptoms that led him to employ a civilian doctor to cultivate the virus among the city's healthy children. Surgeon S. M. Bemiss, Army of Northern Virginia, observed a particularly acute outbreak of abnormal vaccinations among soldiers of the Twelfth and Sixteenth Georgia Infantry Regiments. The problem was so severe that the army's medical director appointed an investigative committee to examine spurious cases. Bemiss found in these regiments over 100 soldiers with ulcers that extended beyond the vaccination site down the arms and throughout the rest of the body. All of the affected men had been vaccinated with lymph taken from the arm of a fellow soldier "of very dissolute habits, who had just returned from a leave of absence" with syphilis symptoms. Many examples of this kind occurred, particularly when soldiers were on furlough and therefore away from military control.[31]

Reports became common of anomalous vaccinations, particularly the coincident appearance of scurvy, syphilis, gangrene, and erysipelas. Even as doctors obtained vaccines and immunized soldiers and civilians, the Confederate army suffered personnel shortfalls. At the battle of Chancellorsville in May 1863, 5,000 soldiers were unavailable for duty because of vaccination-related abnormalities such as ulcerated vaccination sites. Dependable vaccine was in short supply. At Chimborazo Hospital in June and July 1864, 307 vaccinations were administered. Of these, only 134 "took." By February 1864, the increasing number of reports about anomalous vaccinations led Moore to order that one doctor be assigned in every city to vaccinate, gratis, all healthy black and white children who had not been vaccinated previously. The Confederacy, then, was forced to assert control over citizens' bodies in order to manage the integrity of bodily substances. Moore's order, an unusual military intrusion into civil life, served not only to limit the spread of smallpox but also to control the production of pure vaccine matter.[32]

Worse, Confederate soldiers violated the value of doctors' prerogative to manipulate vaccine matter: they vaccinated themselves. Not concerned with the cycle of smallpox or vaccinia, soldiers took lymph from sick comrades directly and applied it by knifepoint to their own arms or the arms of other soldiers. For these troops, success meant that the bigger the resulting sore, the better. Compounding the problem for doctors, when syphilis was present in tandem with vaccinia symptoms, the usual therapies for syphilis did not seem to work. Hospitals began to introduce more vaccination controls, such as providing every released soldier with a ticket detailing when he was vaccinated, where, and the source of vaccine administered (lymph or scab). Upon returning to his regiment, the regimental surgeon inspected the ticket and determined if the soldier could return to duty.[33]

Vaccination problems caused doctors to reassess their own methods through the criterion of *value*: the value placed on lymph or crust, the value of the doctor's observations of the disease's progression through a cycle, and the value placed on the color, size, shape, texture, and odor of skin eruptions. Assessing the value of vaccination in relation to spurious cases raised questions. Did the prevalence of these cases question surgeons' value as healers? Did experience with both genuine and spurious vaccination cases constitute valued knowledge that encouraged doctors to challenge or interfere with the medical supply system or the tactical orders of a military leader?[34]

In their investigation into the reasons why vaccinations become spurious, Confederate doctors were forced to question their assumptions and revisit the principles of vaccination established by Edward Jenner over half a century earlier. As doctors manipulated vaccine matter—in obtaining, storing, and applying it—they created epistemology about how vaccination worked and why in some cases it did not work. Vaccinations that did not take, seemed to cause other diseases, or appeared in tandem with other diseases forced introspection about every phase of the vaccination process (see graphs 1-A, 1-B, and 1-C). Could the lancet that introduced vaccine matter into a soldier's arm be tainted with some other matter? Was the human or bovine source of vaccine healthy and reliable? Was lymph or crust obtained at the right stage of disease symptoms? Did it have the right color, consistency, odor, and texture? What are the best practices for the storage of crusts or lymph? What other environmental or physiological variables might have rendered the vaccination process ineffective or dangerous?[35]

To create conformity in vaccination methods and to minimize the variable handling of sick and healthy bodies (and thus create a platform for generating new knowledge), Surgeon General Moore issued two circulars, in July and October 1863, that outlined standard procedures. The October circular repeated the earlier one but with a preface that faulted doctors for "the pernicious results which have followed the careless employment of impure virus in vaccinating the army." If doctors had propagated the virus in healthy infants, all other problems would have been avoided. The preface reminded doctors that all recruits were to have been vaccinated before reporting for duty.[36]

Artifacts that are biological materials do not necessarily remain under the doctor's control. In the spurious cases, they can be unpredictable or parasitic. To assert control, the Confederacy regulated every phase of vaccination. To designate a lancet for the exclusive purpose of vaccination, doctors were required to break the point off. They were to place a scab between two glass plates, add water, and grind the mixture to the consistency of mucilage. Thus prepared, with his right hand the doctor dipped the broken lancet into the mixture. With the left hand, he took the patient's arm, spread the skin between the fingers over the deltoid muscle, pricked the skin lightly, and then released the skin so that the incision closed. To harvest lymph, the doctor pierced the vesicle at its edge with a conical bone point or quill tip when the vesicle displayed lymph of a "pearly lustre," before the areola appeared. After allowing the lymph to dry, the doctor repeated the process multiple times to anoint the small tool. The quill was split into strips, each wrapped and stored for up to ten days.

The circulars outlined what the physician must do to avoid a spurious outcome. The material requirements were exacting. They effectively instructed how to *guide* the evolution of vaccinia symptoms in the human body, not just how to passively observe them. If an umbilicated vesicle (that is, a small depression atop a pustule or vesicle) showed lymph of "pearly lustre" and after the eighth day "a narrow bright red areola" appeared, then the vaccinia was genuine (the circular even provided a mnemonic for this, "the pearl upon the rose"). Any other result indicated that the vaccination was spurious. If the doctor could not wait for the scab to drop naturally after a few weeks, he covered it with an isinglass plaster before forcing its removal with a lancet. The scab must "be circular or oval, of a light mahogany color, umbilicated, translucent, and when dry, having a resinous fracture." Moore's procedures, therefore, reestablished value and integrity in vaccine matter if doctors—not soldiers themselves—harvested it according to a specific protocol that privileged the value of doctors' training and experience.[37]

Moore's orders applied to vaccinating not only soldiers but civilians as well, thus asserting control over the future of *all* bodies. Moore exercised authority over black bodies by instructing how to assess healthy scabs on them; their scabs should be walnut to black in color, which might vary for mulattos. For this broad exercise of control, doctors were expected to distribute vaccine matter as necessary throughout a national network, even sending it by post. Moore thus required that scabs be encased within guttapercha (a substance derived from latex from Malaysian trees of the sapodilla family, bearing similarities to rubber) capsules for safety. Moore asserted authority over future public health by requiring that soldiers be revaccinated in ten years, and in case of a smallpox outbreak, everyone within the locality must be revaccinated.[38]

Moore's policies transformed the cultural meaning of vaccine matter by creating a new social context for vaccination. By assuming a public health stance beyond military necessity, he reached deep into future civil life. His orders implicitly elevated the status of doctors and extended their control. Tackling spurious cases not only demanded acute observational skills of doctors but also required them to guide the course of disease in human bodies and extract from them substances of dependable value. In assuming this authority, Moore sidestepped routine requisitions protocol, imported lymph from Europe, and dispensed it through his office. He assigned surgeon James Bolton and others to visit plantations to cultivate the virus among healthy children, a system that apparently worked. Yet despite Moore's orders, the wartime upheaval of the South militated against routinized vaccination procedures. Not all doctors observed mandated protocols; many took risks. The insufficient supply of reliable vaccine dogged the best efforts of the Confederacy to maintain an army free of smallpox.[39]

The war ended before Moore could create a summary report on the Confederacy's vaccination experience. Immediately after the war, Joseph Jones solicited observations on spurious vaccination from former Southern surgeons and published his report *Researches upon "Spurious Vaccination."* In it, Jones agreed with Moore that vaccination misadventures were due to "ignorance, and inattention." The report reviewed and affirmed Jenner's precepts, quoted from the experience of foreign doctors, and provided abundant information from former Confederate doctors about their experiences. Jones concluded that spurious vaccinations derived from several circumstances. First, harvesting vaccine matter from soldiers worn from fatigue and the rigors of the campaign with a concomitant poor (possibly scorbutic) diet might not result in vaccinia at all. *Anyone* who may have been exposed to smallpox, including hospital patients, should not be used as a source for new vaccine. Second, harvesting vaccine matter from irregular pustules or ulcers from persons previously vaccinated and who manifested other cutaneous diseases at the time of vaccination led to "injurious effects." Third, the use of decomposed vaccine matter or matter taken from persons with erysipelas or syphilis led to injury, especially in persons "in a depressed state." Fourth, mixing vaccinia and smallpox matter for a vaccine risked the onset of "Small Pox of its worst character." These findings informed postwar vaccination procedures.[40]

Conclusion

If vaccine matter is an artifact through which we glimpse Rita Wright's "underlying mental constructs," the Confederate experience with vaccination, particularly the spurious cases, reveals a challenge to the authority and knowledge of surgeons and their consequent assertion of control. This assertion of control over both military and nonmilitary human bodies extended even to future public health crises. Confederate doctors anchored their knowledge in the original precepts of Edward Jenner but accentuated his insistence that doctors must acquire a "peculiar knowledge" of vaccination. Surgeon Josiah C. Nott agreed that only "educated physicians" should handle vaccine matter; they were expected to observe, monitor, and record the material cycle of vaccination and investigate anomalies. Indeed, after the war, Confederate surgeons applied Jenner's "peculiar knowledge" to defend themselves from war crimes allegations. Confederate surgeons at the Andersonville prison were accused of the deliberate use of tainted vaccine on Union prisoners. Because Jones had investigated prisoners' health at Andersonville, his testimony was compelled in the trial of Andersonville's commandant, Henry Wirz, accused of "pursuing his wicked purpose" of deliberately poisoning prisoners with impure vaccine matter, an accusation Jones did not support.[41]

Jenner's "peculiar knowledge" deepened surgeons' relationship with human bodies. Doctors began to guide people through a course of vaccinia, not merely observe. They commandeered civilian children whose bodies they deliberately infected in order to create vaccine. They stepped beyond their military role to manage public fear and ignorance and recommend public health policy, thus asserting control over *everyone's* bodies. As "universal signifiers," bodies provided disease histories. They made knowledge possible. When bodies experienced spurious vaccination results, they threatened the value of doctors' knowledge. Diseased bodies represented disorganization and lack of control, thus diminishing doctors' social standing and authority.[42]

Surgeons could not practically control all Confederate citizens' bodies for vaccination, much less the diaspora of black Southerners, which made the public health policy challenge acute. Nott, in analyzing the end-of-war smallpox epidemic in Mobile, noted that "the negroes having been suddenly liberated, have ... congregated in towns ... freed from their accustomed restraint and fostering care of their former masters." Not only had many black people not been vaccinated in the first place, but the high mortality of smallpox-infected former slaves caused a panic, driving many whites and blacks who had been vaccinated to seek revaccination. Fleeing the *possibility* of smallpox contagion in the immediate postwar years apparently drove some of the dislocation and migration of the Reconstruction years. Some physicians considered smallpox epidemics a consequence of emancipation, even suggesting that smallpox would extinguish the "Negro race."[43]

Jones and Nott both viewed blacks as subordinate humans, and before the war Nott had acquired a reputation in scientific circles for his polygenist views, expressed in books that posited separate evolution of the world's races. Nott and Jones viewed disease susceptibility in racist terms, but owing to their separate evolution, Nott maintained, blacks were more prone to smallpox contagion and other diseases of "morbid poisons." Both ideologues of white supremacy, Jones and Nott stopped short of theorizing about vaccines borne of black bodies and their influence on white bodies, save to maintain that public health could be best served by controlling the movement and behavior of black people. Control over diseased black bodies—and their diseased tissues—has continued to be a medical issue to the present day.[44]

The postwar epistolary review of spurious vaccination cases by Confederate surgeons may have contributed new material knowledge concerning the safest sources for vaccine matter and the safest methods for storing and administering vaccine. In fact, surgeons' work stimulated culture change, such as the postwar investigation of bovine sources for vaccine, which led to the cultivation of cowpox in Beaugency cattle (which had been successful in Europe). This allowed for scaled-up harvesting of vaccine, free of human scorbutic or syphilitic taint, and enabled the elimination of crusts as a source of vaccine. In short, doctors abandoned the use of humanized virus. By scaling up vaccine production among cows, physicians moved out of the military supply network and created "technology centers" where doctors' knowledge redefined vaccine matter into a commodity for industrial production (Beaugency herds).[45]

The peculiar knowledge surgeons acquired about vaccine matter stabilized practice and led to the establishment of scientific protocols and the introduction of novel methods for studying disease etiology. The empiricism they applied to understanding why vaccination went wrong presaged methods of analysis characteristic of later laboratory-based medicine, particularly microscopy and urinalysis. Surgeon Frank A. Ramsey employed a microscope to determine why a healthy private of the Fifth Virginia Cavalry, upon revaccination, developed a succession of cutaneous eruptions on the left arm and leg. Ramsey searched for microscopic parasites but found none. He found, however, "pus globules floating in a homogeneous fluid," an indication of syphilis. Surgeon J. C. M. Merillat, in Staunton, Virginia, applied urinalysis (using nitric acid added to urine) to distinguish smallpox from rubeola (measles).[46]

The protocols introduced by Surgeon General Moore effectively required Confederate doctors to apply, test, and evaluate vaccine matter and vaccination procedure as a scientific inquiry, that is, as a way to advance knowledge based on standard practices and controls. Did Confederate doctors therefore define a new meaning for the vaccination process, taken collectively, as a scientific instrument? Just as scientific instruments can, vaccination induced material phenomena that were studied and measured. These phenomena led to improved theoretical knowledge about how smallpox and related diseases manifested themselves, were communicated to new victims, and could be managed to a likely healthy outcome. Based on intuition, trial-and-error experimentation, and creation of the technical means to secure or store vaccine matter, Confederate doctors defined rules for the extraction, storage, and application of vaccine matter to ensure its freshness and integrity. By creating a pool of empirical data that led to theoretical elaboration of the value of vaccination and how contagion occurs, doctors created a scientific instrument for knowledge production.[47]

Looking at vaccination through the lens of material culture allows us to see vaccine matter refracted into many of Wright's "mental constructs." It was a repulsive but invaluable substance that was both disease itself and disease prevention. It possessed symbolic power in enlarging the authority of doctors, even to future control over all bodies. It was a fulcrum for galvanizing scientific discourse and investigation. Its value led to the involuntary manipulation of children's bodies in order to achieve a reliable purity. It challenged ideas about the very nature of contagious illnesses. Importantly, in material culture we see an "interconnectedness" between the human manipulation of vaccine matter, its guidance through diseased and healthy bodies, and the construction of "text-based knowledge" in the form of postwar summary monographs such as Jones's and *The Medical and Surgical History of the War of the Rebellion*, the U.S. government–published compendium of what physicians learned from war wounds, injuries, and diseases. The Confederate experience of the manipulation of bodily substances to prevent disease bears analysis as material culture. As material culture, this experience contributes to historical narrative. Jones, in creating his report, recognized the value of incorporating *all* available evidence—textbook authorities, case studies, and testimonies by surgeons of their own observations and experiences—to pronounce vaccination as "the greatest physical boon ever bestowed by a mortal upon the human race."[48]

Notes

I am grateful to Caitlin Angelone of the Historical Medical Library, College of Physicians of Philadelphia, for tracking sources; Kerry Bryan for additional research; Emily Snedden Yates, Mütter Museum, for constructing the graphs; George Wohlreich, MD, Karie Youngdahl, and Guy R. Hasegawa, PharmD, for their comments; Kathleen R. Sands for editorial assistance; and Joan Cashin for her astute editorial guidance.

1. James Bolton, "Spurious Vaccination in the Confederate Army," a paper read before the Richmond, Virginia, Academy of Medicine, 15 November 1866, and included as an appendix to Joseph Jones, *Researches upon "Spurious Vaccination," or the Abnormal Phenomena Accompanying and Following Vaccination in the Confederate Army during the Recent American Civil War, 1861–1865* (Nashville: University Medical Press, 1867). Quotation from Bolton, 139. Bolton regretted that the Confederate medical reports on vaccination "were destroyed by the fire which occurred in Richmond, Va., on the night of its evacuation by the Confederate troops, and that an elaborate paper on Spurious Vaccination, by the writer, was wantonly destroyed by Federal soldiers." Note that the vaccination and smallpox parlance of Confederate doctors is not that of twenty-first-century medicine.

2. Rita P. Wright, "Technological Styles: Transforming a Natural Object into a Cultural Object," in *History from Things: Essays on Material Culture*, ed. Steven Lubar and W. David Kingery (Washington, D.C.: Smithsonian Institution Press, 1993), 243.

3. Jules David Prown, "The Truth of Material Culture," in Lubar and Kingery, *History from Things*, 2. For a critique of the lack of a material culture dimension to Civil War scholarship, see Michael DeGruccio, "Letting the War Slip through Our Hands: Material Culture and the Weakness of Words in the Civil War Era," in *Weirding the War: Stories from the Civil War's Ragged Edges*, ed. Stephen Berry (Athens: University of Georgia Press, 2011), 15–35. See also Joan E. Cashin's study of the compulsion of contemporaries

to collect war relics, "Trophies of War: Material Culture in the Civil War Era," *Journal of the Civil War Era* 1, no. 3 (September 2011): 339–67.

4. Bolton, "Spurious Vaccination," 143.

5. Bolton, 150.

6. Prown, "Truth of Material Culture," 1; Thomas J. Schlereth, "Material Culture Studies in America, 1876–1976," in *Material Culture Studies in America*, ed. Thomas J. Schlereth (Nashville: AASLH, 1982), 3; Steven M. Beckow, "Culture, History, and Artifact," in Schlereth, *Material Culture Studies*, 117; E. McClung Fleming, "Artifact Study: A Proposed Model," in Schlereth, *Material Culture Studies*, 171.

7. See Mark Laird and Karen Bridgman, "American Roots: Techniques of Plant Transportation and Cultivation in the Early Atlantic World," 164–93, and Joel T. Fry, "Inside the Box: John Bartram and the Science and Commerce of the Transatlantic Plant Trade," 194–220, in *Ways of Making and Knowing: The Material Culture of Empirical Knowledge*, ed. Pamela H. Smith, Amy R. Meyers, and Harold J. Cook (Ann Arbor: University of Michigan Press, 2014).

8. Wright, "Technological Styles," 243; Prown, "Truth of Material Culture," 6, 11.

9. Wright, "Technological Styles," 245; Prown, "Truth of Material Culture," 2. To understand the cognitive scheme of the Civil War doctor, see Charles E. Rosenberg, "The Therapeutic Revolution: Medicine, Meaning, and Social Change in Nineteenth-Century America," *Perspectives in Biology and Medicine* 20, no. 4 (Summer 1977): 492–94.

10. Pamela H. Smith presents a case study of artisans whose workshops abided by distinct principles and practices informed by an empirical, systematic understanding of nature. See "Making as Knowing: Craft as Natural Philosophy," in Smith, Meyers, and Cook, *Ways of Making and Knowing*, 17–47.

11. Margaret Humphreys, *Marrow of Tragedy: The Health Crisis of the American Civil War* (Baltimore: Johns Hopkins University Press, 2013), 91–92; Joseph Carson, *Synopsis of the Course of Lectures on Materia Medica and Pharmacy, Delivered in the University of Pennsylvania: With Three Lectures on the Modus Operandi of Medicines*, 3rd ed. (Philadelphia: Blanchard and Lea, 1863), 18, 21–24 (italics in original).

12. Similarly, Alisha Rankin has studied how lay healers in early modern Germany were able to secure pharmacological therapies in competition with professional medical men, who responded by deemphasizing the same therapies and thus reserved their privileged knowledge and abilities. See "How to Cure the Golden Vein: Medical Remedies as *Wissenschaft* in Early Modern Germany," in Smith, Meyers, and Cook, *Ways of Making and Knowing*, 113–37.

13. Many histories of vaccination and smallpox exist, for instance, Michael B. A. Oldstone, *Viruses, Plagues, and History* (Oxford: Oxford University Press, 2000).

14. George B. Wood, *A Treatise on the Practice of Medicine* (Philadelphia: J. B. Lippincott, 1858), 1:387–94, 404–5; W. Beach, *The American Practice of Medicine, Revised, Enlarged, and Improved: Being a Practical Exposition of Pathology, Therapeutics, Surgery, Materia Medica, and Pharmacy, on Reformed Principles* (New York: Charles Scribner, 1855), 1:455; Joseph Jones, *Medical and Surgical Memoirs* (New Orleans: Clark and Hofeline, 1890), vol. 3, part 1, 293. Jones and Wood were allopathic physicians; Beach was an eclectic. Civil War era doctors believed that smallpox could be cycled through a cow, although twenty-first-century physicians disagree.

15. Beach, *American Practice*, 1:20, 458.

16. Wood, *Treatise*, 1:388–92; Beach, *American Practice*, 1:456–58.

17. Wood, *Treatise*, 1:394, 410.

18. Elisha Harris, "Vaccination in the Army," in *Contributions Relating to the Causation and Prevention of Disease*, ed. Austin Flint (New York: U.S. Sanitary Commission/Hurd and Houghton, 1867), 143; *The Medical and Surgical History of the War of the Rebellion* (Washington, D.C.: GPO), part 3, 1:625–28; Jones, *Researches*, 7.

19. Glenna R. Schroeder-Lein, *The Encyclopedia of Civil War Medicine* (Armonk, N.Y.: M. E. Sharpe, 2008), 173, 278–79; James O. Breeden, *Joseph Jones, M.D.: Scientist of the Old South* (Lexington: University of Kentucky Press, 1975), 129–43.

20. H. H. Cunningham, *Doctors in Gray: The Confederate Medical Service*, 2nd ed. (Baton Rouge: Louisiana State University Press, 1960), 21–23. Homeopaths understood disease symptoms to be evidence of the body's attempt to regain equilibrium of its "vital force" and accepted the principle that like cures like. In this approach, a medicine that produces given symptoms in a healthy person can be effective when used on a sick person with the same symptoms. Thomsonians, named for herbalist Samuel Thomson, eschewed allopathic and homeopathic remedies and promoted botanical medicines. Eclectics fused Native American herb-based and European traditions of healing. See discussion of medical training in Shauna Devine, *Learning from the Wounded: The Civil War and the Rise of American Medical Science* (Chapel Hill: University of North Carolina Press, 2014), 5–8.

21. Humphreys, *Marrow of Tragedy*, 92. Many Confederate surgeons recorded how they abandoned army-supplied vaccine matter and sought their own through cows or human infants. Surgeon James Bolton reported that attempts to import vaccine from England failed, and the Confederate surgeon general's office propagated its own among people living on plantations. See Bolton, "Spurious Vaccination," 141.

22. Michael A. Flannery, *Civil War Pharmacy: A History of Drugs, Drug Supply and Provision, and Therapeutics for the Union and Confederacy* (New York: Haworth Press, 2004), 174; Guy R. Hasegawa, "Pharmacy in the American Civil War," *American Journal of Health-System Pharmacists* 57 (March 2000): 482–84; Guy R. Hasegawa and F. Terry Hambrecht, "The Confederate Medical Laboratories," *Southern Medical Journal* 96, no. 12 (December 2013): 1221–30; *American Druggists' Circular and Chemical Gazette* 6, no. 1 (January 1862): 1.

23. Today, smallpox is defined as a variola virus of the genus *Orthopoxvirus*. Parallel to the disease's nineteenth-century cycle, smallpox in the twentieth century observes three phases. Following infection, the disease may incubate for up to two weeks. Symptoms next appear during the prodomal phase, characterized by fever, aches, and malaise for up to four days. The third phase, which varies in severity, features a rash involving lesions (the vesicles and pustules of nineteenth-century description) and the eventual scabbing and scarring when the scabs disappear. Infection most commonly occurs through the "inhalation of infectious respiratory droplets.... Some level of immunity" obtains. Andrea M. McCollum et al., "Poxvirus Viability and Signatures in Historical Relics," *Emerging Infectious Diseases* 20 (February 2014): 177. The circulation of humanized virus through a cow was likely unsuccessful.

24. Descriptions quoted from an 1859 report of the Medical Officer of the Privy Council, London, "Signs of Successful Vaccination and of Successful Revaccination," appended

to Report E, "Value of Vaccination in Armies," in U.S. Sanitary Commission, *Military Medical and Surgical Essays* (Washington, D.C., 1865), 27; "Method of Preserving Vaccine Lymph. By Dr. Husband, of Edinburgh," appended to U.S. Sanitary Commission, *Military Medical and Surgical Essays*, 30; and Jones, *Researches*, 41. Although the 1865 Sanitary Commission report served a need of the Union army, it included descriptions of vaccination techniques that were published before the war in journals known to Confederate doctors.

25. "Method of Preserving Vaccine Lymph," 28–32; J. C. Nott, "Small-pox Epidemic in Mobile during the Winter of 1865–6," appendix to Jones, *Researches*, 159.

26. "Signs of Successful Vaccination and of Successful Revaccination," 27; "New Mode of Preserving Vaccine Virus. By Dr. Collins," appended to U.S. Sanitary Commission, *Military Medical and Surgical Essays*, 31; Jones, *Researches*, 59, 62; Nott, "Small-pox Epidemic in Mobile," 159. Reginald Horsman's biography, *Josiah Nott of Mobile: Southerner, Physician, and Racial Theorist* (Baton Rouge: Louisiana State University Press, 1987), superficially mentions Nott's role in the Mobile epidemic, about which he made the observation discussed (p. 307).

27. Rosenberg, "Therapeutic Revolution," 488; Harris, "Vaccination in the Army," 138. Wood recognized that vaccination does not confer absolute immunity for life, but revaccination may be required. See Wood, *Treatise*, 1:410.

28. Jones, *Researches*, 86, 98, 103; Bolton, "Spurious Vaccination," 142.

29. Frank A. Ramsey, "Abnormalities of Vaccination," report included in Jones, *Researches*, 96. By comparison, Northern physician Dr. Ephraim Cutter experimented with scabs produced in healthy cows at five Massachusetts farms with humanized virus and found that the vaccinia scabs on the cows were identical to those produced in children. *Medical and Surgical History*, part 3, 1:634; correspondence of Dr. S. P. Crawford, 27 January 1867, reproduced in Jones, *Researches*, 4, 99; Harris, "Vaccination in the Army," 159. By comparison, Union army surgeon John H. Brinton wrote to his superior to complain that virus procured through the medical purveyor "has proved in every instance inert," a common complaint in the Confederacy. He asked for permission to purchase cows for the purpose of propagating vaccine. See John H. Brinton Papers 1853–1896, series 3, "Orders & Letters," p. 89, letter written during Brinton's tenure as Superintendent, Director of General Hospitals, Nashville, 1864–5, MSS 2/0269-01 Acc. 1992-078, Historical Medical Library, the College of Physicians of Philadelphia.

30. Bullock and Crenshaw illustrated trade catalog, 1853, Pamphlet Collection, Historical Medical Library, the College of Physicians of Philadelphia (italics in original). Even the North segregated vaccine matter. When United States Colored Troops were vaccinated, one regiment experienced an outbreak of ulcers followed by smallpox making "a fatal sweep" among the black soldiers. To remedy this problem, surgeons located a population of healthy black children in St. Louis, Missouri, to supply improved vaccine. See Harris, "Vaccination in the Army," 144. On smallpox and newly emancipated black people, see Jim Downs, *Sick from Freedom: African-American Illness and Suffering during the Civil War and Reconstruction* (New York: Oxford University Press, 2012), 97–99.

31. Harris, "Vaccination in the Army," 154, 158.

32. *Medical and Surgical History*, part 3, 1:638; Carol C. Green, *Chimborazo, the Confederacy's Largest Hospital* (Knoxville: University of Tennessee Press, 2004), 124–25.

Sharing many common prejudices of the day, both Union and Confederate doctors frequently treated black bodies differently from white ones. They had no scruples about grave-robbing "a dead nigger or two" for dissection. See Joan Cashin, "The Gruesome Case of Henry Eells: Grave-Robbing, Dissection, and Race in the Wartime South," *Journal of Civil War Medicine* 18 (January–March 2014): 2–11.

33. Jones, *Researches*, 89–90; Harris, "Vaccination in the Army," 159; Green, *Chimborazo*, 124. On artifacts as metaphor, see Prown, "Truth of Material Culture," 11.

34. On the value of materials, see Robert Friedel, "Some Matters of Substance," in Lubar and Kingery, *History from Things*, 46. See discussion of value in Wright, "Technological Styles," 248.

35. Davis Baird, *Thing Knowledge* (Oakland: University of California Press, 2004), 144.

36. Surgeon General Samuel P. Moore, circular, "Instructions Relative to Vaccination," 16 October 1863, 1–2. The previous circular, which was published without an admonitory preface, was dated 1 July 1863. The October circular is found at the National Library of Medicine Digital Collections, https://collections.nlm.nih.gov/bookviewer?PID=nlm:nlmuid-101645108-bk, accessed 1 June 2016. The July circular resides at the Abraham Lincoln Presidential Library, Springfield, Illinois. On artifacts as parasites, see Mihaly Csikszentmihalyi, "Why We Need Things," in Lubar and Kingery, *History from Things*, 21.

37. Friedel, "Some Matters of Substance," 46.

38. Moore, "Instructions Relative to Vaccination," 3.

39. Wright, "Technological Styles," 245.

40. Harris, "Vaccination in the Army," 157; Jones, *Researches*, 4, 9. Online versions of Jones's work may be viewed at websites of the Wellcome Library (http://wellcomelibrary.org/item/b22346892); U.S. National Library of Medicine (https://collections.nlm.nih.gov/catalog/nlm:nlmuid-101274216-bk); Google Books (https://books.google.com/books?id=YSA4AQAAMAAJ&pg=PA133&lpg=PA133&dq=researches+upon+spurious+vaccination&source=bl&ots=cUdRFEKfpy&sig=zlQu5CBAiQGcp7ENrtTyVis21AM&hl=en&sa=X&ved=0ahUKEwisvOHtkIrNAhUIGz4KHUS2DMIQ6AEINzAF#v=onepage&q=researches%20upon%20spurious%20vaccination&f=false); and Internet Archive, which is the same as the National Library of Medicine copy. All websites accessed 15 June 2016. Researchers are cautioned that the document in each digital version ends with page number 137. The copy at the Historical Medical Library of the College of Physicians of Philadelphia includes a substantial appendix of almost thirty pages, most of which consists of a paper on spurious vaccination by James Bolton, MD, former Confederate surgeon (see note 1), supplemented by "Small-pox Epidemic in Mobile during the Winter of 1865–6" by J. C. Nott, MD. Jones's report on spurious vaccination was widely read. *The Medical and Surgical History* concluded, weighing Northern and Southern experiences and citing Jones, that the two preeminent causes of spurious cases were impure vaccine and depleted health of soldiers. The report is also cited and discussed in the first volume of the *Sanitary Memoirs of the War of the Rebellion* of the United States Sanitary Commission. Jones himself authored several subsequent monographs on various topics and included his spurious vaccination study in his own memoirs. See *Medical and Surgical History*, part 3, 1:638 (citation of Jones's report), 648 (conclusions); Harris, "Vaccination in the Army," 154–58; and Jones, *Medical and Surgical Memoirs*, vol. 3, part 1,

391–540. This volume contains the original *Researches upon "Spurious" Vaccination* and includes a comparison of smallpox with chicken pox and additional information on the Henry Wirz trial.

41. Wright, "Technological Styles," 243; Breeden, *Joseph Jones*, 156–73; Jones, *Researches*, 13–19. Jones's testimony in the Wirz trial is found at U.S. House of Representatives, *Trial of Henry Wirz*, Exec. Doc. No. 23, 40th Cong., 2nd Sess. (Washington, D.C., 1880–1901), ser. 2, 8:588–632. Consideration of Jones's testimony begins on p. 620 on the Library of Congress website, https://www.loc.gov/rr/frd/Military_Law/pdf/Wirz-trial.pdf, accessed 25 June 2016.

42. Csikszentmihalyi, "Why We Need Things," 23. On bodies as tropes, see Lisa A. Long, *Rehabilitating Bodies: Health, History, and the American Civil War* (Philadelphia: University of Pennsylvania Press, 2004), 12.

43. Downs, *Sick from Freedom*, 97.

44. Nott's two major publications on the evolution of races are *Types of Mankind*, 1854, and *Indigenous Races of the Earth*, coauthored by George R. Gliddon, 1857. See Horsman, *Josiah Nott of Mobile*, 195–217; and John S. Haller, *Outcasts from Evolution: Scientific Attitudes of Racial Inferiority, 1859–1900* (Carbondale: Southern Illinois University Press, 1995), 81–84. The famous case of Henrietta Lacks highlights the racial ideology informing the use of body tissues as artifacts: her cancer cells were cultured and reproduced for research purposes and commercial appropriation without consent of or compensation to Lacks and her family.

45. Jenner quoted in Jones, *Researches*, 11; Nott, "Small-pox Epidemic in Mobile," 147; *Medical and Surgical History*, part 3, 1:648. Beaugency cows are discussed in John Joseph Buder, "Letters of Henry Austin Martin: The Vaccination Correspondence to Thomas Fanning Wood, 1877–1883" (master's thesis, University of Texas at Austin, 1991). For technology centers, see Ross Thomson, *Structures of Change in the Mechanical Age: Technological Innovation in the United States, 1790–1865* (Baltimore: Johns Hopkins University Press, 2009), 4.

46. Jones, *Researches*, 31, 72. Merillat reported his analysis in the May 1864 issue of the *Confederate States Medical Journal*. Discussed in Green, *Chimborazo*, 125.

47. Baird, *Thing Knowledge*, 5. See also Malcolm Baker, "Epilogue: Making and Knowing, Then and Now," in Smith, Meyers, and Cook, *Ways of Making and Knowing*, 408.

48. Baker, "Epilogue," 408; Jones, *Researches*, 9.

Fitted Up for Freedom
The Material Culture of Refugee Relief

SARAH JONES WEICKSEL

In May 1863, an unnamed Philadelphia newspaper correspondent made his way on foot through what he condescendingly referred to as the "odd looking village" of Mitchelville on Hilton Head Island, South Carolina. With amusement he "examined each little hut, variegated with an enormous number of cracks and crevices, which would make a Northern carpenter forever dumb." He patronizingly judged the homes "very comfortable, so the 'aunties' and 'pickaninnies' told me as they displayed with great pride the interior of their imaginative mansions." A year and a half later, in autumn 1864, photographer Samuel Cooley captured an image of two of those small dwellings standing close together on a gravelly, oyster-strewn landscape. The dark void of the open doorways and window contrasts sharply with the brightness of the cabin siding, beckoning the viewer to come closer. But the two-dimensionality of the image stops us short of peering inside that door. A chair sits in the foreground of the photograph, hinting at the belongings of the inhabitants, but the interiors of these homes in the African American refugee community of Mitchelville remain elusive.[1]

These textual and visual depictions of Mitchelville do, however, point to a narrative of refugee communities that looks beyond the destitute conditions that were so often emphasized by relief workers—the predominantly white Northern women and men associated with the army and a range of organizations that considered themselves to be working toward the "relief" of freedpeople. Historians' understanding of refugee life is largely rooted in the records and published reports of relief organizations. To accomplish their work, these organizations required donations of money, clothing, food, books, and other items. Relief workers had an impetus for strategically presenting potential donors with an image of African American refugees that emphasized desperate need and potential for "improvement." Reliance upon relief workers' textual descriptions permits them to dominate the narrative of emancipation, setting a tone of desolation—of a material life seemingly devoid of comforts and lives defined by misery.[2]

The deprivation and struggle of life in refugee camps should not be underestimated, but combining textual, photographic, and archaeological evidence mediates the dominance of relief workers' narratives and allows us to access a modicum of the texture and individuality of refugee life. Uncovering the material landscapes of emancipation does not deny that many black refugees lived in dire, often deadly conditions, nor does it undermine the gravity of their experiences. Combined with textual accounts, the material culture of emancipation provides a route to understanding numerous and at times competing narratives of emancipation that include the hopes and possibilities that motivated black refugees and the ingenuity with which they—quite literally—built free lives. In the unlikely spaces of refugee camps, refugees and relief workers struggled, at a fundamental level, with the puzzles, possibilities, and realities of emancipation. How would the end of slavery affect the material world in which they lived? And how could material goods begin to lend shape to new definitions of freedom? Efforts to address these questions were contested; the answers, muddled.

This essay explores the built environment and material culture of black refugee relief in the 1860s, addressing relief workers' constructed narratives of redemption from the "evils of slavery" alongside refugees' own material, lived experiences. In doing so it captures both relief workers' narrative of degeneracy and the tension between that narrative and formerly enslaved people's own sense of their readiness for freedom. My sources are drawn from three sites to which large populations of freedpeople migrated and lived—Camp Nelson, Kentucky; Mitchelville, South Carolina; and Hampton, Virginia—as well as from additional refugee sites for context and comparison. Focusing on movement, this essay does not seek to address the experiences of those people who remained on plantations. The material worldview from which relief workers approached the challenges of emancipation meant that material goods and the built environment played central roles in their perceptions of freedom and reform. The spaces in which people lived and the things they used were considered powerful pathways to reshape former slaves into free people; the material environment was believed to have profound consequences for the outcomes of emancipation. Relief workers' sometimes conflicting beliefs about the relationship between freedom and the material environment had important effects on refugees' daily, lived experiences. But refugees were not simply the objects of relief. They, too, were actively building a material culture in freedom—a material culture that was far more varied than relief workers' writings would lead us to believe and one that did not necessarily adhere to the gridlines laid out by those relief workers. The material culture of refugees' lives was created through acts of salvage, appropriation, donation, rationing, and protecting. The things to which they had access, ranging from household goods to building supplies, and their physical properties played a role in determining what was possible in freedom; the materiality of those things mattered.[3]

In the wake of slavery's collapse across the South, men, women, and children actively sought to make sense of freedom's possibilities and uncertainties. As they sought to reorder their lives, hundreds of thousands of black refugees found their way to Union lines, were placed on abandoned and confiscated lands by Federal officials, and came together to form their own communities. Most needed food, shelter, and clothing immediately. Some left all property behind, preferring, as white journalist Charles Nordhoff observed, "to lose every thing else in order to assure their liberty." Photographs and illustrations depict refugees en route to these new communities, driving wagons filled with children, the elderly, and unseen belongings; men walking alongside with sacks slung over their shoulders; women balancing bundles on their heads. But what did they carry? What did they encounter when they arrived? What was the material culture they created?[4]

As the number of refugees and amount of occupied lands grew, so too did the number of predominantly white men and women who traveled south to teach; to facilitate the provision of shelter, food, and clothing; and to prepare former slaves to "take their place" in free society. Relief workers' efforts to transform formerly enslaved women and men were based on prejudiced, often overtly racist assumptions about black bodies and minds. Counteracting the negative effects of slavery, reformers believed, required erasing the "marks of bondage" and instilling freedpeople with new habits, routines, morals, work ethics, gender roles, and worldviews to enable them to successfully navigate free life. Such views not only were held by white reformers but also espoused by some African American men and women. As Harriet Jacobs conveyed to William Lloyd Garrison, "They need to be taught the right habits of living and the true principles of life." Which habits and principles were deemed most important for former slaves' education varied: while some reformers focused on the ownership of one's own body and the right to the fruits of one's own labor, others stressed the importance of marriage and familial ties. Historians of emancipation have detailed these relief workers' emphasis on education, familial bonds, and property ownership. But relief workers' approach also had a very material element—and it began with shaping the material environment in which refugees lived.[5]

When Charles Nordhoff traveled through South Carolina in 1863, his assessments of the conditions produced by slavery were bleak, but he nevertheless believed in prospects for reform. He based this observation, in part, on his perception of formerly enslaved people's capacity for embracing cleanliness and neatness as general precepts. He was encouraged that although the people's clothing was tattered, he "found that the rags were clean" and their cabins were not dirty. Cleanliness and neatness were used to gauge an individual's moral uprightness, civility, and even intelligence. Dirtiness was perceived as the "never failing sign of vulgarity"; bodily cleanliness was considered a moral choice for which each individual was responsible. Cleanliness exists in the eye of the beholder and is a historical means of othering; it expresses, as historian Kathleen Brown argues, fear about interacting with other bodies. Like Nordhoff, many relief workers' assessments of prospects for reform were based on unsubstantiated notions— certainly black people were already sensitive to cleanliness and order. The words of formerly enslaved Wayman Williams rang true for many situations when he recalled, "De teacher from de North don't know what to think of all dat." As Williams's words suggest, lack of cultural understanding permeated many of the interactions between relief workers and refugees.[6]

At the center of Northern relief workers' worldview was the belief that material conditions and the physical environment affected the inward condition of a person. This applied not only to individuals but also to the social body. Indeed, in the first half of the nineteenth century, Americans, guided by this worldview, were engaged in a process of reimagining, reforming, and reconstructing the urban built environment—streets, sanitation systems, city plans, and a range of institutions, including cemeteries, government buildings, and penitentiaries—all in an effort to create more ordered spaces, and thereby a more ordered citizenry.[7]

As attitudes toward formerly enslaved people suggest, some members of society were believed to require more extensive reform than even an organized environment could provide. Among them were inebriates, prostitutes, criminals, Native Americans, and the poor. The approach to reforming people through manipulation of their environment and clothing is succinctly articulated in nineteenth-century penal reform movements that sought to rehabilitate offenders. Prison reformers were motivated to improve prisoners' souls through structuring time, space, and employment. This therapeutic vision, architectural historian Dell Upton has observed, was repressive, but "it was an optimistic repression, a misguided attempt to recruit republican citizens from among the downtrodden."[8]

Race and the institution of slavery added other dimensions and expectations to this process of rehabilitation. Formerly enslaved people were perceived and described as suffering from degradation and depravity stemming from a lifetime of enslavement. Relief workers believed that former slaves needed to be rehabilitated by developing many of the same traits that were of utmost concern to prison reformers: industriousness, religiosity, morality, and personal discipline. In short, freedpeople were believed to be the newest members of the downtrodden who needed to develop "mental and corporal habits of virtuous behavior." Improve former slaves' physical conditions, Dr. James Graves argued, "and they will rapidly improve in the moral and religious departments of their nature." Allowing refugees to construct individual houses, another observer argued, was "the strongest motive upon which to act effectively in developing their self-reliance and individuality."[9]

Those physical conditions began with the built environment of self-organized settlements and army contraband camps. Refugee housing was under the purview not only of civilian relief workers but army officials as well, and the appearance of these camps varied depending on location, available materials, and degrees of permanence. When initially formed, camps were composed of army tents and a variety of structures that were interchangeably, and at times derisively, referred to as huts, shanties, lean-tos, and cottages. Refugee settlements were frequently erected in a series of stages. Existing buildings in the nearby vicinity were typically populated first, including deserted houses, abandoned schools, old barracks, barns, and a wide variety of plantation outbuildings. Many camps also began with the use of tents, followed by the erection of cabins. In Corinth, Mississippi, for instance, refugees were housed first in tents but later lived in a combination of tents, barracks, deserted houses, and self-built cabins. Others, however, remained without protection. Even those who did have shelter experienced a tenuous security—shifting policies and changes in command meant that refugees were constantly at risk of eviction.[10]

The impermanent architecture of the United States Colored Troops recruiting station at Camp Nelson, Kentucky, documents the insecurity of refugees' ability to build and protect their homes and belongings. Recruit Joseph Miller brought his family with him when he enlisted because his master said that if "I enlisted he would not maintain them and I knew they would be abused by him when I left." The Millers were housed in an army tent, while other soldiers' families lived in cabins and huts built from material that was "unserviceable to the Government" by the U.S. Colored Troops or at the expense of the female refugees. Nevertheless, on a bitterly cold morning in November 1864, all of these structures were torn down and the inhabitants were loaded into government wagons and driven outside the army camp, where they were left alongside the road. Among them were Joseph Miller's wife and children. After a protracted struggle among army officers, the families were allowed to return to Camp Nelson. But it was too late for Miller's son, who died of exposure soon after being banished.[11]

The destruction of the refugees' dwellings was motivated in part by the perceived disorder of the community. As in many camps, refugees erected structures as new people arrived, resulting in a built environment with a haphazard appearance. The materials from which they were built were drawn from a wide range of inconsistently available sources, including government lumber, castoff tents and canvas sheeting (fabric from which tents were made), and materials salvaged from damaged or deserted structures in the vicinity of the camp. The conditions in many of these camps are well known to historians. As historian Jim Downs has shown, the overcrowded, unsanitary surroundings of many camps exacerbated the spread of disease and refugees' mortality rates. Military officials and relief workers' concerns over refugees' "filthy and close quarters" were not, however, limited to health risks; they were also tied to morality.[12]

Concerns about orderliness and cleanliness of living conditions stemmed from the association of gentility and morality with the ability to control or contain one's body. As Charles Nordhoff reflected, "In our minds this squalor is linked with drunkenness and vicious improvidence; and we unconsciously dislike those who live in this condition. These were my emotions, I confess, when I first entered the cabins of the people here." White relief worker Martha Schofield narrated an address she made to freedpeople in which she "insisted on cleanliness," in part to combat disease, but she also "told them they were done with Slavery & you must give up the curses of slavery & almost the worst thing was filth and the breaking up family ties." That Schofield placed "filth" alongside breaking apart families as the most deplorable results of slavery suggests just how critical cleanliness was to conceptions of a socially acceptable body and home. Indeed, David Franklin Thorpe, a white plantation superintendent, asserted that relief workers needed to "enforce the idea that cleanliness" was "essential to freedom & piety." Such sentiments about order and cleanliness influenced military officials and relief workers as they considered alternatives to the haphazard landscapes of refugee camps and villages. In the case of Camp Nelson, the expulsion of refugees, the destruction of their shelters, and their subsequent readmittance created a context in which military officials and relief workers reimagined refugees' housing, prompting conflict over what type of housing was best suited to recently freed people.[13]

Over time, both civilian relief workers and army officials encouraged the replacement of the impermanent architecture of huts and tents with more solidly built housing in locations with large populations of refugees, among them Camp Nelson and Hilton Head Island. Decisions about the type of structures prompted disagreement: were long barracks or small houses more suitable for recently freed people? While barracks were expedient and could house large numbers of people, this living arrangement did not promote the family-based self-dependence that civilian relief workers sought to encourage. They hoped to avoid, in part, the crowded conditions of camps like that outside Helena, Arkansas, in which only a few feet of space separated the dwellings. One observer noted, "Their cabins consist of an incongruous assemblage of miserable huts no attempt haveing been made toward introduceing any system whatever." As they oversaw the building of new housing, some relief workers sought to arrange the more permanent architecture into orderly rows that resembled a planned community; an orderly landscape was believed to produce orderly people.[14]

On Hilton Head Island, General Ormsby Mitchel favored individual cottages and ordered a map drawn up of evenly spaced lots intersected by roads carved out of a former plantation. He had "all the contraband families provided with boards, nails, hammers, &c." and "told them to build on each lot which had been set off, a house for themselves," forming the town of Mitchelville. A compromise between barracks and single-family housing was attempted at Old Point Comfort, just outside the walls of Fort Monroe, Virginia, where 1,000 refugees lived in three government buildings constructed for their use. One of the buildings was subdivided into small rooms for families, while single men occupied the others. The family rooms were insufficiently heated and the rooms crowded. White relief worker Dr. Le Baron Russell believed that families who lived in houses of their own made "a nearer approach to the condition of free Northern laborers than is possible where they are crowded together in barracks or tents." Living in single-family dwellings, he asserted, "teaches them the value of self dependence, and the habit of relying on their own resources, which are the most important lessons they can learn."[15]

At the Camp Nelson Home for Colored Refugees, opened in January 1865, the barracks-versus-small-house debate was more contentious. Reverend John Fee of the American Missionary Association disagreed with the superintendent of the refugee home over the use of crowded barracks with bunks stacked three high. Fee was dismayed by the prospect of "125 persons in one continuous babel, children crying, mothers fretting." Instead, Fee argued for the construction of neat rows of sixteen-by-twelve-foot cottages that would house eight to ten people. The square footage allocated to each person in these two designs was only nominally different—the barracks permitted fifteen square feet per person, while the cottages granted between nineteen and twenty-four square feet, depending on occupancy. The difference was not about physical comfort or individual privacy; rather, a cottage allowed families space in which to practice and instill the precepts that relief workers thought fitting for free people. Ultimately, the refugee home was a compromise that included barracks, a mess house, and ninety-seven duplex cottages, each thirty-two by sixteen feet and intended to house two separate families.[16]

This effort to order the refugee built environment was readily apparent in the maps drawn up of various camps. A map of Mitchelville, for instance, shows plots of land divided by roads, with houses evenly spaced throughout. Similarly, a map of the Camp Nelson Home for Colored Refugees depicts parallel rows of structures. The barracks at the contraband camp on Mason's Island were also laid out in evenly spaced rows. But the nature of refugee life—and the refugees themselves—defied such gridlines.[17]

Even those communities that were more permanent, including Camp Nelson and Mitchelville, might contain a combination of small houses, military wall tents, Sibley tents, large barracks-style buildings, and, if the camp was situated on a plantation, former slave quarters. A photograph of Camp Nelson includes the schoolhouse, multiple barracks, and cottages outlined on the map—as well as a series of twenty-three tents and several structures made from a variety of materials, resisting the uniformity clearly intended by the erection of the rows of cottages and the manner in which they are depicted on the map.[18]

Relief workers spoke disparagingly of slave quarters, arguing that such living conditions had promoted filth and unnamed ills of slavery. And yet, many refugee houses were actually significantly smaller than the average slave cabin. At Mitchelville, the houses were generally no larger than 220 square feet; at Camp Nelson, 192 square feet—all of which were approximately 100 square feet smaller than typical late antebellum slave cabins. The architectural elements of these houses were also notably similar. A Mitchelville house photographed by Cooley, for instance, bears remarkable resemblance to the exterior of a prewar slave cabin on Point of Pines plantation on neighboring Edisto Island. Both structures feature a facade with a door and a single window. The Mitchelville houses, however, differed in significant ways from many slave cabins. Improvements included glass windows, stoves, elevated floors, and wood plank flooring. Furthermore, the houses were grouped together rather than evenly spaced apart, as were slave quarters, likely representing, as art historian Dana Byrd points out, "a commitment to kin-based organization of space, a privilege denied to slaves."[19]

Mitchelville dwellings had a broad range of architectural features, reflecting both personal choice and availability of materials. One house, for instance, had a brick chimney but lacked paned windows, while another had multiple, though mismatched, paned windows, likely salvaged. A third house had a stove, judging from the pipe that was vented through the roof, as well as a single sash window that allowed the bottom half of the window to be slid open—a luxury at this time. Another building was a small wooden structure with a larger addition made from sheeting typically used for tents. One year later, a teacher described even greater variety: "Some are made of round poles chinked with oyster-shell lime; some of slats; and some of boards, picked up and bought, of every conceivable size, while others are 'pieced out' with old canvas on the chimneys and roof."[20]

Although relief workers and army officials perceived the incongruous nature of refugee camps' built environments as problematic, the variety of structures and their placement evidences refugees' construction of their own material culture of freedom. That material culture was constrained by the availability of materials and the strictures placed upon refugees by military officials, but the resulting built environment nevertheless was part of their enactment of freedom. Horace James, a white relief worker and superintendent of Negro Affairs, reported in 1863 that refugees were eager to build houses of their own design. "Every man," James noted, "knows how to construct his own house, and is ready to do it, if assured of protection."[21]

The built environment and material culture of emancipation were part of a landscape of salvage and appropriation. Building materials could be difficult to obtain due to the restricted mobility of resources, the primacy of military needs, and conflicting attitudes and policies toward freedpeople. The construction of those houses was often a process of salvage and, as a result, bore striking resemblance to the appearance of—and techniques used in—soldiers' winter quarters. Houses and outbuildings in the vicinity of such quarters and camps were often deconstructed, their materials— including sash windows and siding—then used to build soldiers' winter camps. In some instances, those winter quarters became refugee quarters, as in the case of a camp outside Murfreesboro, Tennessee, where nearly 2,000 refugees occupied huts left by soldiers. While architecturally, visually, and at times even literally, refugee camps resembled Union soldiers' winter camps, observers described them quite differently. Impermanent architecture was less problematic for armies of white men whose residency was temporary; the presence of black women and children living there indefinitely was quite different. While soldiers often spoke of the novelty of their self-built huts, rejoicing at the comfort of living under a roof, refugees living in similar circumstances were usually looked upon with pity and even disgust.[22]

The range of circumstances in which people lived is readily apparent in the context of Hampton, Virginia, located a few miles from Fort Monroe, where General Benjamin Butler first declared fleeing enslaved people to be "contraband of war," providing a legal basis upon which contrabands, as rebel property, could be seized and harbored by the Union army. In the vicinity of the fort, people lived not only in the barracks at Old Point Comfort but also in abandoned houses, self-built structures, and a Grand Contraband Camp built from the ruins of the town of Hampton. In the area lying outside Hampton, several houses owned by Confederates were occupied by freedpeople. Among these was the summer home of former U.S. president John Tyler. An Italianate-style house, it became the residence of several refugee families and the principal of the Hampton Colored School.[23]

In August 1861, Confederate soldiers had set fire to the largely abandoned town of Hampton to destroy its usefulness to the Union and prevent the town from harboring runaway slaves. What was once a town of more than 500 dwellings and businesses was reduced to "a mass of charred ruins and towering chimneys." As historian Megan Kate Nelson shows, at the same time as many observers described the ruined town using language of the sublime, others were appropriating materials and "reconstructing the site." While some waxed poetic about the ravages of war, others grasped the material potential of salvaging those charred ruins and towering chimneys.[24]

Describing such activity as rebuilding or reconstructing Hampton does not adequately capture the complexity of what was taking place at this site. Freedpeople were not restoring the town to its former appearance but rather, creating a new built environment out of its ruined landscape. This had practical, material, and symbolic significance. Bricks and stone fragments were salvaged from heaps of rubble and charred wood and combined with government lumber and materials used by Union soldiers to build winter quarters. The ruins themselves played a significant role in determining how this built environment was constructed and arranged. The physical capability of brick to withstand such a conflagration meant that surviving, though damaged, chimneys and walls made up the architectural

Figure 8. Hampton, Virginia, December 1864. (Courtesy of the Library of Congress)

building blocks of many new dwellings. "Their modus operandi," one white New Hampshire soldier wrote, "is to select a good chimney & then build with mud & blocks or old boards a shanty by its side & they have not a house with a chimney but a chimney with a house."[25]

An 1864 photograph of Hampton (figure 8) offers material evidence of this salvaged built environment. In the foreground is a structure made of both milled and rough-hewn boards. Fabric—likely sheeting used for tents—is stretched across sections of the roof, secured to the boards at regular intervals with tacks or nails. One large piece is tented and tacked over the eave of the roof. Lacking visible windows, the structure nevertheless has a brick chimney, a salvaged remnant of the house that once stood there—the remains of which are strewn across the back lot. Directly behind these piles of rubble sits another structure—composed of salvaged boards of varying widths and a fireplace that was not likely built for the structure itself, given that its chimney does not extend above the roof.[26]

The chimney attached to one house has both an exposed lintel (the horizontal structural support above the opening to a fireplace) and a firebox (the interior cavity of a fireplace) clearly visible on the chimney's exterior, suggesting that this was originally a center chimney that served two rooms of a single house—one located on either side of the fireplace. In erecting this new structure, the builders built the house against one side of this chimney, equipping the house with one functioning fireplace, while leaving the other fireplace exposed. Decisions to situate houses in spaces where functional chimneys could be incorporated into the structure were strategic. Chimneys were both time-consuming and complicated to construct—the proper slope of the flue and placement of bricks was the difference between smoke escaping through the chimney and billowing back into the house. In salvaging stone and incorporating surviving chimney stacks into their dwellings, formerly enslaved people were quite literally building their homes from the same material as slaveholders' houses, simultaneously erecting a built environment of freedom on the physical ruins of the Confederacy.[27]

The first iteration of the refugee quarters at Camp Nelson—the huts and tents in which families lived prior to their eviction—was described as chaotic and the people destitute. Indeed, refugees tended to be spoken of as a single group who possessed the same experiences. The material culture of their dwellings suggests otherwise, however. The structures varied in terms of the comfort they furnished the inhabitants. Brick, partial brick, and stick and mud chimneys existed, and some huts had glazed windows. The range of ceramics associated with the huts further points to the varied backgrounds and experiences of the refugees. Among these ceramics were ironware—a less expensive, mass-produced substitute for porcelain—decorated whiteware, and locally made redware. Buttons, military accoutrements, and coins suggest the range of activities that occurred there—laundering and sewing for pay, visits from fathers, and the repurposing of army clothing.[28]

As the Camp Nelson site suggests, contrary to the bleak outlook expressed by relief workers, refugees were not creating a single, monotone vision of free life; their material culture had color, texture, and meaning that stretched far beyond the utility of survival. This material culture was not uniform, combined, as it was, from belongings brought from enslaved homes, secondhand donations, army castoffs, items purchased from sutlers and commissaries using wages, and those appropriated from former slaveholders' houses or abandoned places in the vicinity of new communities. Refugees' belongings simultaneously contained stories of migration and upheaval; generosity and violence; assertiveness, work, loss, and opportunity.[29]

Uncovering the nonarchitectural elements of the material culture of refugee camps requires patching together bits and pieces of the historical record—a glimpse through a window, brief observations, broken pottery shards. What were the interior spaces like in which people shaped free lives? In instances where neither the material nor the textual record offers a direct account of refugee life, it is possible to partly reconstruct tent life by including sources from Union soldiers who lived in the same conically shaped Sibley and rectangular wall tents like those housing refugees. A surviving Sibley tent in the inaugural exhibition at the National Museum of African American History and Culture offers a sense of the weight of the canvas from which it is made, of the effort required to transport and erect the tent, and of the size of the sheltered space it provided. The tent's physical attributes allowed it to provide protection from the elements but with minimal insulation, making warm clothing and blankets all the more necessary for inhabitants.

Soldiers' sketchbooks suggest how refugees' tent spaces might have been arranged — at least in a nominal sense. Massachusetts soldier Herbert Valentine, for instance, illustrated the Sibley tent's interior pulley system and the use of a cone-shaped iron stove, vented through the tent wall. Valentine's sketch shows how life in this tent was necessarily organized around the central support pole and pulleys of the tent. A *Harper's Weekly* print shows ways in which objects could be suspended inside a tent. Clothing, swords, and a towel are hung from a series of short poles attached to the main tent pole, increasing storage space and allowing for better organization.[30]

Wall and Sibley tents could be erected by refugees with semipermanence in mind, employing many of the same features as soldiers' encampments. Among these were stoves or fireplaces vented through tent walls and raised board floors, like those seen in the *Harper's* illustration. Access to enough lumber to lay a board floor significantly improved the comfort of tent life, helping control dampness, promoting cleanliness, and offering a degree of separation from rodents and snakes. In contrast, a photograph of a woman and child in the entrance to a tent outside Helena, Arkansas, depicts life in a floorless tent. The woman sits in a long dress, weeds rising up above her hemline; a young boy stands ankle deep in grass. During rainstorms, the floors of the tent would have become wet when the ground outside became saturated with rain. The presumably wooden chair upon which the woman sits would have begun to warp, rot, and weaken as the wooden legs soaked up the moisture from the ground. Soldiers in the *Harper's* sketch, by contrast, lay with their shoes kicked off, a folding campstool lying on the board floor and a table standing firmly to one side. Such board floors offered both the ability to be swept and greater protection from the elements for one's possessions, which might be placed directly on the board floor with less anxiety of their ruin. Indeed, although one cannot distinguish the items inside the woman and child's Helena tent, a glimpse of belongings piled up, perhaps on a bedstead, suggests the difficulty of caring for one's possessions in a grass-floored tent. The seeming disorganization of goods piled up, off the ground, may have contributed to relief workers' assessment of the disorderliness of refugees' household spaces but was nevertheless necessary to preserve one's belongings.[31]

While the juxtaposition of soldiers' depictions of tents and the photographs of those lived in by refugees suggests the ways in which such spaces were constructed and perhaps organized, archaeological evidence helps to populate those tents with the belongings and daily activities of individuals. Laundry, for instance, was a significant feature of the material landscape of emancipation. This is hardly surprising, given the central role African American laundresses played in supporting Union soldiers encamped in or passing through areas in which refugee camps were located. This material evidence, however, directly contradicts relief workers' textual claims of refugees' inattention to cleanliness. Washtubs and boards, as well as posts with notches and a crossbar for drying clothing, are present in many photographs. In a photograph of Mitchelville, one woman leans over a tub set up on a barrel, her back to the camera, scrubbing a garment against a washboard. She would have completed her task with the use of a heavy heated iron, like one found at the Mitchelville site. This laundry landscape served both military and personal purposes, as indicated by the discovery of buttons made from a wide range of materials, including bone, glass, and stamped military buttons, all of which suggest that the clothing that was washed and repaired was worn by both civilians and soldiers.[32]

Objects can be seen in photographs of windows and doorways at Mitchelville—a curtain hanging across a glass-paned window, a rough-hewn bench propping open a door, a bedstead sitting outside a cabin. These and other objects depicted in the yard and found during archaeological excavations suggest that Mitchelville refugees possessed a range of items that were brought with them from former homes—items that had belonged to them in slavery—and had likely taken from the homes of former masters and mistresses, such as the fancy jewelry and colorful, transfer-printed ceramics found in an excavation. Similarly, the slat-back chair that sits outside one cabin is similar in style to those owned by monied white Southerners. Taking objects left behind in slaveholders' houses required both effort and discernment, limited as refugees were in what they could carry by hand, in head bundles, or, in the best scenario, a wagon. The selection and use of these individual items of former masters' belongings offer a striking contrast to derisive caricatures of freed slaves sliding down bannisters of the plantation house, dancing and inappropriately using the various furnishings in the house. These were objects used to construct free lives.

Looking into a single refugee home, one might discover a range of belongings varying not only in terms of form or function but also in style, pattern, and color. While some people may have owned sets of dishes, more likely they served and ate food from several mismatched pieces—a bone china cup, a dark-brown glazed teapot, a yellow glazed bowl, a white plate with a blue and scalloped decorative edge—all of which were among the items found at a Hampton site. The presence of a wide range of kitchen vessels attests to the varied foodways of Mitchelville's residents, including tea- and coffee-related items, plates and flatware, mixing bowls, pie plates, and a soup tureen. In the context of refugee life, a soup tureen taken from a former master's sideboard might inhabit the same space as a rough-hewn bench, a carved parlor chair, soda-glass bottles, and slates, pencils, and books provided by relief workers. While such incongruity may have been jarring to some observers' eyes, these objects helped to shape and enact their owners' experiences of emancipation. Such a hybrid material culture drawn from many sources was a daily material reminder of lives in transition.[33]

Archaeological excavations at the site of the November 1864 expulsion of Camp Nelson refugees and destruction of their dwellings reveal not only the objects people owned but also the things they lost. The violence and destruction of that moment is preserved in the materials themselves—the burned, misshapen, and charred artifacts, including tableware, ceramics, combs, buttons, and window glass. These objects both are a testament to the violence that occurred at this site and point to the longer-reaching effects of the expulsion. Lost belongings could not be easily replaced. Those possibly brought with people from their enslaved homes—such as a child's doll—could have been items passed between family members or to which memories were attached. The absence of those objects when their owners ultimately returned to live at the Camp Nelson Home for Colored Refugees would have not only made everyday tasks more difficult—combing one's hair, cooking and serving food—but also served as a reminder of the destruction of their homes and the nearly 100 people who died as a result of exposure. Memory was embedded in both the items refugees could still touch and those that were lost, destroyed, or left behind. [34]

Refugees owned and lost a wide range of household goods, and yet relief workers likely provided few of these to them. The pages of donations to relief societies and relief workers' own narration of the process of supplying refugees primarily reference clothing and food—items considered necessities.

The Material Culture of Refugee Relief { 165

Slates and slate pencils are evidence of the education that was so central to relief workers' efforts, and they were likely supplied by them. Porcelain doll parts, marbles, and animal-shaped fragments point to children's play. Most of these toys, dolls, marbles, dishes, and other household items were likely brought with refugees from enslaved homes or master's houses or obtained through their own purchases. Mitchelville residents, for instance, had access to several trading stores that sold food, clothing, and kitchenware.[35]

Relief workers wavered between feeling encouraged, dismayed, and even disgusted by freedpeople's desire for new belongings. Some worried that the development of too fine of a taste could lead former slaves into abject poverty. According to one white visitor, there was a demand for utensils, plates, tinware, better clothing, and hoopskirts. The visitor predicted that, given the opportunity, freedpeople would eagerly purchase household furniture and clothing like that used by "persons of moderate means" in the Northern states. Elsewhere, however, white Union soldier Henry Hayes was appalled that "every cent of their earnings is generally expended in finery or jewelry, rings, braclets, and gaudy glaring, colored dresses, and I should have added earrings, generally monstrous in size and shew." When asked what they purchased with their wages, one white relief worker asserted that freedpeople sought "to gratify the desire for gaudy dress and good things to eat, that is lifes luxuries is generally where the money goes and for those things goes freely." In response to what they considered excessive expenditures, relief workers and others took it upon themselves to educate freedpeople about frugality and temptations of the marketplace. Men were cautioned that a woman could destroy her husband's finances by asking him to buy unnecessary goods that she could do without and that he could not afford. All were instructed, "For the sake of your good name, do not make a splurge in society with jewelry and fine clothes which have not been paid for, and for which you will never be able to pay." Many relief workers saw discretion in purchases as essential to success in freedom. Such beliefs were likely grounded in longstanding stereotypes of black peoples' weakness as consumers incapable of planning and providing for the future. Others, however, were motivated by an underlying, often unspoken commitment to maintaining social distinctions between the races—what they deemed "suitable" for a person to own or wear was directly tied to the color of one's skin and formerly enslaved status. Such beliefs were enacted and reinforced through relief workers' own material culture and built environment.[36]

Although refugees themselves left few textual records of their experiences in camp, one imagines that they noted the disparity between relief workers' living spaces and their own. The housing designated suitable for

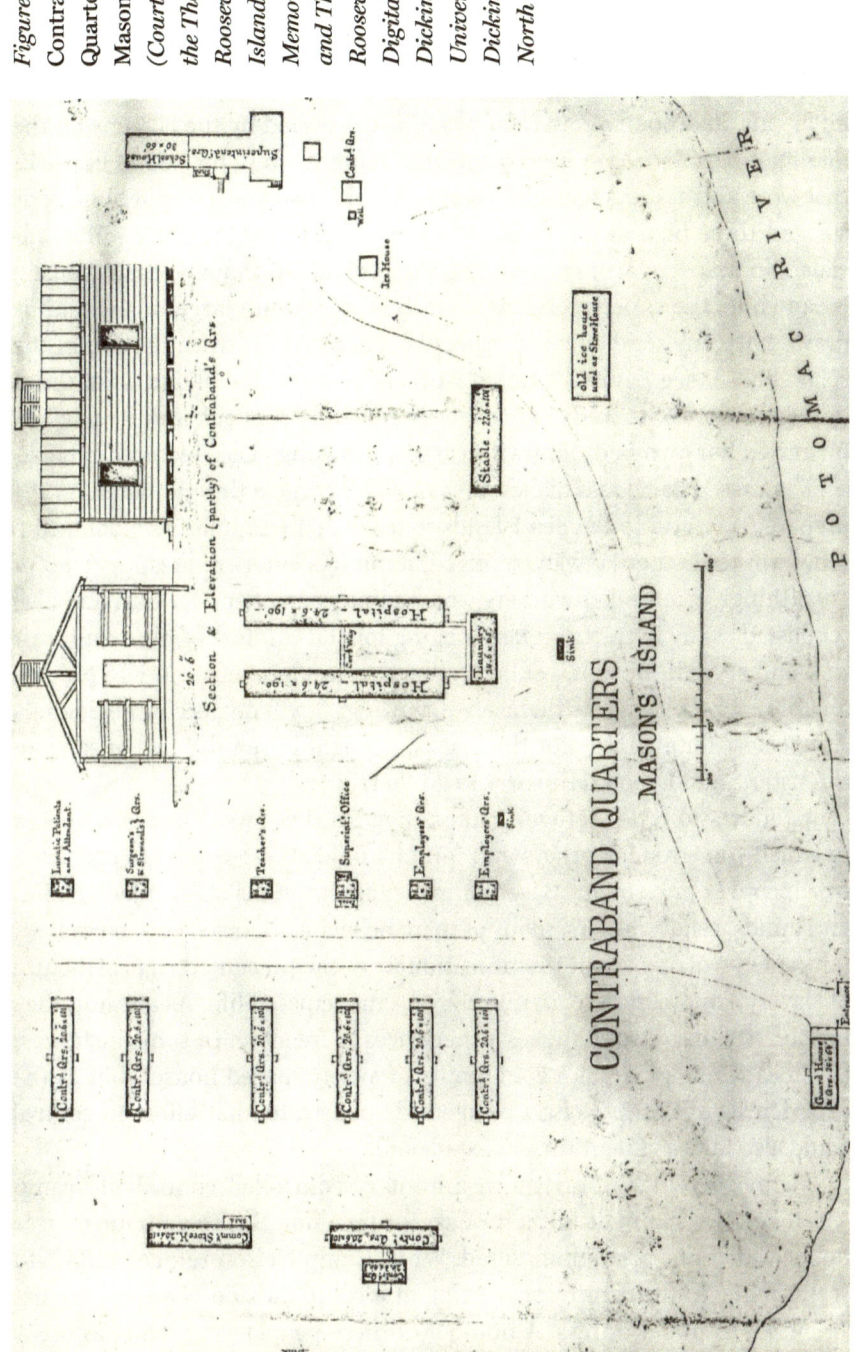

Figure 9. Contraband Quarters, Mason's Island. (Courtesy of the Theodore Roosevelt Island National Memorial and Theodore Roosevelt Digital Library, Dickinson State University, Dickinson, North Dakota)

black refugees by relief workers and military officials reinforced racial and social hierarchies. White relief workers and military officials went to great efforts, however, to ensure their own comfort. In New Bern, North Carolina, for instance, white soldiers occupied the often well-furnished houses of former residents, while refugees "obtained quarters in the out-houses, kitcheons, and poorer classes of dwellings, deserted by the citizens on the taking of Newbern." On Mason's Island, refugees were housed in barracks that were 20.5 feet wide and 100 feet long, with two long rows of bunk beds stacked three high and divided by a narrow aisle. By contrast, white officials and teachers at this camp lived in individual, though small, houses. Meanwhile, the superintendent's quarters were quite large; if the map is drawn with any semblance of scale, his quarters were twice the size of the schoolhouse (see figure 9). Relief workers also worried about the niceties of the interiors of their dwelling spaces. Martha Schofield, a white teacher, furnished her own bedroom with carpet, a looking glass, pictures, a bookshelf, a vase, a flag, glass dishes, towels, a clock, and a thermometer. As she prepared to travel to the Sea Islands to teach at a freedmen's school, white relief worker Esther Hawkes received numerous letters requesting "a lot of good things" from relief workers who had preceded her. Her husband also requested many items from her, longing for the comfort of his own furniture and stove in Boston, yet he hesitated to ask a relief society to provide anything for the refugees themselves, writing, "I will not ask of the Soldiers Aid Society for anything for the blacks; it might lessen the zeal of some of the sisters, and I should be sorry to do that."[37]

As efforts to order refugee camps suggest, these were material spaces in which some relief workers and military officials attempted to constrain freedpeople's movement. Based on racist assumptions about black bodies and minds, relief workers, many of them believing themselves to be well intentioned, worried about the transition from the presumed rigid structure of slavery's oppression to an unfettered, emancipated life. As a result, they took efforts to control refugees' experiences of freedom. In some instances, this meant mapping out a community of evenly spaced houses, but as the experiences of Camp Nelson refugees demonstrate, that effort to control could also take a violent turn of expulsion.

For many refugees, arrival in a military-controlled contraband camp was a decisive moment in their quest for freedom. But the circumstances under which one arrived mattered. While Camp Nelson refugees chose to seek shelter in the camp, some living at a camp outside Natchez, Mississippi, did so under duress. A number of these people were living in occupied Natchez when, under the guise of concern for overcrowding, an order was issued that "no contraband shall be allowed to remain in the city of Natchez, who is not employed by some *responsible white person* in some legitimate business, and who does not reside at the domicile of his or her employer." Anyone attempting to support themselves—whether through washing clothing or working as a drayman—and who did not live at a "responsible" white person's house was to be forcibly removed to the contraband camp located outside the city limits. As a result, numerous people were taken to the camp without shelter or clothing. Such incidents meant that while refugee camps could be the context in which some defined their sense of freedom, that same camp could be an experience of containment and internment for others.[38]

By definition, refugee life is characterized by displacement and movement—of both people and objects. And indeed, for many, these refugee camps were but way stations on a longer journey toward their own versions of freedom. Some continued to points farther north; others turned back to the land on which they had been enslaved or traveled in search of family members. In the decade that followed emancipation, much of the impermanent architecture of tents and hastily built cabins disappeared, but some of the communities endured. Mitchelville, for instance, continued to be populated by its inhabitants well into the late nineteenth century. At Camp Nelson, however, the army's departure brought significant changes. In some cases, former white landowners returned and reclaimed their property. A number of refugees continued to live in the houses, waiting for husbands in the U.S. Colored Troops to return, while others rented land nearby to support themselves. None of the original buildings of Camp Nelson remain, but ancestors of those who once lived there still reside in the community now known as "The Hall." The built environment of the camp continues to shape the movement of modern life in the form of streets that once passed between cottages.[39]

The refugees who built houses on the ruins of Hampton, Virginia, and in its vicinity offer some of the most striking examples of the continuous use of structures built during the war. A series of photographs taken in the 1890s are thought to depict "slab houses" built by 1860s refugees, and comparison to 1860s photographs of similarly built structures support this identification. Named for the slabs of rough planks of timber cut or sawn from logs, these structures were likely repaired and altered in the intervening time. The series of photographs nevertheless attests to the lives built in freedom by the residents of these houses and their descendants. In one photograph, a woman drives a cow-drawn cart, while another woman scrubs laundry in a tub, a child standing on top of something in the doorway nearby. In another photograph, a woman leans against a fence post while two children stand close by and their pet dog lies on the ground. A scrapbook that descended in the family of Hampton refugee Robert Brooks includes a photograph of Brooks and his wife, Edith Batten, seated with their eleven children. The material culture of their free lives is displayed in front of a clapboard house. We cannot know Brooks's refugee appearance, but if he looked at all like the descriptions of the majority of freed enslaved people, he likely had only a few pieces of clothing that were of poor quality. In this photo, he wears a three-piece suit and bowtie, and his daughters wear fashionable dresses, along with lace collars and embellishments. In all of these instances, the built environment of refugee life became long term, and even permanent.[40]

For many refugees, emancipated lives began in a hybrid built environment and material culture made up of belongings carried from enslaved homes; items taken from white Southerners' abandoned houses; secondhand Northern goods; military castoffs; and salvaged objects and architectural elements. At the same time that they provided refugees with access to necessities and small luxuries, relief workers, landowners, and military officials critiqued freedpeople's choices and tastes and placed strictures on their ability to develop new communities and to fashion the material culture of their lives. As one relief worker described, "These poor people have dreadful burdens of oppression & wrong to bear—can't drive a nail to fasten in a glass window, or a plank without forfeiting their necessary articles of furniture to the land owners." Instead, they "learned to fasten with wooden pins as much as possible & so evade the law." Whether part of a sharecropper's contract or a law related to taxes, this mandate meant that freedpeople needed to rely on skill and ingenuity in fashioning living spaces.[41]

Freedom was in part about making choices, from the remarkable to the mundane—from emancipating oneself to choosing to build cabins close together in order to maintain kin groups; from salvaging paned glass windows from masters' houses to selecting items to carry to new homes; from deciding where and when to scrub clothing on a washboard to fastening a window with a wooden pin instead of a nail. Freedom did not, however, mean throwing off all patterns of enslaved life; comfort could also be found in the familiar—in the doll carried by a child; in the redware pot that once sat on an enslaved table; in the trunk containing a dress worn in slavery, preserved as a reminder for future descendants. Together, these objects and houses reveal the muddled boundaries between slavery and freedom in which refugees and relief workers encountered and enacted, in a tangible, material way, emancipation as an ongoing process.

The material culture of emancipation offers a testament to the volatile nature of life in freedom experienced by many, in the form of damaged combs, melted buttons, and charred belongings that lay buried beneath the ground. But material culture also speaks to the kind of life that formerly enslaved people had and envisioned for the future: lives that included the education of themselves and their children; cooking meals and eating food on ceramic plates; choosing the type and location of their work; engaging in leisure activities with families and neighbors; selecting clothing and furnishings that reflected their own sense of style. Drawing together both textual accounts of refugee life and the material world exposes the struggles, possibilities, and lived experiences of emancipation in its many forms. The bleak outlook preserved in relief workers' textual accounts and publications reveals the hardships and racial biases that were part of refugee life. Yet those challenges and prejudices were the context in and backdrop upon which lives were lived out with texture and nuance, sorrow and happiness—the context in which freedpeople constructed vibrant material lives that defied relief workers' gridlines.

Notes

I thank Leora Auslander, Nancy Bercaw, Dana Byrd, Joan Cashin, Kathleen Neils Conzen, Thavolia Glymph, Jim Grossman, Katie Knowles, Brian Luskey, Megan Kate Nelson, Jason Phillips, Yael Sternhell, and Cathy Wright. Support for this research was provided by the Smithsonian Institution, the Committee on Institutional Cooperation, the Clements Library at the University of Michigan, the American Antiquarian Society, and the Division of the Social Sciences at the University of Chicago.

1. Historians have used the term "contrabands" to describe those people who escaped slavery and entered Union lines; the term was common in the 1860s, following the U.S. government's decision to classify former slaves as "contraband of war" to justify its refusal to return slaves to former masters prior to the Emancipation Proclamation. The term "refugee" has described displaced white Southerners. More recently, however, Thavolia Glymph and other scholars have renewed the use of the historical term "refugees" used by teachers, missionaries, newspapers, government agents, and freedpeople themselves. I adopt this terminology in order to more accurately reflect the identity of former slaves as people who were leaving their homes to free themselves and take refuge behind Union lines. "Our South Carolina Letter," *Philadelphia Inquirer*, 18 May 1863, 1.

Despite valuable work on refugees by other scholars, additional research is needed, particularly in regard to housing. See Joan E. Cashin, "Into the Trackless Wilderness: The Refugee Experience in the Civil War," and Thavolia Glymph, "'This Species of Property': Female Slave Contrabands in the Civil War," both in *A Woman's War: Southern Women, Civil War and the Confederate Legacy*, ed. Edward D. C. Campbell Jr. and Kym S. Rice (Charlottesville: University Press of Virginia, 1996), 29–53, 55–71; Chandra Manning, *Troubled Refuge: Struggling for Freedom in the Civil War* (New York: Alfred A. Knopf, 2016). Forthcoming works on refugees include those by Dana Byrd, Thavolia Glymph, and Amy Murrell Taylor. From the military perspective on "contraband of war," see Leon F. Litwack, *Been in the Storm So Long: The Aftermath of Slavery* (New York: Vintage Books, 1980); John David Smith, ed., *Black Soldiers in Blue: African American Troops in the Civil War Era* (Chapel Hill: University of North Carolina Press, 2002); and Barbara Brooks Tomblin, *Bluejackets and Contrabands: African Americans and the Union Navy* (Lexington: University of Kentucky Press, 2009).

2. I use "relief workers" to describe those people—civilian and military—who were actively working to aid freedpeople and manage the transition to freedom. Use of this term is admittedly anachronistic—"relief worker" did not come into use until the late 1870s. These individuals, however, understood themselves to be working toward the provision of relief. It is not my intention to elide the differences between the goals of various individuals, secular and religious organizations, and government agencies or to suggest that their work was always positive; much of their work was characterized by racist assumptions about African Americans. Rather, I employ this term in order to refocus our attention on one of the collective tasks these organizations faced: providing various kinds of aid to people in need.

3. Published works that address material culture and the Civil War include Joan E. Cashin, "Trophies of War: Material Culture in the Civil War Era," *Journal of the Civil War Era* 1, no. 3 (September 2011): 339–67; Michael DeGruccio, "Letting the War Slip through Our Hands: Material Culture and the Weakness of Words in the Civil War Era," in *Weirding the War: Stories from the Civil War's Ragged Edges*, ed. Stephen Berry (Athens: University of Georgia Press, 2011); Joseph Beilein, "The Guerrilla Shirt: A Labor of Love and the Style of Rebellion in Civil War Missouri," *Civil War History* 58, no. 2 (June 2012): 151–79; Jennifer Roth Bucci, ed., *The Civil War and the Material Culture of Texas, the Lower South, and the Southwest* (Houston: Bayou Bend Collection and Gardens, the Museum of Fine Arts, Houston, 2012); Madelyn Shaw and Lynne Zacek Bassett, *Homefront and Battlefield: Quilts and Context in the Civil War* (Lowell, Mass.: American Textile History Museum, 2012); and Sarah Jones Weicksel, "Armor, Manhood and the Politics of Mortality," in *Astride Two Worlds: Technology and the American Civil War*, ed. Barton Hacker (Washington, D.C.: Smithsonian Institution Scholarly Press, 2016). In addition to the authors included in this volume, works-in-progress by Dana Byrd, Ruthie Dibble, Katie Knowles, Megan Kate Nelson, and Ian Stevenson engage material culture studies of the Civil War.

For more on approaches to the study of material culture from the historian's point of view, see Leora Auslander, "Beyond Words," *American Historical Review* 110, no. 4 (October 2005): 1015–45. For an overview of theories and methods, see Ian Woodward, *Understanding Material Culture* (Los Angeles: Sage, 2007).

4. Litwack, *Been in the Storm*, xi; John Eaton, *Report of the General Superintendent of Freedmen* (Memphis, Tenn.: Department of the Tennessee and State of Arkansas, 1864), 18; Charles Nordhoff, "The Freedmen of South Carolina: Some Account of Their Appearance, Character, Condition, and Peculiar Customs," in *Paper of the Day*, ed. Frank Moore (New York: Charles T. Evans, 1863), 12.

5. Harriet Jacobs to William Lloyd Garrison, *Liberator*, 5 September 1862. Historians have largely focused on the work of the Freedmen's Bureau. See, for instance, Paul A. Cimbala, *The Freedmen's Bureau: Reconstructing the American South after the Civil War* (Malabar, Fla.: Krieger, 2005); Mary Farmer-Kaiser, *Freedwomen and the Freedmen's*

Bureau: Race, Gender, and Public Policy in the Age of Emancipation (New York: Fordham University Press, 2010); and Carol Faulkner, *Women's Radical Reconstruction: The Freedmen's Aid Movement* (Philadelphia: University of Pennsylvania Press, 2004).

6. Interview with Wayman Williams in "Federal Writer's Project: Slave Narrative Project," 1936, Texas, Vol. 16, Part 4, p. 182, Library of Congress, Washington, D.C., accessed 28 March 2016, https://www.loc.gov/item/mesn164/; Katherine Ashenburg, *The Dirt on Clean: An Unsanitized History* (Toronto: Vintage Canada, 2008), 2; Kathleen Brown, *Foul Bodies: Cleanliness in Early America* (New Haven: Yale University Press, 2011), 5, 11.

7. Nordhoff, "Freedmen of South Carolina," 17–19.

8. Juliet Ash, *Dress behind Bars: Prison Clothing as Criminality* (London: I. B. Tauris, 2009), 13; Dell Upton, *Another City: Urban Life and Urban Spaces in the New Republic* (New Haven: Yale University Press, 2008), 243.

9. Upton, *Another City*, 268; James P. Graves quoted in James Miller M'Kim, *The Freedmen of South Carolina* (Philadelphia: Willis P. Hazard, 1862); Horace James to Robert Dale Owen et al., 13 November 1863, Samuel Gridley Howe Papers, Houghton Library, Harvard University.

10. Samuel Gridley Howe, "Abstract of Mr. Eaton's Report," [1863], Howe Papers; Chaplain John Eaton Jr. to Lieutenant Colonel Jno. A. Rawlins, 29 April 1863, reprinted in Ira Berlin, Barbara J. Fields, Steven F. Miller, Joseph P. Reidy, and Leslie S. Rowland, eds., *Free at Last: A Documentary History of Slavery, Freedom, and the Civil War* (New York: New Press, 1993), 187.

11. Affidavit of Joseph Miller, 26 November 1864, RG 92, National Archives and Records Administration, Washington, D.C., reprinted in Richard D. Sears, *Camp Nelson, Kentucky: A Civil War History* (Lexington: University Press of Kentucky, 2002), 135–36. For more on the expulsion at Camp Nelson, see Amy Murrell Taylor, "How a Cold Snap in Kentucky Led to Freedom for Thousands: An Environmental Story of Emancipation," in Berry, *Weirding the War*, 191–214.

12. Jim Downs, *Sick from Freedom: African-American Illness and Suffering during the Civil War and Reconstruction* (New York: Oxford University Press, 2012); "Our South Carolina Letter."

13. Brown, *Foul Bodies*, 5–6, 11, 119; Nordhoff, "Freedmen of South Carolina," 18; Martha Schofield Diary, 22 April 1866, Martha Schofield Papers, Southern Historical Collection, Louis Round Wilson Special Collections Library, University of North Carolina at Chapel Hill; David Franklin Thorpe, Memoranda, Notes from Mr. Price's Report, David Franklin Thorpe Papers, Southern Historical Collection, University of North Carolina at Chapel Hill.

14. Berlin et al., *Free at Last*, 214; "Contraband Camp outside Helena, AR," Nebraska State Historical Society, Lincoln.

15. "Our South Carolina Letter"; Le Baron Russell to Edwin M. Stanton, 25 December 1862, Howe Papers. Ongoing work by Dana Byrd explores the spatial history of Hilton Head Island. See Dana E. Byrd with Tyler DeAngelis, "Tracing Transformations: Hilton Head Island's Journey to Freedom, 1860–1865," *Nineteenth Century Art Worldwide* 14, no. 3 (Autumn 2015), http://www.19thc-artworldwide.org/autumn15/byrd-hilton-head-island-journey-to-freedom-1860-1865.

16. John Fee, quoted in Sears, *Camp Nelson*, liv; W. Stephen McBride and Kim A. McBride, "Seizing Freedom: Archaeology of Escaped Slaves at Camp Nelson, Kentucky," reprinted in *African Diaspora Archaeology Network Newsletter*, March 2011, 21.

17. Plan of Mitchelville, its fortifications and environs, 1865, RG 77, National Archives and Records Administration, Washington, D.C.; A. B. Miller, detail of map, Camp Nelson, 1866, Cartographic Section, NARA-II, College Park, Md.; *Contraband Quarters, Mason's Island*, c. 1861, Theodore Roosevelt Digital Library, Dickinson State University, Dickinson, North Dakota.

18. Photograph, *Camp Nelson Home for Colored Refugees*, 1865, Special Collections, University of Kentucky, Lexington.

19. This Point of Pines cabin is now in the collection of the National Museum of African American History and Culture, Washington, D.C.; Byrd, "Tracing Transformation"; Dana Byrd, "Loot, Occupy, and Re-envision: Material Culture of the South Carolina Plantation," in Bucci, *Civil War and the Material Culture of Texas*, 80; Dana Byrd, "Northern Vision, Southern Land," in *The Civil War in Art and Memory*, ed. Kirk Savage (New Haven: Yale University Press, 2015), 27.

20. Samuel Cooley, photographs of Mitchelville, c. 1864, National Archives and Records Administration; A. F. Pillsbury, "Northampton School at Hilton Head," 24 September 1864, *Freedmen's Journal* 1 (1865): 13.

21. James to Owen et al., 13 November 1863, Howe Papers.

22. Walter Totten Carpenter, 11 January 1864, in "A Journey among the Contrabands: The Diary of Walter Totten Carpenter," *Indiana Magazine of History* 73, no. 3 (1977): 204–22, 210.

23. Russell to Stanton, 25 December 1862, Howe Papers; Robert Seager II, *And Tyler Too: A Biography of John and Julia Gardiner Tyler* (New York: McGraw-Hill, 1963); "Encampment and Officers' Quarters at Villa Margaret," *Frank Leslie's Illustrated Newspaper*, 13 July 1861, 131.

24. Alexander Hays, quoted in Megan Kate Nelson, *Ruin Nation: Destruction and the American Civil War* (Athens: University of Georgia Press, 2012), 22; "The Burning of Hampton," *Harper's Weekly*, 31 August 1861, 554; Nelson, *Ruin Nation*, 16, 22–23.

25. Lewis C. Lockwood, *Mary S. Peake, Colored Teacher at Fortress Monroe* (Boston: American Tract Society), 27–28; Nelson, *Ruin Nation*, 25–26.

26. It was recommended that chimneys extend at least two full feet above a roof in order to lessen the possibility of a fire resulting from discharging sparks. *Southern Cultivator*, cited in Amy G. Richter, *At Home in Nineteenth-Century America* (New York: New York University Press, 2015), 92.

27. F. W. Bird, quoted in Nelson, *Ruin Nation*, 25.

28. McBride and McBride, "Seizing Freedom," 11–14.

29. McBride and McBride, "Seizing Freedom," 9–10.

30. Herbert E. Valentine, "Interior of a Sibley Tent," c. 1861–65, Virginia Polytechnic Institute and State University; G. W. Andrews, "Interior of the Tent of a Private in the Cameron Cavalry," *Harper's Weekly*, 21 September 1861.

31. John P. Soule, Stereoview, *No. 379 Contraband Camp, Harper's Ferry, Va., 1862*, Library of Congress; Photograph, *Freedmen Living in Army Tent outside Helena, Ark.*," c. 1861–65, Nebraska State Historical Society.

32. Scott Butler et al., "Archaeological Data Recovery at Mitchelville (38BU2301) Hilton Head Island Airport Improvements Study Area, Beaufort, S.C., Final Report" (Atlanta: Brockington and Associates, 2013), 163, http://www.bcgov.net/mitchelville/pdf/Hilton_Head_Airport_DR.pdf.

33. Grand Contraband Camp Excavation Collection, Hampton History Museum, Hampton, Virginia; Butler et al., "Archaeological Data Recovery," 163.

34. McBride and McBride, "Seizing Freedom," 11.

35. Porcelain doll heads and a range of ceramics were found at the Mitchelville site. Butler et al., "Archaeological Data Recovery," 163.

36. Henry Hayes, 10 June 1864, Henry Hayes Journal, William L. Clements Library, University of Michigan; D. B. Nichols to the Commission, 8 September 1863, United States American Freedmen's Inquiry Commission, box 2, folder 72, Houghton Library, Harvard University; Clinton B. Fisk, *Plain Counsels for Freedmen* (Boston: American Tract Society, 1866), 56–57; Byrd, "Loot, Occupy, and Re-envision," 80; Kathleen Hilliard, *Masters, Slaves, and Exchange: Power's Purchase in the Old South* (Cambridge: Cambridge University Press, 2013), 26.

37. Vincent Colyer to Robert Dale Owen, 25 May 1863, reprinted in Berlin et al., *Free at Last*, 177; *Contraband Quarters, Mason's Island*; Schofield Diary, 6 June 1866, Schofield Papers; Edd to Sister Ett [Hawkes], 2 October 1862, and J. M. Hawkes to Esther Hawkes, 27 July and 3 August 1862, Esther Hill Hawks Papers, Library of Congress.

38. Berlin et al., *Free at Last*, 217–18.

39. McBride and McBride, "Seizing Freedom," 31. For more on the closure of Camp Nelson, see Sears, *Camp Nelson*.

40. Cyanotypes, c. 1892, Charles Herbert Hewins or Jesse Andrus Hewins, Hampton History Museum, Hampton, Virginia; Timothy R. Savage Scrapbook, Community Collection, Hampton History Museum.

41. Caroline Putnam, 14 January 1869, Caroline Putnam Letters, William L. Clements Library, University of Michigan.

There's No Place Like Home
Gender, Family, and the Confederate Alabama Household

VICTORIA E. OTT

Home provided more than shelter for common white families of the Confederate South; it served to create a politicized identity among this often-marginalized population. With much of scholars' attention on the South's slaveholding elites, we are left to ask whether this class group, even with its abundance of firsthand accounts, truly represents the whole Confederate experience. What about the middle and lower socioeconomic classes whose relationship to the domestic material landscape differed in many ways from those whose wealth and social status provided them a comfortable lifestyle? Families of the "plain folk" or "common whites"—comprising independent landowners as well as poor whites—functioned in the margins of the South's economic and political culture.[1] Their position in the region's hierarchy left them with a perception of the material world much different from that of the elite class. Burdened with producing necessities and a few amenities for themselves and their families, they placed a greater importance on the household and the items within it. As the war swept across the Southern landscape and invaded homes, men and women sought to redefine their prewar relationship with the home to demonstrate agency in the elite-dominated world of national politics, secession, and war. From furniture and dishware to livestock and crops, yeomen and poor whites turned to the items most familiar in their lives to help create a Confederate identity within their socioeconomic group. They transformed their relationship to the material possessions necessary for the survival and comfort of their families, painting portraits of the self-sacrificing, maternal woman and the protective male head-of-household dedicated to the support of their loved ones and, by extension, the Confederacy. Yet as the war took a financial, emotional, and physical toll on Southern households, the conditions of those from different socioeconomic classes appeared striking. Non-elites looked to their domestic culture as a symbol and cause of their protest against the war as their material conditions became dire. Because of socioeconomic circumstances, men and women of Alabama's plain folk sought agency in the material culture of domesticity, one most familiar to them.[2]

The Civil War transformed Confederate households in profound and often tortuous ways, from the death of loved ones to the destruction of treasured property. White families, whether rich or poor, played a crucial role in altering the domestic landscape to meet the economic and emotional demands of war. This essay, however, seeks a deeper understanding of the intersection of families and material culture. Alabama's plain folk utilized the home both as a means of production and as a place for possessions needed to navigate the hardships on the home front, create a political identity, and ultimately challenge the validity of the conflict and its cause. Using material culture as a lens through which to examine non-elites raises some significant questions. First, how did they perceive or use certain objects in the creation of a Confederate identity? Second, did their views of objects change during the war? And finally, did some whites decide that certain material possessions were no longer significant while other objects took on greater importance?[3]

This growing field of material cultural studies has opened new forms of analysis in relation to the Civil War experience of civilians and soldiers. Michael DeGruccio examines the fascination people have with the battlefield relics at Gettysburg. Although his focus is more on the public space of postmilitary engagements and less on the private domain of home, he does posit that material culture in the Civil War era "directly or indirectly reflect[s] fundamental belief patterns of individuals and the larger society." He implores scholars to consider more than words and include the objects to "reckon with the symbolic and spiritual power of things." Megan Kate Nelson brings into high relief the tension between what the war destroyed and what it created. Her book *Ruin Nation* includes the narratives of civilians and soldiers, Northerners and Southerners, and free and enslaved individuals. Analyzing the destruction of cities, homes, forests, and bodies, Nelson demonstrates the "power of wartime ruination as an imagined state, an act of destruction, and a process of change." She explores the physical environment and persons as subjects of ruin. Yet it is her examination of the home that demonstrates how the public world of war was brought into the private world of homes. She aptly contends that for wealthy white Southerners, the ruins of the "Big House" gave proof of a villainous, immoral enemy that targeted defenseless women in their intimate spaces. Joan E. Cashin's study of the "trophies of war" collected by Union and Confederate soldiers likewise deals with the practice of pillaging material items of Southern households. She contends, however, that soldiers viewed the possessions they confiscated as souvenirs of their experience as well as necessary items for survival. Yet how does the significance of the physical structure of the home, as well as the things within in it, play a role in the creation of a Confederate identity among common whites?[4]

Other historians writing on the period highlight the intersection of gender and material culture when considering the personal objects of women. Lisa Tendrich Frank's study of the gendered politics of the bedroom concentrates on how Sherman's troops invaded the homes of Confederate women. The incursion into intimate spaces such as the bedroom, she contends, signaled a violation of the "sanctity of female space." In refusing to abide by the rules of male propriety and raiding the most private of settings in the home, Union soldiers attacked "the material indicators of femininity—bedrooms, journals, letters, china, linens, and fancy dress." The response of women in the path of Sherman's men was not to cower from the enemy but rather to reinforce their confidence in the cause for Southern independence. Yet, the focus of her study is weighted more toward women of the elite classes, leaving readers again to ponder whether they can speak for the whole of the female experience. Kristen L. Streater, in her study of Confederate women of Kentucky, brings us a bit closer to a more nuanced narrative of women's wartime lives in relation to their material possessions. She identifies the importance of a "domestic supply line" that enabled women to use the objects within their private world to make public statements of Confederate support. These studies reveal that homes transformed into reflections of newly politicized gender roles.[5]

Fashion as an extension of women's domestic culture likewise played a key role in expressions of political sentiment among Confederate women. Cashin's research into women's clothing in the wartime South demonstrates how high fashion had long been a symbol of the elites' status. Women, as the producers and consumers of clothing, took interest in dress as a marker of their identity. As the region moved into war, wealthy white women found that fashion took on multiple meanings. Whether employing their large hoop skirts to smuggle items across enemy lines or wearing symbols of Confederate support on their dresses, women extracted political meaning from the world of dress, one very familiar to them in the prewar era. These studies of the gendered spaces of women's politicization, however, concentrate primarily on the relationship between women and material culture. What is needed is further examination of the varying experiences of men and women based on socioeconomic status, which this essay addresses.[6]

Alabama presents a unique place of study among the Southern states in regard to time and place. Those pre–American Revolutionary states created out of the British colonies of the region produced a varying set of circumstances different from those produced during the nineteenth-century push into the trans-Mississippi West. Alabama's early beginnings as a frontier of Georgia and its eventual statehood in 1819 meant that it had to catch up to such long-established states as Virginia, South Carolina, and Georgia. As historian Thomas Perkins Abernathy asserts, the formative years of Alabama came not during the colonial period but long after, between 1815 and 1828. The resulting effects meant that the state experienced frontier-like conditions well into the nineteenth century. These conditions created a muting of class differences as elites moving into the state labored to assert their status alongside those seeking the potential for wealth within Alabama's rich and diverse environment. The result was an atmosphere that resisted a true aristocracy, like that found in older Southern states before the Civil War. Class differences and even conflict existed, yet the developing nature of the state tended to keep them beneath the surface.[7]

By the 1840s, however, the areas of northern Alabama and the southeastern region known as the Wiregrass region emerged as strongholds for small farmers and poor whites. The poorest areas, where people had little connection to slaveholding interests and fewer claims to land ownership, were in Winston, Calhoun, and Dallas Counties. The relatively limited development of the state led families, regardless of socioeconomic conditions, to experience the same concerns regarding daily life. Specifically, issues such as family honor, high mortality, moral education, and diet cut across class lines in a state still emerging from its frontier roots. Yet, within this shared experience, class identification did emerge. Planter elites along with the yeomanry set themselves apart from their poor white contemporaries by viewing themselves as refined and well-mannered groups. Poor whites, likewise, pushed against such distinctions by displaying fierce loyalty to family, work, and religion—attributes that afforded them a sense of group honor. Amid this shared frontier experience and growing separate class identification, Alabama's non-elites entered the era of sectionalism and eventually civil war.[8]

Alabama's diverse political landscape shared more in common with the rest of the region. By the 1840s, many planter elites aligned with the Whig Party, while those of the yeoman and poor white communities identified

Gender, Family, and the Confederate Alabama Household

with the language of the "common man" that embodied the principles and ideals of the Democratic Party. The onset of the regional conflict resulting from the debate over the fate of slavery in the newly acquired territories from Mexico, however, opened the door for a political realignment. By the 1850s, with the growing tensions between North and South, Alabama's politics resembled that of many states of the Deep South. Much of the state's voting population threw their support behind the Democratic Party as they sought a safeguard for slavery and found their leader among a new generation of "fire-eaters." The emergence of William Lowndes Yancey as the voice of regional independence gave way to a nascent faction of political leaders clamoring for either protection of slavery by the national government or secession from the country.[9]

The question of secession produced deep divisions over the fate of Alabama in the Union that boiled to the surface by early 1861. The hill country of northern Alabama along with the Wiregrass region became a bastion of Unionism, while those areas where elite power was firmly entrenched held fast to secession as the South's solution to the slavery question. John Inscoe and Robert Kenzer in *Enemies of the Country* bring together a collection of scholars introducing how family loyalty and regional differences within the South produced a strong cadre of Unionist supporters. Building upon their scholarship, Margaret Storey, in her study of Unionism in Alabama, brings into high relief the contentious nature of the secession debate, which gave lie to notions of unanimity for Southern independence. Storey illustrates that a strong loyalist faction existed within Alabama's population. Rather than rely on a regional paradigm to explain the Unionist position, she argues that family honor and a sense of duty brought a minority of Alabamians to lead the charge to remain in the Union. Central to their position was the shared view that "the Union embodied democratic processes that continued to provide fair and just government." Those most vocal Unionists, however, found themselves at odds with the rising tide of Confederates upon passage of the ordinance of secession on 11 January 1861. Those proponents of remaining in the Union retreated underground amid organized vigilante groups seeking to root out perceived traitors to the new Confederate state.[10]

Within this politically charged atmosphere, human spaces—namely the home and all that it encompassed—became tools in constructing a politicized identity. The significance of the home structure especially among Alabama's common whites leads us to view the objects within the home with a greater eye for detail. For the South's women, the environment that permitted their participation in politics and civic affairs blurred the lines between public and private life. Historians point out that war often heightened women's civic activism and created new spaces in which they could express their political beliefs. The politically charged atmosphere that war produced allowed public affairs to invade the domestic arena, while the civic domain became places of informal political exchanges. The same held true in the Civil War South. Women's political participation took place in the domestic setting, where they engaged in war work, hosted patriotic gatherings, and discussed their support for the Confederacy. Even women from yeoman and poor white families found agency in the clarion call to serve the cause and support the military effort. Yet for women of more financial means, their duties included their civic participation outside the household. Their work in the Soldiers' Aid Societies and hospitals enabled women to utilize their domestic skills for the good of the cause. Non-elite women, however, rarely had the free time to volunteer outside the home. Rather, they turned inward to the gendered, physical space of their home and possessions, whether manufactured or raw materials, to express their support for the war. In this atmosphere in which domestic and civic concerns were intertwined, women found political agency in the Civil War South.[11]

Confederate men likewise transformed the home and its material items into a rhetorical device that helped reconcile the call to duty with their absence from the home. Scholars of material culture have asserted that the home served as a tool to navigate large-scale social disruptions. As historian Clifford Clark contends, for example, amid rapid westward expansion and growth of a market revolution, the home functioned as a calming force, a place of stability, and an escape from the uncertain challenges to American democratic principles in early nineteenth-century America. Placing the home in the context of the Civil War, the same holds true for Confederate Alabama. Men turned to the home as a rhetorical subject that justified, in their estimation, enlisting in a war that took them away from their homes and into harm's way. More specifically, men believed that their service fulfilled an honorable duty to defend the physical space of their homes that they saw as a microcosm of a larger Confederate community. As historian James McPherson contends, duty served as a "binding moral obligation involving reciprocity" in which one had a responsibility to serve the country "under whose protection one had lived." Avoiding such service threatened to tarnish a man's public reputation and that of his family. This sense of responsibility drove soldiers from the common whites, who had little investment in the slave institution, to enlist and serve. Domestic relationships became, in part, a motivation for enlisting but also for remaining in the military despite growing economic and emotional hardships at home and the constant grief of a combatant's life as the tide of war turned against the Confederates.[12]

Fathers and brothers were careful to discuss their service with family members in terms of protecting the domestic entity. Equating the cause of Southern defense against outside intruders to the protection of home and family provided a rhetorical tool to help them and others understand why these men should turn their attention to the civil war taking shape. The filial ideals of masculine duty helped them to reconcile service to the Confederacy with the potential for separation and even death. For instance, James Branscomb, from Union Springs, Alabama, wrote frequently to his sister Lucinda Hunter, a widow subsisting on a modest income. With all five of her brothers serving in the Fifth Alabama Infantry, she searched for meaning for their military service, which threatened to tear the family apart. James believed that service to the Confederacy protected both family and home, and in a letter to Lucinda, James attempted to calm her anxieties about his safety and that of her own children by writing that "if neither of your brothers should never return there should be one consoling thought, that we gave our lives in an honorable cause." James, moreover, reminded Lucinda that she too could turn to her family to find solace, citing that "you have some children that I believe will make you happy in after years."[13]

Conversely, the call to arms revealed others less willing to support a war that threatened to disrupt their lives. Emily Moxley of Coffee County protested her husband William's sense of duty to enlist in a local company. The couple had married in 1853 and settled in Coffee County, where William began his medical practice. Emily bore her first child at the age of seventeen and subsequently gave birth to a total of six children during their marriage. William's practice proved less than lucrative in one of the state's economically depressed counties. After Alabama seceded and much to Emily's chagrin, William joined the Bullock Guards and quickly assumed leadership as its captain. From the outset of her husband's service, Emily fell into a deep depression over his absence and the hardships that it would place on the family. As early as September 1861, she wrote to him that "it seems to me that we are all nearly heart broken" and that separation proved "the hardest trial I have ever had, by far." Patriotic encouragement seemed the farthest from Emily's mind when corresponding with William. For this young wife, the fear of losing her husband in battle proved more important than support for a cause that seemed so distant from their lives. After witnessing the death and illness of returning soldiers, she wrote that "I do not know how soon my Dear Husband may come in the same way.... I don't think I could live long if it be the case, for I feel like it would kill me."[14]

The concerns of daily survival likewise resulted in less attention to the impending Civil War. The diary of Sarah Rodgers Rousseau Espy of Cherokee County reveals the constant struggles of her peers in sustaining the domestic economy and less concern with the looming conflict. Espy's husband was a subsistence farmer and raised a modest number of livestock to sell in the community market. The early entries of her diary are primarily concerned with the weather, daily domestic duties, and childcare. After her husband's death in 1860, however, her entries took on a different tone as she struggled to settle his business affairs. Even after she gave power of attorney to a male community member whom she trusted, Sarah recorded a deep fear of being unable to provide for the family. Although her household at one time included two slaves, Espy faced modest and limited financial means at best. Her economic concerns coupled with the emotional stress of losing her husband brought great anxiety about the family's future and less interest in the discussion of war. She wrote in the summer of 1860 that "we are feeling badly and lonely and destitute ... for we are weak and look forward to [a] hard struggle with an unfeeling world."[15]

The demands of sacrifice nevertheless meant redefining one's familiar spaces into a place of support and comfort. Within the structural space of home, non-elites extracted political meaning from regular household items. In doing so, they found a voice in a conflict that, at times, called upon them to sacrifice the security of home and family. In knowing that they could remain connected to the home, men found a powerful source to sustain them through the emotional trials of war. Women likewise, as those left on the home front, received comfort in the knowledge that their domestic production in areas of food and clothing brought relief to those whom they envisioned enduring great suffering. These women sought to define a supportive, maternal identity for themselves by providing the material comforts of home to their male kin on the battlefront.

Southern newspapers emphasized the need for women's domestic production and encouraged them to join supportive organizations. The growth of Richmond's military population, for example, taxed the resources of all public groups to the point where the *Daily Richmond Enquirer* published a general call for all women to help. "We felt ... we should need the cooperation of our sisters," the newspaper implored, suggesting "that in every county and every community societies should be formed at once." For elite women, local soldiers' aid and sewing societies served as the primary organizations in which to gather necessary goods and, in the process, provided women an avenue through which to express their patriotism. But for women of the non-elite class, volunteering in civic organizations placed an undue burden upon their time. They rather had to look inward to the home for items produced there on a regular basis for items that would support the troops on the front. Margaret Miles Gillis, a young woman from Lowndes County, recorded in her diary that as a company of Alabama guards camped out in her small town, an officer "brought out some shirts for us to make for them, and Sis C sis Mollie, sis Sallie and I made one apiece." Resonating from her words was a sense of patriotic pride in her ability to assist the troops, even if they were stationed nearby temporarily.[16]

The women newly politicized by the events of secession and war transformed their normal tasks of household production into expressions of support and self-sacrifice. In essence, while they had always been the manufacturers of household goods, their relationship to those objects changed in the context of war. Patriotism, in part, drove their desire to supply family members on the front. But the need to offer support to specific loved ones on the military front created a new relationship between women and their domestic objects. Foremost among the items soldiers solicited from female kin was clothing. For women of common white households, such contributions to the Confederate war effort made a neat fit with a woman's familial duty to help supply her family, which traditionally relied on female labor. Soldiers from the state's elite mustered in to the army with a relative variety of clothing, while those of less means came into service with merely a change of clothes that they carried "in a sack over their shoulders." Thus, non-elite soldiers depended on female kin to resupply them with clothing. In her diary, Sarah Espy illuminated the invaluable role she played in supplementing the clothing of her sons serving in the Confederate army. Rather than begrudge the added burden to her workday, she saw this as a way to ensure the comfort of her sons despite their separation from the home. Columbus Espy, Sarah's younger son, wrote in September 1861 that he needed clothes, and she acquiesced. Lucinda Branscomb Hunter also wrote frequently to her brothers on the front asking if they needed homemade supplies, in particular clothing.[17]

Women found patriotic meaning in the production of clothing in the home. Producing cloth and clothing provided a comfortable role through which women could express their newfound political identity. Newton Davis, a yeoman from Pickens County, encouraged his wife, Elizabeth or "Bettie," to grow a small plot of cotton "enough to supply you plentiful with spinning cotton and other purposes of home use." Producing clothing in the home was a traditional role for women of the antebellum period. But placed in the context of a struggling economy, a need for self-sufficiency, and a culture of wartime sacrifice, women's clothing production took on a different importance. The same held true for women of the yeoman class. Espy, for instance, recorded in her diary that "we [female friends] are weaving straw bonnets. They are so fashionable and pretty. The blockade of our ports have thrown us on our own resources and nobly we are coming up to the conflict."[18]

Soldiers often discussed issues of food in their letters home. Their expressions of concern over the supply of food to the home indicate a need to assert their role as protector of the family during their absence. Men wrote often to their wives encouraging them to take on greater responsibilities for food production, thus assisting women in redefining their relationship to production and consumption. Scholars have pointed out the consequences of Union and Confederate troops confiscating food from civilians on the Southern home front. The prewar South had enough food to sustain the white population. But when the war reached into Southern homes, food became an extreme source of struggle. The long-term results of soldiers pillaging food supplies meant the potential for hunger, leaving families to seek alternatives for food. Food therefore weighed constantly on the minds of soldiers separated from home, and directions on how to maintain the family's sustenance ensured their continued protective role. Newton Davis, for example, wrote frequently to his wife about the crops and livestock that she attended. "Your Papa wrote me that you had killed a portion of your hogs," he wrote; "I hope you will be fortunate enough to save it all.... It is a very important item at this stage of the game in this Confederacy." In March 1863, Bettie wrote to Newton that their home was in a state of decay and she had contemplated having another modest home built to replace it. Concerned for the material comfort of his family, Newton responded that "I know that it is something that you need very much and I am reminded every hard rain we have of that fact.... You mentioned in your letter how much frightened you were the night of the storm, for fear the house would fall down on your head." John W. Cotton, a yeoman farmer from Coosa County, also wrote to his wife, Mariah, about the condition of their farm. The couple owned a modest landholding of 350 acres meant to support them, their seven children, and one hired hand. He entrusted his wife with the farm but consistently advised her on raising and harvesting the crops, recognizing the value of food as a precious commodity. In an 1862 letter, he expressed concern over the state of their wheat and livestock: "Do the best you can [to] have that wheat and barley thrashed as soon as you can and turn the hogs in."[19]

Soldiers often turned to food and the female kin who produced it to alleviate homesickness and deal with conditions in the military camps. Newton

Davis wrote that rain had soaked him one night after searching for his horse in a storm and he returned to his tent "all wet and shivering with cold and rolled myself up in my blanket, not to sleep but to dream of home, of warm fires, warm beds, and every thing else nice and comfortable." When his wife wrote to him about raising a garden, he again reminisced about domestic culture. "It reminds me of the good old days of yore when you & I used to go down to the garden to sow seed," he wrote. "Oh don't I wish they would come again." Other male kin found a connection to the family by envisioning a return to the home and the normal routine of dining together. James Garrison wrote to his wife that he dreamed of the day when he could return home and enjoy a family meal. As a poor white in rural Alabama, Garrison had very little means of support except for the small family farm. His letters mentioned little of the Confederate cause but rather the hopes of reuniting and resuming life with his wife and children. Garrison likewise missed the food that provided sustenance, which was clearly absent at times on the military front. In April 1863, he wrote to his wife that "I want yew to hav a heap of water melons ... and cornbeef and a few snaps and rosen and a fride chicken." Newton Davis also lamented the absence of home-cooked meals when he quipped that his unit lacked a good cook. "I often long for the good things at home," he wrote Bettie, "and I hope that it will not be long before I shall be permitted to enjoy them." Benjamin Franklin Jackson of Covington County, who served in the Thirty-Third Alabama Regiment, jokingly wrote to his sister that when the watermelons of the farm were ripe, she should "send me on[e] in a letter if you can seal it up." James Crowder of Chambers County wrote to his mother that he looked to her cooking, for which he hoped to survive the war and come home. "I have not eat no corne bread since I eat that up that I started from home with," he lamented. "I wood give a half a dolar for one litle cake of corn bred now just to sea how hit [it] would taste."[20]

Women took to heart the significance of their role in food production, whether with the crops or with cooked items. Left behind to tend to the crops, women of Alabama's plain folk believed that they too contributed to the survival of their families and conceded the importance of their supportive role. By September 1861, Sarah Espy recorded the difficulty in finding basic supplies, a concern that grew throughout the course of the war. She noted that she "must learn to do without such things" or, in her case, take it upon herself to grow basic foodstuffs on the farm. Emily Moxley and her doctor husband, William, had very little income before the war. In addition to his medical practice, their small farm was essential in providing food for the family. The farm took on greater importance after William's absence eliminated his pay as a doctor. One of her neighbors gathered her corn for her and put it in storage but refused to pay for it. She wrote to William that the neighbor's lack of sympathy toward her left their family searching for a means of finding food. "Nobody to do any thing but me, and I cant do any thing by my self," she wrote. "You have lost all you had, and it looks like every thing here will be lost soon." In sum, Emily grew to see her relationship with food production and consumption as a matter of life or death. Mariah Cotton fared better on her farm in her husband John's absence. He entrusted her with the harvest of wheat and rye, as well as with the maintenance of their hogs. She assumed the role as manager of the farm and proved rather successful in keeping their family supplied with food throughout the course of the war.[21]

Women likewise turned to food to do more for the Confederate cause than solely supply provisions for their male kin. Confederate troops passing through a community often looked to the civilian population for the comforts of home, especially a home-cooked meal. Many women obliged, seeing their own sons, fathers, and other male kin in the soldiers whom they were feeding and thus comforting. These invitations to supper with civilian families likewise allowed women to demonstrate their patriotism in less public displays, a good alternative for those with no inclination or time to engage in civic activities. Espy, for example, invited soldiers into her home for dinner on a few occasions. For this woman of modest income and little free time for volunteer organizations, offering dinner and a place to sleep for soldiers gave her a sense of satisfaction that she did her part for the cause. Even as she remarked on limited resources in one of her diary entries, she still invited a cavalry soldier to dine with her family that same day. Just a few months later, she hosted three soldiers for dinner and a place to sleep for the night as they passed through her Alabama community.[22]

By 1863, declining conditions transformed the meaning of material culture within common white households. Government and military officials looked more and more toward the resources from the home front to support the Confederate cause. Non-elite soldiers bore much of the effects of material deprivation, especially concerning food and clothing. Letters from male kin describing scenes of severe deprivation in the camps redefined items typically produced at home as solely a form of comfort as now a matter of life or death. James Branscomb, for instance, remarked on the lack of food in the camps when he quipped that "soldiers are a right happy people when they get enough to eat, but we have not been very happy since we've been here for grist has been scarce." In several letters to his wife, Newton Davis described the uncomfortable conditions made worse by the declining availability of supplies for the soldiers. More and more, he came to rely on Bettie's sewing skills to ease his situation. "My pants have all nearly worn out and I am nearly barefooted," he confided to her. "It is impossible to get any thing here in the way of clothing at all." Paying "sixteen dollars for a very common pair of Grey Jeans pants which would not be worth more than two dollars... in ordinary times" was too much for Newton to bear. He requested Bettie to purchase and send boots and a hat as well as to make shirts for him, all commodities scarce in the declining Confederate economy. He believed, however, that with her on the home front, such items were readily available, not recognizing that she too endured the financial strains of war. Yet when she obliged by sending shirts to Newton, she received his high praise as "a very smart and industrious wife." These connections to home via the material items of the domestic culture provided a sense of security and served a practical purpose, supplementing the amenities that soldiers lacked on the front. Benjamin Jackson expressed his gratitude over the shoes his wife sent him, noting that he was "barefooted or nearly so."[23]

Conditions among Alabama's civilians were little better. Soaring inflation and scarcity of basic supplies brought the state to a crisis level as its population suffered. It became clear that common whites who had fared well enough in the antebellum era now struggled for daily survival. By 1863, numerous letters poured into Governor Gill Shorter's office seeking relief from hunger. The situation grew dire to the point that the state organized relief communities and churches offered assistance. Worse still, the state underwent a shortage in salt supplies—a much-needed commodity in food preservation. Alabama's food crisis revealed the deep class disparities as the wealthy weathered the crisis while the non-elites grew more dependent on the state for assistance. The situation reached a fever pitch when in September 1863 riots broke out in Mobile in which primarily women took to the streets demanding "bread or blood." Seeking to relieve the situation, state officials by 1864 tried to calculate the number of households that received government assistance. Officials reported that the number of indigent families from forty-seven counties totaled 35,393. But even the assistance the government provided did little to reverse the growing resentment among Alabama's common whites toward a war in defense of the interests of the wealthy class.[24]

The presence of Union troops in Alabama exacerbated the crisis in material conditions among non-elite households. By 1863, the Espys, like many yeoman and poor white families of the Confederacy, struggled to obtain supplies for the home, specifically food and clothing. The situa-

Figure 10. Alabamians Receiving Rations, 1866. (Courtesy of the Library of Congress)

tion was made worse still with the invasion of Union troops into Southern households and the practice of commandeering or destroying supplies and material possessions. Sarah recorded in her diary that soldiers had come through her community taking everything "except for a few chickens." The following year, she remarked on the further destruction and deprivation of her dwindling household items and food supply. "There was a company of them," she wrote of the Federal soldiers; "they fed their horses leaving the ground covered with corn and oats; and carried as much away as they could I presume." For this head of a yeoman household, such loss of possessions would take months, if not longer, to replenish in a time of severe inflation and lack of supplies. Espy further stressed the severity of their loss, writing that "they took nearly all the boys fine clothing ... spurs; sheets; towels; pillow-cases; knives and forks, and all other things too tedious to mention." She concluded by noting that the experience left her feeling "helpless as infants." Espy resorted to relying on her community for help, especially to provide food, writing that "we have lost nearly everything, but we have been fortunate in having good friends." Emily and William Moxley spent much of the war struggling to keep their family fed and clothed. Emily and children found themselves in dire straits made worse by a raid of Union troops in their community. In one instance, she wrote to William that Federal soldiers had taken all the hogs except for one and that, as a result, they were now "left in a bad fix a bout meat."[25]

News of home-front conditions and the state of food supply reached male kin on the front and reinforced their need to assert a protective role in their absence. As the war entered its third year, John Cotton grew concerned over the state of his family's food source after hearing of "soldiers wives that has not much to eat." He punctuated his concern by offering to come home if he heard that they were without food: "If I were to here that you had nothing to eat I should come home at the risk of my life." Harris Averett, from Tallapoosa County, wrote to his wife about the declining conditions in the camp. This poor white mechanic dependent primarily on his soldier's pay remarked that the situation had declined to the point that he was starting to sell items that he had received from home just to purchase other goods that he could not afford. He asked her to send items such as butter, potatoes, and ground peas, noting, "I will sell them and send you the money."[26]

The relationship to domestic objects coupled with the conditions of their socioeconomic class ultimately stirred a resistance to the conflict among common whites. Muted class differences common in the frontier-like context of antebellum Alabama gave way to a vocal sense of socioeconomic disparities. Namely, the privations of home goods led to resentment among non-elite women that called into question why they should support a conflict that served the interests of elite, slaveholding Southerners. Those of wealth, for example, found alternatives to staying behind in the face of occupation and possessed more economic resources to weather, at least in appearance, financial downturns. As non-elites felt the material pains of war, they directed their frustrations toward the wealthier families and recognized the inequities in the home-front experience. After a visit to an elite member of her community, Sarah Espy reflected on what she believed was a war waged on the backs of "the workingclasses." When threatened with Federal occupation in December 1863, elite community members possessed the means to retreat from potential danger, while those of Espy's class had little choice but to remain. These class inequities roused in Espy a sentiment that members of her socioeconomic group shouldered an unfair burden of the war. "They are well off," she wrote, "and are going to wealthy friends whereas I, and many others, have no friends and our children even barely boys, are taken from us and put into the serves [service]. There is a great wrong somewhere."[27]

Clearly to Espy and other common whites, the antebellum era of plenty was now replaced by suffering and want, a condition less pervasive among the state's planter elite. Espy also directed her criticisms toward the Confederate government when she wrote about the conscription law that called additional male kin to the front, proclaiming the draft policy "as shameful a one as congress ever passed." She punctuated her anger toward Confederate officials when she criticized them for what she believed were self-serving practices that caused undue burdens on members of her class community. "They also passed a law giving themselves $2700 a year," she wrote in August 1862, "and the greater part of the time they are at home attending their business. I look for a rebellion among ourselves at the rat[e] of going on, for the war taxes the people heavy enough."[28]

Throughout the first two years of the war, before her untimely death in 1862, Emily Moxley expressed conflicting sentiments about the war that caused her husband's extended absence. As the family struggled, Emily became more and more dependent on the assistance of Newton, a white man and neighbor in the community whom her husband had entrusted with caring for the family. Unfortunately, Newton saw the family as more of a burden and seemed less inclined, in Emily's view, to help them. Becoming increasingly frustrated with his lack of attention to the family's financial matters and their growing privation, Emily turned to community members to help provide for her dependents. Newton failed to settle debts owed to William and delayed selling land that could help supplement the family income; Emily noted that "he is not willing to do any thing for me and them." Emily revealed to William that she was now at the mercy of a local merchant to provide supplies on credit and was circumventing Newton's authority to oversee her family finances. Emily also wrote frequently to her husband about the hardships of acquiring necessities for the family. Her writing reflects notions of female dependency rooted in the gendered ideals of the Old South: "I am dependent," she conceded, and punctuated her dependency by explaining how the men of her family and community failed to assist her in properly supplying the home. As the family teetered on the brink of starvation, Emily told William that she would be forced to turn to community assistance: "You don't know how I feel to go [to] any body else for something to eat when I never had it to do in my life. I have all ways had my dear Husband to provide for me and to a head in every thing, and now I have no one that cares for my well fare that is about here." Emily's resentment toward the war led her to question the conduct of Confederate officers, which she saw as adding to the hardships of civilians on the home front. "The officers," she declared, "are in for the money and do not think about the responsibility that rests upon there heads. They ought not to go for money alone."[29]

The material and emotional hardships that Lucinda Hunter experienced on the home front brought her to question her patriotism. She wrote her brother James expressing her discontent with seeing the war through after losing their youngest brother to the military front. James attempted to comfort his sister, writing that "the prospect does look a little gloomy, but wait a while and you will hear of another great victory from Genl Lee's army that will cheer every southern heart." Louis Branscomb, another of Lucinda's brothers, shared his sister's sentiment about the continuation of the war. "I was sorry to find you so low spirited," he wrote to her in October 1863, "but I can't blame you for you have enough to make you so. I must admit that I am in that line myself.... I am getting like you. I am losing all my patriotism."[30]

As the war drew to a close, Alabama's plain folks anticipated returning to their former lives. After families reunited, some broken by death, the prospect of rebuilding life following Confederate defeat provided a way to refocus their energies. Now their daily lives would be filled with recovering from the war. But what did all of this mean to Alabama's non-elites? What meaning had they extracted from four long years of separation, privation, and emotional turmoil? Through the home and the material objects within it, Alabama's common whites found agency in the Civil War experience by creating a supportive, maternal female identity and a protective, paternal male identity. The home provided a structural space to justify their defense of the institution of slavery that served little interest in their daily lives.

Yet the very objects that compelled them to throw their support behind the cause eventually took them to a place of resistance. As in the words of Sarah Espy, they came to see that "there is a great wrong somewhere." The material deprivation and invasion of the household space created a state of crisis among non-elites that led them to question the continuation of the war and fairness of the conflict. The war, in essence, proved a watershed moment for the state's common whites. Gone was the sense of a level playing field wrought by the frontier conditions of a developing state. They came to see the stark reality of class division, even conflict, that had lain dormant in the earlier years of the state.[31]

Notes

1. The title of this essay is from Harris Averett to Linda Averett, 23 August 1863, Harris Hardin Averett Papers, Alabama Department of Archives and History, Montgomery (hereafter ADAH).

I define "common whites" as those non-elites who owned little to no land and fewer than fifteen slaves, if any. To confirm their status, I used the Manuscript Schedules of the Seventh (1850) Census and Eighth (1860) Census of the U.S. Bureau of the Census, available on www.ancestry.com. I also confirmed their nonslaveholding status using the 1850 and 1860 Slave Schedules of the U.S. Bureau of the Census, sources for which were accessed on www.ancestry.com. For the few who mentioned slave ownership, I confirmed that their holdings were fewer than fifteen. In cases of missing census information, I used the editors' information concerning the profile of my subjects in published primary sources.

My definition of common whites derives from the historiographic literature. See Frank Owsley, *Plain Folk of the Old South* (Baton Rouge: Louisiana State University Press, 1949); William Harris, *Plain Folk and Gentry in a Slave Society: White Liberty and Black Slavery in Augusta's Hinterlands* (Middletown, Conn.: Wesleyan University Press, 1985); Bruce Collins, *White Society in the Antebellum South* (New York: Longman, 1985); and Charles C. Bolton, *Poor Whites of the Antebellum South: Tenants and Laborers in Central North Carolina and Northeast Mississippi* (Durham: Duke University Press, 1994). Studies dealing particularly with issues of women and gender include Victoria E. Bynum, *Unruly Women: The Politics of Social and Sexual Control in the Old South* (Chapel Hill: University of North Carolina Press, 1992); and Stephanie McCurry, *Masters of Small Worlds: Yeoman Households, Gender Relations, and the Political Culture of the Antebellum South Carolina Low Country* (New York: Oxford University Press, 1995). Studies relating to the Civil War era tend to focus on reasons why "plain folk" fought and on sources of dissent as wartime conditions worsened. Such studies include Mary Elizabeth Massey, *Ersatz in the Confederacy* (Columbia: University of South Carolina Press, 1952) and *Bonnet Brigades* (New York: Alfred A. Knopf, 1966); Paul D. Escott, *After Secession: Jefferson Davis and the Failure of Confederate Nationalism* (Baton Rouge: Louisiana State University Press, 1992); David Williams, Teresa Crisp Williams, and David Carlson, *Plain Folk in a Rich Man's War: Class and Dissent in Confederate Georgia* (Gainesville: University Press of Florida, 2002); and Mark V. Wetherington,

Plain Folk's Fight: The Civil War and Reconstruction in Piney Woods Georgia (Chapel Hill: University of North Carolina Press, 2005).

2. Elizabeth Varon first coined the phrase "Confederate womanhood" to describe the political agency of Virginia's elite white women as they saw their cause in terms of personal sacrifice and support. Other scholars such as Drew Gilpin Faust and Jacqueline Glass Campbell redirected the notions of the self-sacrificing Confederate woman toward the private, domestic space. Faust demonstrates how increasing hardships on the Southern home front encouraged women to resist the sacrifices needed to sustain the war and, in many cases, protest its cause. Coming to a much different conclusion, Campbell concludes that invading Federal troops in Sherman's march to the sea reinvigorated the rancor and resistance of war-weary women toward the enemy. These studies, however, concentrate primarily on the experience of elite, slaveholding women with little if no attention to the common white woman. Elizabeth Varon, *We Mean to Be Counted: White Women and Politics in Antebellum Virginia* (Chapel Hill: University of North Carolina Press, 1998), 169–70; Drew Gilpin Faust, *Mothers of Invention: Women of the Slaveholding South* (Chapel Hill: University of North Carolina Press, 1996); Jacqueline Glass Campbell, *When Sherman Marched North from the Sea: Resistance on the Confederate Homefront* (Chapel Hill: University of North Carolina Press, 2003). The male conceptualization of the war as a means of protecting the family's honor as well as material well-being are found in Bell Irvin Wiley, *The Life of Johnny Reb: The Common Soldier of the Confederacy* (Indianapolis: Bobbs-Merrill, 1943); Reid Mitchell, *Civil War Soldiers* (New York: Viking Press, 1988); and James McPherson, *For Cause and Comrades: Why Men Fought in the Civil War* (New York: Oxford University Press, 1997).

3. As a literal and as a rhetorical space, the home with its possessions gives us a better understanding of the relationship between subject and object in the creation of identity. Jules David Prown, in his 1982 article, defines material culture as "the study through artifacts of the beliefs—values, ideas, attitudes, and assumptions—of a particular community or society at a given time." A group displays a cognitive awareness when it purchases, creates, or produces objects. The deliberate nature of the items evident in people's lives helps us to understand the culture of societies in specific times of their existence. Thomas J. Schlereth likewise makes a compelling case for the use of material items in understanding human behavior. He contends that objects reveal the behavioral patterns of past individuals and the choices that they made. Schlereth argues that historians are now recognizing how "patterns of home furnishings, foodways, clothing, and organizations of domestic space" give insight into the "social past of middle-class and working-class culture." In other words, according to Schlereth, the objects within the dwelling tell us more about the human experience than textual evidence as they "emphasize ... the diversity of human creative expression and motivation." By applying such a "behavioralistic" paradigm to the families of non-elite households, we can perhaps better comprehend why they chose to use specific items as expressions of Confederate patriotism and, conversely, as declarations of protest. Jules David Prown, "Mind in Matter: An Introduction to Material Culture Theory and Method," *Winterthur Portfolio* 17, no. 1 (Spring 1982): 1–2; Thomas J. Schlereth, "Material Culture Studies and Social History Research," *Journal of Social History* 16, no. 4 (Summer 1983): 115, 117, 124.

Other scholars of material culture have expanded upon the relationship between social groups and objects that focused on the creation of a middle-class identity. The primary contention rests upon the notion that items, specifically those in the home, served to define socioeconomic identities. Whereas American culture seemed more on a level playing field in terms of dwellings and material objects within them in the mid-colonial period, by the nineteenth century, homes clearly became spaces in which the process of creating a middle-class or genteel identity took place. Clifford Edward Clark Jr. in his study of American middle-class homes and Richard Bushman's analysis of new ideas of the genteel identity illustrate the ways in which objects, unattainable to the poorer socioeconomic classes, set upper socioeconomic groups apart from other classes in society. Clark agrees that the home, while important to the individual, became the tool to protecting democracy in the growing nation by the 1800s. Bushman argues that people were performers of gentility and the items in their homes were the props allowing for "the separation of the lower orders." What Clark and Bushman reveal is that the home was more than a shelter but rather a cultural institution in which the process of identity creation took place. Clifford Edward Clark Jr., *The American Family Home, 1800–1960* (Chapel Hill: University of North Carolina Press, 1986), 4, 12; Richard L. Bushman, *The Refinement of America: Persons, Houses, Cities* (New York: Alfred A. Knopf, 1992), xii–xv.

4. Michael DeGruccio, "Letting the War Slip through Our Hands: Material Culture and the Weakness of Words in the Civil War Era," in *Weirding the War: Stories from the Civil War's Ragged Edges*, ed. Stephen Berry (Athens: University of Georgia Press, 2011), 27–28, 29; Megan Kate Nelson, *Ruin Nation: Destruction and the American Civil War* (Athens: University of Georgia Press, 2012), 9, 61–102; Joan E. Cashin, "Trophies of War: Material Culture in the Civil War," *Journal of the Civil War Era* 1, no. 3 (September 2011): 339–67.

5. Lisa Tendrich Frank, "Bedrooms as Battlefields: The Role of Gender Politics in Sherman's March," 33–38, and Kristen L. Streater, "She-Rebels on the Supply Line: Gender Conventions in Civil War Kentucky," 88–90, in *Occupied Women: Gender Military Occupation and the American Civil War*, ed. LeeAnn Whites and Alecia P. Long (Baton Rouge: Louisiana State University Press, 2009).

6. Joan E. Cashin, "Torn Bonnets and Stolen Silks: Fashion, Gender, Race, and Danger in the Wartime South," *Civil War History* 61 (December 2015): 338, 340, 349–350, 353, 357.

7. Thomas Perkins Abernathy, *The Formative Period in Alabama, 1815–1828* (Tuscaloosa: University of Alabama Press, 1965), 170, 178; William Rogers, Robert David Ward, Leah Rawls Atkins, and Wayne Flynt, *Alabama: The History of a Deep South State* (Tuscaloosa: University of Alabama Press, 1994), 113.

8. Wayne Flynt, *Poor but Proud: Alabama's Poor Whites* (Tuscaloosa: University of Alabama Press, 1989), 12, 15–16, 27–28.

9. Abernathy, *Formative Period in Alabama*, 178; Rogers et al., *Alabama*, 150–60.

10. John C. Inscoe and Robert C. Kenzer, eds., *Enemies of the Country: New Perspectives on Unionists in the Civil War South* (Athens: University of Georgia Press, 2001); Margaret M. Storey, *Loyalty and Loss: Alabama's Unionists in the Civil War and Reconstruction* (Baton Rouge: Louisiana State University Press, 2004), 1–17, 21, 56–86.

11. Paula Baker, "Domestication of Politics: Women and American Political Society," *American Historical Review* 89 (June 1984): 620–47; Linda K. Kerber, "Sepa-

rate Spheres, Female Worlds, Woman's Place: The Rhetoric of Women's History," *Journal of American History* 75 (June 1988): 9–39; Cynthia Kierner, *Beyond the Household: Women's Place in the Early South, 1700–1835* (Ithaca: Cornell University Press, 1998), 2; Faust, *Mothers of Invention*, 5–7; Catherine Clinton, *The Other Civil War: American Women in the Nineteenth Century* (New York: Hill and Wang, 1984), 81–82. See also Catherine Allgor, *Parlor Politics: In Which the Ladies of Washington Helped Build a City and a Government* (Charlottesville: University Press of Virginia, 2000).

12. Clark, *American Family Home*, 15–16; Wiley, *Life of Johnny Reb*; Mitchell, *Civil War Soldiers*; McPherson, *For Cause and Comrades*, 22–29; Aaron Sheehan-Dean, *Why Confederates Fought: Family and Nation in Civil War Virginia* (Chapel Hill: University of North Carolina Press, 2007).

13. James Zachariah Branscomb to Louis Branscomb, 27 February 1862, and James Zachariah Branscomb to Lucinda Branscomb Hunter, 27 July 1861, Branscomb Family Letters, ADAH.

14. Thomas Cutrer, ed., *Oh, What a Loansome Time I Had: The Civil War Letters of Major William Morel Moxley, Eighteenth Alabama Infantry and Emily Beck Moxley* (Tuscaloosa: University of Alabama Press, 2002), 1–6, 14, 22, 75.

15. Sarah Rodgers Rousseau Espy Diary, 2 May, 2–6 July, and 13 July 1860, ADAH.

16. *Daily Richmond Enquirer*, 1 August 1861; Margaret Josephine Miles Gillis Diary, 5 May 1861, ADAH.

17. Flynt, *Poor but Proud*, 198; Espy Diary, 27 September 1861, ADAH; James Zachariah Branscomb to Lucinda Branscomb Hunter, 24 August 1861, Branscomb Family Letters, ADAH.

18. Newton Davis to Elizabeth Davis, 20 March 1863, Newton N. Davis Papers, ADAH; Espy Diary, 9 July 1862, ADAH.

19. Schlereth, "Material Culture Studies," 118; Joan E. Cashin, "Hungry People in the Wartime South: Civilians, Armies, and the Food Supply," in Berry, *Weirding the War*, 160–75; Newton Davis to Elizabeth Davis, 24 December 1862, 6 March 1863, Newton N. Davis Papers, ADAH; Lucille Griffith, ed., *Yours Till Death: Civil War Letters of John Cotton* (Tuscaloosa: University of Alabama Press, 1951), vi–vii, 5.

20. I chose to use the original language of the documents rather than make any corrections. Newton Davis to Elizabeth Davis, 11 March 1864, 28 March 1863, Newton N. Davis Papers, ADAH; James Garrison to Harriet Garrison, 22 April 1863, James P. Garrison Confederate Letters, 1862–1863, Manuscript, Archive, and Rare Book Library, Emory University (hereafter MARBL); Newton Davis to Elizabeth Davis, 9 July 1862, Newton N. Davis Papers; Alto Loftin Jackson, ed., *So Mourns the Dove: Letters of a Confederate Infantryman and His Family* (New York: Exposition Press, 1965), 17; James Crowder to Elmira Crowder, 8 July 1861, James Preston Crowder Papers, MARBL.

21. Espy Diary, 23 September 1861, ADAH; Cutrer, *Oh, What a Loansome Time I Had*, 36; Griffith, *Yours Till Death*, 5–6.

22. Espy Diary, 9 July, 21 September 1862, ADAH.

23. James Branscomb to Lucinda Branscomb, 22 October 1863, Branscomb Family Letters, ADAH; Newton Davis to Bettie, 29 July and 29 October 1863, Newton N. Davis Papers, ADAH; Jackson, *So Mourns the Dove*, 73.

24. Flynt, *Poor but Proud*, 38–39, 47; Rogers et al., *Alabama*, 209; *New York Times*,

1 October 1863; Arthur W. Bergeron Jr., *Confederate Mobile* (Baton Rouge: Louisiana State University Press, 1991), 101–2; Cashin, "Hungry People in the Wartime South," 166; "Report on Indigent Families," Public Information subject files, Civil War and Reconstruction Misc., SG 17 131, folder 18, ADAH.

25. The pillaging of food supplies, as demonstrated by Cashin, occurred on both sides of the armies. Confederate and Union troops turned to Southern households for food supply when driven by hunger. For further discussion of food and the Confederate experience, see Cashin, "Hungry People in the Wartime South." See also Espy Diary, 2 September 1863, 2 November 1864, 31 December 1864, 3 June 1864, 4 August 1864, ADAH; and Cutrer, *Oh, What a Loansome Time I Had*, 124.

26. Harris Averett to Malinda Averett, 21 July 1863, Harris Hardin Averett Papers, ADAH; Griffith, *Yours Till Death*, 5.

27. Espy Diary, 18 December 1863, ADAH.

28. Espy Diary, 15 August 1862, ADAH.

29. Cutrer, *Oh, What a Loansome Time I Had*, 23, 47, 83, 91, 30, 83, 128.

30. James Zachariah Branscomb to Lucinda Branscomb Hunter, 7 August 1863, and Louis Branscomb to Lucinda Branscomb Hunter, 25 October 1863, ADAH.

31. Espy Diary, 18 December 1863, ADAH.

The Trophies of Victory and the Relics of Defeat

Returning Home in the Spring of 1865

PETER S. CARMICHAEL

The remains of a lone apple tree, cut down and carved into small pieces by Confederate soldiers, lay along a rutted dirt road that led to the village of Appomattox Court House. Earlier on 9 April 1865, Robert E. Lee had waited under the shade of the apple tree, anxious to hear from Ulysses S. Grant about surrendering his army. Messages between the generals eventually led to a brief meeting between Lee and two Union staff officers who then secured the parlor in Wilmer McLean's house, where Grant dictated the surrender terms to Lee. As soon as the agreement was signed and Lee walked out the door, Union officers "decluttered" the parlor with Yankee efficiency, cutting strips of upholstery from plush sofas, breaking chair legs into small keepsakes, and "appropriating" candleholders and chairs until the room was left barren.[1]

In the meantime, Lee was making his way to his headquarters, slowly riding Traveller down the Lynchburg Stage Road as his adoring troops swarmed around him in an unforgettable farewell. The general said a few words of gratitude, evidently moved by the outpouring of affection from his devoted soldiers, before disappearing over the hillside. Within minutes Confederate relic hunters descended on the apple tree, cutting and hacking away at the limbs and bark so that the slices of wood could become precious commodities of historical and monetary value. A mixture of veneration and entrepreneurialism spawned the cutting frenzy, and the famous *Harper's Weekly* illustrator Alfred Waud sketched Union and Confederate soldiers swinging axes and bargaining over the trophies. The historical magnitude of 9 April 1865 was not lost on the veterans who wanted a piece of history, even if it came at a price.[2]

Such items as the furniture in McLean's house and pieces of the apple tree were more than souvenirs or trinkets of nostalgic symbolism. Soldiers felt incredible emotional attachment to relics at a deeply personal level. At the same time, they appreciated the potential that relics possessed in shaping historical memories and influencing public meanings for years to come. Historians Joan Cashin, Megan Kate Nelson, and Michael DeGruccio, who were some of the first historians to write about Civil War material culture, are in agreement that things possess the power to stir emotions, to affirm or weaken political convictions, and even to guide behavior. Their pioneering works illustrate how ideology is only one source in understanding the inner world of historical actors. The logical outcome of their fine scholarship calls into question the primacy of ideas as the dominant source of motivation. Rather, things themselves have agency, and they possess an intrinsic power to shape behavior, as is evident in the ways that Union and Confederate soldiers responded to the outcome of Appomattox.[3]

At the end of the war, both sides collected objects to validate their military service and the political cause for which they had fought. Returning home from Appomattox with just a few keepsakes testified to the suffering and sacrifices by ex-Confederates. The very absence of things could be a source of shame to some soldiers, but others felt an unconquerable spirit that seemingly resided in their ragged uniforms, busted shoes, and empty haversacks. On the one hand, carrying home a piece of a Confederate banner or a copy of Robert E. Lee's Order No. 9 stirred powerful but conflicting feelings of emasculation and mastery in defeat. Union soldiers, on the other hand, treasured items from ex-Confederates as mementos of a failed rebellion. Pieces of Confederate flags, Southern currency, and even rebel uniforms instilled in Northern soldiers a feeling of manly pride as conquering heroes.

Veterans returning to their Northern or Southern homes also worried that civilians might question their dedication to the cause. They turned to relics to ward off any potential criticisms, believing that material items would stand the test of time. Things, in their estimation, possessed an intrinsic historical truth of valor and sacrifice. These relics, in others words, existed beyond the murky world of interpretation and debate. The things of war constituted an indestructible source of historical evidence that would forever remind future generations of the sacredness of the respective cause and their own personal sacrifices in fighting for it.[4]

The craving for the material objects of war became a preoccupation dur-

Figure 11. Union and Confederate soldiers chopping up the apple tree for Appomattox relics. (Courtesy of the Library of Congress)

ing the last weeks of the Confederacy's existence, when both sides were grasping for things to help them remember the past as they transitioned to a future without war. The demise of the rebel armies, beginning with Lee's army on 9 April and continuing with the surrender of Joseph Johnston's Army of Tennessee on 26 April, Nathan Bedford Forrest's on 9 May, and Kirby Smith's on 2 June, produced a windfall of battle flags, rifles, backpacks, and other articles of war treasured by both sides but interpreted in very different ways. The material elicited a range of conflicting emotions and feelings—despair, futility, optimism, pride, and jubilation—while attesting to the triumph of the Union and the military devastation of the Confederacy. The material culture associated with Union victory and Southern defeat affirms the observations of historians Steven Lubar and W. David Kingery, who argue that material culture can reveal the traumatic consequences of events like a civil war while showing that artifacts are also historical actors unto themselves, always bringing the past into the present. The things that veterans carried home were not forgotten oddities but relics that prompted people to access wartime sacrifices long after Appomattox.[5]

Rather than detailing the surrender proceedings of the various Southern armies or charting the vast multitude of soldier experiences and reactions during the final months of the war, which has been done admirably by other scholars, this essay highlights the surrender experience of a select number of white soldiers on both sides. Two men in particular—the Union's John Smith of the 118th Pennsylvania and Virginian John H. Chamberlayne—receive special attention. Both soldiers take center stage at various points because their writings are exceptional in showing how material culture helped soldiers make sense of the end of the war. Chamberlayne, a graduate of the University of Virginia who had pushed hard for secession while working as a lawyer in Richmond before the war, "skipped" the surrender parade at Appomattox. He joined a band of diehard Confederates who ran to Mississippi during the summer of 1865. Chamberlayne provides the perspective of a radical Confederate who wrote with astonishing introspection while he sought refuge from defeat through self-exile. And on the Union side, the letters of Corporal John Smith, a Philadelphian who was only nineteen when Lee surrendered, detail his journey from Appomattox to the Union Grand Review in Washington, D.C., on 23 and 24 May 1865 with remarkable detail. His letters shine light on the ways that patriotism and profit inspired soldiers on both sides to collect the things of war.[6]

In this essay, my aim—by combining material culture and primary documents—is to explore how Civil War soldiers understood Union victory and the downfall of the Confederacy. I am not concerned with the conditions on the Northern or Southern home front that awaited soldiers as they returned home, nor do I explore the long-term problems of veterans readjusting to civilian life. Those important topics go beyond the scope of this chapter, and there are many fine works that address the numerous layers of the veteran experience. Instead, I begin by reviewing the last week of the war and the events that led to the surrender at Appomattox. An examination of Southern reactions to the collapse of the Confederacy's armies follows, and then I move into the ways that material culture figured into the act of surrendering and how relics shaped Confederates' perceptions of themselves as conquered soldiers.[7]

The Army of the Potomac at Appomattox is the focal point of the next section. The analysis is centered on the ways that material culture shaped how Union soldiers imagined Northern victory and Confederate defeat. The extensive fraternization with Confederates at Appomattox receives considerable attention as a way to locate the amicable and entrepreneurial spirit that prevailed between both sides at the end of the war. This section gives special care to the return of Union soldiers to the battlefields in the Fredericksburg area—a pilgrimage that was not a sacred ritual of nationalism but a poignant reminder of their own harrowing experiences as survivors of organized killing. And by examining the mementos that John Smith collected and sent home for safekeeping, the chapter concludes by focusing on how Smith experienced the Grand Review in Washington and on his exit from the army.

In the week that followed the Confederate evacuation of Richmond and Petersburg on 2 April, the conflict between and the Army of Northern Virginia and the Army of the Potomac rapidly came to an end. Grant's forces hunted down the Army of Northern Virginia with the dogged determination of a veteran army. At every turn, they blocked Lee's attempts to move south while piercing the soft underbelly of the Confederate column with slashing cavalry attacks. By the evening of 8 April, Robert E. Lee had nowhere to go, but his army was like a dying beast, possessing just enough life for one last desperate attack for survival. The Southerners struck early on the morning of 9 April, punched a hole in the Union line before Federal reinforcements filled the gap, and sealed the fate of the Army of Northern Virginia.[8]

Lee had little choice but to accept Grant's demands, as the Union army was poised for a bloody showdown that would have likely resulted in Confederate annihilation. When news of the surrender swept across the Army of the Potomac, members of the rank and file erupted in joy, tossing their hats in the air, rolling on the ground, and blasting horns and beating drums in an unbridled celebration of victory and life as part of the inevitable chain of human progress. After years of frustration and public ridicule, the rank and file of the Army of the Potomac had accomplished what many observers thought was unattainable—the capture of Richmond and the destruction of Lee's forces. All of that changed during the first nine days of April, when Grant had achieved both in what amounted to the knockout blow to the rebellion. At the time, soldiers knew that Appomattox guaranteed the reunion of the nation and the end of slavery. They claimed that their part in this magnificent victory affirmed their belief in Lincoln's words that America was the world's "last best hope." When Grant warned against excessive celebrating, few disobeyed his order out of a soldiery admiration for an enemy who had experienced the similar trials of army life.[9]

When news of the surrender passed through the ranks, many Union soldiers, including John Smith of the 118th Pennsylvania, exercised their new freedoms and headed straight for the rebel camps to acquire a memento of the historically momentous day. Rushing to the scene, Smith crossed a wooden rail spanning a stream swollen by recent rains, lost his balance, and plunged into the waters. "I cried! Cussed!!," he wrote to his mother on 11 April. "But made up my mind I would get a piece of that great apple tree if I fell in forty creeks." When Smith reached the tree, he saw one of Grant's orderlies carry off a limb while other Union soldiers were paying between five dollars and ten dollars for chips. A Confederate standing nearby asked, "'What would you do with it, Yank?' 'Why, take it home as a great relic,' say I to him, so he cut in and cut out big chips." Smith tried to give him ten dollars for the pieces, but the Confederate would not accept the money. "'Here, Yank, with my compliments,'" he said. When Smith returned to his regiment, his comrades hustled off to get their own piece, but they were too late. The tree—including the roots—was gone. They pleaded with Smith to sell some of his pieces, offering as much as five dollars for a wooden sliver, but "I said to them, 'No, go fall in the creek as I did.'"[10]

That Robert E. Lee spent so much time near the apple tree, resting under its branches and occasionally conferring with his staff, invested the space with a sacred aura. For those Union and Confederate soldiers who were fortunate enough to get a hunk of the prized wood, they put very different meanings into their souvenirs that in turn validated their respective service during the Appomattox campaign and the war as a whole. Grant's veterans held up a slice of the apple tree as a tribute to a complete and smashing victory earned by the Army of the Potomac's relentless drive, superior bravery, and exceptional leadership. It is telling that Union soldiers showed no impulse to desecrate the tree site or to do anything that might denigrate their fallen enemy.[11]

Confederate veterans craved shards of the apple tree out of a deep admiration for their commanding general, but the wooden relic could not be disassociated from the painful memories of surrender. How could any soldier forget the defeat of the white South if he owned a slice of the tree? Would not feelings of shame crash down on a Southern veteran every time he came in contact with the wooden trinket? Diaries and letters would suggest that Lee's veterans wanted to distance themselves from the surrender altogether and that relic hunting would have been unthinkable to any self-respecting Confederate. Yet the search for souvenirs provides a different interpretive layer to the popular generalization that all Confederates forever buried their faces in shame. These wooden shards symbolized a once mighty military regime, and any soldier who owned the heirloom possessed a sacred link to the incomparable Robert E. Lee. Moreover, he had proof that he had followed the general to the bitter end.

Lee's men were the first to make a rush on the apple tree, catching the eye of Smith and other Federals who joined the gathering in what turned into a veritable bazaar of trading and selling slices of the apple tree and currency. The Confederates could not get rid of their worthless and burdensome currency quickly enough, and they found a long line of eager buyers among their former enemies who handed out greenbacks for Confederate bills. His desire for Southern money was a little peculiar, but in the future John Smith could display Southern currency as a relic of an extinct nation that had threatened the Union from within.

The trading of currency and the hawking of the apple tree spawned a convivial spirit among the former combatants, and their conversations elicited a range of conflicting Confederate reactions to Lee's surrender. Smith and fellow Pennsylvanian Jacob Zorn described a similar spectrum of Confederate opinions after the surrender. "Some of them feel very indignant in regard to the Surrender," Zorn wrote in his diary, "and express themselves hoping to See the day yet when they will have a chance at us again. Others appear to hail the day when peace will again sound throughout the whole land. They Say they are tired of this war and cant See any use of carrying it on any longer the expressions of the latter are those who done the fighting. and that of the former those who had some easy position and not of the rank and file of the army." N. H. Panghorn, also of the Fifth Corps, heard from many fiery Confederates "that they would meet us again if they got a chance." Lee's veteran comrades told Panghorn that these outspoken soldiers "held bomb proof positions in the army, such as musicians & quartermasters clerks & who were all ways out of reach of bullets in time of a fight."[12]

While Union soldiers found overwhelming material proof of the Confederacy's fall, plenty of Southern soldiers were oblivious to the physical disintegration of their own army. The call of honor awoke some diehard Confederates from the stupor of humiliation that hung over the army. These men fancied themselves as the hotspurs of the rebellion, and in the final months of the war they lived up to their reputations as unconquerable warriors who never grew weary of hearing the music of the shell. They felt they had no choice but to carry on the fight. No floodgate could hold back the rage and humiliation of these fanatics, who promised to follow the Confederate flag wherever it might fly. Virginia's John H. Chamberlayne was one of the few who refused to quit fighting. "McIntosh and myself with several others refused to attend the funeral at Appomattox C.H.," he wrote on 12 April, "& as soon as the surrender was certain we cut or crept our way out, thro' adventures many & perilous wh. I cannot tell of now." Chamberlayne and his party intended to rally with Johnston's forces. If the Army of Tennessee had disbanded by the time they arrived, Chamberlayne would continue to ride to Texas, where the war against the Yankees, he believed, could be waged indefinitely. Still clinging to a romantic view of war, Chamberlayne wrote, "I am not conquered by any means & shall not be while alive. My life is of no further value—Farewell my beloved Virginia—What exile should I fly from himself—The cause was thrown away and such blood."[13]

Chamberlayne's final act of soldiering was full of grand illusions and inspired more by vanity than ideology or politics. He would not allow defeat to crush his dream of eternal fame as a Confederate hero. From the moment he enlisted in 1861, ambition stalked Chamberlayne, pressing him to fight recklessly on the battlefield, but the promise of glory was never fully realized. He spent much of the war incarcerated in a Northern prison camp while his friends from the University of Virginia racked up battlefield accolades. His temperament fueled his impatience for combat laurels while also creating a fiery devotion to the Confederacy. He was drawn to the drama of exile, possibly because of his attraction to Romantic literature. Chamberlayne would follow a plotline after Appomattox that came straight from Lord Byron. The famous Englishman's personal life and published writings turned banishment into a noble adventure. The itinerant life brought fame and notoriety to Byron, but Chamberlayne discovered what it meant to be a man alone. By the end of May 1865, he had reached Mississippi, feeling fatigued in body and disheartened in spirit, but he remained undeterred, still searching for an organized Confederate force to continue the fight. Every morning on his relative's farm in Mississippi, Chamberlayne awoke feeling emotionally numb to the past. All the sacrifices, the suffering, and the bloodshed weighed on the present, an invisible but pervasive force dragging him down and disorienting him to a point where he could "hardly say ... [if] I exist."[14] Even in his abject state of depression, Chamberlayne remained defiant, expressing rage against the North in an apocalyptic fantasy in which the South would rise again. He was no different from defeated people in other nations who believed, as historian Wolfgang Schivelbusch points out, that "the idea of war, death, and rebirth are cyclically linked ... [and] do not allow for absolute eradication." It was not unusual for former Confederates to indulge in revenge fantasies as a way to assure themselves that their honor would ultimately be redeemed.[15]

Like so many former Southern soldiers, Chamberlayne looked for something in the past to rescue his reputation in the present, and a captured pair of Yankee boots helped to restore his self-esteem. "Tho' the country is for a time enslaved," he wrote to his friend Sally, "tho friends are dead & exiled, and no man has a home, & tho I have not a dollar in the world, nor any property but one pair of top boots (with spurs attached), still I can laugh." The boots were the property of a Maine colonel whose person and possessions were captured during the 1862 Maryland campaign when the armies grappled along the South Mountain chain. When Chamberlayne looked at his boots, his mind conjured up memories of a daring adventure. The Yankee shoes became the muse for his epic tale. "We strove with them until night," Chamberlayne wrote, "and we girded our loins in the night season; and we wrestled mightily with them about the rising of the sun, and the voice thereof was the noise of a mighty nation; and we smote them for about the space of two hours, and prevailed against them exceedingly, and took them captive; and took their food, & their raiment, and their horses, and cattle, yea and their creeping things, for a spoil, & for a prey." He admitted to Sally that the story might sound like "nonsense," but the Yankee boots stood as incontestable evidence of the fighting prowess of Confederates, who, even in defeat, used trophies of war to enshrine their individual and collective valor as Southern soldiers.[16]

Military artifacts like Chamberlayne's Yankee boots were not harmless tributes to a chivalric warfare or simple props for nostalgic tales. Relics possessed tremendous emotional power, as they had the capacity to assign meaning to life's experiences. In Chamberlayne's case, the boots materialized gender relations by bonding women to a romantic view of the Confederate soldier as a knightly warrior. Objects could also induce avoidance of the present, as illustrated by Chamberlayne's peculiar attachment to his Yankee boots as a reminder of days of Confederate superiority. The shoes were a source of pride that helped him cope with the shame and humiliation over Appomattox. He feigned surprise to Sally when he stated that he could not understand how the Yankee boots "should walk into... our confab," and yet he purposefully wrote at length about the captured boots to prop up his need for mastery, noting that it was one of his few possessions in the world. Their mere existence, moreover, proved his superiority over a foe that now ruled over him by sheer force and not daring.[17]

Such relics would soothe the wounded pride of Southern men for generations to come, but in the moment of surrender, the vast majority of Confederates returning home were not laden down with war memorabilia or mementos. As Richmond's Carlton McCarthy recalled, "To roll up the old blanket and oil-cloth, gather up the haversack, canteen, axe, perhaps, and a few trifles in time of peace of no value," was all that they could do when leaving Appomattox. Yet McCarthy and his fellow survivors could hold their heads high as they walked home, knowing that they had "faithfully performed their duty." Above all else, the meager possessions of war demonstrated to those at home that they had suffered and sacrificed for the cause. He did not feel the overwhelming sense of disgrace and worthlessness that cut Chamberlayne to his core. Personality and circumstances largely explain why McCarthy embraced the future without bitterness or rancor.[18]

Unlike Chamberlayne, McCarthy had read Lee's farewell address, General Orders No. 9, and the general's words offered emotional sustenance to his soldiers by affirming their place in history as men of unsurpassed devotion to cause and comrade. Lee's staff officer Charles Marshall wrote the proclamation, but Lee edited and ultimately approved the language of the intellectually charged message that framed the Lost Cause explanation of Southern defeat—one that subsequently twisted the pages of history for generations to come. By emphasizing Yankee numbers as the cause of the Army of Northern Virginia's demise, Lee essentially exonerated himself and his men for surrendering while removing Grant and the Union armies as architects of their own victory. General Orders No. 9, as historian Elizabeth Varon writes, "had layers of meaning and deep, tangled roots" that anchored the overwhelming numbers and resources explanation of Union victory as a matter of might over right. The general's words were not combative toward the North, but they were certainly passive-aggressive by suggesting that the Army of Northern Virginia had not been outgeneraled or outfought by the Army of the Potomac but rather worn down by the enemy's ruthless execution of a hard-war strategy that preyed upon the weak and terrorized the helpless. Above all else, General Orders No. 9 enshrined Lee's veterans as a band of loyal brothers whose courage reigned supreme even in defeat.[19]

It is no surprise that the address became a coveted artifact that forever linked a soldier to Lee—the idol of white Southerners—while exalting the rank and file as exemplary men of duty. Copyists at Lee's headquarters sent the original copies to corps and division commanders, and from there it was likely that clerks made copies for brigades and that the process was then repeated at the regimental level. Plenty of copies were nailed to trees or tacked to tent posts for the rank and file to read. Some of these copies even reached the Army of Tennessee by the middle of April, carried by Lee's men as they headed south from Appomattox.[20]

The speedy and wide circulation of the address both inside and outside the Army of Northern Virginia is a shocking fact when considering the rush of practical demands bearing down on soldiers in the midst of disbanding an army. The portability and compactness of the document made it possible to carry on one's body with ease, and if a soldier's military record was called into question, the document offered on-the-spot vindication. The desire to have a copy of the Farewell Address spurred some soldiers to make handwritten copies as a treasured keepsake, but it was also an artifact that possessed the power of touch—it could be held to read and reflect on in order to remember the words of Lee enshrining his small band of soldiers with words of dignity and honor. As soon as a copy of the Farewell Address fell into the hands of Colonel H. Perry, he collected some Confederate stationery and pulled out a bass drum to use as a makeshift desk. With great care, he copied General Orders No. 9 for his own use. When he finished his transcription, Perry visited Lee's headquarters and managed to see the general long enough for an autograph as an incontestable authentication of the document's "truthfulness." Virginian John E. Roller also wanted to take a piece of Appomattox history home, and he instructed an orderly sergeant to make a number of copies before passing the papers among the veterans who were still in the unit. "I thought it due to the men who had served to the close of the war," he noted, "that they should have the fact preserved."[21]

The effect of Lee's General Orders No. 9 suggested equality between former adversaries, a calculated message that could be constructed only by denying what actually had occurred behind the parlor doors of the McLean house. Grant had laid down an unconditional demand to surrender, and Lee had had no choice but to abide by it. Yet the idea of a gentleman's agreement ending the Civil War cannot be rejected as a purely historical falsification inspired by flag-waving nationalism and a militaristic spirit. It is impossible to deny that the actual surrendering of all Confederate forces stretching from Virginia to North Carolina and beyond the Mississippi into Texas was carried out in an orderly and respectful fashion with little to no violence between the opposing forces. The spirit of conciliation is often seen as a uniquely Appomattox phenomenon, but in actuality there was less goodwill shown to Lee's men in Virginia than there was to Confederates at the other surrender sites. Only the Army of Northern Virginia had to participate in a surrendering parade. Union officers who were part of a surrender commission apparently insisted on a formal parade of Confederate infantry marching between opposing ranks of Federal troops. This was a march of shame in the eyes of Lee's lieutenants, a degradation to be avoided, but they had little choice in the matter since the Federals controlled the distribution of the paroles. This slip of paper almost always protected the surrendering Confederates from future molestation by Federal authorities. They could not, in other words, get arrested on the way home and then sent to a Northern prison camp as a prisoner of war.[22]

Under a cold and drizzly rain, Lee's men embarked upon a march that would end with the extinction of their army. The thin procession of Confederate troops passed by the site of the uprooted apple tree and splashed across the North Branch of the Appomattox River before ascending an extremely steep hill that crested at a wide plateau opening up to the village of Appomattox, where 5,000 Federals of the Third Brigade, First Division, Fifth Corps, lined both sides of the road and waited in silence. At the helm of the column rode Confederate general John B. Gordon. His appearance cued Maine's Joshua Chamberlain, who thought that Lee's veterans deserved "the honors due to troops," and he accordingly gave the command "at shoulder," which the Federals executed with soldierly precision.[23]

In recognition of the soldier salute, the Confederates came to shoulder arms as they passed the Maltese Cross, the designated flag of the Fifth Corps. Lee's men continued to march until they reached the left end of the Union line anchored near the McLean house. They then turned to face their former adversaries, stacked their rifles, hung their accoutrements on their bayonets, and rolled up their flags. This process was repeated throughout the day, and by late afternoon the Federals had confiscated some 15,000 rifles and seventy-two battle flags. Scores of Confederates refused to participate in the march; they simply left their muskets in their empty camps before starting for home. Some companies tore their battle flags into small mementos rather than surrender their beloved banners to the enemy. A number of flags were made of silk, often from the wedding dresses of the wives of prominent officers. One Union soldier noted the feel of the banners, remarking that "some few of them were silk, but the most of them were of very course goods." The material carried tremendous emotional and ideological power by reminding Confederates that the struggle was not just a war for slavery; because silk was often associated with the female gender, it also represented a defense of Southern womanhood. Giving up the flags likely touched on Southern male fears that the Yankees would violate the virtue of their daughters and wives. The symbolic power of the battle flag resided in its connection to the blood sacrifices on the battlefield, where so many comrades had given their lives under the banner. To hand over these cherished flags—connected to so many powerful memories—felt like the ultimate act of betrayal of the dead.[24]

By all accounts, Union forces carried out the surrender parade with great solemnity and respect. In victory, of course, it was easier for Northern soldiers to feel sympathy for the enemy, and they had also forged a kinship with an adversary who knew the life of a Civil War soldier—unlike the civilians behind the lines. "Poor Fellows," Union officer Joshua Lawrence Chamberlain of Maine wrote a day after the surrender. "I pitied them from the bottom of my heart. Those arms had been well handled & the flags bravely borne." The things they carried, above all else, embodied the manly spirit of warfare that resonated with Chamberlain and countless other observers that day.[25]

The exceptional silence and solemnity of that day impressed the Confederates deeply, convincing them that they had received the honor due to them as soldiers and as men. Some were so forlorn that they could hardly speak, while others were more expressive, even making witty remarks as they stacked their weapons. Pennsylvanian John Smith overheard one of Lee's men say to his gun, "'My dear wife; I hope that I will never see you again. If you kill as many Rebels as you have killed Yanks you will do very well.'" He then kissed the gun "with the remark 'Good-bye.'" Another Confederate could not part with his musket soon enough: "'Good-bye gun. I am darned glad to get rid of you. I have been trying to for two years.'" To these soldiers, their weapons had become the personification of a comrade who bore witness to battle with a sturdy dependability. Over the course of the war a soldier developed a practical relationship with the tools and materials of war, but the relationship was more than functional. The relics and materials of war were soaked in memories of violence and blood, forged during incredible physical and emotional duress. A rifle, flag, tent, uniform, canteen, or haversack could fill a man with a range of emotions and meanings.[26]

There was little humor when the color bearers gave up their beloved flags. "Many had tears streaming down their faces," Smith observed. "It effected them more than others; the thought of having carried the flag through so many battles and then were compelled to surrender at this time. I tell you, it was an affecting sight, looking at those brave men." The Confederates' filthy uniforms, their bare haversacks, and their banners shredded by Northern bullets offered incontestable evidence of an endurance, devotion, and manly spirit that would forever reside in the things of war. At the same time, Union soldiers visualized Confederate defeat as an irreversible fact. Worn cartridge boxes empty of rounds, the broken scabbards, the tattered shoes, and the frayed battle flags were the remnants of a defeated army and a dead nation.[27] Union soldiers stationed along the surrender route tore off pieces of the captured Confederate flags and sent them home, including the obsessive collector John Smith. He packaged a number of Appomattox artifacts collected from Confederates, among them two printed Confederate songs and a ring traded by "a fine looking Reb." Of all his souvenirs, Smith treasured his piece of "a Rebel flag" with its stenciled letters r and g. "The two letters that are on it," he explained to his mother, "would be ... of the word Fredericksburg, where his regiment suffered horrible losses. Take ... the pieces and when I get home I will tell you all the particulars about them."[28]

Northern soldiers did not become civilians overnight as their Confederate counterparts did at Appomattox. The staggered surrenders of rebel armies necessitated that a substantial number of Union forces remain in the field until the war's work was finally finished. During the third week of May, Confederate forces still operated in the Trans-Mississippi Theater, while a French puppet regime in Mexico edged toward the Texas border. A substantial number of Northern units, as a result, remained on active duty after Appomattox, including the United States Colored Troops, who were consolidated into a single corps and assigned to duty along the coastal areas in the South. Of the one million active Union soldiers in service at the end of the war, approximately 150,000 veterans from General George G. Meade's Army of the Potomac (less its Sixth Corps), General William T. Sherman's Armies of the Tennessee and Georgia, and General Phillip Sheridan's cavalry were available to participate in the Grand Review in Washington, D.C., on 23–24 May, a military procession intended to honor the Union troops and to celebrate the end of the war.[29]

En route to the nation's capital from Richmond during the middle of May, four corps of Sherman's army group traversed portions of the Spotsylvania, Wilderness, Chancellorsville, and Fredericksburg battlefields. The vast majority of the men were encountering the Virginia battlefields for the first time, except for one corps that was primarily composed of regiments that had fought at Chancellorsville. Those survivors of General Joseph Hooker's debacle served as unofficial guides of the field. They told harrowing stories of survival on the spot where their units had fought two years earlier. Returning to the place of such awful violence actually helped some of the men heal from these painful memories of the war. Standing on the killing ground rekindled a connection to the dead by filling the living with tender sentiments for beloved friends and fellow soldiers who had been lost on other battlefields.[30]

Most of Sherman's men did not have a guide, however, and they were left to wander across the woods and fields. With every step, regardless of the direction, they saw trees chewed up by gunfire or skeletal remains protruding from the Virginia soil. Ohioan Marion Roberts, who slipped away from the marching column at Spotsylvania, stumbled upon piles of dead Union soldiers. That night he devoted his entire diary entry to the utter lack of respect and regard shown for the fallen. "Arriving near the spot we saw the timber cut the men were not t[ot]ally covered — and bones would protrude — often a head with gaping jaws, feet hands & c — passing thro' a strip of timber some of the party counted 67 unburied Union soldiers or their skeletons." Hundreds of skeletons, unburied and lying next to each other, marked the spot where they had fallen.[31]

Roberts expressed a recurring motif found in the writings of those who toured the battlefields around Fredericksburg. Their impressions, though varied in details, touched on four similar themes: that the indignities inflicted against the Union dead demanded immediate redress by the U.S. military; that the battered condition of the landscape conveyed the fury of combat as a physical truth; that the individual soldier mattered and that his personal story of suffering and sacrifice resided in the remains of the dead; and that the act of touring the fields elicited opposing feelings of the joy that came with surviving and the mournful sorrow for those who had fallen and would never return to their families. Sherman's men were not bone collectors in search of the macabre.[32]

Sherman's men did not try to purify the battlefield as a heroic space where war regenerated men or the nation. The badly scarred terrain, with its exposed graves and trees gnarled and twisted by artillery fire, reminded veterans of the hell that they had escaped. Every battlefield vista was one of human carnage, making it impossible to forget or suppress images of suffering soldiers who had died an agonizing death. Some skeletons at Spotsylvania revealed the last moments of a soldier's life to a touring Indiana veteran who saw that "some [men] had collected as they lay wounded such sticks and twigs as were within their reach and had striven to erect a barrier to protect them from further injury." Another skeleton had a knapsack strap across the leg, evidently in an attempt to stop a severed artery from hemorrhaging blood. "And now," he concluded, "the leather lying loosely about the bone told pathetically of the vain effort."[33]

Returning to the battlefield prompted Sherman's veterans to remember the fallen as men who had personal life stories that mattered more than any symbolic connection to the Union cause or the end of slavery. The sight of so many graves—without any marker of respect or show of decency—enraged Sherman's touring soldiers. Members of a Pennsylvania unit, while walking over the ground where they had fought at Chancellorsville, could not return to marching column without first caring for the dead. Once they had located their fallen comrades, according to veteran Michael Schroyer, they "picked up the skeletons and brought them home with them." They even found the partial remains of their colonel's corpse, whose body, as Schroyer explained, had soil shoveled up and tossed over his body, a haphazard process known as sodding. "He was lying on his back and was recognized by a tooth brush and several other articles, which were found in his clothing," Schroyer noted. "The bones were placed in a box, put in an ambulance, taken to Washington and then shipped to his home." It was not uncommon for soldiers in Sherman's command, who never fought in the Fredericksburg area, to take out shovels and dig proper graves for the unknown Union dead that they found.[34]

In no way did the sight of trenches, rusty bayonets, or discarded swords awaken a romantic view of warfare among Sherman's bummers. The mangled landscape elicited common phrases like "deplorable losses," "fearful fighting," and "dreadful history" in journals and letters home, where they denounced the inhumanity of killing and refused to mythologize the war. "In our imagination," wrote a Pennsylvania soldier from Chancellorsville, "we could see the awful battle raging; columns moving back and forth, men cheering and cursing and swearing, the cannonading, the volleys of musketry, the moaning and groaning of the wounded, the stampede of the army, the woods afire from exploding shells and filled with the dead and dying, the wounded praying that we would help and save them." And yet Sherman's soldiers were drawn to things that attested to unrecorded acts of bravery, even willing to pay money to see relics that testified to the ferocity of the fighting. Scores of Sherman's soldiers saw the stump of the famous twenty-two-inch oak tree, its massive trunk felled by intensive musketry fire at Spotsylvania's "Bloody Angle." The remains of the tree were on display in a Spotsylvania courthouse building, and the custodian of the relic charged a modest price for a view. At the same time, a steady stream of Union soldiers headed to the actual site of the famous tree. Curiosity, of course, drew them to the battlefield, but the existence of the tree materialized the violence and terror of combat. If there was any question about the killing power of Civil War weapons, the twenty-two-inch oak verified the lethality of the battle while implicitly affirming the bravery of the rank and file for withstanding missiles that carried such a destructive force. Every trench, shell hole, and bullet-riddled tree marked the soldiers' place in time, but these marks, as the men discovered, were not indelible. The unmarked graves, abandoned and uncared for, warned Sherman's men that the battlefield landscape was in the hands of others, that their sacrifices would not always be perpetuated, and that landmarks of heroism and suffering would erode and be forsaken.[35]

By 17 May, the last of Sherman's forces had moved north of the Fredericksburg area, leaving behind a war-ravaged landscape for a victory celebration in Washington. Waiting for his comrades to reach the nation's capital was Pennsylvania's John Smith, whose mania for relics brought in a bonanza of choice items from Appomattox. The campaign had taken a toll on his only pair of shoes, forcing him to march in bare feet, and by the time his unit had reached Richmond, Smith could barely walk. A surgeon sent him to a Washington hospital to recuperate while the rest of the Army of the Potomac completed their overland march across Virginia. Even though he had comrades in adjoining hospital beds, Smith felt unsettled, telling his mother on 8 May that "I feel lonesome being away from the Regt." Yet when he looked around the ward and saw so many wounded and maimed soldiers, he stopped feeling sorry for himself. "I look at them," he added in the same letter, and "I feel grateful that I came through it unharmed with my legs and arms all right."[36]

Smith was not one of the 150,000 white veterans who were part of the Grand Review on 23–24 May. The lacerations and cuts on his feet had not healed, and marching with his unit was out of the question, but the doctors gave him a pass for two days so that he could stand on the sidewalk and celebrate the Army of the Potomac on the first day and Sherman's veterans on the second. Smith was among 100,000 visitors who poured into the city to celebrate the end of the rebellion and pay tribute to their veterans. Smith's eye, as usual, did not just track the people but also focused on the things of war. The torn bunting from Lincoln's presidential box at Ford's Theatre, which had been ripped by John Wilkes Booth's spur when he jumped to the stage after shooting Lincoln, caught his attention as a sad reminder of Lincoln's absence. The passing of brigade after brigade marching in lockstep with veteran precision thrilled Smith, who could barely contain himself when his own regiment, the 118th Pennsylvania, passed by and the crowd erupted in applause. The tattered regimental flag, with a knot of campaign ribbons hanging from the staff, drew everyone's attention, according to Smith, who saw the banners as proof of his regiment's bravery. As a material relic that had passed through the gauntlet of war, it had fluttered in the smoke of battle; it was riddled by enemy bullets; and it was carried by men who had devoted their lives for the honor to be its bearer. The flags kept alive a heroic image of the rank and file as saviors of the Union but at the cost of important context. The campaign ribbons told their own story of hard fighting, and for the veterans, these streamers affirmed how they wanted to see themselves—as dependable soldiers who never shirked in battle.[37]

Smith returned to his regimental camp after the Grand Review, and when he was not occupied with the harmless drudgery of drilling and guard duty, his thoughts drifted to the future. He wondered how family and friends would receive him, even though he knew that he had "earned" his reputation through fighting, having compiled an impressive combat record and a promotion to corporal. Yet Smith worried about preserving his standing as a soldier when he knew that some veterans would come home fabricating tales of heroic adventures and peddling stories for profit, even though they had essentially been "playing" soldier for four years without having to do any of the bloody work. Smith had noticed how established shirkers suddenly worried that they might be exposed as scoundrels when the regiment returned home. They were angling for ways to cover their tracks so that they might be received as combat veterans. "I often told you about the pot robbers men that cook for officers so they wouldn't have to go in a fight," an indignant Smith wrote to his mother. "Would do any thing to keep out of a fight well they are getting brave now and want to come back [to] their company and take a gun [now] the fighting is over." He likely imagined them showing off their weapons to family and friends or prominently displaying them in their parlors, always present to welcome guests to the "home of a veteran." Smith hoped that the War Department, whether intentionally or not, had put up a barrier to the ploys of these quasi-soldiers when it refused to issue new muskets to the troops. Smith understood the cultural power and status a musket imparted to a veteran returning home, since anyone would assume that a man with a rifle must have killed rebels. He wanted the world to know that he was a "fighting man," and he would not let his hard-earned reputation stand on his words alone. He knew that this weapon would help validate his service in the immediate future and tell stories about his history long after he was gone. In one of his final letters before going home, Smith decided that he would purchase his weapon, informing his mother that "as the Government demands $6.00 for the gun I have decided to take my gun home."[38]

Throughout the summer of 1865, Unions soldiers were mustered out of service at a startling rate, but administrative delays continued to keep Smith in the ranks until the middle of July. While waiting for the necessary paperwork to pass through army channels, he occupied himself with checkers, reading, letter writing, and taking stock of his extensive collection of military souvenirs. On 2 July he compiled an inventory of his relics as part of a letter to his mother: "I sent a Rebel jacket by a man by the name of McCarthy. Fix it up and wash it, Mother. Also three rings made from a Rebel shell fuse; I received them at Appomattox C.H. The gold ring that I had on my finger broke while I was on the skirmish line at Gravelly Run. I was firing at the Rebls. I sent you a Rebel $100 note. Save these relics for me." Except for the broken golden ring, Smith did not explain why he collected these items or what they meant to him. He clearly treasured these mementos, but he never instructed his mother as to how she should display or care for them. Maybe Smith intended to keep his mementos in a box so he might release the memories of the military campaigns that had resulted in the capture of Lee's army and effectively ended the Civil War.[39]

In the end, there is no narrative that emerges from Smith's relic collection; we have to put together the pieces of a puzzle that can never be fully reconstructed. The evidence is too fragmentary, but these relics possess interpretive possibilities that open pinholes into the past that cannot be discerned in written sources. Smith's passion for Confederate items, including a shell jacket, is certainly unusual, and Smith must have gone to extraordinary lengths to keep and transport the coat, even asking his mother to clean it so that it might be properly preserved. Maybe these Confederate items were exotic to him, or possibly he treasured them as the fragments of a regime that had fallen to mighty Union armies. Nothing in his Confederate collection hints of vindictiveness toward the enemy, nor do the items capture the trauma of combat. Smith did connect the broken ring to a skirmish at Gravelly Run, pointing out that he cracked it while shooting at the rebels, but he said nothing more about the incident. What is striking is the lack of mementos from his beloved 118th Pennsylvania. Smith did save a piece of a canvas from his shelter tent, but that is the only recorded item connected to his daily experiences in the ranks—a shocking fact, since he felt an incredible bond with his comrades.[40]

One curious item in Smith's collection was a Confederate letter found at Jettersville, a town located along Lee's retreat route to Appomattox. Smith offered a pithy summary of the letter for his mother: "The Reb writes to a friend that he is afraid that this Company will have to go to the front and fight and he don't seem to like that. He don't know what soldiers enlist for." In his own letter, Smith scoffed at this rebel soldier—not because he fought for the Southern cause but because he did not live by the soldier's universal calling to fight. The respect that Smith typically accorded to the enemy grew out of his experience around Petersburg, where he routinely fraternized with Lee's men to trade for Southern stationery, songs, and even buttons. His face-to-face interactions with Southern soldiers might explain why he became such a committed collector of all things Confederate. Smith's Confederate mementos speak to his empathy for the enemy as fellow soldiers who happened to fight on the wrong side. His collection gets to the pulse of a political moderation rooted in Smith's commitment to union. Such a position helped encourage sympathy for the very men who had been trying to kill him for four years.[41]

Smith's exceptional documentation of material culture and his rich letters to his mother sustain such an argument. What if the correspondence did not exist? What interpretive value would his collection possess? While an absence of evidence would certainly close off some lines of inquiry, not all would be lost. This "what if" offers an important reminder that when working with material culture, it is crucial to keep the focus on objects as tools of historical action and not just as mundane things that reflect beliefs. We would do well to remember historian Sara Pennell's warning that to appreciate the full significance of objects, we must recognize that texts cannot always account for the knowledge and emotions inextricably tied to the materiality of the objects themselves. The skeletal remains gathered by Sherman's veterans at Chancellorsville, for instance, embodied the physical sacrifice of departed comrades in ways that language could never capture. Rotting bones of men who had died for their country, scattered carelessly across the ground and denied a proper burial, darkened the mood of Sherman's men toward their former enemies and jeopardized the spirit of reconciliation that came from the terms at Appomattox.[42]

The material artifacts associated with Union victory and Confederate defeat reaffirms James Deetz's argument in his influential *In Small Things Forgotten* that commonplace objects are pregnant with ideological, emotional, and metaphorical power. The physical touch of surrendering a musket, a shard from the Appomattox apple tree, or a piece of a rebel banner cracked open the emotional world of soldiers at the very moment they were leaving a life of killing and destruction. The material culture of defeat does not call into question long-established views about the psychological turmoil of defeat for white Southern men. The desire of Lee's veterans to have a physical reminder of their time in the ranks, however, shows that not all ran away from the memories of war in shame. Ex-Confederates turned to the things of war to confirm their standing as men of honor. Keepsakes such as shreds of battle flags, sidearms, swords, parole passes, and even muskets offered incontestable evidence of having passed through the blood ritual of battle. What little they carried home was not necessarily a source of embarrassment for ex-Confederates, who thought their shoddy physical appearance conveyed their nobility in defeat.[43]

Confederate relics collected at the end of the war served many purposes, but they were more than nostalgic signposts that led to a harmless stroll down memory lane or containers of memories. They could shape behavior, filter perceptions, and serve as conductors of action. The souvenirs of soldiering—as seen in the example of John Chamberlayne—could free the imaginations of former rebels to roam in the dark and dangerous world of reactionary politics during Reconstruction. A Confederate musket over the mantle or a cavalry saber unsheathed during a town parade could inspire feelings of white solidarity in violent acts against African Americans. It is easy to lose sight of the agency that seemingly harmless war relics possessed, since these same mundane objects had acted as peacemakers during the surrender at Appomattox, where a spirit of conciliation prevailed among bitter enemies who had survived four years of cruel and constant death.

Notes

I am grateful for the valuable assistance of Patrick Shroeder, Bert Dunkerly, and Ernie Price of the National Park Service and Kaylyn L. Sawyer, who is a Civil War Institute Fellow at Gettysburg College, and for the editorial assistance of Elizabeth G. Carmichael of Gettysburg.

1. An outstanding analysis of the Appomattox surrender proceedings can be found in Elizabeth R. Varon, *Appomattox: Victory, Defeat, and Freedom at the End of the Civil War* (New York: Oxford University Press, 2014).

2. Varon, *Appomattox*, 90–91.

3. On the importance of things and the expressive power they possessed for Civil War soldiers, see Michael DeGruccio, "Letting the War Slip through Our Hands: Material Culture and the Weakness of Words in the Civil War Era," in *Weirding the War: Stories from the Civil War's Ragged Edges*, ed. Stephen Berry (Athens: University of Georgia Press, 2011), 15–35; Joan E. Cashin, "Trophies of War: Material Culture in the Civil War Era," *Journal of the Civil War Era* 1, no. 3 (September 2011): 339–67; and Megan Kate Nelson, *Ruin Nation: Destruction and the American Civil War* (Athens: University of Georgia Press, 2012), 228–39.

4. On the ways that objects exert agency, see Frank Dikoter, "Objects and Agency: Material Culture and Modernity in China," in *History and Material Culture: A Student's Guide to Approaching Alternative Sources*, ed. Karen Harvey (New York: Routledge, 2009), 158–72.

5. Steven Lubar and W. David Kingery, eds., *History from Things: Essays on Material Culture* (Washington, D.C.: Smithsonian Institution Press, 1993).

6. On Confederates who were in Appomattox denial, see Jason Phillips, *Diehard Rebels: The Confederate Culture of Invincibility* (Athens: University of Georgia Press), especially chapter 5.

7. The transition into veteranhood has been explored in rich and innovative ways

by scholars, some of whom include James Marten, *Sing Not War: The Lives of Union and Confederate Veterans in Gilded Age America* (Chapel Hill: University of North Carolina Press, 2011); Brian Craig Miller, *Empty Sleeves: Amputation in the Civil War South* (Athens: University of Georgia Press, 2015); Brian Mathew Jordan, *Marching Home: Union Veterans and Their Unending Civil War* (New York: W. W. Norton, 2015); Jeffrey W. McClurken, *Take Care of the Living: Reconstructing Confederate Veteran Families in Virginia* (Charlottesville: University of Virginia Press, 2009); David Silkenat, *Moments of Despair: Suicide, Divorce and Debt in Civil War Era North Carolina* (Chapel Hill: University of North Carolina Press, 2011), especially chapters 2 and 5; and Stuart McConnell, *Glorious Contentment: The Grand Army of the Republic, 1865-1900* (Chapel Hill: University of North Carolina Press, 1992).

8. An excellent overview of the Appomattox campaign can be found in William Marvel, *Lee's Last Retreat: The Flight to Appomattox* (Chapel Hill: University of North Carolina Press, 2002).

9. Joan Waugh, "'I Only Knew What Was in My Mind': Ulysses S. Grant and the Meaning of Appomattox," *Journal of the Civil War Era* 2, no. 3 (September 2012): 307-36.

10. John Smith to his mother, 11April 1865, John Smith Papers, Pennsylvania Historical Society, Philadelphia (PHS). For a similar Union account of the famous apple tree, see Jacob J. Zorn diary, 11 April 1865, in *A Sergeant's Story: Civil War Diary of Jacob J. Zorn*, ed. Barbara M. Croner (Apollo, Pa.: Closson Press, 1999), 165.

11. Varon, *Appomattox*, 90-91.

12. Zorn diary, 10 April 1865, in Croner, *A Sergeant's Story*, 165; N. H. Panghorn to his parents, 19 April 1865, N. H. Panghorn Papers, Appomattox National Historical Park, Virginia (hereafter cited as ANHP).

13. John H. Chamberlayne to Edward P. Chamberlayne and Lucy Parke Chamberlayne, 12 April 1865, in C. G. Chamberlayne, ed., *Ham Chamberlayne—Virginian: Letters and Papers of an Artillery Officer in the War for Southern Independence, 1861-1865* (Richmond: Dietz Press, 1932), 322.

14. On the role of ambition and the desire for the approval of women among Confederate soldiers, see Stephen Berry, *All That Makes a Man: Love and Ambition in the Civil War South* (New York: Oxford University Press, 2002). Andrew McConnell Stott, "'What Exile from Himself Can Flee?': Byron and the Price of Exile," *Welcome to the Wordsworth Trust* (blog), 27 March 2014, https://wordsworth.org.uk/blog/2014/03/27/byron-exile/, accessed 24 June 2016; John H. Chamberlayne to Sally Grattan, 1 August 1865, in Chamberlayne, *Ham Chamberlayne*, 329, 333.

15. Wolfgang Schivelbusch, *The Culture of Defeat: On National Trauma, Mourning, and Recovery* (New York: Picador, 2001), 2.

16. John H. Chamberlayne to Sally Grattan, 1 August 1865, in Chamberlayne, *Ham Chamberlayne*, 329, 334.

17. John H. Chamberlayne to Sally Grattan, 1 August 1865.

18. Carlton McCarthy, *Detailed Minutiae of Soldier Life in the Army of Northern Virginia, 1861-1865* (Richmond: Carlton McCarthy, 1882), 160.

19. My insights on General Orders No. 9 draw from the conclusions of Varon, *Appomattox*, chapter 3. For the quote, see p. 70.

20. Email correspondence with Patrick Schroeder, Appomattox Court House National

Historical Park chief historian, 25 April 2016; W. H. Andrews, *Footprints of a Regiment: A Recollection of the 1st Georgia Regulars. 1861–1865*, ed. Richard M. McMurry (Atlanta: Longstreet Press, 1992), 179.

21. The anecdotes from Perry and Roller are taken directly from Varon, *Appomattox*, 104–5.

22. Varon, *Appomattox*, 72–75.

23. Joshua L. Chamberlain to Sarah B. Chamberlain, 13 April 1865, Joshua Lawrence Chamberlain Collection, George J. Mitchell Department of Special Collections and Archives, Bowdoin College, Brunswick, Maine (hereafter cited as BC).

24. On the surrender proceedings, see Marvel, *Lee's Last Retreat*. On the symbolism of Confederate flags and how Confederate banners became sacred emblems, see Robert E. Bonner, *Colors and Blood: Flag Passions of the Confederate South* (Princeton: Princeton University Press, 2002), especially chapters 4 and 5; and John M. Coski, *The Confederate Battle Flag: America's Most Embattled Emblem* (Cambridge, Mass.: Belknap Press of Harvard University Press, 2005), especially chapters 1 and 2. For an example of a battle flag made of silk bridal clothes, see American Civil War Museum, http://moconfederacy.pastperfectonline.com/webobject/84DE6B99-90DB-4FA1-BDE7-971812234980; see also N. H. Panghorn to his parents, 19 April 1865, J. H. Panghorn Papers, ANHP.

25. Joshua L. Chamberlain to Sarah B. Chamberlain, 13 April 1865, Chamberlain Collection, BC.

26. John Smith to his mother, 28 April 1865, John Smith Papers, PHS.

27. Smith to his mother, 28 April 1865.

28. Smith to his mother, 28 April 1865.

29. On the demobilization of Union armies, see Gary W. Gallagher, *The Union War* (Cambridge, Mass.: Harvard University Press, 2011), 8–9.

30. [Noel] Harrison, "William T. Sherman at Spotsylvania, Chancellorsville, and Fredericksburg, May 1865," 4 May 2015, Mysteries & Conundrums: Exploring the Civil War-era Landscape in the Fredericksburg & Spotsylvania Region, https://npsfrsp.wordpress.com/2015/05/04/william-t-sherman-at-spotsylvania-chancellorsville-and-fredericksburg-may-1865/, accessed 22 September 2016.

31. Bradley T. Lepper and Mary E. Lepper, eds., Cyrus Marion Roberts Diary, 16 May 1864, http://www.78ohio.org/Diaries/Capt%20Cyrus%20Marion%20Roberts%20Diary.htm#_Volume_3:__8%20May%20to%2020%20May%201865, accessed 23 September 2016.

32. On the methodology of material culture, see Simon Harrison, "Mementos and the Souls of Missing Soldiers: Returning Effects of the Battlefield Dead," in *Royal Anthropological Institute of Great Britain and Ireland* 14 (December 2008): 774–90.

33. Samuel Merrill, *The Seventieth Indiana: The Volunteer Infantry: In the War of the Rebellion* (Indianapolis: Bowen-Merrill, 1900), 274–75.

34. Larry A. App, Michael Schroyer Diary, 15 May 1865, *Stories Retold Blog Site*, https://storiesretoldvideo.wordpress.com/2013/06/15/chapter-70-may-11-17-1865-stories-from-along-the-homeward-march-the-app-brothers-in-the-civil-war/, accessed 8 May 2016; Henry C. Morhous, *Reminiscences of the 123d Regiment, N.Y.S.V., Giving a Complete History of its Three Years Service in the War* (Greenwich, N.Y.: People's Journal Book and Job Office, 1879), 186–87.

35. My insights into materiality of battlefields and the way historic sites have evolved as commemorative landscapes borrow heavily from Nicholas J. Saunders, "Crucifix, Calvary, and Cross: Materiality and Spirituality in Great War Landscapes," *World Archaeology* 35, no. 1 (June 2003): 7–21; and Michael Schroyer Diary, 15 May 1865. For a similar view, see Jack Bauer, ed., *Soldiering: Civil War Diary of Rice C. Bull, 123rd New York Volunteer Infantry* (San Rafael, Calif.: Presidio Press, 1977), 244–45; and Adin B. Underwood, *Thirty-Third Mass. Infantry Regiment, 1862–1865*... (Boston: A. Williams, 1881), 296–97. The twenty-two-inch oak tree is now on display at the Smithsonian National Museum of American History in Washington, D.C.

36. John Smith to his mother, 8 May 1865, John Smith Papers, PHS.

37. Smith to his mother, 8 May 1865. An excellent account on the Grand Review can be found in Gallagher's *Union War*, especially chapter 1.

38. John Smith to his mother, 13 June 1865, John Smith Papers, PHS.

39. John Smith to his mother, 2 July 1865, John Smith Papers, PHS.

40. For an incisive analysis of soldier material culture, see Nelson, *Ruin Nation*, 228–39. Brian Jordan offers useful insights into the ways that Union veterans used material culture and visits to the battlefield to convey their understanding of the war. See his *Marching Home*, 95–102.

41. On the ways that material culture conveyed the sentiment of union among Northern soldiers, see Gallagher, *Union War*, 54–60. John Smith to his mother, 2 June 1865, John Smith Papers, PHS.

42. Sara Pennell, "Mundane Materiality, or, Should Small Things Still Be Forgotten? Material Culture, Micro-histories and the Problem of Scale," in *History and Material Culture: A Student's Guide to Approaching Alternative Sources*, ed. Karen Harvey (New York: Routledge, 2009), 175–89.

43. For an alternative perspective on the return of the Confederate veteran, see Diane Miller Sommerville, "'Will They Ever Be Able to Forget?': Confederate Soldiers and Mental Illness in the Defeated South," in Berry, *Weirding the War*, 321–39. See also James Deetz, *In Small Things Forgotten: The Archaeology of Early American Life* (Garden City: Anchor Press/Doubleday, 1977).

The Stuff of Defeat
Material Culture and the Downfall of Jefferson Davis

YAEL A. STERNHELL

In July 1874, Jefferson Davis wrote a Washington lawyer and asked him to apply for the return of his personal effects confiscated by the federal government at the closing of the war. Davis was requesting "some letters which are important to me in connection with a question of property in which the government has no interest and there are others valuable only to myself such as family letters running back to the time when I was a schoolboy." In a different trunk, seized in Florida, were "some of my clothes, a few arms of antiquated models only valuable as curiosity to others and to me for the associations connected with them. I should be glad to have that also." At sixty-six, Davis was the insolvent yet unrepentant former president of the Confederate States of America. Before the war, he was a prominent Mississippi planter who had served as a United States senator and secretary of war. He left the Senate in January 1861 when his home state seceded and was elected president by the Confederate Congress one month later. As leader of the rebellion, he threw himself into the job, micromanaging the war effort and refusing to accept the prospect of defeat even when it became an unmistakable fact. His fervor did not abate even once the war was over. Davis continued to defend his actions as president and to insist on the constitutionality of secession.[1]

Thus even in 1874, pleading with his erstwhile enemies for the return of his most cherished belongings could not have been easy. Yet even worse, it was far from a singular occurrence. Jefferson Davis's postwar life was marred by a long series of bitter disputes with friends and foes over his personal effects. His attempts to control the fate of the physical objects and their symbolic meanings embody his experience as the leader of a failed cause. For Davis, defeat had material repercussions that touched even deeper than the loss of his plantation and the difficulty to find remunerative work. Losing the war meant ceding control over his most private possessions and the role they assumed in public life. Remaking his fortunes in the postbellum world often took the shape of trying to win that control back.[2]

The Trunk

Davis left Richmond on the night of 2 April 1865, after it had become clear that the Army of Northern Virginia could no longer defend the capital. An evacuation had been a strong possibility for several days and Davis had already sent his family out of town, but he made no special preparations for his own departure. Only after Robert E. Lee telegraphed that morning and recommended that the government leave did the work of moving the Confederate presidency begin. Davis and his aides hurriedly packed his papers and personal belongings in several trunks and boxes, which were then loaded on the last trains leaving Richmond and headed to Danville, a tobacco town in southwestern Virginia where the Confederate government set up shop and attempted to continue regular operations. After learning on 10 April that Lee had surrendered, Davis and his cabinet took to the road and continued their flight into North Carolina, stopping first in Greensboro and then in Charlotte, where they found out that Joseph E. Johnston had surrendered to William T. Sherman in Bennett Place. At that point, Davis could either offer his own surrender and face the consequences or try to get away from the Union army. Unsurprisingly, he chose to run.[3]

Davis and his retinue continued to Abbeville, South Carolina, and on 3 May they reached Washington, Georgia, where the party split and Micajah H. Clark, Davis's clerk, was placed in charge of the Confederate treasury train, which was headed for the coast. On 22 May, in rural Florida, Clark and his fellow travelers found out that Davis had been captured in Georgia. Clark left Davis's belongings—a leather trunk, two boxes, and a rifle—in the care of the Southern senator David Levy Yulee and his family, who decided the baggage would be safer with a Unionist friend in the neighboring town of Waldo. The Yulees did not disclose the nature of the items to their new minder, and when Federal soldiers came looking for them, they found "the trunk and chests in a store-room adjoining his house, unguarded by even a lock."[4]

Brigadier General Israel Vogdes, the commanding officer, reported to his superiors the capture of Davis's personal property. The most immediately

Figure 12. Jefferson Davis, Beauvoir, Mississippi, ca. 1885. (Courtesy of the Library of Congress)

important items, which he sealed and placed at the top of the pile, were the opinions of members of the Confederate cabinet on the proposed armistice between Generals Sherman and Johnston, submitted to Davis on 17–18 April. Yet there were also many significant telegrams and confidential reports from other Confederate leaders, including Robert E. Lee. The state of the papers bespoke the panic that had swept Richmond on 2 April. As Vogdes remarked in a private message to Secretary of War Edwin M. Stanton, "The haste and disorder in which they were packed is shown by the fact that letters of different dates and different subjects are frequently thrown together, in some cases mixed with ordinary visiting cards."[5]

But even if the official papers were what caught Vogdes's attention, the captured baggage was a treasure trove of information in other ways too. It contained "his private baggage, among which were clothes but recently worn and many of them unwashed. His private papers are in the boxes, and had evidently been thrown in haste and without order, into them." Among the private papers were letters from his wife, brother, and nephews and nieces and some concerning private business. In his official reports, Vogdes did not convey just how personal the items in the trunk were. There were dressing robes, a silk undershirt, winter drawers, towels, razors, toothbrushes, lace shoes, eyeglasses, a gold ring, and the portraits of Davis, his wife, and General Lee. For the past four years, Jefferson Davis had been the Union's public enemy number one. Now Vogdes and his men were getting an intimate look into the Confederate president's hygiene habits, his relationship with his wife, and his business practices. Through his personal effects, the private life of Jefferson Davis was suddenly unveiled.[6]

Davis's belongings—papers, boxes, trunks, and weapons—were stored in the Archive Office, which was established in July 1865 as part of the adjutant general's office in the War Department in Washington, D.C. The Archive Office served as the federal government's repository for Confederate records but was also home to a range of material objects captured by the Federal army in the final days of the war. The staff searched thoroughly through Davis's papers in the hopes of finding incriminating evidence for his involvement in the Lincoln assassination and other assumed conspiracies. Important letters were arranged and cataloged, but the chief of the Archive Office generally deemed the correspondence "not void of interest, but not important as to facts of a historical or legal character." As the federal government became preoccupied with the problems of the postwar era, the private papers and belongings of the Confederate president were left to gather dust amid the vast written record documenting the nation he led.[7]

Nine years would pass before Davis was forced to approach the government and ask for their return. In 1874, the ex-president was involved in a bitter legal dispute over Brierfield, his old plantation in Hinds County, Mississippi. Brierfield had been part of the Davis Bend landholding, which belonged to Davis and his older brother Joseph, now deceased. Joseph had sold the property to Ben Montgomery and his sons, who had formerly been enslaved by the Davis family and were now the leaders of a free black community that was running the plantation as a cooperative. Davis did not have title to the property and was fighting in court to prove that he was the de facto owner and that Joseph had left him the right to rescind the sale and reclaim ownership. Brierfield was probably Davis's best chance to stabilize his finances after years of business failures, bad investments, and unemployment. When the stakes were so high, asking the federal government for a favor was worth a try.[8]

Yet it is more than likely that Davis had other reasons to make the application, even if these were left unstated in his official exchanges. Wresting back control of his most private effects was a way to reclaim his own wartime history. The material objects Davis was seeking had been lost at a moment when he was a desperate fugitive trying to elude the pursuit of the Union army. Their custody by the federal government was a permanent mark of shame, a reminder of his flight, capture, and subsequent imprisonment. Getting them back was a way to erase the memory of that moment in his past. By reclaiming his intimate possessions, he was trying to restore his dignity.

Perhaps to his surprise, response by the government was prompt and willing. In 1874, Reconstruction was dissolving and a new era of redemption and reunion was underway. Even before the November elections that brought Democrats to power in Congress, most Southern states were back under Home Rule and effectively free of Federal intervention. While memories of the war were still fresh in the minds of many individuals, the national government was ready to move on. The War Department, once the epicenter of the struggle against the South, was now preoccupied with new challenges. In June 1874, Congress allocated funding for an ambitious historical project of publishing the official records generated by both the Union and Confederate armies. Soon thereafter, the War Department began coaxing and negotiating with ex-Confederates for the right to copy or buy their wartime papers and would continue to do so for a generation.[9] Under these circumstances, Davis's request for his personal belongings did not fall on deaf ears, and the trunk was returned in September 1874 by Adjutant General Edward T. Townsend. The list of items Davis received included his clothes, personal hygiene items, eyeglasses, keys, opera glasses, the gold ring, and "two envelopes, containing hair, beads, photographs, + c." The papers consisted of personal letters dating as far back as 1831, receipts, recipes, newspaper clippings, and poetry.[10]

While he was happy to get back the mementos and private papers taken in Florida, the business records he was after had never been in that trunk to begin with. With some help from Senator John B. Gordon of Georgia and Representative Charles E. Hooker from Mississippi, Davis kept pressing the War Department to search for additional papers in the hopes that the missing documents would turn up. Secretary of War William W. Belknap responded politely that all the papers the department had kept were of historical value, adding that it did "not seem that any of them could be of use in a suit of law. If Mr. Davis can specify any particular letters or class of letters which have not been returned to him and which he desires to have another examination will be made to see if they are in the possession of the Govt." The bureaucrats managing the historical record of the war resisted occasionally, insisting on their right to preserve in the War Department's files correspondence of Davis with private parties since they contained matters of public and historical interest. Davis, too, maintained a healthy dose of rage toward some Federal officials, especially Adjutant General Townsend, whom he referred to as "that poor snake." Yet all things considered, Davis enjoyed remarkably direct access to the Federal War Department, his sworn enemy for four long years.[11]

This was all the more true following the appointment in 1878 of Marcus J. Wright as the War Department's agent for the collection of Confederate records. Wright had been a general in the Confederate army and remained unabashedly loyal to his former compatriots even as an employee of the Federal government. His dual loyalties were tolerated and often encouraged since his deep ties to the South were exactly what ensured that he would provide the department the invaluable Confederate records Southerners had been clinging to since the end of the war. He and Davis had a very cordial relationship, and Davis expressed "kind regard and esteem" for Wright even in private. In May 1880 Wright appealed to his superiors for the return of additional private papers belonging to Davis, which he had apparently located in the files of the Archive Office. Once again, Wright's request was promptly approved.[12]

Jefferson Davis never regained access to all of the items captured by Union soldiers. In 1913, the War Department still held a mahogany box containing three of his pistols and various accessories. A number of his papers, judged too important to be given up, were also retained in the War Department's archives. And yet receiving the bulk of the material possessions he had lost during the retreat from Richmond proved to be a much simpler task than could have been envisioned in 1865. Nearly a decade after the war, the federal government was in the business of restoring Southern property to its prewar owners. As the formerly rebellious states were regaining their autonomy, the leader of the rebellion was regaining his personal belongings. Returning trophies of war became a means to rebuild the relationship between the federal government and the man who tried to destroy it.[13]

The decision would pay off. In the coming years, as the War Department worked on compiling its massive collection of wartime records, Jefferson Davis proved an invaluable resource. He provided documents that were missing from the Archive Office, deciphered his own telegraphs, and filled in names and dates. While he remained bitter and resentful until the end, he established a working relationship with the federal government that continued until his death. When the compilation came out, Secretary of War Elihu Root singled him out for the aid he offered the department in its task. In many ways, the restitution of the trunk turned out to be a first step in the Federal effort at reconciliation.[14]

The Cloak

Yet there was one object belonging to Jefferson Davis that he would never see again. Incidentally, that object would stand at the center of one of the war's most enduring controversies. Davis was captured on 10 May 1865 in the piney woods near Irwinville, Georgia. After the Confederate government had been formally disbanded a few days earlier, he was traveling in a convoy with his family, his slaves, a number of aides and senior Confederate officials, an armed guard, and a wagon train. While they tried to move stealthily, Union forces were on their tracks. In the early morning hours, the Fourth Michigan and the First Wisconsin Regiments surrounded the Davis encampment and demanded surrender.[15]

What happened next has been the subject of fierce debate for generations. According to a sworn affidavit by Corporal George M. Munger of the Fourth Michigan, the soldiers noticed two women trying to leave the camp. Asking them who they were, one replied that the other was her old mother, who was going to get some water from the branch. Munger observed that "the other person wore a long brownish skirt and a shawl over the head, covering the face and shoulders and coming to the waist, while upon the left arm was carried a tin pail." Yet at that point Munger noticed under the skirt "a pair of high men's boots and feeling sure the dress was a disguise, raised and cocked his gun." Other Union soldiers who were present at the moment of capture corroborated Munger's story, though there were important discrepancies in how they described the item of feminine clothing Davis had on. Munger was most likely stretching the truth when he claimed that Davis was wearing a "skirt." Other affidavits reported Davis as wearing a shawl and a cloak that may have looked like they belonged to a woman. Varina Davis offered a similar version, vouching that she had thrown a raincoat over her husband's shoulders and a shawl over his head.[16] Most of the evidence that has accumulated over the years indicates that these were indeed the items of clothing Davis had on his person when captured. Yet the official report submitted to Secretary of War Stanton by John H. Wilson, the major general in command, ignored the finer details of the incident and stated that Davis "put on one of his wife's dresses and started for the woods." The implication was clear. The leader of the Confederacy was an effeminate coward, unable to face his enemy like a man.[17]

News of the events surrounding Davis's arrest spread immediately and became a national sensation. Within two days, Wilson's report was circulating on the front pages of numerous newspapers, adorned with headlines like "Jeff. Attempts to Escape in His Wife's Clothes!!" A wide array of humiliating cartoons appeared, depicting Davis wearing petticoats, hoopskirts, and women's hats, with captions like "Jeffie Davis, the Belle of Richmond," and "A 'So Called President' in Petticoats."[18] On 15 May, P. T. Barnum, America's master showman, offered the War Department $500 for the "petticoats in which Jeff Davis was caught." When his offer was declined he went ahead anyway and set up in his New York museum a life-size wax figure of Davis wearing a dress similar to the one appearing in the ubiquitous cartoons of the day. In popular culture, the cloak had transmuted into a dress and the shawl into a feminine cap. Davis could have hardly imagined a more embarrassing end to his presidential career.[19]

Davis and his allies did their best to offer a counternarrative. Burton N. Harrison, his private secretary, who was with him that morning and followed him into prison, claimed that the "President had on a water-proof cloak. He had used it, when riding, as a protection against the rain during the night and morning preceding ... and he had probably been sleeping in that cloak." Edward Pollard, the prolific historian of the Confederate cause, denounced the "wicked and absurd story that Mr. Davis was captured disguised in feminine clothes." He too claimed Davis had slept in his clothes and accused Varina Davis of throwing the shawl over his shoulders. In his own memoirs, Davis offered a similar narrative, placing most of the blame on his wife. Expecting an attack from a gang of marauders who had threatened the camp, he went to sleep in her tent, "fully dressed." Just before dawn, his coachman woke him up and reported that there was firing behind the encampment. "As it was quite dark in the tent, I picked up what was supposed to be my 'raglan,' a water-proof, light overcoat, without sleeves; it was subsequently found to be my wife's, so very like my own as to be mistaken for it; as I started my wife thoughtfully threw over my head and shoulders a shawl."[20]

Yet public proclamations like these did little to quash the story. In private correspondence, Davis raged against the "pitiful slander" of his portrayals as a woman and blamed a reporter for the *New York Herald*, who had been on the steamer carrying Davis to Fort Monroe, for spreading the story. The *Herald* remained a source of irritation long after the war. On 12 September 1874 it ran a particularly sarcastic story about the return of Davis's Florida trunk. The *Herald* called the feminine disguise "a part of the history of the rebellion" and recounted how Secretary of War Stanton "was very fond for the time being of holding up and exhibiting to visitors the petticoats that Davis wore when captured." Writing his Washington lawyer, Philip Phillips, Davis wondered whether it would be possible to arrange for someone to refute the *Herald* story by giving an interview to a rival paper and protect him against the "malicious falsehoods" he was the subject of.[21]

The tidbit about Stanton displaying the petticoats to visitors is most likely apocryphal, but Stanton did show an acute awareness of the matter's explosive nature right from the start. While Davis was on his way to prison at Fort Monroe, Stanton instructed Lieutenant Colonel Benjamin Pritchard, commander of the Fourth Michigan, to confiscate from Davis's wife the original clothing Davis had been caught in. Pritchard and Mrs. Davis had had a contentious relationship from the outset, and many of their confrontations revolved around the Davis couple's material possessions. Varina had complained about the disappearance of $80,000 in gold and the theft of her baby's clothing, which Pritchard vehemently denied, and of her own clothing, which Pritchard explained as the confiscation, under orders, of her husband's disguise. Davis later reiterated the accusation that his wife's trunk had been broken into and that articles of women's clothing stolen from it had been used to strengthen the case that he had worn a dress.[22]

What Pritchard actually received from Varina, under protest, was "a woman's light cloak such as is called a water-proof, which she represented was the same worn by her husband when captured, and which was also identified by the soldiers of my command, who were present, as being the same article," as well as "a shawl of hers, stated by her and by her waiting maid to be the one which formed the balance of the disguise." Whether Varina actually conceded to Pritchard that the items formed a "disguise" remains unknown. But by the time the party reached Washington, the version that Davis had been caught in camouflage had attained official status. On 24 May Pritchard delivered the items by hand to the secretary of war in Washington, along with the personal belongings caught with Davis and the papers discovered in the baggage train of his party.[23]

By that point, Davis had already lost control over how his capture was represented and how it would be remembered. With the confiscation of the material items by the War Department, he was surrendering the evidence that could have refuted the legend of his escape in a hoopskirt and bonnet. Even worse, once the cloak and shawl arrived at the War Department, they mysteriously vanished from view. An internal report, prepared in 1935, failed to trace their whereabouts. Yet the crucial date was probably 26 May 1869. That day, the clerks in the Archive Office destroyed the woolen clothing found in a trunk and a box belonging to Davis. The trunk had contained other articles made of wool, like socks and coats. Bezalel Wells, the clerk in charge, did not specify which had been burned. In addition, the Archive Office delivered to the adjutant general an assortment of items from Davis's trunk. The items were listed in an official document and reported to have been deposited in a safe. No mention was made of the cloak or shawl in either report. Twenty years later, a different clerk in charge of the Confederate records could say only that the shawl had been destroyed because it had become moth-eaten but had "no recollection as to when this was done."[24]

The silence of the clerks is surprising considering the importance assigned to Davis's clothing by the secretary of war only a few years before. It was also hardly in line with the level of public interest in the story at that moment in time. In 1869, the capture of the Confederate president was still a hot topic. That same summer in London, Davis was handing out photographs of his attire on the day of his capture, while John H. Reagan, the Confederate postmaster general, published a widely circulating letter defending Davis's conduct and accusing those who were reviving the story of trying to use it for political gain.[25] The controversy would remain alive for decades, as the principal actors in the drama of that morning in Georgia continued to give wildly different accounts of what had transpired and the press continued to publish them.[26]

And yet the cloak was nowhere to be found. Was it because the garment was very similar to Davis's own, as he had claimed, and exposing it would have revealed the official account as a falsehood meant to disgrace the Confederate president? Or was it pure negligence? In any case, Davis was his usual livid self in complaining about the secreting of the controversial clothing by the federal government. Writing a supporter in response to another testimony by a Union soldier claiming to have seen Davis in a dress,

Material Culture and the Downfall of Jefferson Davis   { 231

he fumed that Adjutant General Townsend, "whose feat has been to keep watch and ward ... over the cloak and shawl taken from my wife when a prisoner," could have easily cleared up the matter had he chosen to.[27]

The great irony was that even as Davis succeeded in regaining possession of other items he had lost in the war, the most crucial ones for his legacy were gone. Davis understood well that even though his cloak and shawl were actual objects, they also existed in a mythic realm in which they could be easily transformed into a skirt, a dress, or any other imaginary item of feminine attire. Both the material objects and their afterlives in text and image had eluded his control. The story of his downfall, dressed in women's garments and trying to flee, became a hallmark of Civil War lore. The most vehement denials were useless in the absence of the material items on the one hand and in the face of the public's entrancement with the myth on the other. After four years of military and political leadership, his reputation was defined by two items of clothing he had put on in a moment of panic at the crack of dawn. Defeat, for Davis, was made of cloth.

The Letter

Davis should have presumably had less trouble regaining ownership over personal effects that ended up in the hands of ex-Confederates. And yet as it turned out, the same men who served and supported him during the war had their own agendas when it came to his material possessions. This became painfully clear by the fall of 1865, when Varina Davis, who was managing the family's finances while her husband was in jail, tried unsuccessfully to force Watson Van Benthuysen, a member of the presidential retinue, to return a sum of roughly $1,500 he had saved for her and their children when the remnants of the Confederate treasury were divided in Florida on 23 May. Van Benthuysen denied and evaded Varina and the Davis aides who implored him to hand over the money to a woman who was trying to feed four children and sustain her husband in jail. Only in the summer of 1867 did he relent and transmit the funds to Davis through his former secretary, Burton Harrison. Dealing with Van Benthuysen and his two brothers, "three of the basest wretches I have ever heard of," in Varina's words, taught the Davis couple a valuable lesson. In the aftermath of defeat, even former confidants could not be trusted.[28]

Papers were less inherently valuable than specie, but they were almost as coveted. While many of Davis's records ended up in the War Department's Archive Office, others were never discovered by the federal government and were left in the hands of the men and women who happened to hold them at the end of the war. Years later, when he tried to recover the records for his *Rise and Fall of the Confederate Government*, which would come out in 1881, Davis realized that he was as helpless in trying to reclaim material belongings left in the hands of his allies as he was when attempting to wrest them from his enemies.[29]

Part of the issue was that Davis's presidential archive had been highly disorganized to begin with. Davis tended to keep important papers in his office in the customs house or in a room in the Confederacy's executive mansion, where they piled high on his desk with no identifiable system.[30] When the clerk Micajah Clark packed up Davis's archive on the morning of 2 April as the Union army was approaching, he stuffed the papers in several different trunks without making a log of which document had been placed where. One of the trunks used actually belonged to Davis's private secretary, Burton Harrison, who had left town a few days before as an escort to Varina Davis and her children.[31]

The frenzied evacuation of Richmond and the meandering retreat into the Deep South did much to exacerbate the chaos in the presidential records. The disintegration of the archive began in Abbeville, South Carolina, where Clark along with two other Davis aides worked feverishly to reduce the size of the presidential wagon train by burning what he later defined as "many unimportant papers," repacking the rest along with the presidential stationery and leaving it at the home of Judge Monroe, under the care of Monroe's daughter, a Mrs. Leovy, and her sisters. On their next stop in Washington, Georgia, the rest of the archive was once again divided. Clark took some of the papers with the treasury train to Florida, where they ended up in the boxes discovered in the unlocked room in Waldo. Davis kept some of the papers in his own valise. The trunk belonging to Burton Harrison was left in the hands of a Mrs. Robertson, at whose house Harrison had stayed a few days earlier when he passed through town with Varina Davis. After learning that Davis had been captured, Clark returned from Florida to Abbeville, where he spent nearly a week examining the papers and destroying a great many. What he did retain were papers from senior politicians and generals and those that seemed to throw "any light upon the history of the country and the struggle." The papers left with Mrs. Leovy and Mrs. Robertson survived the war, and both women eventually sent them to Harrison's new home in New York.[32]

Davis knew all along that Harrison was the keeper of some of his most important records, but only in 1872 did he write him to ask for their return, explaining that there was no longer any danger in his possession of his own records. When Harrison did not respond, he wrote again, in January 1874, after having begun to arrange his papers. Specifically, Davis was anxious to find letters he had received, which he assumed were in the collection turned over by Mrs. Leovy. Once again he did not hear back. Nearly two years passed before Davis tried again. This time, he seemed inclined to believe that Harrison was not simply ignoring him but that the shipment may have gotten lost in the mail. Harrison, in New York, maintained an icy silence.[33]

A few months later, however, ignoring the question of what happened to Davis's papers ceased to be an option. In February 1876, *Scribner's Monthly* published a highly personal letter Robert E. Lee had written to Jefferson Davis under the tantalizing headline "A Piece of Secret History." In the dispatch, written on 8 August 1863 from Camp Orange, Virginia, Lee was offering his resignation following the failure of his Pennsylvania campaign. In touching prose, Lee gave voice to the mental and physical exhaustion he was feeling. "No one is more aware than myself of my inability for the duties of my position. I cannot even accomplish what I myself desire. How can I fulfill the expectations of others?" While nearly two more years would pass before Lee would actually surrender, the letter was an early omen of an impending defeat. The editors remained vague on the question of how they had obtained the letter and simply noted that they were publishing the piece "in the language of sectional friendliness in which it reaches us."[34]

Davis was furious. The publication of the letter confirmed that his missing papers were not lost but intentionally concealed by people who understood their value and wanted to profit from it. "If one lives long how many of those trusted will be faithful to the end?" he complained to his wife. Davis had good reason to feel personally betrayed. Harrison had been one of his closest aides, close enough for Davis to have entrusted him with the responsibility of escorting his wife and children out of Richmond when the end was nigh. Now, their relationship had been upended. Harrison was in New York, settled and prosperous, while Davis was dislocated and poor. Yet even worse, Harrison was the de facto owner of Davis's prized possessions, the wartime papers that were key to commemorating the Confederate past. His distress was still apparent a year later, when he once again approached Harrison.

> I wrote to you, at intervals, three times asking you to send to me the letters you got from Mrs Leovy.... As you told me that the papers had been put in a place of absolute safety, it is fair to assume that you know or can learn who had access to them after you took charge of them, and it is but reasonable that I should look to you to trace if practicable and restore to me the letters and papers which have been pillaged. You will realize

their importance to me now, as you did when for their safe keeping you claimed to have possession of them.[35]

Davis had concrete reasons to want his letters back. In October 1876, he signed a contract with D. Appleton & Co. in New York to publish his memoirs "at the earliest practicable date." The memoirs were a once-in-a-lifetime opportunity to vindicate himself in the court of public opinion and shape his image in the eyes of future generations. They were also the rare promising financial prospect for Davis, who at that point was effectively homeless and unemployed. He was residing in a cottage on a Mississippi plantation owned by Sarah Dorsey, a widowed admirer, to the great chagrin of his wife, Varina. Appleton committed to paying 10 percent of the retail price on the first 20,000 copies, 12.5 percent on more than 20,000, and 15 percent after 30,000.[36] The unauthorized publication of Lee's resignation letter was particularly alarming since the missives from Lee were the records Davis was most interested in. Lee was the South's premier military leader and a national figure without which no history of the war could be complete. The personal correspondence between them was uniquely valuable, Davis argued, since the two men enjoyed such a close relationship that Lee expressed his thoughts to him freely and his letters were read by no one else. Yet these particular documents also had an emotional value that went beyond their utility for the writing of a good historical narrative. Davis was distressed by the fact that these private letters, exchanged between confidants, had been made public without his consent. Davis had valued his personal bond with Lee enough to keep his picture along with that of Varina in his personal trunk. Lee was now dead, and the letters they exchanged were the only material remnants of their wartime camaraderie. Their pilfering by others was a personal loss as well as a painful reminder of how far he had fallen from wartime leader to postwar nonentity.[37]

As pleading with Harrison had clearly proved futile, Davis in late 1876 dispatched his assistant, ex-Confederate officer William T. Walthall, to confront Harrison directly and try to obtain the papers he was keeping. In the aftermath of the visit, Harrison finally responded to Davis and gave him a full account of what had happened to his papers since they were packed by his clerk, Micajah Clark, and another aide, John Taylor Wood, on 2 April 1865. The letters from Lee never were in the boxes left with Mrs. Leovy in Abbeville, he claimed, but in the trunk left with the Robertsons in Washington, Georgia. "Sometime after I had removed to New York, Mrs. Robertson forwarded the trunk to me here. When I opened it here, I became aware (for, so far as I can recollect, the first time) that some of your papers were in it- and among them, I saw a number of letters from General Lee." Since Harrison was living "first in one boarding house and then in another" he stored the papers that had traveled from the South in a warehouse until the summer of 1870, when another Southern expatriate, Charles C. Jones Jr., offered to keep the items in his house in Brooklyn. Jones, a scion of an eminent Georgia family, was a well-respected planter, politician, historian, and ex-Confederate officer who seemed like the right person to take care of the papers. His house, so he said, had already served as a repository for other valuable objects. At no point, Harrison claimed, did Jones receive authority to publish the papers or to make any other use of them, though it was understood that he would look through the trunk and arrange the papers in a way that would ensure their safety from mice and mold.[38]

Harrison never saw the papers again until Walthall arrived in New York and the two went over to Jones's Brooklyn home. Jones handed over "the less valuable" papers belonging to Davis and informed the men that "those were all there had been in the trunk!" None were from Robert E. Lee. Harrison confronted him about the published resignation letter, telling him that he "remembered that letter very well, expressed my surprise that it had been published and asked where were the other letters from General Lee which had been in my trunk. Col. Jones replied that there were no letters from General Lee in the trunk when it reached his house."[39]

And yet Jones did not deny his responsibility for the publication of the letter. He informed Walthall and Harrison that he had received it on loan "from *somebody* (not specified) in Richmond." In August 1877 he finally responded to a written request from Walthall and named the person who had given him access to the letter. It was Captain James O'Donnell, "then in New York City, but said to be of Richmond Virginia, and who was introduced to me by John R. Thompson Esq. whom you know certainly by reputation." O'Donnell had a number of official letters addressed by Lee to Davis, among which was the "Gettysburg letter of which I took a copy, and for preservation had it published in Scribner's Monthly." Jones claimed that after Walthall's visit he had written O'Donnell but received no response. "Where he is now I know not."[40]

Davis, Walthall, and Harrison embarked on a mission to locate the mysterious Captain O'Donnell and the collection of Lee letters he ostensibly held. They wrote a number of well-connected Virginians, who made additional inquiries, but to no avail. No one had ever seen or heard of O'Donnell, including Lee's son and his secretary. "All my detective intentions have been utterly baffled by this Hibernian Nominis Umbra," Walthall complained. One correspondent guessed that the name of O'Donnell was an assumed one and that the said Mr. Thompson would not have associated with such doubtful characters. Walthall suspected that O'Donnell was not a doubtful character but a myth.[41]

As the months went by, it became clear that he had been right.[42] Jones was an ardent Confederate who devoted his postbellum life to writing the history of the South, but he had no qualms about stealing from and lying to the former Confederate president in order to retain ownership of the papers that had fallen into his lap. This left Davis in the peculiar position of having to cajole Jones into returning the letters if he ever wanted to see them again. Harrison suggested taking advantage of the fact that Jones had gone to Georgia in the hopes of becoming the president of its university: "He can't realize that [ambition] if a half dozen leading citizens of the State, such as I have mentioned, have any reason to think ill of him in such a case as this." Harrison was also counting on the possibility that Jones, now back in the South and surrounded by Southerners, might have a change of heart. Away from the materialistic and cutthroat environment of the city, he might be convinced to respect Davis's claim to his wartime papers. In any case, it was clear to Harrison that Jones was now the de facto owner of the documents. There was a real danger of their destruction, he avowed, "if the pursuit of them be not conducted with diplomatic regard for the feelings of the custodians of them." Harrison advised that Davis write Jones a "polite letter" and that Walthall would follow up and *"take charge of the negotiations."*[43]

Harrison, by that point, was once again in the good graces of his former boss, as Davis was satisfied with his explanation of what had happened to the papers under his charge. This gave him license to make another practical suggestion: "Even people who prize such things as autographs (and the autograph hunter is apt to be unreasonable) can probably be prevailed on to furnish you copies, and to give you access to the originals, if they refuse to surrender those originals to you." Harrison wanted to separate the material form of the historical document from the text. Davis would be able to write his history, but those who cherished the original pieces of paper would not have to give them up.[44]

Harrison's conciliatory approach toward Jones and other relic hunters might have had something to do with the fact that he too was holding on to some of Davis's papers and was disinclined to give them back. Harrison explained to Davis that he and Walthall had gone through the contents of the trunk at Jones's house, but after a few days, when the trunk was sent to his own home, his wife, the writer Constance Cary Harrison, searched through it and miraculously found "several letters and dispatches, among which is the letter written by General Lee to the Secretary of War, shortly before the lines around Petersburg were abandoned." Harrison, despite being on a mission to locate other missing records by Davis, was not planning to return the originals. "I send you, with this, copies of all those letters and dispatches. My wife hopes to keep the originals, as mementoes. She has, I think, no other letters or papers of any interest in reference to the war. I have none whatsoever. The copies which are enclosed, I have myself carefully compared with the originals they are made *literatim*.... If you desire the originals, my wife will, of course, cheerfully surrender them to you." Throughout the letter, Harrison, a practicing lawyer, uses distinctly noncommittal language to describe his connection with the papers, even in regard to the simple question of whether his wife was or was not in possession of additional Davis records in their shared home. Later on in the letter, he admits to also having kept a bound volume of the *Statutes at Large of the Confederate States 1861–1864*, "which was on your table at the Executive Office, still has your book marks in it, and has been kept by me as a memento of you. It shall be sent to you if you desire it." At that point in his life, Harrison had no actual need for these books and papers. Despite knowing that Davis was writing a history of the war, he did not even attempt to offer an excuse for why he insisted on retaining important papers and books other than the desire for documents as memorabilia. This inconsistency reflected the complicated feelings he still harbored toward Davis. Physically and emotionally, the two men had grown far apart. Yet Harrison was obviously still deeply attached to his memories from the war period and to Davis's books and papers in particular. While the bitter man writing from the Deep South seemed increasingly alien, the material objects left from their time together were obviously too precious to be returned. For Harrison, like other ex-Confederates of his generation, the material objects had an affective value that trumped his commitment to returning to Davis what was ostensibly rightfully his. While the Confederacy had been long gone and these men had moved on with their lives, the war was an event of a lifetime, and the papers left in its wake were a physical, tangible link to a time when they were young, energetic, and full of hope for an independent South. Davis had no chance to retrieve the actual relics from these men. All he could hope for was access to the text in the form of a copy.[45]

The close relationship between Davis and Lee made the publication of the secret resignation letter an exceptionally hard blow. But it was not the last time Davis saw his private correspondence appear publicly without his consent. In 1882, another personal letter to a confidant surfaced. This time it was a missive to Colonel James Chesnut, dated 11 November 1861, discussing an accusation by General P. G. T. Beauregard that Davis refused to authorize a battle plan he had submitted. Davis tried to use his contacts in the War Department to prevent the letter from being published in *The War of the Rebellion: A Compilation of the Official Records of the Union and Confederate Armies*, which was under preparation at the time, but was informed that the letter had already appeared in volume 2. Writing Marcus J. Wright, he accused Beauregard's friend and chief of staff, General Thomas Jordan, now also in New York, of furnishing copies from Beauregard's papers under a false identity. "But my surprise is as to how either of them got the letters I wrote to Chesnut, which was personal and which on account of my great regards for Chesnut I am sorry to have had made public."[46]

Nearly twenty years after the fact, Jefferson Davis was still trying to assemble the material possessions he had lost in May 1865. At times, it was an effort to reclaim cherished mementos and financially significant documents. At others, it was a struggle over objects that would define his legacy as the person who had led a powerful but unsuccessful rebellion. Consistently, he discovered that the fate of his material belongings was both unpredictable and out of his control. Papers disappeared and then reemerged; a cloak that was a prized possession mysteriously got lost while worthless items of clothing and toiletries were kept intact for years. Close allies turned out to be entirely unreliable, while the federal government was often more cooperative and transparent in its handling of his things. Regardless, what Davis came to realize was that as a vanquished leader, his belongings were no longer his own. The most intimate of effects and the most private of papers were turned into public property, as both enemies and friends treated them as they pleased and used them for their own ends. For Davis, regaining their possession often embodied a broader attempt to regain his bearing in the postwar world. In his lived experience, this was the meaning of defeat.

Notes

1. Jefferson Davis to Philip Phillips, 13 July 1874, folder 230, box 4, Jefferson Davis Papers, entry 1, RG 109, National Archives and Records Administration, Washington, D.C. (hereafter Davis Papers, NARA). Biographies of Jefferson Davis include William J. Cooper, *Jefferson Davis, American* (New York: Knopf, 2000); Felicity Allen, *Jefferson Davis, Unconquerable Heart* (Columbia: University of Missouri Press, 1999); and William E. Dodd, *Jefferson Davis* (Lincoln: University of Nebraska Press, 1997).

2. On the role of material objects in shaping Civil War culture, see Simon Harrison, "Bones in the Rebel Lady's Boudoir: Ethnology, Race and Trophy-Hunting in the American Civil War," *Journal of Material Culture* 15 (December 2010), 385–401; Joan E. Cashin, "Trophies of War: Material Culture in the Civil War Era," *Journal of the Civil War Era* 1, no. 3 (September 2011): 339–67; Megan Kate Nelson, *Ruin Nation: Destruction and*

the American Civil War (Athens: University of Georgia Press, 2012); and Michael DeGruccio, "Letting the War Slip through Our Hands: Material Culture and the Weakness of Words in the Civil War Era," in *Weirding the War: Tales from the Civil War's Ragged Edges*, ed. Stephen Berry (Athens: University of Georgia Press, 2011), 15-35. Some seminal works in the history of material culture more generally are Adrian Forty, *Objects of Desire: Design and Society from Wedgwood to IBM* (New York: Pantheon Books, 1986); Ian Hodder, ed., *The Meaning of Things: Material Culture and Symbolic Expression* (London: Routledge, 1989); W. David Kingery, ed., *Learning from Things: Method and Theory of Material Culture Studies* (Washington, D.C.: Smithsonian Institution Press, 1996); Arjun Appadurai, ed., *The Social Life of Things: Commodities in Cultural Perspective* (Cambridge: Cambridge University Press, 1986); and Leora Auslander, "Beyond Words," *American Historical Review* 110 (October 2005), 1015-45.

3. On the retreat of the Confederate government from Richmond, see William C. Davis, *An Honorable Defeat: The Last Days of the Confederate Government* (New York: Harcourt, 2001), 62-75; Herman Hattaway and Richard E. Beringer, *Jefferson Davis, Confederate President* (Lawrence: University Press of Kansas, 2002), 391-93; Cooper, *Jefferson Davis*, 523-24; Nelson Lankford, *Richmond Burning: The Last Days of the Confederate Capital* (New York: Penguin, 2002), 77-79, 91, 104-5; Burke Davis, *The Long Surrender* (New York: Random House, 1985), 30-32, 44-53; and Michael B. Ballard, *A Long Shadow: Jefferson Davis and the Final Days of the Confederacy* (Jackson: University Press of Mississippi, 1986), 43-49.

4. C. Wickliffe Yulee, *Senator Yulee of Florida: A Biographical Sketch* (Jacksonville: Florida Historical Magazine, 1909), 29-30; U.S. War Department, *The War of the Rebellion: A Compilation of the Official Records of the Union and Confederate Armies*, 128 vols. (Washington, D.C.: GPO, 1880-1901), ser. 1, vol. 47, pt. 3, 653-56 (hereafter *OR*). Quote on p. 653.

5. Israel Vogdes to E. M. Stanton, 17 June 1865, folder 231, box 4, Davis Papers, NARA; *OR*, ser. 1, vol. 47, pt. 3, 651.

6. Inventory of private property of Jefferson Davis captured at Waldo, Florida, folder 230, box 4, Davis Papers, NARA.

7. U.S. Department of War, General Orders No. 127, 21 July 1865, box 1, entry 441, Orders and Regulations of the Archive Office, Records of the Archive Office, RG 109, National Archives and Records Administration, Washington, D.C. (hereafter Records of the Archive Office, NARA); inventory, P. T. Beauregard personal baggage, folder 230, box 4, Davis Papers, NARA; report of Francis Lieber, Chief of Archive Office, 18 January 1866, folder 1, box 1, entry 436, Records of the Archive Office, NARA.

8. Cooper, *Jefferson Davis*, 615-20, 643-44, 675.

9. On the federal government's publication project and its political implications, see Yael A. Sternhell, "The Afterlives of a Confederate Archive: Civil War Documents and the Making of Sectional Reconciliation," *Journal of American History* 106 (March 2016): 1025-50.

10. Dunbar Rowland, ed., *Jefferson Davis, Constitutionalist: His Letters, Papers, and Speeches*, 10 vols. (Jackson: Mississippi Department of Archives and History, 1923), 7:404; William W. Belknap to John B. Gordon, 15 March 1875, book 3, Letters Sent, entry 435, Records of the Archive Office, NARA; inventory of books, papers, and effects

of Jefferson Davis, returned to him by Adjutant General E. D. Townsend, 9 September 1874, folder 230, box 4, Davis Papers, NARA.

11. Lynda Lasswell Crist, ed., *The Papers of Jefferson Davis*, 14 vols. (Baton Rouge: Louisiana State University Press, 2012), 13:240; Belknap to Gordon, 15 March 1875, book 3, Letters Sent, entry 435, Records of the Archive Office, NARA; A. P. Tasker to General Townsend, 14 February 1878, folder 230, box 4, Davis Papers, NARA; Rowland, *Jefferson Davis*, 8:293.

12. Rowland, *Jefferson Davis*, 8:293; George M. McCrary to the Adjutant General, 11 February 1879, folder 230, box 4, Davis Papers, NARA; Marcus J. Wright to Robert N. Scott, 11 May 1880, folder 230, box 4, Davis Papers, NARA; Marcus J. Wright, receipt for Davis Papers, 1 June 1880, folder 230, box 4, Davis Papers, NARA.

13. Jeff Davis relics, 3 December 1913, folder 230, box 4, Davis Papers, NARA. On restitution of wartime property not as a means of building bridges between former enemies but as a means for disentanglement and closure, see Simon J. Harrison, "War Mementos and the Souls of Missing Soldiers: Returning Effects of the Battlefield Dead," *Journal of the Royal Anthropological Institute* 14 (December 2008): 774–90.

14. Elihu Root, preface, *OR*, ser. 1, vol. 130, xi; Robert N. Scott to Jefferson Davis, 12 September 1879, 19 December 1879, 8 January 1880, 4 November 1882, 13 November 1882, book 2, entry 707, Letters Sent, Records of the War Records Office, entry 94, National Archives and Records Administration, Washington, D.C.; Scott to Secretary of War, 11 May 1880, book 2, entry 707, Records of the War Records Office.

15. Benjamin D. Pritchard deposition, 27 May 1865, folder 231, box 4, Davis Papers, NARA. Accounts of the capture are in Cooper, *Jefferson Davis*, 573–75; Joan E. Cashin, *First Lady of the Confederacy: Varina Davis's Civil War* (Cambridge, Mass.: Harvard University Press, 2006), 161–63; William C. Davis, *Jefferson Davis: The Man and His Hour* (New York: HarperCollins, 1991), 636–38; and W. Davis, *Honorable Defeat*, 299–304.

16. George M. Munger deposition, W. H. Harrison Crittenden deposition, and James J. Bullard deposition, all 27 May 1865, folder 231, box 4, Davis Papers, NARA; Cashin, *First Lady of the Confederacy*, 161.

17. J. H. Wilson to Edwin M. Stanton, 13 May 1865, folder 231, box 4, Davis Papers, NARA. On the political and cultural meanings of clothing throughout history, see Valerie Steele, *Fashion and Eroticism: Ideals of Feminine Beauty from the Victorian Era to the Jazz Age* (New York: Oxford University Press, 1985); Alison Lurie, *The Language of Clothes* (New York: Holt Paperbacks, 2000); Diana Crane, *Fashion and Its Social Agendas: Class, Gender, and Identity in Clothing* (Chicago: University of Chicago Press, 2000); Elizabeth Wilson, *Adorned in Dreams: Fashion and Modernity* (London: Tauris, 2003); Michael Zakim, *Ready-Made Democracy: A History of Men's Dress in the American Republic* (Chicago: University of Chicago Press, 2003); and Kate Haulman, *Politics of Fashion in Eighteenth-Century America* (Chapel Hill: University of North Carolina Press, 2011).

18. "Later!!," *Evening Star*, 15 May 1865; Joseph Hoey, "Jeffie Davis, the Belle of Richmond," 1865, image retrieved from the Library of Congress, https://www.loc.gov/item/2008661830/ (accessed 2 August 2016); Gibson & Co., "A 'So Called President' in Petticoats," 1865, image retrieved from the Library of Congress, https://www.loc.gov/item/2008661797/ (accessed 2 August 2016.)

19. P. T. Barnum to Edwin M. Stanton, 15 May 1865, folder 231, box 4, Davis Papers, NARA. On the gendered meanings of Davis's capture, see Nina Silber, *The Romance of Reunion: Northerners and the South, 1865–1900* (Chapel Hill: University of North Carolina Press, 1993), 29–37.

20. Burton Norvell Harrison, "The Capture of Jefferson Davis," *Century Illustrated Monthly Magazine*, November 1883; Edward Alfred Pollard, *Life of Jefferson Davis with a Secret History of the Southern Confederacy* (Philadelphia: National Pub. Co., 1869), 523; Jefferson Davis, *The Rise and Fall of the Confederate Government*, vol. 2 (New York, 1881), 701.

21. Rowland, *Jefferson Davis*, 8:53, 7:405; "Jeff Davis' Capture," *New York Herald*, 12 September 1874; Davis to Phillips, 26 September 1874, in Crist, *Papers of Jefferson Davis*, 13:241–42.

22. Benjamin D. Pritchard to Edwin M. Stanton, 1 June 1865, folder 231, box 4, Davis Papers, NARA; memorandum for Mr. Powell, administrative assistant, 5 April 1935, folder 230, box 4, Davis Papers, NARA. See also Silas S. Stauber, 31 May 1865, folder 231, box 4, Davis Papers, NARA; and Rowland, *Jefferson Davis*, 7:405–6, 8:36. On the Davis family finances, see Cashin, *First Lady of the Confederacy*, 171–72.

23. Pritchard deposition, 27 May 1865, folder 231, box 4, Davis Papers, NARA; Nelson A. Miles to C. A. Dana, 24 May 1865, folder 233, box 4, Davis Papers, NARA.

24. Inventory, Jefferson Davis personal baggage, undated, folder 230, box 4, Davis Papers, NARA; Bezalel Wells, memorandum, 26 May 1869, folder 230, box 4, Davis Papers, NARA; list of property of Jefferson Davis turned over from Archive Office to General Townsend, 26 May 1869, folder 230, box 4, Davis Papers, NARA; memorandum for Mr. Powell, administrative assistant, 5 April 1935, folder 230, box 4, Davis Papers, NARA.

25. Cashin, *First Lady of the Confederacy*, 189; John H. Reagan, "Circumstances Attending the Capture of President Davis," *Charleston Courier Tri-weekly*, 26 August 1869.

26. See, for example, "Jeff Davis Was Disguised," *Emporia Daily Gazette*, 28 March 1895; "Capture of Jeff Davis," *Milwaukee Journal*, 9 April 1895; "Jeff Davis's Disguise," *Indiana State Journal*, 24 May 1899.

27. Rowland, *Jefferson Davis*, 8:36.

28. The correspondence concerning the fate of the Confederate gold is voluminous and complex. Some key documents showing the conflict with the Van Benthuysen brothers over the missing funds are found in the Burton Norvell Harrison Papers, Manuscript Division, Library of Congress, Washington D.C. (hereafter Harrison Papers): Micajah H. Clark to Varina Davis, 15 January 1866, folder 3, box 6; John W. Scott to Micajah H. Clark, 26 January 1866, folder 18, box 7; Micajah H. Clark to Varina Davis, 27 January 1866, folder 3, box 6; Tench Tilghman to Varina Davis, 24 February 1866, folder 20, box 7; Watson Van Benthuysen to A. Y. Stokes, 9 May 1867, folder 21, box 7; Jefferson Davis to Watson Van Benthuysen, 5 July 1867, folder 24, box 7; and Burton N. Harrison, memorandum, 21 August 1885, folder 21, box 7. Varina Davis quote is in Crist, *Papers of Jefferson Davis*, 12:109.

29. While historians of material culture often distinguish themselves as studying objects rather than documents, there is a growing understanding that papers too are objects and that it is impossible to divorce the text from the material on which it is inscribed. For this distinction, see "AHR Conversation: Historians and the Study of Material Cul-

ture," *American Historical Review* 114 (December 2009): 1356. On papers as objects, see Lisa Gitelman, *Paper Knowledge: Toward a Media History of Documents* (Durham, N.C.: Duke University Press, 2014); Cornelia Vissman, *Files: Law and Media Technology* (Palo Alto: Stanford University Press, 2008); Bruno Latour, *The Making of Law: An Ethnography of the Conseil d'état* (Cambridge: Polity, 2010); Ben Kafka, "Paperwork: The State of the Discipline," *Book History* 12 (2009), 340–53; and Will Slauter, "Write Up Your Dead," *Media History* 17 (Winter 2011), 1–15.

30. Burton N. Harrison to Jefferson Davis, 24 May 1877, Jefferson Davis folder, box 6, Harrison Papers.

31. Micajah Clark to William T. Walthall, 28 August 1877, Jefferson Davis folder, box 6, Harrison Papers; Harrison to Davis, 24 May 1877, Jefferson Davis folder, box 6, Harrison Papers.

32. Micajah H. Clark to Burton N. Harrison, 20 February 1866, folder 4, box 6, Harrison Papers; Burton N. Harrison to Col. Darr, 5 January 1897, folder 5, box 6, Harrison Papers; Crist, *Papers of Jefferson Davis*, 13:241; Harrison to Davis, 24 May 1877, Jefferson Davis folder, box 6, Harrison Papers.

33. Crist, *Papers of Jefferson Davis*, 13:107, 13:187; Jefferson Davis to Burton N. Harrison, 14 November 1875, Jefferson Davis folder, box 6, Harrison Papers; Rowland, *Jefferson Davis*, 7:466.

34. "A Piece of Secret History," *Scribner's Monthly*, February 1876, 521, 522.

35. Crist, *Papers of Jefferson Davis*, 13:388–89; Jefferson Davis to Burton N. Harrison, 19 May 1877, Jefferson Davis folder, box 6, Harrison Papers.

36. Crist, *Papers of Jefferson Davis*, 13:375. On the uneasy relationship between Varina and Sarah Dorsey, see Cashin, *First Lady of the Confederacy*, 218–24.

37. Crist, *Papers of Jefferson Davis*, 13:501. Harrison confirmed the existence of a direct channel of communication between Davis and Lee in his letter from 24 May 1877, Jefferson Davis folder, box 6, Harrison Papers.

38. Harrison to Davis, 24 May 1877, Jefferson Davis folder, box 6, Harrison Papers. For a complete history of Lee's resignation letter, see William Harris Bragg, "Charles C. Jones Jr., and the Mystery of Lee's Lost Dispatches," *Georgia Historical Quarterly* 72 (Fall 1988), 429–62. See also Dallas D. Irvine, "The Fate of Confederate Archives," *American Historical Review* 44 (June 1939), 823–41.

39. Harrison to Darr, 5 January 1897, and Harrison to Davis, 24 May 1877, Jefferson Davis folder, box 6, Harrison Papers.

40. William T. Walthall to Burton N. Harrison, 9 June 1877, folder 21, box 7, Harrison Papers; J. William Jones to William T. Walthall, 9 August 1877, folder 12, box 7, Harrison Papers.

41. Rowland, *Jefferson Davis*, 8:535–36; Walthall to Harrison, 9 June 1877, folder 21, box 7, Harrison Papers. See also the following in the Harrison Papers: William T. Walthall to Burton N. Harrison, 20 August 1877, folder 21, box 7; Charles Williams to Burton N. Harrison, 14 December 1877, folder 24, box 7; E. H. Skinker to Burton N. Harrison, 26 October 1877, folder 18, box 7; and Jefferson Davis to Burton N. Harrison, 16 October 1877, Jefferson Davis folder, box 6.

42. Bragg proves this conclusively in "Charles C. Jones Jr., and the Mystery of Lee's Lost Dispatches."

43. Harrison to Davis, 24 May 1877, Jefferson Davis folder, box 6, Harrison Papers; Crist, *Jefferson Davis*, 7:547.

44. Jefferson Davis to Burton N. Harrison, 13 July 1877, and Harrison to Davis, 24 May 1877, Jefferson Davis folder, box 6, Harrison Papers.

45. Harrison to Davis, 24 May 1877, Jefferson Davis folder, box 6, Harrison Papers.

46. Robert N. Scott to Jefferson Davis, 24 November 1882, book 2, entry 707, Letters Sent, Records of the War Records Office. The letter appears in *OR*, ser. 1, vol. 2, 513–14; Jefferson Davis to Marcus J. Wright, 16 March 1882, folder 11, series 5, Marcus J. Wright Papers, Southern Historical Collection, Wilson Library, University of North Carolina at Chapel Hill.

Contributors

LISA M. BRADY earned her Ph.D. from the University of Kansas in 2003 and is a professor of history at Boise State University and the editor in chief of the journal *Environmental History*. She is the author of *War upon the Land: Military Strategy and the Transformation of Southern Landscapes during the American Civil War* (University of Georgia Press, 2012) and of several articles, including "Life in the DMZ: Turning a Diplomatic Failure into an Environmental Success" (*Diplomatic History*, 2008) and "From Battlefield to Fertile Ground: The Development of Civil War Environmental History" (*Civil War History*, 2012).

PETER S. CARMICHAEL is the Fluhrer Professor of History and director of the Civil War Institute at Gettysburg College. He is the author of *The War for the Common Soldier: How Men Thought, Fought, and Survived in Civil War Armies*, forthcoming from the University of North Carolina Press.

JOAN E. CASHIN received her doctorate in American history from Harvard University. She is a professor of history at Ohio State University, and she is the author or editor of five books and many articles on nineteenth-century American history. Her next monograph, *War Stuff: The Struggle for Human and Environmental Resources in the American Civil War*, is forthcoming from Cambridge University Press.

EARL J. HESS holds the Stewart W. McClelland Chair in History at Lincoln Memorial University, Harrogate, Tennessee. Author of more than twenty books, his *The Rifle Musket in Civil War Combat: Reality and Myth* (University Press of Kansas, 2008) and *Civil War Infantry Tactics: Training, Combat, and Small-Unit Effectiveness* (Louisiana State University Press, 2015) deal with the use of weapons in the Civil War in ways that support a material culture perspective.

ROBERT D. HICKS is the director of the Mütter Museum and the Historical Medical Library and the William Maul Measey Chair for the History of Medicine, both at the College of Physicians of Philadelphia. He holds a doctorate in maritime history from the University of Exeter, United Kingdom, and degrees in anthropology and archaeology from the University of Arizona. He is the editor of the forthcoming *Civil War Medicine: A Surgeon's Experience*.

VICTORIA E. OTT is the James A. Woods Associate Professor of American History at Birmingham-Southern College. She is a scholar of the American Civil War, the Old South, and U.S. women's history. She is the author of *Confederate Daughters: Coming of Age during the Civil War*, and which was published by Southern Illinois Press in 2008. Her more recent publications include "Voices from the Margins: Non-elites in Confederate Alabama," in *The Yellowhammer War: The Civil War and Reconstruction in Alabama* (University of Alabama Press, 2013) and "Love in Battle: the Meaning of Courtship in the Civil War South," in *Children and Youth during the Civil War Era* (New York University Press, 2012).

JASON PHILLIPS is the Eberly Professor of Civil War Studies in the Department of History at West Virginia University. He earned his doctorate in history from Rice University. He is the author of *Diehard Rebels: The Confederate Culture of Invincibility* (University of Georgia Press, 2007) and the editor of *Storytelling, History, and the Postmodern South* (Louisiana State University Press, 2013). With Brian Luskey, Phillips edited a special issue of *Civil War History* (June 2017) devoted to material culture. Phillips's current book, *Looming Civil War: Imagining the Future in Nineteenth-Century America*, is forthcoming from Oxford University Press.

TIMOTHY SILVER is a professor of history at Appalachian State University, where he teaches courses on American environmental history and the history of America's national parks. He received his Ph.D. in early American history from the College of William and Mary. He is the author of *A New Face on the Countryside: Indians, Colonists, and Slaves in South Atlantic Forests, 1500–1800* (Cambridge University Press, 1990) and *Mount Mitchell and the Black Mountains: An Environmental History of the Highest Peaks in Eastern America* (Chapel Hill: University of North Carolina Press, 2003). With Judkin Browning, he is the coauthor of a work tentatively titled *The Civil War: An Environmental History*, forthcoming from the University of North Carolina Press.

YAEL A. STERNHELL received her Ph.D. from Princeton University in 2008 and is currently an associate professor of history and American studies at Tel Aviv University. Her first book, *Routes of War: The World of Movement in the Confederate South*, (Harvard University Press, 2012) was a cowinner of the Francis B. Simkins Prize from the Southern Historical Association and a finalist for the Lincoln Prize. Her next book, on the Civil War archive, is under contract with Yale University Press. An article drawing on her findings from this project, "The Afterlives of a Confederate Archive: Civil War Documents and the Making of Sectional Reconciliation," was published in the *Journal of American History* in 2016 and won the Organization of American Historians' Binkley-Stephenson Award.

SARAH JONES WEICKSEL received her Ph.D. in history from the University of Chicago in 2017 and is currently an Andrew W. Mellon Postdoctoral Fellow at the Wolf Humanitites Center at the University of Pennsylvania and a research associate at the Smithsonian's National Museum of American History. She holds an M.A. in American material culture from the Winterthur Program at the University of Delaware and a B.A. in history from Yale University. She is the author of several articles and essays, including "The Dress of the Enemy: Clothing and Disease in the Civil War Era," *Civil War History* (June 2017); and "'Peeled' Bodies, Pillaged Homes: Looting and Material Culture in the American Civil War Era," in *Objects of War: The Material Culture of Conflict and Displacement*, edited by Leora Auslander and Tara Zahra (Cornell University Press, 2018). She is currently at work on a book manuscript, "The Fabric of War: Clothing, Culture, and Violence in the American Civil War Era."

RONALD J. ZBORAY is a professor of communication and director of the graduate program for cultural studies at the University of Pittsburgh, where MARY SARACINO ZBORAY is a visiting scholar in the Department of Communication. They have coauthored several essays on antebellum U.S. and American Civil War–era print culture, including "Cannonballs and Books: Reading and the Disruption of Social Ties on the New England Home Front," in Joan E. Cashin, editor, *The War Was You and Me: Civilians in the American Civil War* (Princeton University Press, 2002), and "Beyond the Market and the City: The Informal Dissemination of Reading Material during the American Civil War," in James Connolly et al., editors, *Print Culture Histories beyond the Metropolis* (University of Toronto Press, 2016). They have also coauthored four books: *A Handbook for the Study of Book History in the United States* (Center for the Book, Library of Congress, 2000); *Literary Dollars and Social Sense: A People's History of the Mass Market Book* (Routledge, 2005); *Everyday Ideas: Socioliterary Experience among Antebellum New Englanders* (University of Tennessee Press, 2006); and *Voices without Votes: Women and Politics in Antebellum New England* (University of New Hampshire Press, 2010). Ronald Zboray is also the author of numerous articles on antebellum U.S. publishing and reading and *A Fictive People: Antebellum Economic Development and the American Reading Public* (Oxford University Press, 1993). Ronald and Mary are coediting *U.S. Popular Print Culture to 1860*, volume 5 of *The Oxford History of Popular Print Culture*.

Index

Page numbers appearing in *italics* refer to illustrations.

Abel (a slave), 38
accidental death, 107–8, 113, 115–16, 117
actor-network theory, 3–4
advertising for vaccine matter, 131–32
African Americans: books as shields and, 77; at Harpers Ferry, 19–21; refugee camps and built environment, 152, 154, 155, 156, 158, 159, 160, 161, 162, 166, 170; vaccinations and, 138, 143, 148n30. *See also* African Americans and relics; artifacts; emancipation; ex-slaves; freedpeople; housing, refugee camps; refugees; slavery; slaves
African Americans and relics: in the antebellum era, 20–21, 38, 39; civilians during the Civil War, 45–46, 174n19; postwar, 170; soldiers during the Civil War, 47, 77
agency: home and, 176–77, 192; objects having, 3, 199, 218; women and political, 180–81, 194n2
agriculture, 4, 18, 35, 39, 57, 58–59, 70, 137, 179
Alabama, 5, 27, 83, 176–97, *189*
Albany Chronicle, 79
Alexander, Edward Porter, 102
allegiances, political, 5–6, 19
American Bible Society, 82, 91
American Civil War Museum, 220n24
American Missionary Association, 157–58
American Tract Society (ATS), 80–81
amicide, 107–8, 113, 115–16, 117. *See also* friendly fire
Anderson, Osborne, 18–21
Andersonville prison, 142
animals, 63, 67, 69, 126

Antietam, memorialization of the battle at, 63–65, 70, 73n18
Antietam Creek, 53, 56–57, 59, 60–63, *61*, 69
Antietam National Battlefield: as an artifact, 53–71; the battle and, 59–63, *61*, 65–67; overview of, 53–55; park at, 63–65, 69–70, 73n21; place of, 55–59; Union soldier occupation and, 67–69
Antietam National Cemetery, 54, 64
Appalachian Mountains, 56
Appomattox: apple tree at, 198–99, *200*, 203–4; surrender at, 198–99, *200*, 201–5, 207–11, 218
Appomattox surrender, defeat relics from: apple tree relics as, 198, 203–4; Lee's Farewell Address copies as, 207–8; overview of, 198–201, *200*, 217–18; surrender parade and, 209–10
Appomattox surrender, victory trophies from: apple tree relics as, 203; overview of, 198–201, *200*, 217; surrender parade and, 211; Union soldier John Smith and, 203, 214, 215–17
archaeological excavations, 35–36, 100, 164, *165*
architecture, 3, 7. *See also* built environment; historic buildings; historic preservation
Archive Office, Washington, D.C., 225, 227–28, 231, 232
areolas, 128, 133, 140
Arlington plantation, 37, 40, 42, 44, 45, 46
arms. *See* weapons
Army of Northern Virginia, 130, 138, 202, 207, 208, 209, 223

{ 249 }

Army of Tennessee, 137, 201, 205, 208
Army of the Potomac, 85, 202–3, 207, 211, 214
Articles of War, 40
artifacts, 35; aesthetic aspects of, 99–100; African Americans and, 1–2, 4, 6, 20–21, 38, 39, 45–46, 47, 77, 174n19; buildings as, 7, 40–45, 58, 65, 154–62, 213; a definition of, 35; desire for, 41–42; family history and, 3, 37, 38, 39, 44–45; as an inspiration, 39–40, 41; protection of, 40–45, 65, 91–92, 125–27, 140; revealing intention, 99; from Revolutionary War, 34–46; soldiers and, 4, 5, 6, 35–39, 41–47, 63, 91–92, 99–118, 131, 139, 198–218, 228–29; utilitarian attitudes toward, 45, 99. *See also* historic houses; historic preservation; monuments; relics; souvenirs; statues
artifacts of white Northerners: antebellum, 3, 13, 26, 39; during the Civil War, 4, 40–47, 76, 178; postwar, 5, 6, 92, 91–92, 116–17, 199, 201, 203, 211, 213, 214, 216
artifacts of white Southerners: antebellum, 3, 22, 34–35, 38; during the Civil War, 4, 5, 40–47, 76, 178; postwar, 5, 6, 91–92, 141–42, 198–99, 201–4, 206–7, 217–18, 237, 238
artillery: as artifacts, 100; emotional embrace of, 102, 113–14, 117; friendly fire and, 115–16
Ashby, Turner, 27
Association of Army and Navy Surgeons of the Confederate States, 131
Atchison, David, 15
Audoin-Rouzeau, Stéphane, 101
"Austrian Musket in Action" (Gaskill), 104, *105*
Averett, Harris, 190

Badger, William, 45
Bangor Young Men's Bible Society, 75, 82
Banks, Nathaniel P., 91
Barker, Roberta, 24–25
Barnum, P. T., 229
barracks, used to house refugees, 155, 157, 158, 160, 168
Bartram, John, 125
Batten, Edith, 170
battlefields, 2, 35, 75, 77, 114, 221n40; as landscapes, 35, 39, 40, 53–71, 211–12, 221n35; in Kansas, 13, 27, 28, 29n1, 67; in Maryland, 6, 7, 53–74; materiality of, 53–74, 221n35; in Mississippi, 101, 106, 113, 116; in North Carolina, 35; in Pennsylvania, 45, 65, 81, 90, 91, 177; as sources of relics, 16, 114, 35–36, 46–47, 124, 177; in Tennessee, 63, 90, 106, 114; in Virginia, 83, 101, 138–39, 202, 211–14, 217. *See also* Antietam National Battlefield; Black Jack, battle of; Crater, battle of the; Franklin, battle of; Gettysburg, battle of; Stones River, battle of
Baxter, Richard, 78–79
bayonets, 101
Beard, Grace, 44
Beauregard, P. G. T., 238–39
Becker, Annette, 101
Beckwith, Margaret, 5
Belknap, William W., 227
Bemiss, S. M., 138
Ben (a slave), 20
Bennett Place, surrender at, 223, 225
Berry, Cora, 47
Bibles damaged by bullets. *See* books: as shields
Black Jack, battle of, 13, 16, 27, 28, 29n1
Blair, Charles, *12*, 17, 18
Bleeding Kansas, 17, 32n25
Bliss, Robert Lewis, 105
Bloody Angle, 213
Bloody Lane, 62, 63, 70
bodies. *See* human bodies
body armor, 102, 110, 111, 117

Bolton, James, 123, 141, 145n1, 147n21
Book of Common Prayer, 81
books: bullet impact and divine protection of, 85–87, *86*; cultural-intellectual history of, 78–80; enshrining of, 90–92; press coverage of, 87–90; reasons for wearing and placement of, 83–85; as shields, 75–92, 80–83, 92
Boone, Arthur, 47
Booth, John Wilkes, 26, 214
Boston Investigator, 75
Boswell, James Keith, 85
bovine vaccines, 123, 128, 137, 143. *See also* vaccine matter
Bowie, Rezie, 14–15
bowie knives, 13–15, 17–18, 21, 23, 28, 30n7, 115
Braddock House, 42
Brady, Lisa M., 4, 6, 7
Bragg, Braxton, 114
Branscomb, James, 182, 187
Branscomb, Louis, 192
Bridgford, David Benjamin, 91
Brierfield plantation, 226
Brinton, John H., 148n29
Brockett, W. B., 13, 16
Brooks, Robert, and family, 170
Brown, John, 6; battle of Black Jack and, 13; fund-raising tour of, 16–17, 18; Harpers Ferry raid and, 19–23; Pate's knife and, 13, 16–17, 24, 27–28, 33n38; pikes of, 6, *12*, 17–18, 22, 23–25, 26–27, 28, 29; in prison and execution of, 27
Brown, Kathleen, 154
Brown, Mary, 26
Brown, Watson, 22
Bruggeman, Seth, 39
Buffalo, N.Y., 74
Buford, Samuel, 15
buildings, historic, 40, 42, 43, 45, 65. *See also* architecture; built environment; historic preservation
built environment, 4, 70; antebellum, 58; during the Civil War, 4, 63, 152–58; postwar, 152, 213. *See also* architecture; historic buildings; historic preservation
bullet-in-the-book stories. *See* books as shields
bulletproof vests, 102, 110, 111, 117
Burnside, Ambrose, 62
Burnside's Bridge, 54, *61*
Bush, Elliot N., 110
Bushman, Richard, 195n3
Butler, Benjamin, 160
Byrd, Dana, 159
Byrne, Terence, 21
Byron, Lord, 205

campaign ribbons as relics, 214–15
Campbell, Jacqueline Glass, 194n2
Camp Nelson, Ky., 152, 155–58, 162, 165, 168, 169
Camp Nelson Home for Colored Refugees, 157–58, 165; expulsion of refugees from, 156–57, 165, 168, 173n11. *See also* refugee camps
camps, refugee. *See* refugee camps
canons. *See* artillery
"Caroline Gray," 80
Carson, Joseph, 127
Cashin, Joan E., 4, 54–55, 76, 145n3, 178, 199
Cassidy, John, 81, 82
Catholics, 58, 81
Catlin, James K., 108
Cayce family, 35
Cedar Hill house, 1–2, *2*
census, federal, 39, 193n1
Cephas, Charles, 21
ceramics, 58, 162, 166, 175n35
Chamberlain, Joshua Lawrence, 209, 210
Chamberlayne, John H., 201, 205–7
Chancellorsville, battle of, 83, 138–39, 217
Chesnut, James, 44, 238–39
Chesnut family, 44

Index { 251

Chickamauga and Chattanooga National Military Park, 64
children, 100, 182, 186, 191, 233, 234; as authors, 77; as refugees, 153, 156, 158, 160, 166, 170; as sources of vaccine matter, 123, 137–39, 141, 142–43, 145, 148n30; war relics and, 100, 101
Chimborazo Hospital, 124, 137, 138, 139
chimneys, 159, 160–62, 174n26
churches, 53; antebellum, 27, 58–59; during the Civil War, 34, 41, 43, 60, 61, 62, 63, 188
cholera, 69, 74n28
civilians, 2, 100; antebellum, 16, 22; during the Civil War, 42, 43, 45, 66, 90, 157, 188; postwar, 55, 67, 70, 90, 199, 202, 211. *See also* soldiers and civilians
Clark, Clifford Edward, Jr., 181, 195n3
Clark, Micajah H., 223, 233, 235
cleanliness as a cultural symbol, 154, 156, 163, 164
clothing: in combat, 109–10; refugees and, 162, 163, 164, 165, 166; soldiers' need for, 188–90; war support production of, 184–85; women's, 4, 5, 178; worn by Jefferson Davis at his capture, 229–32
collecting: consumer culture and, 2–3; by Union soldier John Smith, 202, 203, 204, 211, 216–17; war relics, 16, 22, 24, 39, 46–47, 178, 199, 218; of wartime records, 225, 227
Collins, John, 81, 89, 90–91
Colt, Samuel, 18, 26
combat boots found by Joshua Chamberlayne, 206–7
common whites, 193n1. *See also* yeomanry
Confederate States Medical and Surgical Journal, 131
"Confederate womanhood," 194n2
confluent smallpox, 128–29. *See also* smallpox

Congressional Committee on Military Affairs, 64
consumer culture of antebellum era, 2–3
contraband camps. *See* refugee camps
contraband of war, enslaved people as, 157, 160, 168–69, 171n1
Cooley, Samuel, 151, 158
Corby, William, 43
Corinth, Miss., contraband camp in, 155
Cotton, John W., 185, 190
Cotton, Mariah, 185, 187
Counts, Walter Henry, 83
cowpox, 127, 128, 130, 132, 137, 143
cows, 127, 132, 137, 143–44, 146n14, 147n23, 148n29
Cox, Jacob, 41, 59–60
Cox, Thomas, 86
Crater, battle of the, 101
Crawford, S. P., 137
Cromwell, Oliver, 79, 94n13
Cromwell Bible story, 79–80, 87
crosses, 111
Crowder, James, 186
crucifixes, 111
Crystal Palace exhibit, 3
Cumberland Valley, 56
currency, Confederate, 199, 204
currency, Union, 42, 188, 203
Curtis, Finley P., 105
Custis, Parke, 37, 38, 40, 44
Cutter, Ephraim, 148n29

D. Appleton & Co., 235
daguerreotypes, 5. *See also* photographs
Daily Richmond Enquirer, 183
Dame, Harriet, 47
Dangerfield, John, 20
Danton, Georges Jacques, 26
Daston, Lorraine, 3–4, 24
Davidson, James Innes, 102–3
Davis, Bettie, 184, 185, 186, 188
Davis, Jefferson, 224; career of, 222–23; cloak and shawl of, 229–32; as

Confederate President, 40; fleeing and capture of, 223, 228–30; and historic preservation, 40; letters and official papers of, 222, 223–25, 232–39; memoirs of, 233, 235; personal archive of, 233; trunk with personal property of, 223–28
Davis, Joseph, 226
Davis, Newton, 184, 185–86, 187–88
Davis, Varina, 229–30, 232, 233, 235, 243n36
Davis Bend landholding, 226
De Bow's Review, 15
Deetz, James, 3, 217
DeGruccio, Michael, 4, 54, 76, 177, 199
Delano, Sterling P., 108
Democratic Party, 180, 226. *See also* politics, electoral
de Rochambeau, Comte, 42
Devereaux, Seth K., 75
disease: Antietam and, 68, 69; cholera, 69, 74n28; cowpox, 127, 128, 130, 132, 137, 143; human remains and, 68. *See also* smallpox; vaccination; vaccine matter
distinct smallpox, 128. *See also* smallpox
Distinguished Flying Cross, 112
doctors. *See* medicines; physicians; smallpox; vaccine matter
Dorsey, Sarah, 235, 243n36
Dougherty, Eli, 82, 88, 91
Douglas, James P., 113–14
Douglass, Anna Murray, 1–2, 3
Douglass, Frederick, 1–2, 3, 28
Downs, Jim, 156
Doyld, Willie, 47
Drake, Brian Allen, 4
dress. *See* clothing
Dunker Church, 61, 62, 63

Eastern Dispensary, 132
East Woods, 58, 61
emancipation: Northern, 39; relics of, 39, 45–46, 47; smallpox and, 138,
143; wartime proclamation of, 63, 64, 77
Enfield rifles, 105–6
English Civil War Bible tales, 78–80, 88
environment: Antietam National Battlefield and (*See* Antietam National Battlefield: as an artifact); overview of material culture and, 4, 6; smallpox and, 128
environmental history, 6, 7, 53, 55, 69, 70
epistemology and vaccinations, 126–27, 128, 139–40, 143–45
erysipelas, 125, 138, 142
Espy, Columbus, 184
Espy, Sarah, 183, 184–88, 190, 191, 193
Europe, 7, 17, 23, 57, 111, 125, 137, 141, 143, 147, 147n20
Europeanists, 9n5
Evangelical Magazine, 79–80
Evans, John, 79
Everyday Life of the Man under a Musket on the Firing Line and in the Trenches (Gaskill), 104, *105*
ex-slaves, 5, 6, 143, 152–71. *See also* African Americans; freedpeople; slavery; slaves
eyewitnesses to the Revolution, 36, 46

Farewell Address: by George Washington, 40; by Robert E. Lee, 207, 208
farmers. *See* agriculture
farming at Antietam, 58–59
fashion, 4, 16, 170, 178, 185
Faust, Drew Gilpin, 194n2
Fee, John, 157–58
flags, 15, 168, 208; Confederate, 47, 199, 201, 205, 209–10, 211, 217–18, 220n24; Revolutionary, 37; symbolic power of, 210; Union, 5, 43, 214–15
Fletcher, George, 84
Floyd, John, 26–27
folk culture, 3, 36, 39, 46, 87, 112
Foltz, Theobold, 104

food and foodways, 194n3; antebellum, 6, 16; during the Civil War, 66–67, 69, 70, 138, 151, 153, 165, 166, 183, 185–90, 197n25; postwar, 171
Ford, Marion, 45
Forrest, Nathan Bedford, 201
Fort Monroe, 157, 230
Foster, Davis, 83
Foster, Jacob T., 108
Founders, the, 40–44. *See also individual Founders*
Fourth of July, 35, 37
Fowle, John, 46
Frank, Lisa Tendrich, 178
Franklin, battle of, 106
Frederick the Great, 37
freedpeople, 151–71. *See also* African Americans; ex-slaves
Freeman, Elizabeth, 39
Free State Hotel, 18
French, William, 62
French and Indian War, 80
friendly fire, 107–8, 113, 115–16, 117. *See also* amicide
Fritz, Levi, 83
future, the: public health and, 141, 142; weapons as symbols of, 24, 26, 28, 29

Gambill, Jesse, 47
Garrison, James, 186
Garrison, William Lloyd, 17–18, 26
Gaskill, J. W., 104, *105*
Geffert, Hannah, 21
gender: antebellum, 38, 102; during the Civil War, 46, 112–14, 153, 176–93; postwar, 46–47, 153, 206, 209. *See also* masculinity; women
General Orders No. 9, 207–8, 219n19
Gettig, Samuel R., 91
Gettysburg, battle of, 45, 81, 90, 91, 177
Gettysburg National Battlefield, 65
Gillis, Margaret Miles, 184
Glassie, Henry, 3, 35
Glymph, Thavolia, 171n1

Gordon, John Brown, 62, 209, 227
Grand Contraband Camp, 152, 160–62, *161*, 165, 169–70
Grand Review in 1865, 211, 214–15
Grant, Ulysses S., 198, 202–3, 208
Graton, Edward R., 88
grave robbing, 22, 32n25, 149n32
Graves, James, 155
Grayson, George Washington, 110
Great Appalachian Valley, 56
Green, Israel, 32n24
Green, Shields, 20
Greene, Nathanael, 42, 43
guns. *See* weapons
gun use, training on, 103

Hagerstown Pike, 53, 60
Hagerstown Valley, 56, 59
Haimes, John, 36
"Hall, The," Kentucky, 169
Hampton, Va., 152, 160–62, *161*, 165, 169–70
Harpers Ferry, Va., 18–23; aftermath of revolt at, 20–22, 26–27; revolt at, 18–20; souvenirs from, 22–23, 32n25
Harper's Weekly, 81, 84, 163, 198
Harrison, Benjamin, 43, 64
Harrison, Burton N., 229, 232, 233–38
Harrison, Constance Cary, 39, 237–38
Harrison, Simon, 16, 33n36
Harrison, William Henry, 42
Hartzell, John Calvin, 102
harvesting vaccine matter, 126–27, 141, 142. *See also* smallpox; vaccination; vaccine matter
Hawkes, Esther, 168
Hayes, Henry, 166
Hayes, Rutherford B., 46
Hazen, William B., 63, 73n18
Heidegger, Martin, 112
Helena, Ark., refugee camp, 157, 163–64
Henry, Patrick, 35, 42
Henry IV, 24

Herald of Freedom, 18
Herr, William, 91
Hill, A. P., 62
Hilton Head Island, S.C., 151, 152, 157–59, 164–65, 166, 169, 175n35
historic preservation, 36; antebellum, 3, 17, 28–29, 35, 38, 39; during the Civil War, by civilians, 6–8, 42, 63–64, 90, 170; during the Civil War, by soldiers, 7–8, 42, 90, 91, 114; postwar, 5, 6, 7–8, 47, 54–55, 64–65, 90, 92, 208, 216, 227. *See also* architecture; built environment; historic houses
Hodder, Ian, 3
Holmes, George Frederick, 15
Holmes, Oliver Wendell, 39
Holt, David, 104
home invasions, 178, 188–90, 197n25
honor, 14, 25, 27, 179, 180, 181, 194n2, 205, 206, 208, 209, 214–15, 217
Hood, John Bell, 65–66
Hooker, Charles E., 227
Hooker, Joseph, 60, 211
Hopper, John, 26
Horn, Mary, 45
households: clothing and, 184–85, 187–88; food and, 185–88; overview of, 176–77, 192–93, 193n1; protective role of men and, 181–82, 190; and resentment by whites of Confederate elites, 190–92; social disruption and, 181–83; Union raids of, 188–90, 197n25; war recovery and, 192; of white Confederates in Alabama, 176–93; white women's war support and, 183–84. *See also* gender; objects; women
houses, historic, 42–43. *See also* Greene, Nathanael; Harrison, William Henry; historic preservation; Monticello; Mount Vernon; Washington, George
housing, refugee: material culture of, 162–64; salvage and appropriation for, 159–62, *161*; soldier and relief worker disparity of, 166–68, *167*; structure and layout for, 155, 157–56, *167*. *See also* African Americans; barracks, used to house refugees; built environment; refugee camps
housing boom in wartime North, 7
Howard, George P., 82
Howe, Samuel Gridley, 33n38
human bodies: control of, 5, 6, 34, 66–67, 133–45, 153, 154; as material entities, 5, 6–7, 22, 34, 68, 103, 111–12, 153–54, 168; and medical care, 123–27, 132–42, 144–45. *See also* human remains
human remains: at Antietam, 68; as relics, 16, 22, 34; in Virginia battlefields, 212–14, 217
hunger: among soldiers, 184–90, 196n25; among wartime civilians, 184–90, 196n25. *See also* malnutrition, among Confederate troops; starvation, among Lee's soldiers
Hunter, Alexander, 66
Hunter, Lucinda, 182, 184, 192

identity: class and, 179, 195n3; gender and, 178, 183, 192; politicized, 176, 177, 180, 184, 194–95n3; race and, 19–21, 22–24, 38, 39, 47, 155, 170–71, 204, 217–18
Indians. *See* Native Americans
Ingalls, George K., 75, 82
Ingersoll, Frank, 90
Ingraham, Edward H., 116
inscriptions: on books, 83; on guns, 114–15
In Small Things Forgotten (Deetz), 217
instruments, medical, 125–26, *136*
Interior Department of the United States, 65, 73n21

J. H. Gemrig, *136*
Jackson, Benjamin Franklin, 186, 188
Jacobs, Harriet, 153

Index { 255

James, Horace, 159
James, William, 3
Jamison, David Flavel, 25–26
Jefferson, Thomas, 42. *See also* Monticello
Jenner, Edward, 127, 132, 137, 139, 142
Johnston, Joseph E., 201, 205, 223, 225
Jones, Charles C., Jr., 236–37
Jones, Joseph, 130–31, 133, 137, 141–42, 143, 145, 149n40
Jones, Lucy, 84
Jordon, J. C., 104
Jordon, Thomas, 239
Journal of Material Culture, 100
Joy, Jody, 112

Kagi, John, 19, 20
Kansas, 14–15, 17, 18, 28–29
Kansas-Nebraska Act, 14, 16
Keegan, John, 31n11
Kershaw, Mary, 38
Kingery, W. David, 201
kitchenware, 3, 46, 165, 166
knife of Henry Clay Pate, 13, 16–18, 19, 27–28, 29, 30n7, 33n38
Korean War, 116

Lady of the Lake, 81
lancets, 126, 133, *136*, 140
landscapes: antebellum, 35, 39, 71n2; as artifacts, 101; during the Civil War, 40, 53–64, 159, 160, 176, 212, 213–14, 221n35; as material culture, 72n14, 101; postwar, 47, 64–71; of refugee camps, 156–57, 164. *See also* Antietam National Battlefield; battlefields
Lange, John, 44
Latour, Bruno, 3, 14
Leasure, Daniel, 84
Ledlie, James Hewett, 85
Lee, Mary Custis, 44, 46
Lee, Richard Henry, 35, 36
Lee, Robert E., 34, 43, 44, 45, 130; battle of Antietam and, 60–62, 66–67; Farewell Address of, 207–8; Harpers Ferry and, 32n24; letters to Jefferson Davis from, 234–38; postwar, 46, 199, 204; relics of, 46; resignation letter of, 235–37; surrender at Appomattox of, 198, 202, 203–4, 207
Lee, Theodoric, 36
Leovy, Mrs., 233–34
Letcher, John, 25
Libby, Jean, 21
Lieber, Frances, 40
Lieber Code, 40
limestone, 56, 59, 70
Lincoln, Abraham, 1, 11n14, 41, 63, 64, 203, 214, 225; assassination of, 225
Lincoln, Mary Todd, 1
Livermore, George, 80–81
Logan, Wilton B., 85, 91
long-range fire, 106–7
"Looking Back: The Civil War in Tennessee" (exhibit), 5
L'Ouverture, Toussaint, 23
Lubar, Steven, 201
lymph, 123, 125–30, 132–33, *136*, 137–41
Lyon, Caleb, 42

Macon, Edgar, 43
Madison, James, 43
malnutrition, among Confederate troops, 66–67. *See also* hunger; starvation, among Lee's soldiers
Maney, George, 114
Mangum, Martha, 83, 84, 89
Mangum, William Preston, 83, 85, 88, 89
Mangum, Willie, 89, 91
Mankon Kingdom, 109
Mansfield, J. F. K., 60
Manual of the Christian Soldier, 81, 82
Marion, Francis, 36
Marshall, Charles, 207
Martin, Michael F., 82
Martin, William T., 43

masculinity, 14, 18, 21, 24–25, 26, 27, 28, 113, 182, 199, 210. *See also* gender; women
Mason's Island, 158, *167*, 168
material culture: defined, 3, 35, 194n3; of fighting, 111–12; gender and, 38, 47, 178; sources for, 4–5; vaccination and study of, 125–27, 144–45; warfare study and, 99–101, 177–78. *See also* material culture studies; materiality
material culture studies: in the field of history, 4–8, 28–29, 54–55, 76, 99–101, 177–79, 194n3, 199, 239n2; in other disciplines, 3–4, 99–100, 112, 124, 125, 194n3, 217, 240n2
materiality, 3, 86, 87, 100, 103, 153, 217, 221n35. *See also* artifacts; objects; physical contact with artifacts; sense of touch; souvenirs; tactile pleasure in touching objects
materia medica, 126–27, 136
Mather, Cotton, 79
matter. *See* materiality; objects; physical contact with artifacts; relics; sense of touch; souvenirs; tactile pleasure in touching objects
Maynard, R. L., 46
McAloon, Peter A., 88
McCall, George A., 114
McCarthy, Carlton, 207
McClellan, George B., 60, 62
McCracken, Grant, 38
McKim, James Miller, 26
McLean house, Wilmer, 198–99
McPherson, James, 181
Meade, George G., 211
Mechanics' Institute, 3
Medical and Surgical History of the War of the Rebellion, The, 145, 149n40
medical history and smallpox: antebellum, 125, 127–28; during the Civil War, 137–43; postwar, 145. *See* vaccination; vaccine matter

medicines: applied to bodies as a talisman, 109, 110, 111
memorials, 36, 63–64, 70
memory, 6; collective, 4, 7, 29, 37, 38, 39, 47, 48, 64, 86, 117, 201, 208, 212, 217; individual, 1, 6, 7, 17, 29, 83, 165, 226, 231, 236
mental constructs, 124, 125, 142, 144
Merillat, J. C. M., 144
Merrill, Charles W., 83, 85, *86*
Mexican War, 80
miasmatic theory of disease, 68
Midwest, 15
military policy on artifacts, 40, 225, 228
Miller, David, 58
Miller, Joseph, and family, 155–56
Mitchel, Ormsby, 157
Mitchell, W. S., 124
Mitchelville, S.C., 151, 152, 157–59, 164–65, 166, 169, 175n35
Mollohan, Harrison, 82–83, 90
money. *See* currency
Monocacy, battle of, 7
Montgomery, Ben, 226
Monticello, 42. *See also* Jefferson, Thomas
monuments, 29, 36, 63, 73n18, 100. *See also* statues
Moore, Francis T., 108
Moore, Junius, 91
Moore, Samuel Preston, 131, 137, 138, 139, 140, 141, 144
mortality from smallpox, 127, 130
Moshenska, Gabriel, 100
Mount Vernon, 34, 36, 37, 40–41
Moxley, Emily, 182, 186–87, 190, 191–92
Moxley, William, 186–87, 190
Mulberry plantation, 44
Mumma family, 53, 59, 60, 62, 63
Munger, George M., 228–29
Murfreesboro, Tenn., 63, 159
museums, 2, 7, 37, 39, 40, 45, 90, 91, 92
music, 75, 89, 204

Index { 257

Napoleon, 115
Natchez, Miss., 168–69
National Battlefield Sites, 64, 65, 70. *See also* Antietam National Battlefield: as an artifact
national cemeteries, 54, 63–64
National Museum of African American History and Culture, 5, 163, 174n19
National Park Service (NPS), 54, 55, 65, 70
Native Americans, 35, 57, 110–11, 115
natural artifacts. *See* Antietam National Battlefield: as an artifact
Neese, George, 45
Nelson, Megan Kate, 4, 160, 172n3, 177, 199
New Bern, N.C., 168
Newby, Dangerfield, 22
New England: antebellum, 16, 29, 39, 43–44; during the Civil War, 83
newspapers as shields, 80, 84
New Testament, 81, 82, *86*, 91
New York Herald, 230
Nicodemus Hill, 60
Nord, David Paul, 87
Nordhoff, Charles, 153, 154, 156
North Carolina Museum of History, 47
North Woods, 58
Nott, Josiah C., 133, 142, 143, 150n44

objects, 35, 39, 43, 76, 92, 99, 113, 163, 225, 226, 239; appeal of, 1–7, 23, 45, 46, 177; distinction between, 36, 38, 99, 112, 164, 170, 218, 232; as historical evidence, 4–5, 25, 37, 38, 46, 47, 77–78, 101, 118, 217, 218; household, 3, 5–6, 38, 44, 46, 47, 164, 165, 178, 180, 184, 190, 192, 194n3, 195; symbolism of, 4, 6, 7, 16, 27, 34, 42, 47, 89, 103, 109, 112, 117, 165, 177, 193, 199, 206, 217, 223, 238
occupation by Union soldiers at Antietam, 67–69
O'Donnell, James, 236–37
Old Point Comfort, Va., 157, 160

Old Steve (a slave), 45
oral tradition, 35, 38

Panghorn, N.H., 204
Panic of 1857, 18
paroles, 209
Pate, Henry Clay, 13, 15–16, 27–28, 29n1, 30n7
Pate's knife, 13, 16–18, 19, 27–28, 29, 30n7, 33n38
Peale, Charles Willson, 36, 44
Pennell, Sara, 217
Percy, Henry "Hotspur," 24–25
performative actions, 112
Perry, H., 208
Perry, John, 45
Phillips, John G., 104
Phillips, Philip, 230
Phillips, Wendell, 22, 26
Phlox, 125
photographs: during the Civil War, 92, 153, 164, 169; postwar, 169, 225. *See also* daguerreotypes
physical contact with artifacts: antebellum, 37; during the Civil War, 41–42, 44–45, 165; postwar, 47, 54, 208, 217. *See also* materiality; objects; relics; sense of touch; souvenirs; tactile pleasure in touching objects
physicians: allopathic, 131; eclectic, 131, 146n14, 147n20; homeopathic, 131, 147n20; Thomsonian, 131, 147n20. *See also* medicines; vaccine matter
Pickens, Andrew, 43
Pickens, Francis W., 43
pikes: history of, 17, 30n11; of John Brown, 6, *12*, 17–18, 22, 23–25, 26–27, 28, 29; versus spears, 23
Pinckney, Charles Cotesworth, 44
Pinckney, Harriott, 44
Pitts, Helen, 2
plain folk. *See* common whites; yeomanry
pocket-size books as shields. *See* books as shields

Pogue, Levi S., 104
Pohick Church, 41, *41*, 43
Point of Pines plantation, 158
political symbols, objects as: antebellum, 1–3, 6, 14, 17–18, 27–28; during the Civil War, 34–35, 42, 47–48, 54, 64, 181, 183, 199; postwar, 47–48, 231
politics, electoral: antebellum, 6, 14, 15, 28, 176, 179–80; during the Civil War, 176; postwar, 64, 226
Pollard, Edward, 229
Polley, J. B., 104
postwar trauma, 201, 206
preservation, historic. *See* historic houses; historic preservation
prisoners of war: antebellum, 13; during the Civil War, 40, 86, 142, 154, 205, 209; postwar, 226, 229, 232
prisons, Civil War, 7, 142, 154, 155, 209, 230. *See also* Andersonville
Pritchard, Benjamin, 230–31
Prosser, Gabriel, 23
Prosser, Solomon, 23
protocols, medical, 125, 137, 141, 144
providence, belief in, 87, 88, 89
Prown, Jules David, 99–100, 194n3
public memory. *See* memory
pustules, 124, 128–30, 133, 140, 142, 147n23
Putnam family, Israel, 43–44

race: collective memory and, 38; refugee relief workers and, 153, 155, 166; vaccine matter and, 137–38, 143, 149n32; white supremacy and, 14–15, 28, 143. *See also* African Americans; identity; ex-slaves; freedpeople; slavery; slaves
Ramsey, Frank A., 137, 138, 144
Reagan, John H., 231
realpolitik, 14
Reconstruction, 6, 64, 143, 218, 226
Red Hill, 35
Redpath, James, 28

refugee, use of term, 171n1
refugee camps, 151–75; control of, 168–69; daily activities and belongings at, 164–66, 175n35; disparity of soldier and relief worker housing at, 166–68, *167*; dwelling material culture of, 162–64; environment, order, and virtue at, 154–57; floors of refugee homes, 159, 163–64; housing salvage and appropriation at, 159–62, *161*; housing structure and layout at, 155, 157–56, *167*; overview of, 151–53, 170–71, 171n1–2; post-emancipation, 169–70. *See also* African Americans; built environment
refugees, education of, 153–54, 166, 171
refugees, familial ties and, 153–54, 156, 157, 159, 170
refugees, morality and, 155, 156
relics, 4–7, 13–14; collecting of, 1–2, 4–7, 16, 22, 24, 28–29, 39, 46–47, 178, 199, 218; a definition of, 35; veterans as, 36. *See also* African Americans and relics; Appomattox surrender, defeat relics from; artifacts; battlefields: as sources of; campaign ribbons as relics; children: war relics and; Douglass, Anna Murray; Douglass, Frederick; emancipation; human remains; Lee, Robert E.; Lincoln, Abraham; Lincoln, Mary Todd; materiality; objects; physical contact with artifacts; sense of touch; shackles worn by slaves; slavery; souvenirs; Sprague, Rosetta Douglass; tactile pleasure in touching objects; things; trophies, war; Washington, George; weapons; women
relief organizations, 151–52, 172n2
relief workers: disparity between refugees and, 166–68; environment and, 154; material environment and, 156–57; overview of, 151–53, 172n2; refugee household goods and, 165–66

Index { 259

religion, organized: antebellum, 58, 179; during the Civil War, 81; postwar, 111
Republican Party, 73n35. *See also* politics, electoral
Researches upon "Spurious Vaccination" (Jones), *134–35*, 141–42
revaccination, 137, 141, 143, 148n27
Revised United States Army Regulations of 1861, 40
Revolutionary War artifacts, 34–47
Revolutionary War as inspiration for Civil War, 39–40
Richards, Paul, 109–10
Richardson, Frank L., 110
Richardson, Israel, 62
Richmond Examiner, 45
rifles: musket, 103, 104–5, 107, 108; smoothbore, 105, 106
riots in Mobile, Ala. 188
Rise and Fall of the Confederate Government (Davis), 233
Roane, William, 35
Roberts, Marion, 212
Robertson, Mrs., 233, 235
Rogers, William P., 111
Rohrbach's Bridge, 59, 60, 62
Roller, John E., 208
Roosevelt, Franklin Delano, 73n21
Root, Elihu, 228
Roulette, William and Margaret, 59
Roundheads, the, 83–84
Ruffin, Edmund, 22–25, 27
Ruin Nation (Nelson), 177–78
Russell, Le Baron, 157
Rust, Albert, 25
Rust, Horatio, 17, 18–19, 26

Sanborn, Franklin, 30n7
Saunders, Nicholas J., 100
Savannah, Ga., 37, 87
"Saved by a Newspaper," 80
"Saved by a Testament," 75
scabs, 123–26, 128, 133, *136*, 141, 147n23, 148n29

Schivelbusch, Wolfgang, 206
Schlereth, Thomas J., 194n3
Schofield, Martha, 156, 168
Schroyer, Michael, 213
Scott, Sir Walter, 81
Scott, Winfield, 34, 44
Scribner's Monthly, 234, 236
secession: Alabama and, 180; Davis and, 222; Revolution as inspiration for, 39–40; South Carolina and, 25–26, 28
secular book-shields, 81–82, 83, 85, 89
self-vaccination, 139
sense of touch, 37, 41–42. *See also* materiality; physical contact with relics; tactile pleasure in touching objects
sensorimotoricity, 102, 103, 107, 112, 117
settlements, refugee. *See* refugee camps
Seven Years' War, 80
sewage disposal, 67–68, 73–74n28
sexually transmitted disease, 125, 133, 137, 138, 139, 142, 144
shackles worn by slaves, 45–46
Shakespeare, William, 24
Sharpsburg, Md., 57–58, 59–60, *61*, 63, 67–69
Shenandoah Valley, 45, 56
Shepherd, William T., 106
Sheridan, Phillip, 211
Sherman, Roger, 43
Sherman, William T., 43, 211, 223, 225
Sherman's troops, 178, 194n2, 211–14, 217; march through Virginia battlefields, 211–14
Shorter, Gill, 188
short-range firing, 106, 107
Shrader, Charles R., 115–16
Shuler, Rosa, 83
Sibley tents, 158, 163
Sierra Leone, warriors of, 109, 110–11
silk, 37, 209–10
Sillitoe, Paul, 114–15
slab houses, 169
slave cabins, 46, 158–59

slave revolts, 20, 23, 25. *See also* Brown, John; Prosser, Gabriel; Prosser, Solomon; Turner, Nat; Vesey, Denmark

slavery, relics of, 5, 6, 45–46, 47

slaves: antebellum, 39; during the Civil War, 45–46, 152, 171, 212–13. *See also* Abel; Ben; Brown, John; ex-slaves; freedpeople; Harpers Ferry, Va.; Horn, Mary; Old Steve; refugees; shackles worn by slaves; slave cabins; slave revolts; slavery, relics of; soldiers; soldiers and civilians; women

smallpox, 7, 123–25, 126, 127–30, *129*, *134–35*, 146n14, 147n23. *See also* medical history and smallpox; vaccinations; vaccine matter

Smith, John, Union soldier, 201, 203, 204, 210–11, 214–17

Smith, Kirby, 201

Smith, Mark M., 4

Smith, Merritt Roe, 106

Smith, Timothy B., 63

Smith, W. J., 124

Smithsonian National Museum of American History, 221n35

smoothbore muskets, 105, 106

Sneden, Robert Knox, *61*

snipers, 107

soldiers: battlefield trauma of, 216; bravery of Confederate, 63, 111, 205, 206, 207, 213; bravery of Union, 41, 63, 111, 203, 206, 213, 214; skills of, 103–4; as targets, 107–11; winter camps of, 159–60. *See also individual soldiers*

Soldiers' Aid Societies, 181

soldiers and civilians, 2, 66, 69, 123, 164, 177; antebellum, 16, 22; during the Civil War, conflict between, 55, 67, 141, 185, 192; during the Civil War, cooperation between, 42, 43, 68, 76, 83, 84, 86, 90, 92, 138, 164; postwar, 199, 211

soldier salute, 209

Souldier's Pocket Bible (1643), 80

Southern Unionists, white, 5, 10n12, 43, 47, 180

souvenirs: antebellum, 1, 16, 22, 23, 26, 37; during Civil War, 16, 42, 47, 106, 178; postwar, 5, 199, 203, 204, 211, 216, 218. *See also* artifacts; materiality; objects; physical contact with artifacts; relics; sense of touch; tactile pleasure in touching objects

spears of John Brown, 6, *12*, 17–18, 22, 23–25, 26–27, 28, 29. *See also* pikes

Spotsylvania, battle of, 211, 212, 213

Sprague, Rosetta Douglass, 1

spurious vaccinations, 138–42

Stamford Advocate, 90–91

Stanton, Edwin M., 225, 230

Star of Empire, 16

starvation, among Lee's soldiers, 66–67. *See also* hunger; malnutrition, among Confederate troops

statues, 29, 34, 41. *See also* monuments; Washington, George

Statutes at Large of the Confederate States, 238

Stearns, George, 17

Stearns, Mary, 17

Stephens, Aaron, 21

Stephens, Alexander, 40

Stephenson, Philip Daingerfield, 115

Stones River, battle of, 63, 90, 114

Storey, Margaret, 180

Stout, S. F., 137

Stradivarius, 7

Streater, Kristen L., 178

Stringfellow, John, 14–15

Strother, David Hunter, 21, 27, 41

Stroud, Ellen, 68

Stuart, J. E. B., 21–22, 31–32n24

Sumner, Edwin, 13, 62

Sunken Road, 59, 60, *61*, 62

surgeons. *See* physicians

surrender parade at Appomattox, 209–11

Index { 261

surrenders: at Appomattox, 198–99, *200*, 201–5, 207–11, 218; at Bennett Place, 223, 225
swords, 14, 23; belonging to Frederick the Great, 37; belonging to Gabriel and Solomon Prosser; belonging to George Washington, 19, 21, 37; belonging to W. B. Brockett, 16, 17

tactile pleasure in touching objects, 37, 41–42
Taft, Horatio, 42
talismans: in American Civil War, 5, 76, 80, 83, 86, 102, 109, 110, 117; in other wars, 110, 111
targets, soldiers as, 107–11, 115–16, 117
technological determinism, 106
Tennessee State Library and Archives, 5
"thing politics," 14, 28–29
things: agency and power of, 199; distinction between objects and, 112; politics and, 14, 28–29. *See also* monuments; objects; relics; souvenirs; statues
Thom, Joseph Pembroke, 91
Thompson, David, 62–63
Thompson, John R., 236
Thoreau, Henry David, 17, 28, 33n38
Thorpe, David Franklin, 156
Tilley, Christopher, 3
tools, medical, 125–26, *136*
Toombs, Robert, 54, 62
Townsend, Edward T., 226–27, 232
Trans-Mississippi West, 19, 110, 179
trauma, war-related, 68, 201, 216
trench art, 100, 101, 111
trophies, war, 16; battlefields and, 213–14; from Harpers Ferry, 22; as symbols of valor, 206–7. *See also* Appomattox surrender, victory trophies from; artifacts; memory; objects; souvenirs; relics
Turner, Nat, 23
Tyler, John, 160

Unionists, white Southern, 5, 43, 47, 180
United States Colored Troops, 148n30, 155–56, 211
University of Wisconsin experiment, 108
Unseld, John, 22, 32n24
Upton, Dell, 154–55

vaccination kit, *136*
vaccinations: in the Confederacy, 123–45; conclusions on, 142–45; experience of, 130–37, *134–35*, *136*, 148n27; material culture and, 125–27, 144–45; overview of, 6–7, 123–25, 145n1; smallpox and, 127–30, *129*; sources of vaccine matter and, 137–38, 148nn29–30; spurious, 138–42
vaccine matter, 123, *136*; epistemology creation and, 126–27, 128, 139–40; harvesting, 126–27, 141, 142; sources for, 131–32, 137–38, 147n21
vaccinia, 123, 124, 128, 130, 132–33, 137, 139–40, 142
Valentine, Herbert, 163
value criterion for vaccinations, 139
Van Benthuysen, Watson, 232
Varon, Elizabeth, 194n2, 207
Vermilion, William, 110, 111
Vesey, Denmark, 23
vesicles, 123, 125, 128–30, 132–33, 140, 147n23
veterans of the American Civil War: Confederate, 6, 64, 198–99, 201, 204, 207, 208, 209; Union, 6, 64, 91, 111, 199, 201, 203, 211, 212, 214, 215, 217, 221n40
veterans of the American Revolution, 36, 39
Vicksburg, siege of, 101, 106, 113, 116
Vietnam War, 4, 116
Virginia Historical Society, 46
Vogdes, Israel, 223–25

Waddell, Alfred, 38
Waddell, Fanny, 47
Walthall, William T., 235, 236–37
War Department of the United States, 64, 65, 73n21, 215, 225, 226–28, 229, 231. *See also* Archive Office, Washington, D.C.
Warnier, Jean-Pierre, 103, 109, 111–12
War of the Rebellion, The, 239
war trophies. *See* trophies, war
Washburn, Emory, 80
Washington, George: family of, 19, 36–37, 38–39, 43, 44, 46; memorials to, 36, 41; possessions and relics of, 36–37, 44, 45; public focus on, 38–39, 40–41; remains of, 16, 34; self-awareness as historical figure, 36. *See also* Mount Vernon; statues
Washington, John Augustine, II, 34
Washington, Lewis, 19, 20–21, 37
Washington, Martha Custis, 38, 43
Washington, Mary Ball, 41, 45
waste disposal, 67–68, 73–74n28
water carriage systems, 67–68, 69
Watkins, Frederick, 90
Waud, Alfred, 198
weapons: antebellum gun culture and, 101–3, 117; emotional attachment to, 5, 112–15, 116–18, 210, 215; engraving on, 21, 112, 114–15; naming of, 102, 112–14, 117; overview of material culture of, 101–2; as relics, 16, 22, 24, 26, 35, 100, 106, 124, 177, 210; soldiers as targets of, 107–11, 115–16, 117; soldiers' skill in using, 103–4, *105*; soldiers' yearn for the "best," 104–7. *See also* swords
Wells, Bezalel, 231
West Woods, 62
Whig Party, 179. *See also* politics, electoral
White House, Virginia, 43
widows, 26, 36, 182, 235

Williams, Lawrence A., 44
Williams, Wayman, 154
Wills, Charles, 43
Wilson, John H., 229
Wiregrass region of Alabama, 179, 180
Wirz, Henry, 142
Wisconsin Veterans Museum, 111
Wola of New Guinea, 114–15, 117
women: African American Northern women, 7, 39; African American Southern women, 1–2, 4, 7, 45, 46, 156, 160; common white Southern women, 7, 178, 181–93, 194n2; elite white Southern women, 4, 38, 44, 164, 178, 183, 194n2; home, domesticity, and, 177, 178–79, 183–85, 186–93, *189*; material culture and, 7; political agency and, 178–79, 180–81, 183–84, 194n2; war relics and, 1, 5, 7, 38, 41, 43, 44, 45, 46, 47, 83, 84, 192; white Northern women, 2, 7, 18, 151. *See also* gender; households; masculinity; *individual women*
Wonders of the Invisible World (Mather), 79
Wood, John Taylor, 235
World War I, 100, 111, 115–16
World War II, 100
working-class whites. *See* common whites; yeomanry
Wright, Marcus J., 227, 239
Wright, Rita P., 124, 125, 142

Yancey, William Lowndes, 180
yeomanry: antebellum, 17, 35, 37, 176, 179; during the Civil War, 176, 177, 178, 180, 181, 184–85, 186, 188, 190, 191, 192, 193; postwar, 192. *See also* common whites
Yokota, Kariann, 27
Yulee, David Levy, 223

Zorn, Jacob, 204

www.ingramcontent.com/pod-product-compliance
Lightning Source LLC
Chambersburg PA
CBHW030532230426
43665CB00010B/857